D0427234

Shaplen
A turning wheel

950.42
8589

A Turning Wheel

Books by Robert Shaplen

The Face of Asia (Introduction)
The Road from War
Time out of Hand: Revolution and Reaction in Southeast Asia
The Lost Revolution
Toward the Well-being of Mankind: 50 Years of the Rockefeller Foundation
Kreuger: Genius and Swindler
A Forest of Tigers
Free Love and Heavenly Sinners
A Corner of the World

1500

A Turning Wheel

Three Decades of the Asian Revolution
as Witnessed by a Correspondent
for The New Yorker

by ROBERT
SHAPLEN

, 1917-

DS
35
S44

DISCARDED

Random House   New York

EL CAMINO COLLEGE LIBRARY

Copyright © 1973, 1974, 1975, 1976, 1977, 1978, 1979 by Robert Shaplen

All rights reserved under International and Pan-American Copyright Conventions. Published in the United States by Random House, Inc., New York, and simultaneously in Canada by Random House of Canada Limited, Toronto.

Grateful acknowledgment is made to *The New Yorker* for permission to reprint "Letter from Saigon." Copyright © 1975 by The New Yorker Magazine, Inc.

Library of Congress Cataloging in Publication Data

Shaplen, Robert, 1917-
A turning wheel.

Includes index.
I. Asia—History—20th century. I. Title.
DS35.S44   950'.42   79-4781
ISBN 0-394-41752-6

Manufactured in the United States of America
9 8 7 6 5 4 3 2
First Edition

Random 13/79 9962

To my wife, June Herman Shaplen,
and to my three children, Peter, Kate and Jason,
who have shared with me
the mysteries and joys of Asia

Acknowledgments

This book is primarily the product of my own research and is based on thousands of interviews over many years in all the countries of North and Southeast Asia. It would be impossible to list all the people who gave me the benefit of their time and offered me valuable insights and observations, as well as vital factual and background information; some of them, particulary Vietnamese, are now dead. My thousands of pages of transcribed notes serve as a testimonial to their patience and as a record of history in the making.

A number of friends were of special help through these years in improving my understanding of the complicated trends and events in their native or adopted countries. They include Soedjatmoko, in Indonesia; William Klausner, in Thailand; F. Sionil Jose, in the Philippines; Bernard Krisher, in Japan; and Jim Haussman and Steve Bradner, in South Korea.

Government officials, from Prime Ministers and Presidents to lower-ranking bureaucrats in specialized fields, were often invaluable sources, but much of my material was obtained from those outside government, including ordinary workers, peasants and soldiers; businessmen, schoolteachers and academics, as well as literary and cultural critics. Many of them are mentioned by name in the book, but for reasons of security and their own protection many others—such as opposition political leaders and dissident fighters for human rights—are referred to anonymously. I extend my thanks to all of them.

Scores of books about Asia, and particularly about Vietnam, have been written over the past twenty years, and I have read many and referred to some. A number of books about Japan were of help to me in comprehending that unusual society, and I have quoted from them and from interviews with their authors. In analyzing the American occupation of Japan, the early part of which I covered, I found a number of historical accounts and memoirs helpful, among them *Postwar Japan to the Present*, edited by Livingston, Moore and Oldfather. But here, as elsewhere, wherever possible I sought to interview the principals involved in historical as well as contemporary events. The help given me by the Foreign Press Center, in Tokyo, in providing interpreters was especially appreciated.

Accounts of meetings and important statements of speeches in Communist countries, to which direct access was often difficult to obtain, were published in the daily reports of the Foreign Broadcast Information Service of the United States government, and I regularly subscribed to this valuable source. *Far Eastern Economic Review* and *Asiaweek*, both magazines published in Hong Kong, were consistently useful for background between visits to the various countries.

It would have been impossible to write this book without the opportunity given me by William Shawn, the editor of *The New Yorker*, to live and work in Asia from 1962 through 1978. His constant encouragement, and the time he allowed me to prepare long articles for that unique magazine, were the substance and foundation of my rewarding Asian experience. Portions of more than a hundred articles that appeared in the magazine have been used in writing the book, but they have been refashioned and woven into original material. The conclusions and judgments are my own.

I also owe a debt of gratitude to William Knapp, my long-time friend and editor at *The New Yorker*, and to the staff of the magazine's library for research material they collected for me over the years. My thanks go in equal measure to Mrs. Carol Brandt, my friend and agent, and to Joseph Fox, my editor at Random House.

Finally, I must thank my wife, June Herman Shaplen, who was patient beyond the call of matrimonial duty during my long periods of absence from our home in Hong Kong, and who regularly gave me the benefit of her editorial experience and of her own cogent observations of Asia.

R.S.

Contents

Introduction

I set foot in Asia for the first time early on the morning of October 20, 1944, near Tacloban, Leyte, in the Philippines, where I landed as a war correspondent with the First Cavalry Division. The landing was easier than we had anticipated— the area had been thoroughly "softened up" by heavy artillery, rocket barrages and strafing planes—and by the time we walked through the surf and onto the debris of the beach, strewn with shattered coconut trees and heavy with acrid smoke, most of the Japanese had either been killed or had fled, though there was considerable fighting afterward, and some monumental sea battles. But what I remember most was the response of the Filipinos. Even as the rifles were still crackling, they kept pouring from everywhere and nowhere, running down the roads and out of the jungle to hang garlands on us, to shove fruit, whiskey, themselves and their children at us in what was the warmest and most spontaneous greeting I have ever received. The phrase I kept hearing, over and over again, was "Lovely Americans, lovely Americans."

More than thirty years later, as I fled Saigon under North Vietnamese rocket fire, I rode by bus to the helicopter pad through streets that were packed with Vietnamese staring sullenly or crying out to us to take them along; some of them clung to the sides of the bus until they dropped off in exhaustion. We were scarcely regarded as "lovely Americans." The Vietnamese had come to detest us for what we had done to their country and for now deserting them, saving our own skins while, except for those we took with us or helped escape on their own, the vast majority had no choice but to remain and greet their victorious Communist brethren from the North who arrived the next morning by tank, by jeep and on foot. The looks of contempt and hatred as well as frenzy on the faces of those Vietnamese that last morning still haunt me.

What had happened over those thirty-odd years to provoke such an abysmal change in attitude, to cause love to turn to hate? The question is, of course, simplistic, unfair and pejorative, since Americans today retain a reservoir of good will throughout Asia; nevertheless, the contrast lingers in my mind and inspires all sorts of thoughts about what we, as a nation, have achieved or failed to achieve in Asia since World War II.

The answers are complex and contradictory, and the record is obviously mixed. If we look at it chronologically and rationally, I would say that the five most momentous events in Asia in the past three decades, in all of which we played a certain role, have been the resurrection of Japan, begun during the American occupation, when we created an altogether new democratic set of concepts for the Japanese, implemented them, and then gave Japan back its independence and watched it become a major world economic power; the Chinese revolution and the victory of the Communists in 1949 over the Kuomintang we had so futilely supported; the development of nationalism in Southeast Asia in the postcolonial era, which has followed an erratic course and, over recent years, has increasingly and disappointingly veered toward authoritarianism; the Korean War of 1950–1953, which was the last "patriotic" war we engaged in and which in many ways was the product of both World War II and the Cold War that followed; and, finally, the disastrous Vietnam war, which led to our also becoming deeply embroiled in Laos and Cambodia.

In assessing the impact and influence we had over these five major events, I would risk saying that the only two in which we actually played a conclusive role were the development of Japan and the war in Korea. Despite our long and costly involvement in Vietnam, we simply delayed the Communist victory there, which was perhaps inevitable as far back as 1946. As for China, though we tried to bring the opposing sides together during the abortive mission headed by General George C. Marshall in 1946–1947, there was in fact little we did, or could do, to avoid the victory of the Chinese Communists, despite what the fulsome propaganda of the old "China lobby" has maintained. As for the nationalist revolutions that took place in Southeast Asia after World War II, we had an obvious impact in the Philippines, to which we granted independence in 1946, but elsewhere our role was generally inspirational in support of nationalism and freedom, rather than material. What took place in the other nations of the region as the Dutch and the British divested themselves of their colonial possessions with varying degrees of stubbornness and grace was bound to take place anyway because there was no stemming the nationalist thrust.

Looking back over thirty-five years, I remember the enthusiasm and excitement of the days when the Pacific war was drawing to a close, and the exhilarating atmosphere of political adventure and zeal at the time of victory and immediately thereafter. A sense of American power, even of rejuvenated manifest destiny, was in the air, and out of the liberation of the Philippines and the surrender and occupation of Japan, followed by our temporary occupation of northern China, came a fresh identification with Asia as a place teeming with a tantalizing variety of people and with all sorts of alluring opportunities for exploration and discovery. In many ways, it was a time of unabashed naïveté or ingenuousness, when anything and everything seemed possible. If one looked beneath the surface, however, there were already disquieting signs and portents.

After spending the initial occupation month in Japan, I went to China with occupying Marine forces. We left Okinawa in transport ships, which took us to the Taku bar outside of Tientsin, and then proceeded up the Hai River in small amphibious boats, past the remains of the old forts that had been built in the days of the Boxer Rebellion or before. About a mile or so from the sea the river narrowed, and the banks were jammed with thousands of screaming and waving Chinese, most of them brandishing Kuomintang flags. Here, once again, we received a tumultuous welcome, but unlike that in the Philippines, this one was patently staged for our benefit by our Kuomintang allies, who, though still based in Chungking, had obviously given orders to their soldiers and to ordinary peasants and townsfolk to turn out en masse and greet us. I remember feeling that this was a shame; if left to themselves, the people would probably have responded of their own accord.

After a few days of celebration in Tientsin, I boarded a train for the short ride to Peking, that loveliest of cities, where we wandered around the old imperial palaces, and alleys, compounds and markets. I began to fall in love with China, even though, or maybe because, it was already a revolutionary cauldron. Moving down the coast by boat and plane, I reached Shanghai, another of the world's great cities but a complete contrast to Peking, with a turbulence and excitement of its own, and a sense of its independent role that still obtains in Communist China today. In the immediate postwar days—and nights—Shanghai reverted quickly to its prewar status as a teeming, raunchy treaty port with its own cosmopolitan style, which enabled it to blend profit, pleasure and politics with a kind of gangster grace. This was to be my home for the next two years, during which I traveled extensively around Manchuria and to many other places in China, and through Southeast Asia. Most of the correspondents lived on the top three floors of the Broadway Mansions on Soochow Creek, overlooking the so-called Bund, the waterfront; part of the busy harbor, and the downtown area where the big Chinese business hongs and the foreign banks and commercial bastions were located. Directly below us, along the sides of the creek, huddled together or scuttling about like water bugs, were hundreds of sampans, and from our nest-like perches high above, we had a constant bird's-eye view of the daily existence of this segment of city life, the boat people, whose lack of privacy and boisterous competitiveness provided a zestful and uninhibited example of how the vast majority of the Chinese lived.

The longer I stayed in Shanghai, the more disturbing it was to witness the stark contrasts between rich and poor. While the wealthy Chinese who had returned from the western provinces, and the wealthy foreigners who had returned from abroad, or the ambitious newcomers who had come to Shanghai for the first time as postwar carpetbaggers, slid about in shiny black oversize sedans and occupied sumptuous flats and houses in the old French quarter, it was not uncommon on cold mornings to see the frozen dead bodies of beggars and infants on the city's downtown streets.

In Nanking, not far to the north, where Chiang Kai-shek had re-established his shaky capital, General Marshall was trying to get him to agree to set up a coalition government with the Communists. Marshall was the most impressive American I have ever met, combining a deep knowledge of history and a high intellectual grasp of complicated situations with a tremendous judgment of other men's character and motivations, and with an abiding patience and understanding. But I never felt he had much of a chance of bringing together the two sides in the emerging civil war, and it soon became apparent to most of us that the Communists would win the war, not only because of the disorganization, corruption and lack of unity and will of the Kuomintang but because the Communists suffered none of these handicaps and had planned their conquest of China carefully.

Both in Nanking and Shanghai we met from time to time with Chou En-lai, who was then the chief Communist negotiator between Marshall and the Kuomintang. We usually saw him late at night in Shanghai, in a house in the French quarter, where he would serve us tea and answer questions until the early hours of the morning. Even in those days Chou, a vibrant, magnetic and handsome man, spoke more English than he would let on, and he would often correct his interpreters, one of whom, a thin, tubercular man named Chiao Kuan-hua, later became Foreign Minister of the People's Republic of China. Chou always answered our questions freely and frankly. Sometimes he gave us short lectures, which were less didactic than informative and demonstrated his confidence in victory and in the ability of the Communists to rule China effectively. He was invariably persuasive, witty and urbane—qualities that, among others, he afterward demonstrated as Premier in his dealings with foreigners.

In October 1946 I was fortunate to travel to Yenan, the Communists' mountain stronghold in northern Shensi province, where I met Mao Tse-tung, General Chu Teh and the other top Communist leaders. I spent three hours with Mao one morning, during most of which he discussed ideology and answered questions about the negotiations. He was highly critical of the refusal of the Kuomintang to make any concessions, as well as of the Americans for supporting the government with arms, but, prophetically, he also said, "Our hope rests on the shoulders of the American people." Mao wore a brown suit, with a small cap perched on the top of his head. His almost feminine, babyish face made him look like a little boy grown up, but though he smiled and laughed frequently, the tenor of his dialogue was solemn and serious, and his expression showed that he was weighing carefully the meaning of every word. One felt that the weight of the surrounding hills and caves on the mountainside, where he and his cohorts lived, and of the whole future of China lay on his broad, round back, and that he enjoyed carrying it all. Mao and Chou En-lai balanced and served each other well, then and later, but I remember feeling that if it was Mao who sparked the revolutionary engine, Chou was the one who deserved to be called "the Great Helmsman," for even in those days he tried to keep to a moderate course when Mao pushed too hard.

Prior to my visit to Yenan I had made my first trip in the summer of 1946 through much of the rest of Asia, traveling from Shanghai to Hong Kong, to Saigon, to Bangkok, to Rangoon and to Calcutta, from where I flew back over the Himalayan hump to China. Hong Kong, where I was later to live for sixteen years, had a population then of only 600,000, compared to 4.5 million today, and it had just begun to regain its British pride as a crown colony after being occupied, under relatively benevolent conditions, by the Japanese. The old British hongs—Jardine, Matheson and Butterfield & Swire—were back in business; the British ran the government and made their profits, but the Chinese, who comprised 98 percent of the population, dominated the day-by-day commerce. If they were still banned from the plush clubs, their graceful junks, with their multicolored sails, commanded the spacious harbor, and the narrow streets of the colony overflowed with scurrying Chinese who always seemed to be going in several directions at once.

Saigon, three hours farther south by plane, was altogether different, a tropical garden city. With its beautiful tree-lined streets and old stucco houses, it gave the appearance of tranquillity, but the atmosphere was, in fact, already tense, and the Vietminh guerrillas around town were actively conducting ambushes against the returning French soldiers and throwing grenades in the city's cafés and restaurants. One sensed that the French, who had begun to make all the military and some of the political mistakes the Americans later would repeat, were not only a hundred years behind the times but stubbornly determined to pursue their outworn colonial dreams to the point of self-destruction. Ho Chi Minh had just left Hanoi for Paris, where he hoped to implement the agreement he had signed in March whereby France had recognized his new northern republic as part of a vague new French Union, but he returned empty-handed and bitter, and in his absence the French had announced the creation of a "Provisional Government of Cochin-China" in the South, an effort to isolate Ho's new government and torpedo his negotiations for economic aid. It was already apparent that war would come to Indochina, but on this first visit, during which I began my long emotional involvement with the country, I had no idea that Vietnam would consume so much of my time and energy over the next twenty years.

Bangkok looked drab compared to Saigon, and it wasn't nearly as exciting. Its gold-domed Buddhist temples, shrines and royal gardens were lovely to contemplate, but the city as a whole lacked vitality and character; so did the Thais, compared to the Vietnamese. Not that they weren't friendly, smiling and accommodating, but behind the smiling faces it was difficult to find much substance. The Thais had managed to avoid being overrun by the Japanese by declaring themselves an ally of Japan, but the strategy hadn't worked as well as they had hoped. The Japanese had confiscated everything in sight for use in the war and left the economy to stagnate, and now that the war was over, Thailand faced the problem of making friends again with the Western Allied powers. The British had been the major influence before the war, but now they had far less money than the Americans, who began moving their dollars into Thailand long before the heavy military and other investments of the Vietnam war. At the time of my visit Pridi Phanomyang, one of the few competent civilian statesmen Thailand can claim, was Prime Minister and was doing his best to patch things up with the allies while trying to create a functioning democracy amid conditions of political instability of the sort that would consistently plague Thailand. A month or so before my arrival, the young King Ananda Mahidol had been found dead in his palace bedroom with a bullet wound in his head. The mystery of whether it was an accident, suicide or murder has never been cleared up, despite commissions of inquiry, but two years later, when the military dictatorship of Pibul Songgram was back in control, the government claimed that Ananda had been murdered, and Pridi, accused of complicity, fled Thailand to avoid being arrested. For many years he lived in Canton under the Chinese Communists, until he moved to France in the seventies.

In those days all of Asia was astir with political activity. Rangoon, when I stopped there for a few days, was a place full of promise but also beset by problems. General Aung San, the young commander of the Burma National Army, had just begun negotiations with the British that would soon lead to independence, though not before he had been murdered by his political rivals. He was succeeded by a close comrade, the gentle, deeply religious U Nu, who concluded the independence talks but ran into trouble with the Communists and hill tribes opposed to some of the concessions granted the British, such as the right to use airfields in case of emergencies. When U Nu was unable to pacify these opposition elements, the country drifted into a state of disorder and rebellion that has lasted ever since. Still, U Nu did manage to keep Burma on the course of parliamentiary democracy until 1962, when General Ne Win led a coup against him and set up a new "revolutionary" government with himself at the head. Soon it became an outright military dictatorship.

Thus, on that first trip through Southeast Asia, I began to witness the violence and unrest that would continue to plague the area for most of the ensuing three decades. It was apparent that the defeat of the Japanese did not mean that Asians would enjoy the peace they so much deserved. The new nationalist or revolutionary movements that existed everywhere quickly revealed an ideological factionalism and a lack of cohesive leadership. The outstanding exception to this was the Vietminh movement of the North Vietnamese, guided by the almost metaphysical force and organizational genius of Ho Chi Minh and his tight group of doctrinaire Communists, who would eventually lead the country to victory over both the French and the Americans. But there were other exceptions as well: Malaya, later Malaysia, would make a more or less orderly passage from colonialism to independence; and the Philippines, which, before Ferdinand Marcos declared martial law in 1972, was democratic to the point of chaos. But these nations, too, would suffer periods of violence and rebellion. Elsewhere, the general pattern of nationalist development was erratic, full of turmoil, and as time passed, frequently stultifying. The result was that brilliant demagogues like Sukarno in Indonesia, or colorless and crafty military men of the stripe of Ne Win in Burma, took over their countries and prosecuted their revolutions or counter-revolutions, which were autarchic and often despotic.

As the trend toward authoritarianism, in varying degrees, became increasingly pervasive, the early revolutionary zeal lost its thrust and was replaced by different forms of guided democracy, which were far more guided—and frequently misguided—than democratic. Though it stayed alive, the spirit of nationalism became more raw and was sullied by time and events. And as the world became more complicated and burdened by social and economic problems, politics as such lost much of its dynamic appeal. Beset by personal woes and given little real opportunity to express their opinions and take part in the political process, the racially mixed populations of most of the Southeast Asian nations drifted in a political and social void; economically they remained for the most part immersed in poverty. By default or otherwise, they watched sung or unsung leaders usurp the prerogatives of power, while the revolutions of rising expectations benefited the privileged rather than the needy.

Yet as I write this book, begun in Hong Kong and completed in the United States, thirty-five years after my landing in Leyte, there are encouraging signs. China and the United States have normalized relations, as China and Japan have drawn closer, and the Chinese seem determined to pursue a moderate and modernizing course after the ravages of the Cultural Revolution and the death of Mao. The Japanese are beginning to recover from their recession and are trying to adapt themselves to a lower growth rate while competing with the United States and Western Europe for business with China. The Vietnamese, having invaded Cambodia and engaged the Chinese in a nasty border war, remain the stormy petrels of Southeast Asia, as the North Koreans are in Northeast Asia.

This huge continent is still in a state of transition, and it is so vast that it is often easy to forget how varied it is, and what a compendium of civilizations it represents. Its cultural watersheds overlap and blend, but national differences remain a matter of pride for Asians. They are also a source of continuing fascination for those who, like myself, have tried to explore the social and political issues and the human forces at work in the various countries. These elements keep changing, as they do elsewhere, but the Asian experience has always seemed to me to be particularly fluid and open-ended. To pursue it and to try to comprehend its changing facets is both a joy and a challenge.

Robert Shaplen
Princeton, New Jersey
May 1979

Indochina—
An End and
a Beginning

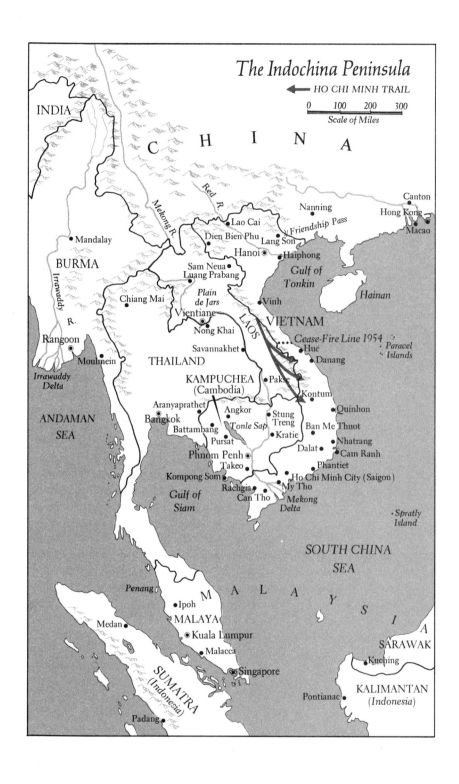

The Indochina Peninsula

← HO CHI MINH TRAIL

0   100   200   300
Scale of Miles

INDIA

C H I N A

Canton

Nanning

Hong Kong

Friendship Pass

Macao

Mekong R.

Red R.

Lao Cai

Dien Bien Phu

Lang Son

Hanoi

Haiphong

Mandalay

BURMA

Sam Neua

Luang Prabang

Gulf of
Tonkin

Hainan

Irrawaddy

Chiang Mai

Plain
de Jars

Vinh

Vientiane

VIETNAM

Nong Khai

LAOS

Rangoon

Savannakhet

Cease-Fire Line 1954

Paracel
Islands

Moulmein

THAILAND

Hué

Danang

Irrawaddy
Delta

KAMPUCHEA
(Cambodia)

Pakse

Kontum

ANDAMAN
SEA

Aranyaprathet

Angkor

Stung
Treng

Quinhon

Bangkok

Battambang

Tonle Sap

Kratie

Ban Me Thuot

Pursat

Dalat

Nhatrang

Phnom Penh

Cam Ranh

Takeo

Phantiet

Kompong Som

Ho Chi Minh City (Saigon)

Rachgia

My Tho

Gulf of
Siam

Can Tho

Mekong
Delta

· Spratly
Island

SOUTH CHINA
SEA

Penang

M   A   L   A   Y   S   I   A

Ipoh

MALAYA

SARAWAK

Medan

Kuala Lumpur

Kuching

Malacca

Singapore

SUMATRA
(Indonesia)

Pontianac

KALIMANTAN
(Indonesia)

Padang

Vietnam—
Conquest and Turmoil

 I arrived in Saigon one hot sunny morning in mid-June 1946 aboard a rickety old Royal Air Force transport from Hong Kong, and I left for the last time at three o'clock on the acrid afternoon of April 29, 1975, in a Sea Stallion helicopter flown by the United States Marines which I boarded under Communist rocket and small-arms fire at the American defense compound at Tan Son Nhut Airport. Fifty minutes later the big helicopter, which was overloaded with eighty Americans and Vietnamese (we had been ordered to jettison all our baggage except for one small piece) landed on the deck of the aircraft carrier *Okinawa*, twenty miles out in the China Sea. The wash of the rotor and the exhaust of the chopper, and of another helicopter that landed fifteen minutes later with only Vietnamese aboard, all but blew the old men, women and children off the carrier deck, and the young Marines had to rush out and grab them as they slithered about and guide them to safety below. That, to me, was the end of the war, and that was when my own tears welled.

There was plenty to weep about, but the fall of Vietnam was not the end of the fighting. There was to be no end to the Vietnamese revolution. Many of us had predicted that a third Indochina war would soon take place, perhaps an internal political or religious struggle accompanied by fresh guerrilla outbreaks, or an ethnic conflict that could conceivably spread beyond Vietnam's borders to Laos and Cambodia. But few imagined that less than four years later, on January 7, 1979, 100,000 Vietnamese troops, acting in the name of perhaps 10,000 "new" Cambodian Communist insurgents, would capture the capital of Phnom Penh after a climactic two-week surge through the eastern part of the country, and overthrow the radical and tyrannical revolutionary Khmer Rouge regime of Prime Minister Pol Pot, which had established itself a fortnight before the North Vietnamese captured Saigon. Nor that the conquest of Cambodia by the Vietnamese, although a border war had been going on since 1975 and had spread and become more violent in 1977, would culminate as swiftly as had the earlier conquest of South Vietnam and the fall of Saigon, thereby once again taking by surprise not only the Americans but the Russians and the Chinese as well. There was one important difference: while Moscow and Peking had both backed Hanoi before, this time they were on opposite sides of the Communist fence. The Russians supported the Vietnamese, and the Chinese the Cambodians.

If the United States, on the other hand, supported neither and was not directly involved, its actions in Cambodia during the Vietnam war had helped create the conditions of chaos and destruction that led to the Khmer Rouge victory in the spring of 1975, and now to this startling epilogue. The Americans, and the Western nations as a whole, were concerned about its implications for the rest of Asia and about the further reactions of the two mutually hostile Communist powers. The Chinese, for their part, having sent the overthrown Cambodian regime considerable military and economic aid, and dispatched thousands of military advisers to encourage its ill-fated resistance, were chagrined and embarrassed. Beyond that, they were angry at their former Vietnamese allies, to whom they had cut off all economic assistance over the Cambodian issue, and over the flight, under Vietnamese duress, of 170,000 *hoa chiao* (Chinese who had been forced to adopt Vietnamese citizenship) across the Vietnam border into southern China. Conversely, the Russians, who had solidified their relationship with the Hanoi government since the end of the Vietnam war, were elated. They had recently signed a new treaty affording the Vietnamese more economic and military assistance, and agreeing to consult with them in any military crisis. In fact, even though they hadn't expected Hanoi's troops to move quite so fast, the Russians had probably given them the green light in Cambodia, particularly in view of the heavy Chinese build-up of the Cambodian army, from about ten divisions in mid-1975 to about twenty-five at the end of 1978. The Vietnamese and the Russians both believed that this new Cambodian force was bound to be directed against Vietnam sooner or later, and that Vietnam would be faced with a two-front war if the Chinese then attacked from the north. Some observers, regarding the new conflict from the viewpoints of Moscow and Peking, looked upon it as a proxy war between the two major Communist powers.

Proxy war or not, the Vietnamese grab of Cambodia was bound to heighten tensions throughout Southeast Asia and to stimulate further the already growing Sino-Soviet contest for influence in the area. This would not exclude Indochina itself, which remained a festering sore. While the Vietnamese seemed well on their way to dominating all of it, they had, rather precariously, overextended themselves and faced difficult problems of control and consolidation. Though they had early on gained a strong hold over Laos, resistance to their overlordship there, while sporadic and uncoordinated, was continuing; and now that Cambodia had fallen under Hanoi's sway, the Chinese might lend fresh support to anti-Vietnamese guerrillas in both countries. If the Chinese did assist remnants of the Pol Pot regime, or any new resistance groups in Cambodia, the most feasible way to do so, particularly in view of the Vietnamese capture of Cambodia's major airfields and the port of Kompong Som on the Gulf of Siam, which had been the main port of entry for

Chinese aid, would be through smaller ports on the gulf or via the difficult overland route through Laos and Thailand. Early in 1979 there were indications that such resupply was taking place, but on a small scale.

Moreover, the Vietnamese still had their hands full at home. Economic mismanagement, corruption and food shortages, aggravated by severe floods in the Mekong Delta in 1978, had made more difficult the political consolidation of the North and the South under the unified Socialist Republic of Vietnam. Differences within the normally cohesive Politburo in Hanoi— between the hard-liners who favored the Cambodian invasion and the moderates who were against it, and wanted to concentrate on domestic matters while mending fences with China—posed a disturbing party conflict that Vietnam could ill afford. And on top of that, a build-up of Chinese and Vietnamese forces on the Sino-Vietnamese border was already threatening to break out into a full-scale war—a threat that, as it turned out, would soon materialize, further delaying economic progress in Vietnam.

All of Southeast Asia, especially Thailand, Cambodia's neighbor, watched with growing trepidation as the Vietnamese troops rammed their way through the Cambodian provinces. Despite Hanoi's expressed pledges to respect the area's peace and neutrality, the other nations wondered anew what the ultimate aims of the Vietnamese were, whether they would not, sooner or later, attempt to spread their still unfinished and compulsive revolution farther south. Whatever the countries of ASEAN (Association of Southeast Asian Nations, comprising Indonesia, Malaysia, the Philippines, Singapore and Thailand) thought of the dictatorial and bloody Pol Pot regime, it had served as a buffer against further Vietnamese expansion. This was an argument in which the United States, which had severely condemned the Pol Pot government for its mass killings and its flagrant abuse of human rights, concurred. On a global scale, Washington was worried about what effect the collapse of Cambodia would have on its recently announced normalization with China and on its still tenuous negotiations with the Soviet Union over another SALT agreement and a number of other issues, including the reduction of conventional arms. In sum, the fall of Cambodia threatened to Balkanize Indochina and perhaps the rest of Southeast Asia as well, and if the feared spillover effect took place, its implications could become extremely serious. Although unlikely, the possibilities of a larger war, or a triggering series of flash-point outbreaks that could spread from the Sino-Soviet border across to Korea and down through Southeast Asia into the Indian Ocean and South Asia, were not to be ignored.

If the Vietnamese had indeed acted as Moscow's surrogates in Cambodia, was this a Russian response to the establishment of closer ties between Peking and Washington, and perhaps to the new Sino-Japanese treaty of peace and friendship as well? Would Cambodia, with its ample rice and rubber, prove to be a prize or a plague to the Vietnamese as another group of faceless men with names like Heng Samrin, Penn Sovan and Chea Sim tried to run a less dictatorial, destructive and doctrinaire government in the face of perhaps prolonged guerrilla opposition? These and other questions could not immediately be answered, but there was little doubt that a new and dangerous dispensation in Southeast Asia existed, and that Thailand in particular, as a result of its proximity and its inability to hold back what could be a further flow of refugees and insurgents of various persuasions, would inevitably be affected by the turn of events. Not only anti-Communists fleeing from Communists, but Communists of one stripe fleeing from those of another, as well as right-wing groups seeking to gain a foothold for a comeback from Thai soil along the loose Thai-Cambodian border, constituted a new threat to the tenuous stability of Thailand, a country that had too many troubles of its own to relish serving as a sanctuary for conflicting revolutionary forces ranging across the whole political and ideological spectrum.

The new Cambodian invasion inevitably carried me back to the American invasion of May 1970, and to the subsequently disclosed secret bombing of Cambodia ordered by President Richard Nixon in 1969. I had strongly opposed the 1970 invasion, which I covered at the time, not only because it laid waste an innocent country trying to survive the pressures of the Vietnamese, who were using it as a haven, but because the incursion was bound to fail in achieving its aims and would simply widen the war in ways that could not conceivably, even in military terms alone, help the cause of the Americans and the South Vietnamese. It merely sucked the United States into a deeper swamp. The chances are that without it, Cambodia would have gone Communist anyway, though in a gentler, less bloodthirsty way. However, to assume that the Vietnamese would not eventually have made an effort to dominate it would be illusory: the centuries-old racial animosity between the Khmer (Cambodians) and the Vietnamese, which had its inception in their having originated from different ethnic watersheds and in their competition to establish hegemony over one another, was deep and bitter. But what the American–South Vietnamese invasion of Cambodia in effect did, somewhat ironically, was hasten the end of the second Indochina war. Contrary to Secretary of State Kissinger's hopes, it failed to encourage Vietnamization in South Vietnam, and instead heightened disillusion and disgust back home in the United States, thus helping pave the way for the American withdrawal and the North Vietnamese victory. In this sense, Cambodia was an Achilles heel.

The End of the Vietnam War

When the victory took place, it was over as quickly as a nightmare. Whatever remembrances, doubts and recriminations lingered, the long torment had ended—except for those Vietnamese left behind who, during the following years, tried, successfully or just as often unsuccessfully, to escape the country by boat, and who created one of the most heartrending human tragedies in history.

Certainly for me, as for other Americans who had spent most of the past thirty years in the Pacific during World War II and then in Asia afterward, the fall of Vietnam represented the end of an era. The war had in fact, embraced several eras, or phases, of the larger American experience in Asia since the end of World War II, which could be linked together in a sort of downward slide. During the early phase of the Vietnamese nationalist-Communist revolution, a handful of Americans working for the Office of Strategic Services played a brief and romantic role in South China and in the jungles of Vietnam as supporters of Ho Chi Minh in his struggle against the Japanese occupation forces during the Pacific war; these Americans were then with Ho in Hanoi for a few euphoric months after September 1945, when he captured and held the city with only a thousand or so Vietminh troops. The second phase saw the return of the French to Vietnam in 1945–1946 and the outbreak of the French Indochina War in November and December of 1946. Despite the military assistance the United States gave to the French without sufficient regard for the political consequences and Vietnam's future, this period culminated in France's abject defeat by Ho's forces in 1954. The third phase saw the Americans in effect replace the French in Indochina in what was thought at the time to be a legitimate and logical move to stop the spread of Communism throughout Southeast Asia.

For the Americans, the real trauma of Vietnam began when this third phase led to their deep overinvolvement after 1961 and their inability to comprehend not only the Communists they were fighting but the Vietnamese they were supporting. For the Vietnamese, on both sides, the three phases blended and formed a revolutionary mosaic of conflict and continuity, and as the conquest of Cambodia in 1979 testified, the saga of the revolution was continuing in what undoubtedly would be self-generating cycles of further struggle and sacrifice to achieve ever-expanding and perhaps unattainable goals.

If Vietnam was a finished chapter for most Americans after April 1975, the war continued to evoke multiple memories and images, heroic as well as shameful. As the dust of defeat settled—the greatest defeat the United States has ever suffered in any foreign war, politically and psychologically even more than militarily—the judgments and appraisals began to come more clearly into focus. The line between violence and compassion, between meanness and mercy, began to be better understood. Even all the errors of omission and commission that were made, all the unnecessary killing and destruction wrought, were, if not forgiven or forgotten, placed in a broader historic context and perspective. One hoped that in time they would produce a more practical and sensitive awareness of the limitations of power, of the difference between responsibility and response.

In the darkest moments of the war and in the months that followed, I felt that, beyond the lost and ruined lives, the United States would learn little or nothing from Vietnam. I am still not sure that the full lessons will be learned, and it may never be completely possible to "heal the wounds of the war," neither those of the Americans nor those of the Vietnamese. Some scar tissue will inevitably remain. But a graft of recognition—a slowly emerging cognitive awareness of what it all really meant, of how beyond confusing pride with purpose, and damaging their own hearts and heritage, the Americans tarnished their own image and suffered a diminution of character and creed—gradually began to take place.

From the outset Vietnam was damaging and dangerous because the challenges it presented were as exotic and enticing as its pitfalls were perilous. The challenges were also difficult to grasp and define, in part because Vietnam, at the end of World War II, was a comparatively small unknown country seething with nationalist rebellion and caught up in a contagious and exciting swirl of contending political and religious forces. I still believe, as I have noted in earlier books, that the catalogue of American mistakes in Vietnam began in the mid-forties, when the United States should have gambled on trying to arrange a deal with Ho Chi Minh, which he sought from both the French and the Americans. Then, during the fifties, had the United States not supported the French so foolishly and futilely in their outworn effort to retrieve an already lost empire, the Vietnamese revolution might not have been "won" but it might at least have evolved less discordantly and disastrously. Vietnam would probably still have gone Communist, but it could have emerged as a real Asian Yugoslavia, both independent sooner, and at far less cost, and less dependent on the Soviet Union today. In any event, Vietnam need not have been a quagmire, and it could have been a proper revolutionary proving ground instead of a scarred and bootless battlefield.

Nothing was ever simple about either Vietnam or the Vietnamese, and nothing is solved, if the effort to understand what happened there, and what has happened since the Americans left in such an undignified fashion, is confined to saying that they had no business being there in the first place. More was at stake than the morality of intervention in a distant land. If the United States is to learn anything about its role in Asia and avoid repeating the sort of mistakes made in Vietnam, it has to consider its experience in the larger framework of its relationship historically to all of Asia since the Pacific war, to Japan and to Korea as well as to Vietnam and the rest of Southeast Asia. This became particularly true after the Chinese Communists captured China in 1949, and the Western world, especially the United States, misread and overreacted to their external revolutionary dialectic and purpose.

The question of whether the United States might have accomplished more in Vietnam by doing less will bedevil historians for some time to come. Certainly a formula of properly conceived counterinsurgency assistance, limited and supervised economic aid, plus more consistent and firm pressure for political and social reforms, should have been more forcefully attempted back in the early days of the regime of President Ngo Dinh Diem, after 1954 and prior to 1961. It was then that America's direct role in the second Vietnam war began to increase without adequate planning and foresight; Vietnam became the unrequited and in many ways the insatiable mistress of the United States, and the extraordinary love-hate relationship began that led to misery and disaster for both countries.

At that point Washington was so concerned about the spread of Communist influence through Vietnam to Thailand and elsewhere in the region that it lost sight of its political and emotional bearings. The increase and misuse of additional aid led to a loss of faith in Diem and prompted the Americans to encourage and ultimately secretly to support the coup against him and his scheming brother, Ngo Dinh Nhu, in November 1963, though President John F. Kennedy and others were deeply upset over the unanticipated assassination of the two men. Unfortunately, the illusion that backing the coup would demonstrate American interest in substantial reforms in South Vietnam was quickly destroyed by a weak or nonexistent response to the chaos that set in afterward. Not only did the United States lack any post-coup planning, as did the Vietnamese, but as events unfolded the Americans revealed an abysmal and increasing paucity of understanding both of the complicated politics and of the social and cultural mores of the Vietnamese.

Why the Americans Failed

Granted that the South Vietnamese were extraordinarily and probably congenitally divisive, Washington either should have used the leverage it had to force reforms more strongly or, once the Vietnamese proved incapable of putting their house in order and fighting a successful counterinsurgency war against the Communists, should have reduced its aid and refrained from becoming more militarily involved. I felt this in the early sixties, as did many if not most of the early American military advisers who were assigned all over the country, and I came to believe it even more strongly in later years, though I continued to believe that the United States had a genuine political commitment in Vietnam, which unfortunately it misconstrued and mishandled. At the very least, the dispatch of large numbers of American troops should have been dependent on a firm political quid pro quo from the Vietnamese—to put their political house in order and initiate social and economic reforms. And if, after Diem, Washington still felt that Southeast Asia was of vital concern to the non-Communist world, which I also believed (as I do today), Washington should have broadened its regional approach and policy more sophisticatedly and effectively from the outset and not just concentrated on "saving" Vietnam from its inevitable revolutionary catharsis.

Instead, having given up any real hope of internal reform by influencing the revolving-door Vietnamese governments of 1963–1965, Washington made the tragic decision to fight a bigger war. This began early in 1965, with the start of the bombing of the North and the dispatch of the first contingent of American Marines to Danang; by mid-1965 direct participation included the the sending into action of the first large-scale ground forces as, in effect, the attempt was made to substitute American power for native weakness and incapacity. In the end, this was probably the most disastrous American decision of the century.

In the last thirteen years of the guerrilla war that blended into the big war, I was based in Hong Kong and was in and out of Vietnam constantly, spending about half my time there. Though I traveled extensively around the country and went out on a number of military operations—logging thousands of miles in helicopters, visiting firebases, sleeping at night in the jungle and spending occasional weeks trying to comprehend the sheer military aspects of the war —my major concern was the deteriorating political and social scene. I still believe that this was the core of the problem, and that the war was essentially a political rather than a military one, which is to say that it was unwinnable militarily but could have been ameliorated and compromised sooner.

Almost from the beginning, the South Vietnamese suffered from poor morale or sheer incapacity to mount and sustain successful operations against a dedicated, determined and highly propagandized jungle-wise enemy. With rare exceptions, the South Vietnamese forces at all levels were riddled with corruption or were victims of ambitious scheming by ranking officers, who in turn were involved in the larger power contests in Saigon. When the Americans made the mistake of taking over the main burden of the fighting in 1966–1967—and demonstrated that having fought the wrong kind of war to begin with, they did not even know how to fight the wrong kind of war right —they also reacted with growing confusion and lack of rational response to the endemic instability of Vietnamese politics. By their misconceived efforts to introduce Western techniques of management and planning into the conduct of the war, in such areas as pacification as well as in military matters, they simply confused the Vietnamese further and inhibited what might have been a more natural political and social development in the South. By computerizing the war with body counts and hamlet evaluation schemes, the Americans dehumanized it further, beyond death and defoliation, and corrupted themselves as well as the Vietnamese. Even if the South was bound to succumb to Communism, it might have been able to retain a greater revolutionary identity of its own had the United States overwhelmed it less with its lumbering presence.

This is not to say that everything the Americans did was wrong. There were, for example, a considerable number of imaginative young State Department and economic-aid officers who worked in the countryside on pacification and other matters, and who were able, in their own unique way, to comprehend the true revolutionary situation and to facilitate schemes to deal with the Communists. But, invariably, either the Vietnamese counterparts of these Vietnamese-speaking Americans were transferred or the Americans themselves were, or left for home after their relatively short tours of duty were up. Some of them kept coming back out of infatuation by or obsession with Vietnam, but in almost all cases their second, third or even fourth attempts to put worthwhile ideas into practice brought diminishing returns and ultimately renewed frustration.

At the national political level, the procession of American ambassadors and their vast, incestuous staffs always astonished me with the narrowness of their vision and their scant knowledge of the odd mixture of romanticism, deviousness, opportunism and greed of most Vietnamese politicians, especially of those the United States chose to deal with. If anything, the Vietnamese knew and understood even less about the Americans, though they tantalized themselves with fantasies. Sooner or later most of them fell into the trap of believing that the Americans could do anything: organize a coup, make or break a new political party, manipulate Buddhist bonzes or Catholic priests as if they were pawns on a chessboard. While in a position to use political pressure to some degree, the United States unfortunately either failed to apply it at all when it was most necessary or used it in the wrong way at the wrong time to help the wrong people.

It was of course a mistake at the outset to believe that the United States could introduce a Western system of democracy into an Asian country such as Vietnam, with its convoluted history of struggle against the Chinese, its own dynastic conflicts and its divisive and enervating colonial and postcolonial experience. It was even more foolish to suppose that this could be done in the midst of a bitter war. The South Vietnamese—unlike their Northern compatriots, who knew what victory was and had their own concepts of independence—had never really tasted either conquest or any sort of genuine freedom. They had been subjugated for so long that the idea of democracy, if it sounded or seemed appealing, was more chimerical than real. As they tried to fathom it their experimental moves, their American-inspired and orchestrated elections, their maverick constitutions and political party maneuverings and laws became an increasingly hollow and shabby charade. On top of all this, the South was composed of more diverse political and religious elements than the North, and the Southerners in general were accustomed to an easier and slower way of life, with plenty of food available, as well as luxuries introduced by the French and then by the Americans—all of which created additional psychological problems that made it impossible to build a solid, cohesive and functioning governmental structure. Certainly there was no chance to superimpose a Western democratic system on an antipathetic Asian framework or to blend American habits and customs with the far different and more elusive attributes of the Vietnamese.

The fact is, the Americans were all along much more optimistic about the war than the vast majority of Vietnamese I knew, including ordinary peasants who always carefully hedged their bets and made their own accommodations with the Communists, whenever that was necessary, which it often was. It was the Americans who created the myth of the coonskin cap and ultimate victory and who refused to face up to reality; much as the South Vietnamese talked of wanting to avoid Communism, they were simply incapable of making enough sacrifices and working together effectively enough to do so. Unable to adapt themselves to American methods, military or political, as one of my Vietnamese friends commented sadly toward the end, "We didn't even have the courage to speak up to you." Surely, if they were ever to have a chance, they should have been made far more self-reliant from the outset than the United States permitted them to be. If they were to have guns, for example, they should have been given the best guns the Americans had, M-16 rifles, far sooner than they got them, which was not until after the 1968 Tet attack of the Communists; and at the same time they should have been trained to train themselves, not imitate the Americans or depend on them for almost everything, from cartridges to cigarettes. The whole array of American-imposed panaceas—the Strategic Hamlet program, the Phoenix program for killing Vietcong agents, and so on—were the product of American "think tanks" and were invariably masterminded from the White House basement, without sufficient recognition of Vietnamese social and economic conditions, or of Vietnamese culture and mores. The trouble was that when the big war took over, the social planning went awry, and the lack of political judgment and plain common sense on the part of the Americans led them time and again to back leaders simply because they were amenable to doing things "the American way," no matter how corrupt and ineffectual they and their entourages might be.

As an American friend of mine who had spent many years in Vietnam ruefully remarked at the end, "Have we been kidding ourselves all along about the abilities of the Vietnamese soldiers? We should have asked ourselves long ago how an army can go on functioning when it is simply a business organization in which everything is for sale—from what you eat to a transfer or a promotion. We never encouraged the Vietnamese to fight aggressively, to take the offensive. We fought the war for them and made them overdependent on air support. We prepared them for a conventional war when the Communists were fighting unconventionally, and then, when the Communists adopted conventional tactics, the South Vietnamese didn't know what to do. The fact that they had no leadership was largely our fault; we made them followers— so successfully that even the soldiers who were willing to fight got killed or wounded as a result of incompetence, or lost by default." Somewhat earlier in the war one of my closest Vietnamese friends had put it even more cogently and prophetically. "You Americans think you have given the Vietnamese a better material life," he said. "Most of the equipment you've poured in here will end up as scrap . . . The Vietnamese like to raise monkeys. You have seen them, in the animal markets, in homes, in the parks. What you have done here is create a monkey climate of your own. The only Vietnamese you really know —the ones you have always dealt with—are monkeys who copy what you do. Why don't you at least help us get rid of the monkeys before you go!"

As the war dragged on, through the ill-fated invasion of Cambodia in May 1970, and the fiasco of the Laos incursion in 1971, followed by the Communist Easter offensive in Vietnam in 1972, and as the objectives of the North Vietnamese to capture all of South Vietnam one way or another became ever more clear, it also became ever more apparent that domestic pressures as well as failures or stalemates in the field would force the Americans to somehow extricate themselves. At the Paris peace talks in October 1972 (which I attended) Secretary of State Kissinger and Le Duc Tho, the North Vietnamese negotiator, drew up the basic agreement, which, though it was not put in force until the more specific cease-fire agreement was signed in January

1973—following the violent Christmas carpet-bombing of the North—spelled the end for the South Vietnamese. I wrote at the time that Kissinger and Tho had "brilliantly, if rather brutally, contrived" the agreement—brutally because, while the Americans agreed to withdraw from South Vietnam, nothing was said about North Vietnamese troops withdrawing, which amounted to a tacit acceptance of their continued presence in the South. The agreement imposed on the Saigon government also meant that the United States had started to pull the rug out from under President Nguyen Van Thieu by finally telling him that they had done everything they could for him (though he would still receive some military hardware and economic aid) and that it was now up to him to prove that he could keep South Vietnam from going Communist.

This was something I had never thought Thieu had the slightest chance of doing. In countless long arguments with American officials through the years I had maintained that Thieu was an unpopular, vacillating and conniving leader who could never pull the country together, let alone control the bickering members of his own palace guard. The Americans defensively insisted—until the last few weeks, when it was too late—that there was no one better than Thieu and that, anyway, he had been elected and re-elected in open, honest votes, which to me had rather seemed ineffectual and unconvincing demonstrations of a dictatorship pretending to be a democracy. What the Americans had done was effectively paint themselves into a corner with Thieu. If they had intervened earlier to get rid of him, they could at least have created the kind of dialogue among Vietnamese political leaders—and there were some honest patriotic nationalists around—which might have led to the formation of a decent civilian government, even one that in wartime would perforce have had to have some sort of military council sitting on top of it. By 1973 it was too late to promote such an effort, even if the American establishment had wanted to do so. And even if such an effort had been made, it probably wouldn't have altered the outcome of the war, but at least its resolution would doubtless have come sooner, under less demeaning circumstances.

The question of whether the Hanoi government ever seriously considered a negotiated settlement of the war has been widely debated. Despite their avowed intention to conquer the South (which all their captured documents and their secret party resolutions made abundantly clear), they were at various times willing to negotiate an end to the costly conflict, as the history of abortive international efforts shows, including several that involved East European diplomats and a motley collection of travelers to Hanoi. On at least two occasions the initiative was Hanoi's. Some of these "openings" were later proved to be phony, and in the final analysis Hanoi would probably never have accepted any terms that would not have ensured its victory, much as it wanted the Americans to get out of Vietnam.

If a coalition government of some sort had been created, it would surely soon have been dominated by the far better organized Communists, with the

Northern leaders of the Laodong (Workers) Party, now the Communist Party of Vietnam, simply using their Southern agents of the National Liberation Front (NLF) and later of the Provisional Revolutionary Government (PRG) as their momentary instruments—to be discarded, as indeed most of them afterward were discarded, when the takeover became complete. The process of domination, however complicated under some of the projected terms of the Paris agreement, conceivably would have taken from three to five years. But such a hiatus would have enabled many thousands of Vietnamese who were unable to leave Vietnam at the end of the war, or to escape by hazardous boats afterward, to emigrate more normally. Hundreds of thousands of lives might have been saved if a negotiated agreement had occurred as early as 1971 or 1972. But by the third week of March 1975, and perhaps even earlier, it was beyond question that Hanoi had decided to go for broke and take Saigon by force.

The Fall of Saigon

According to accounts subsequently verified by the North Vietnamese themselves, the Communist command in the South, known as COSVN (Central Office for South Vietnam), had as far back as August 1974 begun formulating a long-range plan for what was at first projected as a limited General Offensive. In November and December the Hanoi top command, led by General Vo Nguyen Giap and his deputy, General Van Tien Dung, sorted out the options more carefully, formulating a three-phase plan. The first phase was a series of attacks in the Delta and against the province of Phuoc Long, northeast of Saigon. Phuoc Long fell early in January, the first of eighteen South Vietnamese provinces to be militarily captured, and the North Vietnamese were surprised and gratified when the reaction in Washington was far less strong than the Communists had anticipated. At the outset of the cease-fire in 1973 the Americans had poured a large amount of military hardware into South Vietnam, but thereafter, to the dismay of the South Vietnamese, they began diminishing their support and failed to abide by the basic agreement to replace weapons and other equipment lost on a one-for-one basis, with the result that army commanders began hoarding ammunition and other supplies, which scarcely increased their capacity to resist North Vietnamese attacks. In sharp contrast, two weeks before the capture of Phuoc Long, General V. G. Kulikov, Chief of Staff of the Soviet Armed Forces, visited Hanoi, and the Russians then agreed on a three- or four-fold military-aid increase.

The North Vietnamese command ordered the start of their second phase —an attack on the city of Ban Me Thuot, in the Central Highlands—at dawn on March 10. Though some government troops fought surprisingly well, the city fell to the Communists in three days. What began as an orderly retreat eastward by government troops and civilians, mostly in trucks and cars, bogged down fifty miles from the coast, where a damaged bridge had to be repaired. With food and water short, fighting broke out between undisciplined government Rangers and local townspeople. Then elements of the 320th North Vietnamese Division began pouring artillery fire into the rear of the column, and panic started. Many people were killed or wounded, and most of those trying to get to the coast never made it.

The day after the fall of Ban Me Thuot, Thieu met with his top commanders and set forth a strategic concept that involved the possible abandonment of the lightly populated, Communist-dominated provinces of Pleiku and Kontum, north of Darlac province, of which Ban Me Thuot was the capital. The general in charge of the corps area interpreted Thieu's concept as a tactical order and started the withdrawal at once, at which point the government's tactical-command structure fell apart. The Communists, who as their third phase had planned an attack on Tayninh province, on the Cambodian border northwest of Saigon, thereupon changed their plans and decided to strike heavily in the north, at the cities of Hué and Danang. They took swift advantage of the confusion caused by Thieu's reversing himself on which city to defend more forcibly—he opted belatedly for Hué, which had more sentimental but less strategic value than Danang. As a result the worst panic of the war broke out as soldiers fought refugees to get out of Danang by road, by sea or by air. Soldiers shot civilians who were blocking their way as they tried to board planes, and sometimes shot one another in struggles to climb onto barges and escape by water. No one thought any longer of making a stand.

By the end of the month both Hué and Danang were gone, and a chain reaction led to the quick collapse of the coastal provinces to the south. The North Vietnamese themselves were surprised by the swift success of their campaign, which had cost the Thieu government nearly half of its main divisions, large additional elements of Rangers and other groups, untold numbers of territorial and local forces, half of its air force, and as much as $1 billion worth of equipment. With eighteen Northern divisions in the country at this point, the preponderance of North Vietnamese strength was now described by one American as "so overwhelming as to be ludicrous."

The North Vietnamese moved quickly in Hué and Danang and in the other coastal province cities they captured to set up new revolutionary administrations, which generally consisted of a People's Revolutionary Committee, a Military-Political Committee and a Military Management Committee. The structure of these three basic committees was reminiscent of the old Vietminh organizations established in the South between 1946 and 1954. At the same time, as they swept along in their drive southward, members of the underground revolutionary committees created by the Communists over the past several years began to surface in the countryside. However, while the underground apparatus in the various cities and in the countryside played a part in the quick conquest of about three fifths of South Vietnam in a month's time, it could not be said that this amounted to the General Uprising the Communists had always talked about. There was no mass movement, no mass reaction as such. The victory was a blunt military achievement, though in many places the government troops had fled in panic as the Communists simply walked in and took over with virtually nothing except loudspeakers, a few tanks and truckloads of their own troops, and they lost very few men on their drive south.

By April 4, in accordance with the decision made at the late-March meeting of COSVN, the word had been passed along at lower-level cadre meetings throughout the South that the aim was now "total victory," with the attack on Saigon to begin by mid-April. By about April 20 the National Security Agency, in Fort Meade, Maryland, had begun to receive intercepted Communist communications that fully substantiated this attack plan. These offered proof that the North Vietnamese were placing as many as thirteen divisions around the capital, that they had missiles capable of functioning over a radius of thirty nautical miles and emplaced close enough to Saigon to hit the city if necessary. If the Communists had ever been serious about giving the fumbling Saigon government time to reorganize itself, which by this time was certainly no longer the case, they formally ran out of patience on April 22, the day after President Thieu was finally prevailed upon by American Ambassador Graham Martin, with the help of French Ambassador Jean-Marie Merillon, to resign.

For several days before April 21 and 22, when the Communists stiffened their propaganda line and started cutting off the roads leading into Saigon, there was a seeming pause in their attack and in their propaganda, too. Through French and East European channels, and probably through Moscow as well, the United States had given assurances to Hanoi that the man the Communists had for some time indicated they might negotiate with, General Duong Van Minh, would be chosen to head a new government. Minh had been chief of state for three months after the 1963 coup against Diem, which he helped lead; after the next coup that overthrew him, he went into exile in Thailand for five years, and upon his return moved slowly back onto the political scene as a figure sympathetic to the non-Communist but ardent nationalist "third force," supported by many Buddhist leaders and favoring reconciliation and peaceful coexistence with the Communists.

In any event, if the Communists ever regarded Minh as anything more than a decoy—and in retrospect this seems doubtful, certainly not after the March COSVN decision—the scenario that belatedly brought him to the presidency, on the evening of Sunday, April 27, had been played out much too slowly, with the South Vietnamese bickering about "legality" and "constitutionality" while the roof was falling on their heads. Thieu's immediate successor had been Vice President Tran Van Huong, the once popular mayor of Saigon, who, at seventy-one and infirm, had every bit of Thieu's stubbornness but little of his acumen and adroit manipulative ability. Once having achieved the presidency, Huong was in no mood to relinquish it. Minh, as stubborn as the rest of them, insisted that he be made head of state again, or else President, and he refused to become Prime Minister under Huong. As the heavy weight of legality hung over Independence Palace—just as every last shred of independence was vanishing—and as the South Vietnamese Assembly met and bickered about inconsequential details of transfer of power to Minh, the vaunted

American-style democracy, which Washington had foisted upon South Vietnam, was revealed in this ultimate moment as totally ineffectual.

The role played at the end by the Americans was peculiarly ambivalent. Beyond delaying any action on getting Thieu to quit (Martin had talked Vice President Nguyen Cao Ky out of mounting a mini-coup against Thieu) the ambassador, who had always performed diplomatically as a lone wolf, had held back on recommending the complete evacuation of Americans, of their Vietnamese employees, and of political friends, because he was afraid that such a move would cause panic among the population and influence the Communists' choice between military and political action. He did not realize, or would not admit, that the choice of military action had already been made. In fact, his military analysts had told him for weeks that the situation was deteriorating very rapidly and that the Communists were fully prepared to begin an attack on Saigon. He not only stubbornly refused to accept this intelligence but even dispatched an economic report to Washington that emphasized the wealth of the rest of the country, especially the Delta, which he thought could be saved, and which, he said, still merited foreign investment. Members of the embassy, on the other hand, had been trying for weeks to convince him that the only hope of compensating for the worsening military conditions was to force the creation of a suitable Saigon government, which would negotiate from weakness but might at least save lives and arrange an orderly American withdrawal and a surrender with some dignity.

At the root of his hesitation—and this was part of his refusal to order an earlier evacuation which could have been better controlled and would have got more Vietnamese who had worked for the Americans out of the country— was his misguided hope that Congress would still somehow vote South Vietnam enough aid to rally its soldiers and continue fighting. (Later, aboard the Navy communications ship *Blue Ridge,* looking like a ghost of his former confident self—he was then suffering from mild pneumonia—Martin defended his position, while admitting his deep "professional as well as personal involvement." He told the assembled correspondents, "The verdict of history will be that we didn't have to leave Vietnam the way we did"—meaning that the fault was not his but Congress'. He was a man who chose to go down with his ship, blaming the abrupt final crisis on the storms of political controversy back home and not, in any way, on his own procrastinations and his forlorn miscomprehension of what was going on in Vietnam during the last month of the denouement. His behavior in the final month was the paranoid culmination of his career as an ill-fated Cold Warrior.)

By April 26 the PRG radio was broadcasting demands that all Americans, including Martin himself, leave the country, and that before going, they dismantle the "puppet government and its machinery completely"; it declared that a third force could no longer serve any useful function beyond "bringing the people over to the revolutionary side." This clearly spelled out that the Communists were no longer interested in a tripartite government under the terms of the Paris agreement but only in dealing directly with a new regime that was ready to surrender. When Minh was finally approved unanimously by the faltering South Vietnamese Assembly as President—Huong having reluctantly stepped down—he spoke of the need for reconciliation but also ordered the army to "keep your spirit high, your ranks intact, and your positions firm," so as "to defend the territory that is left," and he ordered all officials and the police "to continue fulfilling your duties and to watch vigilantly to prevent sabotage." The Communist radio quickly let it be known that the speech was "insufficient."

There was no longer any doubt that the die was cast. Shortly after six o'clock on the evening of April 28, the Communists pulled their neatest ploy: they manned four captured government A-37 fighter-bombers with captured government pilots, who were angry about having been abandoned by Thieu's troops and had undoubtedly been subject to some rapid "re-education," and after refueling at Pham Rang on the coast, the planes proceeded to Tan Son Nhut, where they bombed the headquarters of the Vietnamese air force. The irony of the Communists' using American-donated planes flown by disaffected government pilots to attack the capital was not lost on the Vietnamese in Saigon. From the airport, one of the planes flew over Independence Palace —an action that created panic downtown, with soldiers firing wildly at it— and then all four planes flew northward, strafing Route 1. The incident occurred just after President Minh had been formally installed in the palace, in a typically elaborate South Vietnamese ceremony marked by the removal of the flags and seal of the Second Republic and their replacement by Minh's personal symbol, a stylized lotus.

At four o'clock the next morning, Tan Son Nhut and the principal suburbs of Saigon were bombed, shelled and rocketed, and numerous fires broke out on the city's outskirts. From the roof of the Caravelle Hotel we watched North Vietnamese tanks and vehicles move down Route 1, their lights brazenly shining, toward the capital. American officials, rushing to the embassy in the dark early-morning hours, suspected that the end had come, yet few took the precaution of packing even an overnight bag, for they believed they would at least have a chance to go to their lodgings again. The chance never came. They spent the morning burning and shredding documents, and they also burned several million dollars' worth of U.S. currency. By dawn, crowds of Vietnamese were seeking to get into the embassy, and the panic to get out of Saigon was spreading throughout the city. Offshore, the ships of the Seventh Fleet, most of which had been stationed there for five days or a week, were already on full alert to lift out the remaining 1,400 Americans in Saigon.

As a dozen or so members of the embassy staff dashed around town to collect Vietnamese politicians and intellectuals who had been placed on a special evacuation list, other officials, both at the embassy and at the Defense Attaché Office at Tan Son Nhut, gathered some of the Vietnamese employees of the Americans and their families, and piled them on buses bound for the DAO area—the main embarkation point by air. About 40,000 Vietnamese, including bar girls who had been "vouched for" by individual Americans, and corrupt business and government officials, had been evacuated by transport planes during the previous ten days. Though some further planning had belatedly been done in the final week, the last-minute effort to get as many Vietnamese employees or friends of the Americans out as possible by helicopter was an ad hoc proposition, and it was amazing that as many got out as they did. Had firm contingency plans been prepared in advance by Martin and his staff, many more, including 60,000 or 70,000 key employees of the embassy, the AID mission and the CIA, could have been rescued in time. The fact that so many Vietnamese got out on their own, in fishing boats, or in some cases in barges made available by their American friends, to be picked up at sea by American transports, was a tribute to their own ingenuity and daring.

In the fifteen minutes before I left my room at the Hotel Continental, around eleven o'clock in the morning, two of my best Vietnamese friends visited me. One of them eventually got aboard a helicopter from a nearby rooftop. The other, an ardent anti-Communist nationalist and one of the main underground leaders in the Buddhist fight against Diem in 1963, didn't make it. I later heard he had either been shot or committed suicide, as did a number of other friends who made a conscious decision to remain behind, believing that even though their lives might be imperiled under the Communists, life in Vietnam was still preferable to being a destitute alien in some strange, faraway country. Some of these friends later changed their minds and were among the 10,000 who managed to escape from Vietnam by boat in the next two years, before the major exodus of boat people began after 1977. By 1979 it had reached more than 200,000, and the numbers kept increasing each month. The vast majority of postwar refugees settled in the United States. Others went to France, Germany and Australia, or remained in camps in Thailand and Malaysia, hoping to be accepted somewhere eventually.

The North Vietnamese Take Over

North Vietnamese tanks and troops entered Saigon in force on the morning of April 30, and about 12:15 P.M. the surrender ceremony took place at Independence Palace; after delivering a short speech, ex-President Minh, whose tenure had been one of the briefest and saddest in the history of any country, was allowed to return to his house nearby, where he resumed his avocation of raising orchids. According to Europeans and Americans who stayed behind, among them a number of foreign correspondents, the city was extremely quiet for the first two or three days. The streets were empty and shops were boarded up, and there was a general sense of trepidation. But then, as the new Communist officials gave orders for business to continue as usual, the shops reopened, and so did the restaurants and cafés. Within a week or so, the sidewalk vendors—most of them peddling goods stolen earlier from the American Post Exchange or looted from the homes of fleeing Americans—returned, and the thousands of *bo doi* (North Vietnamese soldiers wearing baggy green trousers and shirts and pith helmets as they patrolled the streets) could not believe their eyes at the vast amounts of goods on display, ranging from wine, liquor and cigarettes to spare machine parts, shiny tool sets, electric typewriters, adding machines, stereo sets, cameras, radios and watches. In their wildest imagination, the *bo doi* admitted, they had never dreamt of such things being available.

Having suddenly achieved their goal of three decades, the Communists were in no hurry; they now moved slowly, and with some degree of uncertainty, to establish their authority. According to Neil Davis, an Australian correspondent who worked for the National Broadcasting Corporation and who remained in Saigon for three and a half months, the predominant feeling in Saigon during these early months was one of bewilderment on the part of most of the population, which was puzzled by the absence of revolutionary fervor and change. But, as Davis perceptively added, they were also increasingly apprehensive that their personal freedom was bound to be more circumscribed and their traditional easy way of life severely altered if not altogether obliterated in the months and years ahead, and their fears proved well founded.

As the mood momentarily relaxed in the first weeks, lithe Saigon girls reappeared in their dainty *ao dais* (silk trousers and robes) or in bright summer dresses, and this panoply of color and the conviviality that accompanied it entranced the *bo doi,* who ran the risk, as Hanoi was to become increasingly aware, of being subverted by the warmth and riches of the South after so many years of harsh disciplined life in the North or in the jungle. While the *bo doi* behaved well for the most part, much better than the soldiers of the old South Vietnamese army ever did, the Saigonese quickly became aware that they spoke with authority and held the power of life and death in their hands. While they were gentle in taking care of drunks, drug addicts and prostitutes —the crackdown against these elements did not begin in earnest until after Davis left—the *bo doi* demonstrated a quick, angry response at other times. To cite one incident, two young old-regime "cowboys" (as members of youth gangs were called) rode by on a motorcycle and snatched an old woman's purse. When she screamed as they rode off, a *bo doi* calmly stepped out into the street, and standing face-on to the onrushing motorcycle, killed the two cowboys with two direct shots. The old woman cried, "I didn't want them killed, it was only two hundred piastres." By the same token, Davis reported, a number of *bo doi* began to be mysteriously killed, either by cowboys or by what were the beginnings of a small but persistent resistance movement. "All in all," Davis noted, "the *bo doi* are like strange transplants, and in their own way they seemed to me just as bewildered by Saigon as Saigon was by them."

As elsewhere, the North Vietnamese quickly established a Management Committee to run Saigon (the name of which was changed to Ho Chi Minh City) and it was headed by one of their war heroes, suave, bespectacled General Tran Van Tra. Except for attending a few receptions and an occasional press conference, General Tra and the committee stayed behind the scenes but handed out an increasing number of edicts and regulations, limiting travel out of the city without permits, ordering the closing and confiscation of shops if the old owners had fled the country or gone into hiding, and most important, ordering everyone to register with the new authorities. On May 15 a big victory parade took place, when for the first and only time in the early months the Saigonese got a glimpse of the top North Vietnamese leaders, including the aged President of North Vietnam, Ton Duc Thang, and Politburo members Le Duc Tho and Pham Hung, the top man in the South both during the war and after. At one point during the first few weeks General Vo Nguyen Giap, the military hero of the thirty-year revolution who had directed the campaigns against both the French and the Americans, was in town for two or three days, but he never appeared in public.

During the early weeks of the takeover—what Davis described as "a peculiar sort of limbo period"—the two chief topics of discussion in Ho Chi Minh City were the future of the Provisional Revolutionary Government and the timetable for unifying the two halves of the country. At the outset, the North Vietnamese red flag with a yellow star was prominently displayed in most places at similar staff length with the PRG's blue-and-red flag with a yellow star. Although the North Vietnamese Politburo was uncertain in the immediate postwar period about what kind of permanent or semipermanent government it wanted to establish in the South prior to unification, it clearly was not going to relax its control. During the first four months it sent down thousands of its own cadres to administer the South, where Communist cadres had been badly decimated during the long war, and besides, it was doubtful that Hanoi trusted them to control the situation. While PRG ministries were formally established (Huynh Tan Phat, a former Saigon architect who had headed the PRG in the jungle, became Prime Minister of the new government, and Nguyen Huu Tho, a lawyer and the other chief Southern revolutionary hero, became its "adviser"), these top officials seldom appeared in public in Ho Chi Minh City and spent most of their time traveling around the countryside in low-key showman roles.

The fact that both Vietnams applied for membership in the United Nations —applications which, many thought foolishly, were vetoed in the Security Council by the United States—was a sure sign that Hanoi was initially playing it both ways. If two Vietnams had been accepted, that would have given Vietnam two votes in the General Assembly and might have delayed the process of unification by two or three years. Most Southerners would have preferred this—at the very least it would have given them some degree of leverage with the Northerners, if only temporarily. Aside from instinctively wanting to avoid being dominated politically by the North, they were definitely against the agriculturally rich South having to support the poorer North with rice and other products. "We'll have to pay if we unify" was a phrase often heard in the cafés, where, despite the ubiquitous *bo doi*, conversation was surprisingly free in the beginning. But as far as Hanoi was concerned, once the two-Vietnams approach had been rejected it had every reason to proceed faster with unification; the National Liberation Front went through the trappings of holding a conference and selecting a new committee for Ho Chi Minh City headed by Tho, but the behind-the-scenes Northern bosses there, notably Pham Hung and General Tra, slowly but surely moved to do away with the old paraphernalia and panoply of Southern independence.

In the months that followed, more and more Northern cadres were placed in top administrative positions, and the network of revolutionary management committees was extended all over the country. What the North Vietnamese called "breaking the machine" not only replaced the old regime structure but pushed the PRG into the background. According to Father André Gelinas, a French-Canadian Catholic priest who had lived in Vietnam for twenty-eight years and remained in Saigon for fifteen months after the takeover, what amounted to a coup against the PRG took place on July 19 and 20 when its headquarters in town was surrounded by the police. Other Westerners still there, however, maintained that this was just a precaution against a repetition of anti-Communist demonstrations that had taken place on those dates in previous years to commemorate the "National Day of Shame," denoting the signing of the 1954 Geneva accords ending the French Indochina War and giving recognition to the Hanoi government. Opposition already existed in various parts of the country by this time, particularly in areas along the Cambodian border populated by so-called Khmer Krom and by members of the Hoa Hao religious sect, most of whom were anti-Communist; among some elements of the Cao Dai sect in Tayninh province; and in the Central Highlands among the Montagnards, independent-minded tribal elements who had never got along with the lowland Vietnamese. Isolated pockets of resistance also existed in other parts of the country, where small groups of former government soldiers were holding out. None of this activity was serious enough to cause the new government much concern, but it continued sporadically over the ensuing months. Considerably more serious was the growing friction with the Cambodians, which began in the immediate postwar months along the border of the Delta provinces and for the most part resulted from attempts by the Cambodians to conduct raids and seize villages they claimed were rightfully theirs historically. This was the inception of the border war that, by the beginning of 1977, stretched all the way southward from Tayninh to the Gulf of Siam, and that would culminate in the Vietnamese seizure of Cambodia early in 1979.

The Process of Unification

In late 1975 and in the spring of 1976, the North Vietnamese proceeded methodically to prepare for the unification of the two halves of Vietnam. On April 25, a few days short of the first anniversary of the Communist victory, elections were held for a new joint North-South National Assembly in what was described as part of the process of "state unification." A total of 605 candidates were nominated by the Fatherland Front in the North, and the National Liberation Front in the South, and of these, 492 were elected (249

Northerners and 243 Southerners). The North Vietnamese announced that the new National Assembly would be "an organic part of the dictatorship of the proletariat, not a bourgeois legislature." Father Gelinas described the election in Ho Chi Minh City as not an electoral campaign as such but "a general mobilization of people's minds, which took the form of a barrage of propaganda in the press, radio and television, and on the street loudspeakers." Though the lists in each district included two or three more names than the number to be chosen, he added, Communist cadres told the people whom to vote for, and he quoted one such cadre as saying, "It's exactly our duty to clarify your liberty and to help you to act really freely by indicating the people who will best represent you." The voting turnout was nearly 100 percent— perhaps due to the fact that an individual's voting card, after being stamped, became his identity card, without which he would be unable to buy rice at government prices. Most victorious candidates received majorities of 96 percent or better.

The first meeting of the new Unification Assembly was held in Hanoi in the last week of June and the first week of July 1976, and on July 2 the Socialist Republic of Vietnam was formally created. Ton Duc Thang, despite the fact that he was weak and old, was re-elected President, and Pham Van Dong, the pragmatic revolutionary veteran, remained Premier. As a sop to the Southerners, Nguyen Huu Tho was named a second Vice President and Huynh Tan Phat became a Vice Premier, along with three other Southerners, including Madame Nguyen Thi Binh, who had been the PRG's peripatetic Foreign Minister, and Pham Hung, who kept his high status in the Politburo and remained the overall boss in the South. Hanoi became the capital of the new unified Vietnam, and the national flag and national anthem were the old North Vietnamese ones. The total number of provinces in the country was reduced from sixty-one to thirty-five, and most of the Southern provinces were consolidated and renamed.

The reasons for rapid unification soon became apparent. The North was having more difficulty swallowing the South than it had anticipated, and for administrative as well as security purposes, unity was considered necessary. Despite regional and religious differences, Ho Chi Minh and his fellow Communist leaders had always played upon the theme of "Vietnamese-ness," of a single people striving toward common aims, and they had done this far more successfully than the bickering Southerners and the proud but divided Central Vietnamese. And once unification became a reality, the new government in Hanoi wasted little time doing away with what remained of the Southern revolutionary groups. Late in January 1977 the National Liberation Front, which after its creation in 1960 had pretended through the years to be a bridge between Communists and non-Communists as well as the spearhead of the General Uprising that never took place, was unceremoniously buried. The PRG was already dead, and the Alliance of National, Democratic and Peace Forces, which had been set up in 1968 as a supposedly independent organization but had simply been another adjunct of the underground People's Revolutionary Party, the branch of the Laodong in the South, now also was abolished. A new national Fatherland Front (an expansion of the old one in the North) was created as the overall mass organization, incorporating elements of the former Southern front organizations. The Laodong itself was replaced by what it had always been—the Communist Party of Vietnam. The pretense was over, and if the memory of a separate Southern revolutionary movement lingered in the minds of some disillusioned Southern nationalists or national Communists, it would be a long time, if ever, before such ideas or ideologies would have a chance to be expressed.

All during the war, for sixteen years, the North Vietnamese had failed to call a party congress. Finally, in mid-December 1976, with the two halves of Vietnam by no means yet "unified" despite formal reunification, the Fourth Party Congress was summoned in Hanoi (previous congresses had been held in 1935, 1951 and 1960). It was attended by just over a thousand delegates, who represented 1.5 million party members (double the number in 1966), and its main purpose and achievement was to reaffirm ideological guidelines, approve the new Five-Year Plan (1976–1980) and make certain organizational changes in the party. Although the Politburo was enlarged from thirteen to seventeen members, including three alternates, all but one of the old-guard leaders who had been in power for up to thirty years and had led the way to victory over the French and the Americans (only Ho Chi Minh was dead) were re-elected, and the enlargement was largely a reflection of the Southern branch of the party having been absorbed (the three new full members were experienced administrators from the South). Sixty-eight-year-old Le Duan, first among equals since Ho's death, became secretary-general of the party instead of first secretary, and all the other old revolutionary heroes, including Truong Chinh, Pham Van Dong, Pham Hung, Le Duc Tho, Vo Nguyen Giap, Nguyen Duy Trinh and Le Thanh Nghi, were renamed with great acclaim in a festive atmosphere. They were all old men, averaging sixty-five years in age, and if some of the younger party leaders, hardly known in the West, had hoped to be given a chance to emerge, they were disappointed. However, quite a few of them, mostly Northerners but including some Southerners and Centrists, were elected to the new Central Executive Committee, which was enlarged from an estimated 57 to 138 members, and their average age dropped by about six years.

If a power contest existed beneath the surface—over the last three decades there had been doctrinal differences, particularly between Le Duan and Truong Chinh, but they had seldom surfaced, the big exception having been the struggle over land reform in the mid-fifties—it was not in evidence at the congress, which was essentially a victory celebration. However, four of the old veterans seemed to gain in power and stature: Pham Hung and Le Duc Tho (Tho had shared the Nobel Prize with Henry Kissinger for negotiating the peace), who were both Southern-born and had been the dominant figures in the South through the years, gained political stature and could be regarded as potential heirs to Le Duan; in the vital economic field, Trinh and Nghi assumed greater importance. That cagy, far-wandering diplomat, Premier Pham Van Dong, whose charm had captivated Westerners at the Geneva Conference of 1954 and even earlier, more than held his own at the age of seventy (he is likely to become President eventually), and it was he and Le Duan, along with Trinh and Tho, who made the major speeches at the congress, and afterward, that outlined the bold economic aspirations of the new Socialist Republic of Vietnam and set the new political guidelines. It was also these four who in a series of declarations before and during the congress severely criticized the party cadres, especially the younger ones, for such character faults, in Le Duan's words, as "loafing, callousness, irresponsibility, arrogance, authoritarianism, and bureaucratism." Tho warned of "opportunist elements infiltrating the party and assuming power with a view to seeking fame and wealth" and revealed that "tens of thousands of unqualified members" had, in fact, been expelled from the party. Trinh, cast in the new role of economic czar as well as retaining the Foreign Minister portfolio, attacked the cadres for adopting postwar attitudes espousing "the easy life," while the soldiers in the South, along with the cadres, were severely criticized for "being bewitched by material lifestyles." The dangerous temptations the *bo doi* and the cadres faced in the South were summed up in the phrase "money-guzzling." In the months that followed, reflecting the admonitions of the party leaders, two minor reshuffles of jobs in the Politburo took place, as well as the beginnings of a new purge of party members that indicated a reduction in total membership of as much as 10 percent and gave further proof of the worries about party discipline and the need for harder work and concentration.

In lengthy, rambling speeches at the congress by Le Duan, Pham Van Dong and others—Le Duan's alone was 240 pages long—the continuing supremacy of the Communist Party was clearly set forth, and the new ideological line of building "a model socialist world" and then progressing through phases of abolition of private property and collectivism to the new "Communist society," was elucidated. Le Duan spoke of the new Five-Year Plan as having "at the same time to do away with the heavy sequels of thirty years of war and to reorganize an originally poor and backward country." He re-emphasized the basic targets of the plan, including the production by 1980 of 21 million tons of rice, partly through the reclamation of 1 million hectares to supplement the 5 million hectares already under cultivation; the production of 1 million tons of sea fish, the planting of 1.2 million hectares of new forests, the raising of 16.5 million pigs; increasing engineering industry output two and a half times, and so on. Pham Van Dong said that all this would require a total investment of 30 billion dong, or about $7.5 billion, and that the annual rate of growth in the various fields would range between 13 and 18 percent. For a nation with a shattered Northern economy confronting a complex class structure in the South marked by an admitted "small-producer mentality" and an individualistic-minded peasantry, this was a tall order, made all the more difficult to fulfill because of the shortage of domestic technology and the ability to absorb outside help, even if it was obtainable at the rate anticipated, which it wasn't.

The South Proves Hard to Digest

In the months that followed, a deeper awareness of the problems that lay ahead and a more rational approach to them began to be expressed, although the hortatory, revolutionary line continued to be proclaimed, accompanied by constant admonishments, in particular, to the workers to make greater efforts. In a speech in Hanoi in September 1977, marking Vietnam's thirty-second National Day, Pham Van Dong declared, "There are those whose revolutionary nature has changed or decayed, and who are no longer worthy of the great cause of our people. We definitely will not tolerate skeptical, backward and pessimistic thinking. Nor can we accept fear of difficulties and hardships, selfish claims for privileges and special advantages, and manifestations of bureaucracy, authoritarianism and their consequences. 'A single worm can spoil a whole pot of soup!' Our people are determined to rid themselves of this kind of worm by any and all means!" Two bad years of crops (a third was to follow in 1978) had spurred the leaders to a fresh awareness of the primary importance of agricultural development, forestry and fisheries, and while the long-range objective of producing machinery and building up heavy industry remained, it was now stressed that such undertakings as irrigation works to stimulate food production came first, and that industrial projects that would stimulate agriculture were the most important plans to be pursued.

At the same time the urgency to develop raw materials and produce for export to obtain more foreign exchange was recognized, as was the need to satisfy the growing demand for consumer goods in the impoverished North, which had now seen how much better living conditions were in the South. Pham Van Dong, for instance, stressed the development of light industry "to supply consumer goods to the farmers so as to encourage them to boost agricultural production with zeal and efficiency." The quicker agricultural development took place, the more rapidly could the labor force be shifted to industrial enterprises, he said, and he emphasized the importance of the district as "a managing level in all fields, dealing directly with the provinces and to some extent with centrally run offices."

Even before unification was accomplished, the North Vietnamese had taken steps to restructure the South, socially and economically. Once the process of registering all citizens was completed, especially of old-regime officials and officers of the old army, the first groups of men were sent out to re-education camps, and eventually about 400,000 were subjected to re-education and labor reform. Long-term re-education, with no cutoff date, was prescribed for former military officers, former cadres and personnel in the fields of intelligence, public security, the Phoenix program and the Chieu Hoi program (the "open arms" program for surrendering Communists during the war), former members of old political parties, and those simply charged with owing "a blood debt" to the people. Separate treatment was accorded to prostitutes, juvenile delinquents and social misfits such as the "Saigon cowboys." Prostitutes, for example, some of whom were still patrolling the streets of Ho Chi Minh City in 1979, were sent to special schools for "restoring the dignity of women," where, in addition to attending lectures, they were taught handicrafts. As for the drug addicts, who numbered at least 200,000 during the war, they were sent to special centers, where after being treated medically, including by acupuncture, they underwent courses in gymnastics and occupational therapy, which included self-criticism sessions to help them establish their "self-respect" and keep them from returning to opium and heroin, which were still available.

According to Nguyen Cong Hoan, a former National Assemblyman under the Communists before he escaped by motorized junk to Japan and subsequently testified before the House of Representatives Subcommittee on International Organizations, the new government at the end of 1976 published an eight-point policy statement concerning the above groups of people. It stipulated that those who "show progress" might be released in three years, but there was no definition of how progress should be measured. Hoan added that the re-education camps for long-term prisoners were located "in remote areas, usually in the wooded or mountainous back country." Such camps were also called "production socialist reform camps," and those sent there were regarded as prisoners who were subjected to forced labor as well as indoctrination. A second, somewhat less stringent category of camps known as collective reformatories were basically re-education and thought-control centers, while a third category, the *hoc tap* (study) camps, were generally for short-termers and sometimes were only day centers. The government ran some model camps and displayed these to occasional visitors. Hoan, who as a National Assemblyman had been able to visit a number of the camps, corroborated what refugees and others who were able to smuggle out letters to relatives or friends abroad said: that the prisoners in the first camp category suffered from "extreme physical deprivation" and were "ill-treated in many ways," not only by being subjected to forced labor of all sorts but by having to go out hunting by hand for land mines left over from the war. He said he knew of seven large prison camps, and many smaller ones, in his native province of Phu Yen alone, where there were at least 6,000 prisoners, and where, he said, 700 persons had been executed, most of them in the immediate aftermath of the war. He added that additional numbers of prisoners had died in jail or committed suicide, while others had been sent to North Vietnam and no one knew what had become of them.

Hoan's testimony was the most specific and severe, along with that of Nguyen Van Coi, a former provincial representative from Quang Duc province, who escaped after spending time in three prison camps, in the last one of which, in the U Minh forest in the Delta, he said he had been chained by his ankles to a tree most of the time. Even discounting some of the more lurid accounts that have come from such witnesses, there was ample documentation to substantiate the fact that the Communists, while they did not engage in an outright bloodbath, dealt particularly harshly with those they considered incorrigible enemies of the new regime. Certainly many of these, as well as others who were old and weak, died in the camps from disease, malnutrition, overwork and lack of any amenities, including medicines, but how many may never be determined. In mid-1976 Hanoi officials told visitors that 95 percent of the 1.5 million persons who had been given re-education as of that date had been released, and early in 1977 the Vietnamese ambassador in Paris said that "at most some fifty thousand detainees were still held because of the gravity of their crimes." But there was no way to prove these figures, either. Nor was it easy to obtain and verify information about prominent non-Communist and "third force" leaders who had voluntarily chosen to remain behind in Vietnam or had been unable to escape at the end of the war. Some of these well-known political persons were imprisoned in Saigon while others were allowed to remain free but were kept under various forms of house arrest. One of the latter, for example, was Thich Tri Quang, the ardent Buddhist monk who had led the 1963 demonstrations against Diem and had later strenuously opposed Thieu. Others, among them my old friend Dr. Tran Van Tuyen, the former opposition leader to Thieu in the old National Assembly, were jailed, and according to letters smuggled out by friends and relatives, were known to have died there, or as in the case of another well-known monk, Thich Thien Minh, in re-education camps.

Four French correspondents who visited Saigon late in 1978, including three who had written favorably about North Vietnam during the war, corroborated that what amounted to a "Vietnam gulag" prison network existed and said that despite the release of a million or more South Vietnamese after they had been "rehabilitated," thousands of others, among them many former Vietcong soldiers, were still disappearing into agricultural "work camps." (Hoan claimed that "many others" were "openly executed.") There was sufficient evidence from refugees and additional sources to warrant the conclusion that some outright executions had indeed taken place. The fact that thousands of people had disappeared from their homes and were never seen again was more than circumstantial evidence that many of them had died, from illness or by their own hand or otherwise. Thus, if no bloodbath comparable to that in Cambodia took place, the elimination of unwanted and undesirable elements was carried out over a long period in a sustained and subtle fashion, and in doing so, the new government was guilty of human rights violations on a wide scale.

Control over individuals' lives, both in the cities and in the countryside, began early in 1976 when the governmental apparatus was tightened and various new committees were formed to function between the central management at the top and the revolutionary committees at the bottom. In Ho Chi Minh City a new Municipal Revolutionary Committee was set up, headed by a well-known Communist, Vo Van Kiet, replacing the initial Military Management Committee. Nine subcommittees or departments were established under the committee—dealing with security, administration, economy, health, welfare, information, culture, education, and liaison with the Chinese. Administratively, the city was divided into 17 precincts or districts, 91 wards, or subdistricts, and 492 sub-wards. Solidarity units, or block units, of about twenty families each existed within the wards, and it was at this level that indoctrination, including meetings every night, was held, on everything from a recital of American atrocities to discussions of local cleanliness and health and neighborhood discipline.

Father Gelinas was most graphic in describing the census that took place in the summer of 1976, when every adult had to describe his monthly activities for the previous seven years—"where you lived, what you did, what you thought and why you thought it, the names of people you knew and of those for whom you worked, etc." On each form, Gelinas said, "you had to list the names of five people who could guarantee the accuracy of your statements." This report then had to be read publicly before the block committee, and if neighbors caught any errors, it had to be done over again. Ten days later, according to Gelinas, without having taken any notes, each person had to answer the same questions all over again, and in some cases the process had to be repeated a third time, with the authorities double-checking every piece of information, so that ultimately they came to know "everything about everybody" in the neighborhood.

Prior to the census, the most important event was the first currency reform. After all bank accounts had been frozen, in June 1975, it was suddenly announced early in September that within twelve hours all money had to be exchanged for new South Vietnamese dong, the equivalent of the currency used in the North. All old currency was declared to be worthless thereafter, and each family could only obtain about $225 worth of the new dong. The "reform" caused a rapid spiraling of food prices, partly because farmers refused to sell their products to the government at fixed rates and grew only what they needed for themselves and their families. Under rationing regulations, everyone was entitled to at least nine kilograms of rice a month, at about nine cents per kilogram (those who did hard physical work got more), but to supplement this, those who could afford it bought extra rice on the new black market that quickly sprang up at about eight or ten times the official price. Meat and chicken became virtually unobtainable, and fish was hard to come by, too. As the inflation soared, and the freewheeling economy of the South, accustomed to American largess, continued amid the usual hoarding and speculation, the government moved more drastically to halt it. In March 1978 a national inventory of all private business establishments was conducted, and a vast amount of hoarded food and other supplies were confiscated, with the owners receiving payment for them at set prices; the proceeds were ordered placed in the national bank, to be used henceforth only for approved production purposes. Early in May the government unified the monetary system throughout the country and issued new banknotes. Each person was allowed to keep only 100 of the new dong (50 dong for rural people), and the residue had to be deposited in the national bank, to be withdrawn "for personal or production needs in accordance with prescribed procedures."

The new measures hit the South hard. If the inflation was halted, the traditional free market was all but ended, which particularly affected the Vietnamese and Chinese middle-class traders, let alone the wealthier ones, and it was these elements that by mid-1978 began the big new refugee exodus, which the government made no effort to stop and, in fact, condoned. Payments and bribes of $3,000 or $4,000 in gold to government officials and Chinese organizers of escape groups, and the monthly figures of those fleeing in boats to Malaysia, Thailand and other countries soared as the plight of the refugees grew worse and finally commanded world attention. The United States agreed to raise its quotas for the boat people to 14,000 instead of 7,000 a month; but this only solved part of the problem of the continuing heavy outpouring from Vietnam, with some 75,000 refugees ending up in Malaysia alone, which, like Thailand, accepted them temporarily but with increasing rancor. In 1978–79 half a million or more wanted to escape.

Curbs on currency, and the crackdown on private enterprise, brought the economies of the North and South closer together, but did little to solve Vietnam's basic economic problems, aggravated by a paucity of foreign aid, particularly after the Chinese cut off their assistance in July 1978. And what made things still worse was the bad agricultural situation. Although the 1975 rice crop had been good, drought, cold weather, typhoons and mismanagement had caused the poor results of 1976 and 1977, and the country, with its total of 50 million people, faced a shortage of about 2 million tons of rice, or one fifth of the normal rice crop. The Five-Year Plan calling for the production of 21 million tons annually was considered by most analysts to be much too ambitious, given the problems of management and discipline Vietnam was facing. In order to match the annual growth in population, at the rate of about 3 percent, food production had to increase by that much alone just to keep up with the growing number of mouths to feed. The situation continued to deteriorate in 1978, when disastrous floods in the southern Delta caused a loss of 2.6 million tons of rice; it was estimated that, overall, the country would have a deficit of 3.5 million tons for the year ending in April 1979, which was in excess of a third of its annual requirements. This forced the government to use its meager foreign-exchange earnings to import large amounts of grains from abroad instead of new machinery it sorely needed.

Southern Resentment Mounts

Confronted by food shortages that sometimes reached famine proportions (in Ho Chi Minh City, the stipulated ration of nine kilograms of rice actually consisted, late in 1978, of only one kilogram of rice, the rest being wheat, flour, sweet potatoes and cassava), the government moved to collectivize production in the South. It issued orders for all forms of "capitalist exploitation" of land and farm equipment to be abolished by mid-1979. "Rich peasants"—those who had more land than they could cultivate—were told to surrender their surplus acres, which the government would "requisition purchase," along with tractors and other equipment. Plans to nationalize the land were drawn up in order to achieve what Le Duan described as "political and economic collective mastery." Given the mood of the Southern peasants, who had started to sabotage what crops they had left or to feed them to their pigs rather than sell them to the government at the low fixed prices, it would not be easy to collectivize the land without the use of draconian measures. The government indicated it was not averse to using such measures, and there was already talk of forced grain collections.

The boldest and most far-reaching step the Communists of the new Vietnam undertook after their victory was massive relocation of the population. According to Douglas Pike, a State Department expert on Indochina, this was a long-term project which, if carried to completion over the next decade, would result in as much as four fifths of the total population moving to new homes. Pike predicted that the scheme "will have a more profound effect on Vietnam than anything that has ever happened in its long history." Particularly affected was the South, which was to be de-urbanized by the movement of 5 million city dwellers to the countryside and the transfer of another million from one rural area to another. Complementing the de-urbanization was a plan for what was called "rural urbanization," as a result of which about 160,000 hamlets were to be reorganized into 20,000 district-size towns, or "centralized villages," geared to better agricultural production. The first step in this proposed social and demographic restructuring began just after the end of the war, when 350,000 persons were repatriated from Ho Chi Minh City to their native villages. These were people who had fled to Saigon during the war, to escape the bombing or to find better jobs, and while some of them returned to their homes voluntarily others were "persuaded," or in effect forced, to leave the city by having their rice rations withheld if they refused to go. Another 300,000 were similarly moved from Danang and other large cities by the end of 1976.

An additional 350,000 persons were sent from Ho Chi Minh City to so-called New Economic Zones (NEZ). The government had hoped to move more than a million to such zones by the end of 1976, but the target wasn't met. The city's population was reduced by about 700,000 in all by mid-1977, which left it with about 3.2 million people, still far above the government's goal of bringing it down to 2 million or less. Unemployment remained a serious problem, with as many as 600,000 out of work in the winter of 1978. Directed from Hanoi by the General Department of State Farms and New Economic Zones, the chief aim of the NEZ drive was to return some 500,000 hectares (a hectare is two and a half acres) of war-abandoned land to cultivation. In addition to sopping up the unemployed and underemployed, the purpose of the program was to afford work for the more than 1.5 million members of the South's former armed forces and police. In all, there were to be about five hundred NEZs in the South, located in all the Southern provinces but primarily in large plains areas between Ho Chi Minh City and the Cambodian border, as well as in the highlands and their foothills. Theoretically, each family that arrived in a NEZ village of some 5,000 people was supposed to get a plot of land of at least an acre; lumber, and thatch or tin-roofing to build a new house; six months' supply of rice and salt; a month's supply of milk tins per child, plus five more months' supply eventually to be repaid; a water storage jug; mosquito netting; a kerosene lamp and two cooking pans; farming and carpentry tools; seed, fertilizer, and when available, some breeding stock, including pigs and water buffaloes.

Despite glowing government reports about the NEZs, their success was at best extremely uneven, and for the most part they were deeply resented by those uprooted, who were dispatched to the zones on short notice, sometimes as little as twenty-four hours, with large families often dispersed. The new arrivals usually found themselves in a barren wilderness, without any of the government's promised facilities and gifts. Lack of water, medicines and sanitation was among the major complaints, and "housing" was often nothing but bamboo huts without walls or floors and only banana leaves for roofs. Food rations proved meager. Life in general was described as miserable by those who wrote to their friends and relatives left behind in the city. Whether the poor preparation—first by the army, which was supposed to clear the ground and build roads, and then by paramilitary youth teams, which were to lay out plots, build houses, dig wells and stockpile tools—would eventually improve remained to be seen, but the initial impact of the NEZs on most people was almost as shattering as the re-education camps on those sent there. When they could, individuals and whole families paid bribes to Communist officials to keep from being shipped to the zones, or once there, they bribed their way back to the cities.

Among the subjects the Communists had most difficulty dealing with was religion, which had always been a strong force in the South. While accepting the existence of religious groups, the North Vietnamese refused to accord them social or political status in any organized sense that could threaten the doctrinal hegemony of the Communist Party. The party sought to resolve this issue by combining a pretense of freedom with subtle harassment and repression.

At the end of the war there were 1.5 million Catholics in the South, many of them originally Northerners who had fled after 1954, and their children, later born in the South. The Communists allowed them to go to church, but discouraged them from doing so with propaganda. According to some Jesuit priests who stayed in Ho Chi Minh City for a year and a half after the takeover, between two and three hundred priests and at least two bishops were in prison in 1976, some of whom were later released. The Jesuits reported a conflict between the younger priests willing to cooperate with the Communists and the older hierarchy of the church trying to survive on its own firm grounds of religious freedom. Some anti-Communist Catholic activists conducted a number of demonstrations, at least two of which were broken up by soldiers. But bit by bit, the leading Vietnamese Catholics compromised with the Communists. In October 1977 Archbishop Nguyen Van Binh, who went through a week of re-education courses, was allowed to attend the Synod of

Catholic Bishops at the Vatican, where he said that the Catholics in Vietnam were determined to coexist with the Communists and had decided to "help reconstruct society." The Church would not hide the differences between Marxism and Christianity, he added, but he asked, cryptically, "Does St. Paul's position—to be a Jew with the Jews, and Greek with the Greeks—apply to Christians living in a Marxist environment?" A year later, in an interview in the French Communist newspaper *L'Humanité,* he went further. People were not imprisoned in Vietnam "for religious reasons," he said, and "after three years of contact one has seen reality very well. Things have become much better. The Communists are not so cruel, not so bad, as people would say. Our Church is not subject to persecution. If we have no mistrust, but just open our hearts, we will be better understood. Christ has told us to love all our fellow beings. He did not say, 'Don't love Communists, don't love atheists.' "

The Communists were more wary initially in dealing with the South's predominantly Buddhist population. Five million Southern adults, almost half the adult population in the South, were practicing Buddhists in 1975, and another 40 percent were nominal believers. Soon after the takeover, a National Buddhist Liaison Office was established at the Xa Loi pagoda in Ho Chi Minh City to deal with Buddhist affairs. Of the two Buddhist groups that existed at the time, many members of the moderate faction, the Vietnam National Buddhists, fled the country. The more activist An Quang group at first tried to work out a *modus vivendi* with the Communists, who had long fostered their own Buddhist mass organizations in the North. More important than these organizations, however, was the new Six Harmony Buddhist Council, run by Thich Thien Hao, a National Assembly delegate from Ho Chi Minh City and a former leader of the National Liberation Front who surfaced after the 1968 Tet offensive. The party tried to convince the Buddhists of the merits of socialism and Communism even more assiduously than it did the Catholics, urging changes in the Buddhist lifestyle, such as substituting productive labor for the traditional solicitation of alms, and so on.

The response of most Buddhists in the South was one of passive resistance, what they called "a strategy of weakness." But beginning late in 1976 and continuing throughout 1977, individual Buddhists resumed an activist role. In November 1976 several Buddhist nuns and monks in Can Tho, in the Delta, immolated themselves by fire, an act reminiscent of what a number of Buddhists did during the days of their rebellion against Diem. Five months later the Communists closed the An Quang pagoda in Ho Chi Minh City and arrested at least six national Buddhist leaders—Thich Tri Quang among them. In the fall Thich Man Giac, one of Tri Quang's associates, fled to Paris and reported that the Buddhists' efforts to cooperate with Communists had failed and that the country was in the throes of an anti-Buddhist campaign. This seemed to be the case, although the Communists, conscious of the world-wide strength of the Buddhist movement, would no doubt concentrate on eliminating the influence of those Buddhists they felt were engaging in dissident activity while continuing to appease the majority of Buddhist bonzes (priests) and permitting the population to practice Buddhist rites. The potential resistance of the Buddhists, both passive and active, remained a factor the Communists might well have to contend with in the future, as was also true of those elements of the Hoa Hao and Cao Dai sects which kept up active resistance, but there were no signs, in 1978, that this opposition was as yet serious enough to cause the Communists much concern.

Another problem the Communists had to deal with when they took over the South was what they described as "the depraved, reactionary, degenerate, enslaving old culture." During the first weeks an organized demonstration led to the burning of decadent Western literature—books and magazines ranging from lurid detective and boudoir novels to sexy pictorial monthlies that used to be sold in the American post exchanges and were everywhere to be seen on streetside stalls. For a fortnight or so, all this stuff disappeared and in its place came dictionaries, technical manuals and Communist tracts. Then all the old books and magazines slowly reappeared, but not for long. A second clean-up campaign was begun in earnest, and a list of proscribed authors and books was announced. Thereafter nothing could be published without the government's permission, and most of what appeared in public was imported from Hanoi, primarily political tracts, technical books and pamphlets.

It was not easy for the Communists to change the lifestyle and loose habits of a city as big and sprawling as Ho Chi Minh City, including the large Chinese commercial area of Cholon, and progress was slow. At the outset, horse racing at Phu Lam, near the airport, which had continued until almost the very end of the war, was abolished, but cockfights were held for some time. Western movies disappeared and in their place, shown in about fifty movie houses in Ho Chi Minh City, came films and newsreels from the North, and these were played each evening on television, too. The old downtown Rex Cinema specialized in films about the Soviet Union and Eastern Europe. The Rex Hotel and the old Majestic Hotel alongside the Saigon River, as well as the Caravelle (renamed Independence Hotel), were meant to be the chief hostels for foreign tourists, which the Communists by late 1977 had begun to cultivate in their search for more foreign exchange. The old colonial Continental, where I first stayed in 1946 and where I continued to stay throughout my many years in Saigon, was renamed Hotel of the General Uprising and became a billet for the armed forces and government officials.

If the Communists found it difficult to change the face of the city in a hurry, there were certain elements of the population whose influence they did move to eliminate quickly, particularly writers, artists and intellectuals of the old regime, including university and high school teachers. Such people, along with what remained of the old South Vietnamese army and the "army of beauty, ladies of easy virtue," were collectively described by the Communists as "the three armies" that were most harmful to the revolution. While experts in scientific subjects were acceptable (American-trained technicians in the South were, in fact, among its most valuable assets for the North), intellectuals in the field of liberal arts, such as sociologists and teachers of literature, were anathema, and these people, if they were not sent to re-education camps, as many teachers were, were subject to indoctrination courses on the nature of Vietnamese Communism and socialist discipline. Some of these sessions were turned into Chinese-type "denunciation meetings," at which "counterrevolutionaries and local tyrants" were denounced, while others were devoted to self-criticism. As for the press, all the old newspapers (there had been more than a score at the end of the former regime) were promptly closed down, and a new government paper, *Giai Phong* ("Liberation"), was published, while about 60,000 copies of *Nhan Dan,* the major Hanoi daily, were flown to Saigon each day as soon as regular air schedules were established. A third paper, *Tin Sang,* published by former anti-regime National Assemblyman Ngo Cong Duc, who had fled the country under Thieu and returned when the Communists came, was the only semi-independent voice and was permitted to express occasional criticism under self-censorship.

As for education, all schools in the South were closed when the Communists arrived and were reopened only gradually, beginning with the elementary schools. Cadres sent down from the North brought special directives to incorporate schools into the Northern state system, and Northern teachers took over many classes at the junior and senior high school level, helping to indoctrinate the former Southern teachers who managed to avoid the re-education camps. When the universities were reopened, the sons and daughters of the working classes were allowed to enroll, but all but a few students with middle- and upper-class backgrounds were excluded, and all students were required to spend a third of the school year working on farms or doing other constructive labor. Liberal-arts courses were abolished, and fifteen separate new colleges were set up and attached to various ministries. Thus, by mid-1976 the educational system had been thoroughly revamped to serve the purposes of the state, and no semblance of freedom of expression on the part of students remained. It was no accident that many of the refugees who fled the country by boat, and to whom I subsequently spoke in camps in Thailand and Malaysia, were college students who had found the new system unbearable. Others, who had not been allowed to return to school, fled because they wanted desperately to continue their education in the United States or in France, or anywhere else where they would be accepted.

The Russians, Americans and Chinese

The more people fled Vietnam, the more isolated, in other respects, Vietnam seemed to become. When the final campaign to take over Cambodia began on Christmas Day 1978, the country's only major ally was the Soviet Union, with which, early in November 1978, the Vietnamese had signed a twenty-five-year treaty of friendship and cooperation during a high-level visit to Moscow by Le Duan and Pham Van Dong. The treaty—which primarily gave the Vietnamese much-needed economic assistance for repairing their major railways and bridges, for building a ground satellite communications station, and for training technicians and skilled workers in various fields—contained grandiose clauses mutually pledging political cooperation "to consolidate the world socialist system" and to consult immediately "in case either party is attacked or threatened with attack." Whether there was more to it than that, whether the Russians had taken advantage of Vietnam's economic predicament to bind it more closely to the Soviet Union militarily and obtain the right to increase their radar stations on the Sino-Vietnamese border and their reported tactical missile bases on the Gulf of Tonkin and possibly farther south in Cam Ranh Bay, was not certain, but the pact sent shockwaves all over Asia and disturbed the United States and the Western alliance.

A further question could be asked: Would Hanoi, despite its long wartime dependence on the Russians and its ideological ties that had certainly been as close and probably closer to Moscow than to Peking for many years, have accepted this somewhat blatant postwar bear hug if the United States had been more willing to improve relations with Vietnam and if the Hanoi-Peking relationship had not deteriorated so badly? The answer is "Probably not." But whatever specific quid pro quo the Soviet Union obtained, military or otherwise, it bound to its side Southeast Asia's largest if somewhat reckless military power, gave its approval to Hanoi's attack on Cambodia, and won a diplomatic and strategic victory over its archenemy Peking, which was backing the discredited Cambodian regime of Pol Pot. For the moment, this suited Vietnam's purpose, although the dangers of arousing the Chinese on the Sino-Vietnamese border remained. Over the longer range, the pact with Moscow broke down the careful fences Hanoi had been building with the five nations of ASEAN and raised fresh doubts among them about the ultimate aims of the Vietnamese in Southeast Asia. A new Moscow-Hanoi alliance with military overtones that promptly catapulted Vietnamese forces through Cambodia to the borders of Thailand scarcely gave credence to Hanoi's pledges to the ASEAN countries only a few months before that it would respect their territorial integrity, security and neutrality.

The United States, by opting for normalizing relations with Peking ahead of establishing ties with Hanoi, was certainly a factor in the new dispensation. In September 1977, after Washington agreed to lift its earlier vetoes, the Socialist Republic of Vietnam, the sixteenth largest country in the world and the third largest Communist nation, had become the 149th member of the United Nations. The process of normalizing relations with America had already got under way at meetings held in Paris in May and June of that year, largely as a result of a mission to Hanoi in March headed by Leonard Woodcock, who later became the first United States ambassador to the People's Republic of China. The Woodcock mission succeeded in obtaining the promise of the Vietnamese to help track down the remains of some eight hundred Americans still listed as missing in action, but the Vietnamese maintained their position that the Americans should "heal the wounds of war" by paying $3.25 billion in reconstruction aid, plus another $1.5 billion in commodities as pledged in 1973 by President Nixon at the time of the

Paris peace talks. The official United States position was that since the Vietnamese had violated the Paris agreement by attacking in force in South Vietnam, the pledge was no longer valid, and a possible compromise both on the amount of aid and the means of funneling it to the Vietnamese, through international organizations, was made more difficult by the House of Representatives' reaffirming the American decision not to give Vietnam any economic assistance.

There was little doubt that the Vietnamese needed the Americans more than the Americans needed them, though Washington would also benefit from the establishment of relations with Hanoi as part of the process of redefining its role in Southeast Asia. During 1978 the Vietnamese dropped their conditions for exacting reparations and cooperated further in tracking down the missing war dead, but Washington did not prosecute the issue of normalization, and President Jimmy Carter even quietly allowed the trade embargo with Vietnam to stand, though many American businessmen in Hong Kong and in the United States, including oil companies that wanted to explore Vietnam's offshore deposits, were eager to see the embargo lifted. The Vietnamese had already issued an attractive investment code that offered foreign companies a fair return on joint ventures, tax incentives, the right to remit profits, and a pledge not to nationalize any foreign-supported ventures for ten to fifteen years.

As the chances of establishing some sort of a relationship with the United States diminished, the close relationship with China ("as lips to teeth" had been the wartime phrase) came apart. Through the fall of 1977, when Le Duan was warmly received in Peking, they were satisfactory, and the Chinese, who had given the Vietnamese more than $10 billion in aid over two decades, were still giving them substantial amounts to repair the war damage and help alleviate food shortages. But the harsh treatment accorded to Chinese traders and artisans that followed the crackdown on private enterprise in Vietnam in the spring of 1978 (which started the exodus to China in the north, and then from Ho Chi Minh City in the south) soon led to a series of shooting incidents along the Sino-Vietnamese border, particularly in the Friendship Pass sector between the two countries. Efforts to patch up the quarrel and arrange some sort of orderly migration failed, and on July 3, 1978, less than a week after Vietnam had joined the Soviet-sponsored Council for Mutual Economic Assistance (Comecon) in Eastern Europe, Peking announced that it was ending its economic aid projects and withdrawing its advisers. The Vietnamese had already been ordered to close their consulates in three southern Chinese cities. Both the Chinese and Vietnamese sent more troops to the border, and the hostile atmosphere increased with the exchange of repeated accusations and warnings. Moscow offered Hanoi its "resolute support" against "attacks and blackmail," and as the tension mounted it seemed increasingly likely that the Chinese might launch a punitive attack on Vietnam. Rival claims to the Spratly and Paracel islands in the South China Sea between Vietnam and China did nothing to heal the break between the two countries, which for the time being, though diplomatic relations were not broken, seemed all but irreparably damaged.

The Vietnamese were receiving some assistance from non-Communist countries in Western Europe and from Japan, including grants, and government and private-bank credits, but they badly lacked technological capability and knowledge and were bogged down by red tape and mismanagement. Shipments that came into Haiphong often piled up on the docks—Hanoi itself admitted and criticized these transportation and communication bottlenecks. As for Southeast Asia, having maintained tenuous relations with other countries of the area after the war, fencing with ASEAN and accusing it from time to time of being a military alliance supported by the United States rather than an economic grouping, Hanoi began a serious effort in 1976 and 1977 to mend its fences. It sent its top-level diplomats on reassuring tours to the ASEAN capitals, and this culminated, in September 1978, with a trip through the region by Pham Van Dong, during which he made his pledge that Vietnam would not back insurgency movements in the ASEAN countries. Led by Malaysia, and then Thailand (which had earlier established diplomatic relations with Vietnam), new agreements for trade and technological exchanges were signed. Though mutual suspicions remained, a more substantial relationship on a bilateral basis between Vietnam and the Southeast Asian nations appeared to be emerging.

The Attack on Cambodia

Under these circumstances, and given the many problems they faced both at home and abroad, what prompted the Vietnamese to reverse this course and launch their lightning offensive against Cambodia?

Above all, it was an almost Pavlovian reaction to the long-burning ethnic conflict. It was also a cool, calculated military and political decision based on a number of factors, among them growing economic and social difficulties in the southern Delta area adjacent to Cambodia. A resentful peasantry already antipathetic to Hanoi's efforts to enforce greater discipline was further disturbed, though perhaps also titillated, by an increasing influx of anti–Pol Pot refugees from Cambodia's tyranny, and by the fuzzy but endemic anti-Communist border activity of the Hoa Hao religious sect and the Khmer Krom dissidents of mixed Cambodian and Vietnamese blood. Beyond that, the Vietnamese sensed that time was running out, that the Cambodians, who had initially incited the border skirmishes at the end of the Vietnam-American war, were likely to remain daring and disputatious at the same time that they began crawling out of their shell, making approaches to the outside world, and this included putting out diplomatic feelers in Southeast Asia. A contentious though fellow-Communist Cambodia, seeking a new identity of its own, was anathema to troubled Vietnam, still trying to put its own house in order after the hasty unification of the North and South. And, finally, with the support of the Soviet Union, the Vietnamese undoubtedly felt that they could take a chance with the Chinese, that any reaction by Peking to an attack on its wanton and often inconvenient ultra-Maoist protégé would now be unlikely, or under the terms of the new Hanoi-Moscow treaty, would be containable. As things turned out, this was something of a miscalculation.

One could also say that the Vietnamese were simply compulsive, that they were driven revolutionaries, that after so many years of warfare, against the French and then against the Americans, their revolutionary wheels could not stop spinning. Their own sense of manifest destiny, of the ever-expanding frontier, their perhaps willful but intoxicating vision of an Indochina Federation controlled by strings pulled in Hanoi, was a heady stimulant; and as both Laos and Cambodia showed increasing signs of becoming fractious, the Vietnamese responded in the fashion of bullies, determined to keep the minions in line. Conversely, the minions at home, including a restless army dissatisfied with the meager rewards of victory over the Americans, and smarting under the guerrilla thrusts of the surprisingly adept Cambodians, might be revitalized by another quick taste of blood, especially if the blood were that of an ancient enemy.

Disputes between the yellow-skinned, primarily mainland Vietnamese and the darker-skinned Khmer and the Chams (descended from the people of the ancient kingdom of Champa) who were historically proto-Malayan or Indonesian in origin, and were later Hinduized, dates back centuries. Though they were allies against the Americans, the war did not diminish their age-old hatred of one another. During the war, when the Vietnamese used Cambodia as a sanctuary and trained Khmer Rouge cadres in Hanoi, and later fought against the troops of the Lon Nol government that replaced Sihanouk in March 1970, they clashed frequently with the Khmer Rouge troops too. At the same time they established what in effect was a permanent foothold in the northeastern part of the country. At the end of the war the border between Vietnam and Cambodia, historically unclear and made more so by the French, became amorphous as a two-way traffic took place: Cambodians who had taken refuge in Vietnam moving, or being forced, back into Cambodia, and Vietnamese living in Cambodia fleeing into Vietnam as anti-Vietnamese feelings rose. The first border incidents took place in the summer and fall of 1975, when the Cambodians raided towns in the southern Delta, claiming they were Khmer territory. The Vietnamese responded by seizing the Poulo Wai group of islands in the Gulf of Siam, which were reported to contain oil deposits. Cross-border raids by both sides, accompanied by bloody atrocities, occurred sporadically in 1976 and 1977, and by the end of 1977 it became apparent that a full-scale border war was in progress. It sputtered out for a time during the first part of 1978, after the Cambodians claimed to have won a "great victory" and recovered most of the territory seized by the Vietnamese. The Vietnamese withdrawal, however, most observers believed, was attributed as much to a subtle warning from Peking as to battlefield action, although the Cambodians, adapting guerrilla tactics in response to the conventional attacks of the Vietnamese, inflicted considerable punishment on the invaders. At one point the Cambodians rejected a Vietnamese offer for a cease-fire and a territorial settlement, though, when the tide turned in favor of the Vietnamese, the Phnom Penh government professed a willingness to talk peace. Hanoi's attitude then stiffened, and most analysts in Thailand and elsewhere believed that the Vietnamese, who had begun to train Cambodian prisoners and refugees as a paramilitary and then as an outright military force, intended to carve out a cordon sanitaire inside Cambodia and establish "friendly" local administrations which, in time, would "bleed" farther into Cambodia and help subvert and then promote the collapse of the Pol Pot regime. Few believed, however, that Hanoi would risk an all-out attack of its own against Phnom Penh and other Cambodian cities, for fear of finally provoking a major Chinese attack on Vietnam's northern border.

But the analysts were proved wrong. The Vietnamese had all along been waiting for the dry season. The Christmas Day attack was launched primarily from the Central Highlands and proceeded rapidly along eight key Cambodian highways in a manner astonishingly similar to the final attacks in Vietnam in 1975. Both were planned by General Van Tien Dung, the army chief of staff, under the overall direction of Defense Minister Vo Nguyen Giap, who four days before the campaign started had spoken of using a "strategic offensive" to execute the "historic mission" of defeating "the aggressive war of the reactionary clique in Phnom Penh." According to Nayan Chanda, of the *Far Eastern Economic Review* (the best of the Indochina analysts who wrote the clearest political and military reports on the war and on the general situation in Vietnam, Cambodia and Laos), Dung adopted the same tactics he used in Vietnam, what he called the "blooming lotus" method of hitting directly at the center of key cities, destroying the Cambodian command headquarters there, and then fanning out to hit outposts on the perimeter. Using Soviet tanks and planes, including MiG-21s and American A-37s and F-5s left over from the war (this was a difference between 1975 and 1978, since only a few planes were utilized against Saigon and this time as many as fifty sorties a day were flown), more than 100,000 Vietnamese troops fighting in large units struck at the key city of Kratie on the Mekong, and then outflanked another important city, Kompong Cham, on the other side of the river. They trapped 30,000 Cambodian soldiers, almost half the army, and then smashed them with heavy-artillery fire and bombs. Complementing this attack into central Cambodia were thrusts through the northeastern and southeastern parts of the country. After capturing Takeo, another vital city in the southeast, five Vietnamese divisions, supported by intense air cover, advanced along three highways toward Phnom Penh, which was surrounded early on January 7 and then quickly entered and seized. The Vietnamese forces, as Chanda pointed out, thereupon continued their "blooming lotus" tactics by mopping up the smaller peripheral towns and seeking out the scattered units of the defeated and bewildered Cambodians.

Just as they had done in South Vietnam during most of the war, until toward the end, the North Vietnamese denied that they were in Cambodia.

They credited the hastily organized 10,000-man "army" of the Kampuchean National United Front for National Salvation with the victory—some Western analysts later said these forces only totaled 5,000 originally. KNUFNS' central committee was headed by the little-known Heng Samrin, a former regimental commander and political commissar in the Khmer Rouge forces. The day before Phnom Penh was captured, the central committee made public an eight-point policy statement, drawn up on January 1 for the "liberated areas," and on January 11 the Kampuchean People's Revolutionary Council proclaimed the founding of the People's Republic of Kampuchea (see the chapter on Cambodia for further details). An estimated 30,000 or so remnants of the Khmer Rouge army, mostly holed up in the northwest and in the Cardamom Mountains and Elephant Range southwest of Phnom Penh, vowed to continue the fight. The mountains and range could become a formidable redoubt, and if these forces could obtain supplies from the Chinese via the sea route, in the Gulf of Siam, or across the Thai border, some analysts believed they could make good on their threat to fight a "protracted people's war of resistance." But most observers felt that even though they rallied and recovered some territory, their days were numbered and that at least a third or half of the Vietnamese forces would remain in captured Cambodia indefinitely to safeguard the victory and supervise the administration of the new government.

Pol Pot was reported to have taken refuge initially in the northwest, near Battambang, but Foreign Minister Ieng Sary fled to Thailand and was allowed to fly on to Hong Kong and then to Peking, where he pressed the cause of the defeated Khmer Rouge with his Chinese friends before returning to Cambodia. The man left in charge of resistance in the field, in the southeastern mountains, was Son Sen, the former Defense Minister, who had visited Peking shortly before the attack and was apparently forewarned that the Chinese would not intervene in Cambodia if the Vietnamese attacked, and that he would have to depend primarily on his own guerrillas.

Two days before Phnom Penh fell, Prince Norodom Sihanouk, the former King, Prime Minister and Chief of State of Cambodia, who had been a virtual prisoner of the Pol Pot regime for three years under what amounted to house arrest, was allowed to leave the city and fly to Peking, where he held a six-hour press conference in typical Sihanouk style, gesticulating wildly, laughing, crying, and in his squeaky voice letting it be known that though he held no brief for the Pol Pot regime, he would represent it at the United Nations in New York in denouncing the Vietnamese invasion and demanding that the Vietnamese forces get out of Cambodia. Sihanouk was allowed to speak at the UN, where others too decried the invasion (as did the ASEAN nations collectively), but nothing substantive was accomplished, chiefly because of the Soviet veto in the Security Council. Possession anyway was nine parts of the law, and the law in this case—that of outright conquest—had been written and applied by the Vietnamese themselves.

It was difficult to judge the long-term impact of the startling Vietnamese conquest of Cambodia. From the beginning Hanoi must obviously have weighed the drawbacks of further upsetting the already upset Chinese and of alienating the ASEAN countries, while gaining the opprobrium of most of the rest of the world, including the United States. If the Russians were smirking over having given the Chinese a setback in the area, they had also run the risk of setting off a chain-reaction situation in which, knowing the Chinese might act to slap the Vietnamese down on the Sino-Vietnamese border, they would have to decide what to do to help their Hanoi allies, either in Southeast Asia itself, or in northern Asia or along the still-bristling Sino-Soviet border. Whatever happened, by encouraging Hanoi to strike into Cambodia, Moscow had damaged the cause of Asian stability and had raised fresh doubts about its motives in the Far East. The key to what might happen next remained in Thailand, for if the Vietnamese chose to support the Thai Communist guerrillas, contesting the Chinese for influence among them, the overall outlook for peace and stability would become still gloomier. The domino theory, if too simplistic, still had some validity, and both the Malaysians and Singaporeans were extremely worried about what might happen next. I have always preferred to think in terms of a "bleeding" theory rather than of falling dominoes, and if the Vietnamese revolution, with fresh blood in its veins, now bled across the Cambodian border into Thailand, and if the complex refugee flow aggravated the picture further in time, all the ASEAN nations would sooner or later be affected. On the other hand, if the Vietnamese, having done their deed in Cambodia for their own reasons, eventually withdrew and tried to repair the damage done to their own relations with ASEAN, some sort of equilibrium could be re-established, but there was no doubt that their pious statements would henceforth be taken with a solid grain of salt.

China Attacks Vietnam

The Chinese invasion of Vietnam that began on February 17, 1979, and lasted seventeen days in its initial offensive phase, added a major new dimension to the already tenuous situation. In view of the months of friction along the 700-mile border between the two countries and the preparations for war by both sides, the attack came as no surprise, but the question everyone asked was why the Chinese chose to launch it just after having consolidated their new relationship with the United States and as they were about to start their bold new modernization plan. Vice Premier Teng Hsiao-ping's excoriation of the "polar bear" during his successful trip to the United States was one thing, but baiting the bear in open defiance, and embarrassing his new-found American, European and Japanese friends, whose economic help he so much needed, was something else again.

Peking's main motivation was probably its determination to prove its *machismo*, to make clear that it was not a "paper tiger" and, as Teng had forewarned during his American trip, to "teach the Vietnamese a lesson." The centuries-old hostility between China and Vietnam, and Peking's conviction that the Vietnamese were becoming too bold and were moving too fast to consolidate their hold on all of Indochina, undoubtedly were other factors. The Chinese also must have felt that they had to respond to Russian "adventurism" in Africa and the Middle East (the Horn of Africa, Angola, Iran, Ethiopia, Yemen, etc.), as well as in Asia, including the whole area extending from Afghanistan to Vietnam and the rest of Southeast Asia. Moreover, the recent flexing of Soviet naval muscles in the western Pacific was certainly worrying the Chinese, as it also worried other Asian nations, particularly Japan.

The attack, though limited from the outset "in time and space," as the Chinese indicated, was a fairly large incursion that ultimately sent approximately 100,000 troops into Vietnam, with about as many held in reserve on the Chinese side of the border. Opposing the dozen invading divisions were six regular Vietnamese divisions, including the famed 308th, which had successfully fought against both the French and the Americans, but only a few of these 60,000 troops were committed to battle; the burden of defense was borne by 70,000 regional and local forces. Though outnumbered by the Chinese, the more mobile Vietnamese fought well and kept the attackers from advancing as swiftly as Peking had hoped. The Chinese said from the start that they would not make an effort to capture Hanoi or Haiphong, and it appeared that their geographic objectives were half a dozen key towns ten to twenty miles below the border, including Lao Cai in the west and Lang Son in the east, all of which they eventually succeeded in capturing before beginning their slow withdrawal at the conclusion of their "punitive" effort, but they did not succeed in luring the Vietnamese into a major battle, which was their tactical objective. Ultimately both sides claimed military victory, but both claims were dubious. By using as many troops as they did, the Chinese were eventually able to overpower the Vietnamese and seize the towns they wanted after inflicting considerable damage. But their army, which had long been considered an ill-equipped defensive force with virtually no experience beyond China's borders (the comparable brief attack on northern India in 1962 had been much easier to prosecute against little opposition), did not distinguish itself. The far better equipped and more experienced Vietnamese, chiefly the tough regional troops, held off the Chinese for the better part of a week, even without the use of Vietnam's first-rate air force, which Hanoi was reluctant to commit against Peking's inferior but larger number of planes.

The apparent architect of the invasion was Teng Hsiao-ping, who must have had his own reasons for launching it. Certainly among them was his desire to benefit from normalization of relations with the United States and to use that as a weapon against the Russians, whom he and other Chinese leaders had long been accusing of seeking world hegemony, a favorite Chinese deprecatory code word. When he was visiting the United States he constantly repeated his warnings about Soviet ambitions, including the use of the Vietnamese as surrogates—he referred to Vietnam as "the Cuba of the East" in emphasizing the need to restrain Hanoi's ambitions as well. When the invasion took place,

Moscow charged "collusion" between Washington and Peking, ignoring the fact that President Carter had sought to restrain Teng from attacking Vietnam, though perhaps not as forcefully as he might have. While they had believed Teng's declarations about teaching the Vietnamese a lesson, the Americans had hoped that he would not strike so soon after his return to Peking, which gave the Russians an obvious propaganda opening at a time when Washington was eager to balance normalization with China off against preserving and solidifying détente with Moscow, particularly with the SALT II talks reaching a climax.

The Russians demonstrated unusual restraint when the invasion took place, mainly warning the Chinese to "stop before it is too late," and they lived up to their treaty with Hanoi by consulting with the Vietnamese but confined their military response to sending a dozen vessels, including one missile cruiser, into or toward the South China Sea and to dispatching a dozen cargo flights and some cargo ships with military hardware to Vietnam. There were reports of Soviet troop movements along the North China borders, but no incidents took place, though if the invasion had lasted much longer, a limited Soviet military response in Manchuria or in Sinkiang in western China was considered possible if not probable. No doubt for this reason, Teng halted the invasion after the capture of Lang Son and ordered the Chinese troops to start withdrawing under protective artillery fire. For his own domestic reasons too, Teng did not choose to risk arousing his political opponents in China, who had probably been against the attack from the start and who were by no means averse to seeing Teng come a cropper as a result of it. If he had prolonged the invasion, Teng would surely have risked his political future and endangered his modernization plans as well. The Russians, hoping this might happen, thus had a further reason for showing restraint, and Teng was undoubtedly also aware of that.

The Chinese had hoped that their attack would force the Vietnamese to withdraw troops from Cambodia and that their withdrawal from northern Vietnam could then be tied to a Vietnamese agreement for an international conference on Cambodia that might eventually lead to elections, with Sihanouk ending up the winner. While such a conference may ultimately take place (the Americans and the ASEAN nations, among others, have supported the idea), Hanoi showed scant inclination to let go of Cambodia, although the Russians airlifted some Vietnamese troops from South Vietnam and from Cambodia to the Hanoi area during the period of the Chinese invasion. The Vietnamese quickly replaced them with new conscripts. As the Chinese withdrew from the north, Hanoi ordered a state of full mobilization amid signs that the border issue would not be that easily settled. While the Vietnamese wanted to establish a neutral border zone several kilometers in depth, the Chinese implied that they might try to retain several areas in northern Tonkin below the border which had been seized by the French late in the nineteenth century and had later become part of independent Vietnam. There were also signs of Chinese troop activity in northern Laos, where Peking had been building roads for the Laotian government for seventeen years under the protection of a number of its own battalions. Urged on by the Vietnamese and the Russians, the Lao now demanded that the Chinese construction crews withdraw, at least temporarily, but the whole picture in northern Laos remained murky and there were increasing reports of the Chinese arming some of the rebel tribal elements including the Meo, who had fought with the Americans during the Vietnam war. In sum, the situation along the borders between China and Vietnam and Laos seemed likely to remain tenuous indefinitely, and a resumption of hostilities at any time could be expected, whatever tentative agreements were reached.

It was difficult to make a judgment as to who had benefited most from the Chinese incursion. If the Chinese had proved that they weren't paper tigers and had made good on their promise to teach the Vietnamese a lesson, the lesson was scarcely driven home forcibly. Both sides claimed to have inflicted "heavy" casualties on each other, but the Vietnamese lost more in manpower and property destruction—Lang Son, Lao Cai and the other towns the Chinese had captured and then given up were all but destroyed, mostly by artillery, and scores of bridges and industrial facilities, chiefly manganese phosphate and other mines, were blasted by shells. As aggressors, the Chinese had to some extent taken the curse off the Vietnamese for having been the aggressors in Cambodia, but the ASEAN nations remained worried about what the Vietnamese might do next, though they hoped the Chinese invasion would inhibit any further immediate aggression by Hanoi. The momentary benefactors appeared to be the Russians, who were respected for having shown restraint, though fear of Russian ambitions to dominate the Asian seas remained; it had been no secret that Moscow wanted to establish a naval base at Cam Ranh Bay in southern Vietnam, which the Hanoi government had so far refused to concede, through Russian ships were anchoring there occasionally. More important, Western intelligence sources reported that the Russians had received concessions in the northern port of Danang and had also been granted rights to use the large airfield there built by the Americans.

As far as the Vietnamese themselves were concerned, the big question was whether they would be able to strike a proper permanent balance between their revolutionary convictions and their desire to concentrate on internal reconstruction and development and on building complementary and peaceful competitive relations with all the other nations of Asia, including the ASEAN countries, with Japan, and when the dust died down, with China as well. More than anything else, Hanoi remained eager to establish new relations with the United States, which would help them economically and make them less dependent on the Russians. This would be in Washington's interests, too, and it seemed only a matter of time before the Carter Administration's earlier backing off from accepting such relations—a decision apparently reached for domestic political reasons that only partly had to do with the determination to normalize first with China—would be reappraised.

Beyond these diplomatic ploys lay the primary question of how well the

Vietnamese, with whatever outside assistance they received over the coming years, would be able to solve the problem of adjusting to peace after more than thirty years of waging war. The difficulties of joining the two culturally disparate parts of the country were almost too tremendous to contemplate: to carry out the vast experiment of shifting around so much of the population, to reconcile class and doctrinal differences that were bound to remain, and at the same time to achieve even part of the ambitious economic goals over the next two decades. Some observers in Hanoi (Communists as well as Westerners) were pessimistic about the chances of the Vietnamese prospering. Their shortcomings were cited as including a confused and demoralized bureaucracy, the inability to regiment a diverse people of so many different religious beliefs and social customs, and technological deficiencies. It would surely take a generation to deal with such matters in any conclusive way.

Another imponderable concerned the new generation of leaders who would take over from the aging members of the Politburo. Now that the fight for independence and unification had been won, would they have the same sense of dedication and zeal that their remarkable predecessors had had? Or would they succumb to disunity and factionalism among themselves, or perhaps to another form of foreign adventurism, which their response to Cambodia's ill-fated challenge to their hegemony in Indochina perhaps foreshadowed?

Proud and xenophobic, despite their fresh attempts to reach out to the rest of the world, the Vietnamese are still basically survivalists. They have survived for centuries against combinations of enemies, and they have successively thrown back the Chinese, the French and the Americans. This sense of national survival undeniably runs deep and is in most ways commendable, but it also contributes to an attitude of ultradefensiveness, and to an odd mixture of bravado and fear that tends to enhance Vietnamese suspicions of outsiders. In this sense, as Asians, and particularly as Asian revolutionaries, they are closer to the Chinese than to the Russians, but this, in turn, also accounts for their fear and suspicion of the Chinese.

Having known and watched the Vietnamese for thirty years, my own feeling is that they could strike the necessary balance between their domestic aspirations and requirements and their foreign hopes and fears, but that the danger of their overreacting, intentionally or accidentally, to what happens in the rest of Southeast Asia is still a perilous factor. If the authoritarian societies in the region begin to break down, and fresh revolutionary opportunities and imperatives arise, it would be too much to expect the Vietnamese to ignore them, particularly in view of the contesting Russian and Chinese presence. One cannot, therefore, over the long term, diminish in any evaluation the revolutionary dynamics inherent in Vietnamese history, or in the Vietnamese psychology. Certainly, one way or another, the impact of the new Socialist Republic of Vietnam will be a force to be reckoned with in Asia.

Cambodia—
Trouble in the
Isolation Ward

The agony of Cambodia will go down as the most tragic episode of the second Indochina war and its aftermath. However one juggles the figures of the dead—and true numbers were hard to come by—death was rampant and pandemic. Between March 1969, when the secret American B-52 bombing of the country began, and January 1979, when the tyrannical Pol Pot regime was overthrown by the Kampuchean National United Front for National Salvation (a sudden creation of the invading Vietnamese), about 2 million people lost their lives. Of these, an estimated 800,000 were killed by bombs and artillery and as a result of the ferocious ground fighting during the big war. At least a million—and some estimates ran to nearly twice that many—were murdered or died from disease and starvation after the Communists took over and instituted what can only be described as one of history's greatest reigns of terror marked by draconian forced internal migrations in the name of political purification and rapid rustication of the urban population.

In 1970 Cambodia had a population estimated to be between 7 million and 8 million. The Communists maintained in 1978 that the total was nearly 8 million, a figure widely regarded as high because the rulers of the country wanted to make it seem bigger than it was, not only to deny the deaths that had taken place but because they wanted to attain a population goal of 15 million to 20 million in a decade or so. This was a bravado ambition based on their fear of again being attacked by their voracious neighbors, chiefly Vietnam, which had destroyed the once powerful Khmer empire that held sway from the ninth to the fifteenth centuries and had included most of what later became South Vietnam as well as Laos and Thailand.

Their fears, as it turned out, proved well founded. The Vietnamese all-out attack on Cambodia that began on Christmas Day 1978, following three years of sporadic border warfare, was a calculated move that combined ethnocentric vengeance with brazen imperialism, and it created as much turmoil and recrimination in Asia and elsewhere as was caused by any single action or event of the long Vietnam war, including the American–South Vietnamese invasion of Cambodia in May 1970. Both sides excoriated and denounced each other in the harshest terms, accusing each other of adopting Hitlerian tactics and of being guilty of every sin from rape to cannibalism. While most Cambodians, and most of the rest of the world as well, were glad to see the overthrow of the Pol Pot dictatorship, widespread dismay and anger greeted the Vietnamese effort to destroy through outright aggression a neighboring country, however reprehensible its oppressive rule. With both fitting irony and tragicomic drama, it was left to Prince Norodom Sihanouk, the former chief of state, who was freed from three years' house arrest in Phnom Penh at the last minute, to plead the defeated government's case before the world while more vociferously condemning the Vietnamese. Sihanouk performed his task with all his old-time zest and aplomb, and simultaneously salvaged his own tormented conscience. Using all his natural theatrical talents, and falling back on his own vast experience of acrobatic diplomacy with the Vietnamese, the Chinese, the Russians and the Americans, the wily, articulate Prince bitterly attacked the Vietnamese for their perfidy while making it clear that he spoke not in defense of the Pol Pot regime but of Cambodia and himself as the personification of the Khmer tragedy.

The question that nobody could answer, and that would probably remain unanswerable for some time to come, was how much freedom of action and maneuver Hanoi would permit the new Phnom Penh government of Heng Samrin, the forty-four-year-old President of the Kampuchean People's Revolutionary Council. It became quickly apparent that Hanoi was determined to move even more rapidly than it had done in Laos to embrace the new Cambodia tightly in its fold. Under a twenty-five-year treaty of friendship and cooperation drawn up in mid-February 1979 between the two countries, including "cooperation in national defense," the Vietnamese would be able to garrison their troops in Cambodia for as long as they deemed fit. Given the continuing resistance of the scattered but considerable number of Pol Pot forces, now turned guerrilla fighters—an estimated 30,000—it was likely that at least seven or eight Vietnamese divisions would stay on indefinitely, which, with logistic reinforcements, might mean 60,000 or 70,000 men. By making the Vietnamese presence "legal" (Hanoi had earlier denied it had any troops in Cambodia and had given all the credit for the victory to the armed soldiers of Samrin's Front for National Salvation) Prime Minister Pham Van Dong, who came to Phnom Penh in person to sign the new treaty, relieved himself of the embarrassment of pretending the Vietnamese weren't there, but he also created fresh risks, both for himself and Samrin. However much he cited the need to maintain stability in Cambodia, the ASEAN nations would scarcely welcome a doubling of the number of Vietnamese troops stationed east and south of Thailand—40,000 or 50,000 were already on what looked like permanent assignment in Laos. And more serious, from the political standpoint, was the problem of the Samrin government obtaining genuine national support in its own right and image. This became rapidly apparent as the Vietnamese took over virtually all administrative tasks and sent Deputy Foreign Minister Vo

Dong Giang to Phnom Penh as its effective proconsul. Such moves, however, simply postponed an ultimate Cambodian solution. The deep-seated anti-Vietnamese feelings in Cambodia would not subside simply because the Vietnamese had helped get rid of Pol Pot and his bloodthirsty group. No Khmer nationalist, of "whatever stripe," as Pol Pot himself used to say, could hope to establish a popular government under any form of Vietnamese hegemony or control. Thus, the longer the Vietnamese stayed, the greater would be the chances of new insurrectionary activity, whether led by the Khmer Rouge or by other resistance elements, including old right-wing forces such as the so-called Khmer Serei, that would still emerge. And this, in turn, because of the loose borders that existed between Thailand, Cambodia and Laos, would enhance the dangers of any new insurgency or insurgencies spilling over.

But there was another side to the coin. Simply because it had followed the coattails of the Vietnamese into Cambodia, Samrin's new regime would not necessarily cater or pay homage to them indefinitely—as the neighboring Lao leaders, such as Prime Minister Kaysone Phomvihan and others who had Vietnamese wives or parents and were actual members of the Communist Party of Vietnam, had done. And the more nationalistic and independent, as well as reformist and humane, the new Cambodian rulers proved to be, the less cause the Vietnamese would have to maintain an iron fist, especially in full view of newly suspicious ASEAN, let alone Japan, the United States and the West European nations. The ardently nationalist Khmer were a different breed from the pliable Lao and could be expected to be capable, with some outside technological help, of building their own form of socialism and of running the country efficiently, once they got their priorities straightened out and restored a sense of sanity after the debacle of the Pol Pot era.

Much, of course, would depend on the·caliber of the new leadership and on its determination to maintain its own identity and pride, even in the face of meeting certain Vietnamese demands, such as shipments of rice to alleviate Hanoi's food shortages. At the outset, not much was known about Samrin, a thin, intense man with the mien and manner of the late Houari Boumedienne, of Algeria, or about the other new leaders, but there seemed nothing to belie their genuine Khmer nationalism, despite their opportunistic collaboration with the Vietnamese. Early official accounts said that Samrin was born in Prey Veng province in 1934 of a poor peasant family, and that after joining the revolutionary movement in 1959, he became a regimental commander. Following the Khmer Rouge victory in 1975 he was named commandant and political commissar of the 4th Division, and was then promoted to deputy chief of the general staff and a member of the party's executive committee for the eastern region of Kampuchea. In May 1978 he was apparently one of the leaders of a major coup attempt mounted against Pol Pot with the backing of the Vietnamese. A series of earlier attempts, in 1975 and 1976, had been bungled, and in 1977 there were several more revolts, including one by young Khmer Rouge field-grade officers and four or five provincial chiefs seeking to ameliorate the harsher aspects of the revolution but to retain its basic objectives. All of these failed and led to harsh reprisals and fresh purges.

The May uprising took place in three eastern provinces that comprise Region 203, near the Vietnam border, and Samrin was the leader in Kompong Cham province. Prior to the revolt, a fresh purge within the military and civilian ranks of the Khmer Rouge itself as well as among remnants of the old regime had been ordered by Pol Pot, and many additional thousands of people had been killed, which at the time was reported by refugees, including Khmer Rouge officer-defectors, who fled to Thailand. After the failure of the coup Samrin escaped to Vietnam, along with Chea Sim, who was to become Minister of the Interior of the new regime, but the chief figure in the May rebellion was said to be a man named So Phim, a former Khmer Rouge Central Committee member and vice chairman of the State Presidium. For a number of months So Phim had been mentioned in connection with the anti–Pol Pot plots—he had turned against the regime after a purge in his Region 203 headquarters, which Pol Pot had ordered shelled. According to reports after Phnom Penh was captured in January, So Phim had been Hanoi's first choice to head the new government. But he was said by members of the new regime to have been "heroically" killed in action. Other reports claimed he had been executed by Pol Pot after the failure of the May coup. There was a third possibility: the fact that he was known to be particularly close to the Vietnamese, who gave him their own name, Muoi Xu, might have resulted in his being killed by his fellow plotters because of his too strong Vietnamese views.

Pol Pot Accused

When the new regime took power, it issued a statement declaring that "from now on, Kampuchea is truly independent and free, and the Kampuchean people are truly masters in their country and of their own future." The clique headed by Pol Pot and Ieng Sary, the Deputy Prime Minister and Foreign Minister, was accused of having "betrayed the national interests, monopolized the gains of the revolution and set up the cruelest dictatorial regime ever seen in history. It transformed Kampuchea into a hell on earth covered with blood and tears, a Kampuchea which constituted a danger to peace and stability in Southeast Asia and a tool to serve the expansionist aims of the foreign reactionary forces"—obviously meaning China. The statement, issued in the name of the new Kampuchean People's Revolutionary Council, pledged to carry out the eleven-point program that had been proclaimed a month earlier by the liberation front (KNUFNS) when it was established "in the liberated area." The program contained promises to allow people to return to their native homes; to restore complete freedom of choice to marry; to reinstitute the use of currency and banks, and of an eight-hour workday with fair pay; to "carry out a foreign policy of peace, friendship and nonalignment" and to put an end to the border war with Vietnam; not to allow "any foreign military base or military equipment into Cambodia"; and after holding new elections and writing a new constitution, to create "genuine socialism" and "strengthen solidarity with all revolutionary and progressive forces" in support of "national independence, democracy and social progress against imperialism, colonialism and neocolonialism." The tone and language of the program were similar to that of the old National Liberation Front in Vietnam during the war and smacked of having been drawn up in Hanoi.

On the eve of the capture of Phnom Penh, early in January, the KNUFNS put out another policy statement, which again sounded as if it had been written or at least approved by Hanoi. It called for the election of "self-management committees" composed chiefly "of those who have suffered at the hands of the Pol Pot–Ieng Sary clique," and these committees, similar to those set up throughout Vietnam after April 1975, were to "ensure social order and security [and] defend the village(s); prevent the enemy's counterrevolutionary propaganda from sowing division among the people," and organize new "solidarity production teams" to restore normal agricultural conditions. All the categorical divisions of the population into young and old, married and unmarried, male and female work squads were to be abolished, as well as "all the old administrative, coercive and secret-police organizations." New primary schools would be built for all children from seven to ten years of age, as well as crèches and nurseries, and local public health programs would be introduced. Freedom of religion would be restored, and pagodas and temples damaged or destroyed by the Pol Pot government were to be rebuilt and reopened. Persons who worked for the former regime were to be welcomed back, and after being scrutinized by the self-management committees, would be "issued certificates and will enjoy all citizens' rights," while former "enemy" troops who were captured or surrendered would receive "five days of re-education," after which they would be allowed to return to their families and assigned to production teams. In what was an obvious dig at the Chinese, the statement added that "foreign officials and military advisers who work for the Pol Pot–Ieng Sary regime who cross over to the revolutionary forces will be welcome and well-treated."

Even assuming that the new regime could establish its *bona fides* and win the loyalty of the population with its temporizing measures, it would take months to reverse the course of the revolution, and if resistance by the Pol Pot forces continued, the task might never be accomplished and Cambodia could easily drift into a semipermanent state of chaos. In that event, the worst fears of Sihanouk—who had long ago described the Vietnamese as "eaters of Khmer soil"—would be justified, and the country would either become a total Hanoi satellite or continue to seethe in a revolutionary maelstrom and eventually break up. My own guess, in the spring of 1979, was that the new government had a better than even chance to survive and succeed, if it held together politically, though some resistance seemed bound to continue and could become increasingly serious if it received help from the Chinese. The greatest problem Samrin faced was the lack of experienced cadres, including technicians, teachers, doctors—all categories of professional people—almost all of whom had either been killed under Pol Pot or died under forced labor, while some had managed to flee the country. In this sense, the Vietnamese were in the best position to help, however one appraised their motives. More than 35,000 Cambodians had fled to Thailand after April 1975, compared to the 330,000 who sought sanctuary in Vietnam, and it was undoubtedly these people, among whom were experts of various kinds, who would be more likely to return, willingly or unwillingly, than those in Thailand. The latter, if they had not already departed for new homes, would wait to see how the wind blew. No doubt the Vietnamese had thought of these large numbers of captive Cambodians when they made their decision to go all out and seize Phnom Penh. But even so, just as the Pol Pot revolution was Cambodian and not Chinese, despite Chinese help and the adoption of some Chinese slogans and models, the new revolution, if it held its ground, would ultimately prove to be Cambodian and not Vietnamese, however long Vietnamese troops remained in the country.

Any appraisal of what has happened in Cambodia in the past decade must start with the Vietnam war. There are those who would place the original and main burden of the blame for the Cambodian holocaust on the Americans, and specifically on President Nixon and Secretary of State Kissinger for having widened the scope of the war in the spring of 1970 by invading Cambodia, a year after they had begun the secret bombing and conducted it, unbeknownst to the rest of the Administration, let alone Congress and the public, from the White House basement and later from a hideaway room in the American embassy in Phnom Penh. Before Congress intervened to force a halt, in August 1973, more than half a million tons of bombs had been dropped on Cambodia. Lacking up-to-date maps, the Americans used old ones to the scale of 1:50,000 on which they cut rough bombing patterns in the shape of ill-defined "boxes," with the result that since it was impossible to obtain adequate identification of new or relocated villages inhabited by peasants who had fled earlier bombings, unknown thousands were killed in the designated target areas. In coordinating the attacks, which often ran to sixty B-52 sorties a day, the embassy acted as a communications-relay point, with American officers using a radiophone system that linked the Cambodian general staff, the U.S. Seventh Air Force, and both battlefield command-and-control planes and forward air-control planes. But most of the time the bombers, at 30,000 feet, had no knowledge of what they were actually hitting.

This cruel private war, which I watched unfold and which dismayed me and the majority of Americans and caused deep divisions within government ranks, was almost as unfortunate an adventure for Nixon as Watergate; in fact, it contributed directly to the congressional moves for his impeachment which provoked his resignation. The ostensible purpose of the B-52 attacks was to "save" American lives in Vietnam by forcing the North Vietnamese to widen their defensive tactics while at the same time the process of Vietnamization in South Vietnam would be hastened, enabling the Americans to withdraw troops faster. It is highly debatable whether either of these designs worked. The North Vietnamese, already deeply involved in Cambodia for many years, retreated deeper into Cambodia and did for a time become further committed. But then, though they continued to fight some of the major battles against the troops of Lon Nol after Sihanouk's overthrow in March 1970, they turned the war over to the Khmer Rouge, a generic term that at the time embraced various Communist factions and non-Communist elements, including the Khmer Rumda, the old liberation forces that had supported Sihanouk.

Initially the Khmer Rouge only totaled 4,000, but it soon grew to 20,000, plus another 20,000 support elements, and these troops improved in quality and capability with the help of several thousand North Vietnamese political and military officers, and 3,000 or 4,000 Khmer Rouge cadremen who had been trained in Hanoi over the prior decade, and who returned to the Cambodian jungles to become the nucleus of the new and less diffuse Khmer Rouge army (later these returnees would become the victims of one of Pol Pot's many purges). Despite their Cambodian ploys, and notwithstanding the Paris peace talks and cease-fire agreements of 1973, which they were unable to extend to Cambodia, the Americans could not avoid the ultimate North Vietnamese offensive that drove them ignominiously out of South Vietnam at the end of April 1975, two weeks after they had fled, in much smaller numbers but just as abjectly, from Phnom Penh shortly before the Khmer Rouge entered the city in force.

Notwithstanding the costly Cambodian fiasco, the ugly, criminal behavior of the Cambodian Communists who took over the country, of the small shadowy group of men who led the Communist Party and of the young, often teenage peasant soldiers they commanded like medieval legions, could not solely be attributed to earlier American misdeeds, and even less could it be condoned by any moral standards. It remained strange and inexcusable that the ardent advocates of human rights in the West generally tended at first to ignore what was happening in Cambodia; it was only after the heavy preponderance of evidence became insurmountable and incontestable that the rest of the world seemed to sit up and take notice. The Communists, in fact, had earlier dealt ruthlessly with the peasants in the more than half of the countryside they occupied even before they marched on Phnom Penh, conscripting those able to fight, including boys as young as eleven and twelve, and forcing the rest to move to New Villages, where rigidly run cooperatives became the crude model for the vast social upheaval and reorganization that took place after the war. Khmer Rouge leaders subsequently disclosed that their plans to evacuate the cities after victory and to wipe out every vestige of the old society, with its French colonial background and later American trimmings, had been formulated while they were still in the jungle, contrary to what Ieng Sary claimed when he said that Phnom Penh's population of 2.5 million had been told to evacuate because of the prevalence of "spies" and because the city was going to be bombed by the Americans. Actually, the idea for the evacuation, and for the rustication of the country, had been formulated back in 1959 by Khieu Samphan, who became chairman of the State Presidium when the Khmer Rouge took over, and later President of Kampuchea. In his dissertation that year as a student at the Sorbonne, entitled "The Economy of Cambodia and Its Problems of Industrialization," Samphan set forth the theory that since Cambodia had been kept underdeveloped by the French, who extracted raw materials from it in return for high-priced consumer goods, the country's future could only be solved by methodically using "the dormant energy" of its peasant masses to clear and irrigate new land.

Unlike the Americans, the Communists brooked no compromise. If what they did demonstrated a Neanderthal-like pattern of behavior, there was a peculiar method in their madness. The American commitment to Cambodia, on the other hand, was certainly far less than it was to Vietnam, and what was done to the country surely showed madness in the method. Cambodia was simply regarded as a military pawn, a small country of no value beyond the fact that it abutted Vietnam and thus provided sanctuaries for North Vietnamese troops and supplies—Kissinger was subsequently quoted as saying "I fail to see the moral issue involved" in the destruction of Cambodia.

The ineffectual Khmer leaders like Lon Nol were even sorrier figures than the ones the Americans so futilely backed in Vietnam. Those members of the American establishment who strongly if privately opposed what the United States was doing to the country hoped that some sort of coalition government could eventually be formed, as they had hoped for Vietnam, and that the more nationalist-minded leaders of the Khmer Rouge—men like Hou Youn and Hu Nim, who were later purged by Pol Pot—could be persuaded to turn against the hard-liners. Those who had such hopes thought that Sihanouk might return from his haven in Peking, where he had become the titular head of the Cambodian government-in-exile under the benign protection of Premier Chou En-lai. Sihanouk was still widely regarded as a God-Prince by many peasants in Cambodia; but if there was some chance to bring him back, Kissinger muffed it by refusing on two occasions to meet with the Prince during trips to Peking; when he later sent one of his aides to Sihanouk's residence, Phnom Penh was already under heavy rocket fire and about to collapse. (Ironically, long after, in the spring of 1979, Kissinger, as a private citizen, visited Sihanouk in Peking.) Sihanouk, however, had never harbored any illusions about his future role. He had frequently said that once the leaders of the Khmer Rouge took over, they would "spit me out like a cherry stone."

As events turned out, the Communists subjected him to slow, symbolic regicide. He was welcomed back to Phnom Penh early in September 1975, still as chief of state, and the Communists used him briefly as a sort of ambassador-at-large, allowing him to go to the United Nations a month or so later, where he claimed that the Khmer Rouge were above all "nationalists" and that, as a patriot, he had agreed to retain his post because he was needed to provide "unity, stability and legitimacy." But the following April, after the adoption of a new constitution and the "election" of a new 250-member Legislative Assembly, he was discarded and replaced by Khieu Samphan; and it was then, though he lived comfortably with his wife, Monique, and their two children, first in his old palace and then in a guest house, that his three years of house arrest began. Thereafter, until he made his final sortie in January 1978, he watched, no doubt with dismay and grief, the slow, purposeful destruction of the ancient Khmer cultural and historical traditions he had fought so fervently and so long to protect and preserve. The Communists, if they were also Khmer (they renamed the country Democratic Kampuchea, using the old name), had no use for those values, symbols or shrines of a lost empire epitomized by the beautiful ruins of Angkor Wat. Their idea of the new Kampuchea was to obliterate the past altogether, and they set about doing it with such a blood-crazed zeal and blind determination that they might just as well have been creating new settlements in the craters of the moon.

Flight from Phnom Penh

Sihanouk had at least been spared the horrors of the first few days of Phnom Penh's occupation, when its entire population was ordered to leave the once gracious but now seething, tortured city and take to the highways in whatever manner they could to unknown destinations. In addition to the 2.5 million who streamed out of the capital in all directions, another million inhabitants were similarly ordered out of other cities. Sydney Schanberg, of the *New York Times*, one of the correspondents who remained behind when the Khmer Rouge entered Phnom Penh, wrote of people moving out of the city en masse "in stunned silence—walking, bicycling, pushing cars that had run out of fuel, covering the roads like human carpets, bent under sacks of belongings hastily thrown together when the heavily armed peasant soldiers came and told them to leave immediately." The Communists made no exceptions, and simply told the people that the city had to be "reorganized" in the face of the American bombing threat. The worst victims of the blanket order to leave were the sick and wounded and dying in the hospitals. Jon Swain, of the London *Sunday Times*, described his visit to one of the hospitals: "People by the dozen were bleeding to death in the corridors, the floors of the ward were caked with blood. The hot, fetid air was thick with flies—the sight of these swarming over the living and the dead, over the anguished faces of those who knew they were doomed to die, churned the stomach and made the mind reel. . . . Upstairs it was worse. The dead and the dying lay in pools of their own blood. The long corridor outside the operating theater was literally awash with it." The following morning, April 18, Swain wrote of the Khmer Rouge "tipping out patients like garbage into the streets. Bandaged men and women hobbled by the Embassy (the French Embassy, where the correspondents and all others who had remained behind had been ordered to stay). Wives pushed wounded soldier-husbands on hospital beds on wheels, some with serum drips still attached. In five years of war this is the greatest caravan of human misery I have seen. The Khmer Rouge must know that few of the twenty thousand wounded will survive. One can only conclude they have no humanitarian instincts."

The grisly story of misery and death caused by the Khmer Rouge (or what mysteriously after the war was called the Angka Loeu, or Organization on High, until in April 1977 the Communist Party of Kampuchea formally surfaced) came principally from the Cambodian refugees who escaped to Thailand, since the larger number in Vietnam were inaccessible. The testimony and evidence offered by these refugees, including stories of their often harrowing escapes through minefields and pursued by Khmer Rouge patrols, admittedly had to be carefully weighed against their own prejudices. However, in the case of the Cambodian escapees particularly, the accounts they gave, often in great detail, of what had taken place in Cambodia were too consistent to create any doubts that mass killings did indeed occur and that hundreds of thousands of others died from illness and starvation. Since many if not most of the refugees escaped from northwestern Cambodia, where the killing and dying were greater than elsewhere, it was difficult to extrapolate figures for the country as a whole, but there was enough evidence from other sources as well to warrant the conclusion that the bloodbath was extensive and that privation, above all insufficient food and medicines on top of abject living conditions and forced hard labor, caused the deaths of huge numbers of people in virtually all provinces of the country, especially of older men, women and young children.

Late in 1976 and early in 1977 I interviewed a score or more of the refugees at the camp in Aranyaprathet, on the Thai side of the Cambodian border, and I spoke with others who were living illegally in Bangkok—that is, they had avoided registering in the camps and had fled to the city to find work at wages far lower than were paid the Thais. I also interviewed a number of Western diplomats and Thai officials, some of whom had access to special intelligence about what was going on in Cambodia, including information obtained from high-flying reconnaissance planes, satellites and radio intercepts. Two writers for *Reader's Digest*, John Barron and Anthony Paul, who interviewed about three hundred refugees in writing a book published in 1977 called *Murder of a Gentle Land—the Untold Story of Communist Genocide in Cambodia*, reached the conclusion that "at the very minimum, more than 1.2 million men, women and children died in Cambodia between April 17, 1975, and January 1, 1977," most of them as a result of disease and starvation. While the book was polemical in style and lacked a broad perspective, the sheer weight of evidence offered further proof of the brutal intention of the Cambodian Communists to start from scratch after the war, to create their own kind of revolution in their own fashion and in their own revengeful image from the bones and ashes of the past. A much more thorough, reflective and analytical book was written by François Ponchaud, a French missionary who lived in Cambodia for ten years and left in the last convoy of foreigners from the French embassy on May 8, 1975. Ponchaud, whose book was translated into English and published in the United States in 1978 under the title *Cambodia: Year Zero*, had interviewed ninety-four refugees in depth and kept a detailed account of all Communist radio broadcasts. He initially estimated that the number of dead in Cambodia after the war "certainly exceeds one million" and described the Khmer revolution as "irrefutably the bloodiest of our century." In an author's note for the English translation, he wrote: "A year after the publication of my book I can unfortunately find no reason to alter my judgment."

The violent and destructive nature of the revolution, predicated on the theory, as expressed by Radio Phnom Penh in January 1976, that "two thousand years of Cambodian history have virtually ended," surprised many Westerners as well as Asians, for some such drastic event as a bloodbath had been expected to occur in Vietnam, if anywhere. The Khmer had generally been thought of as a gentle people, who, having been innocent, if major, victims of the war, simply wanted to be left alone and to preserve what was left of their old empire. Another, less widely publicized view was expressed all along, to the effect that beneath their calm exteriors the Khmer had always harbored a streak of cruelty and vengeance both toward their own countrymen and toward others—especially, of course, toward the Vietnamese. Moreover, in a historical sense, the Khmer had always been somewhat isolated culturally, and had never really "belonged" to the Indochinese cultural scene. In fact, their heritage derived from a Polynesian-Indonesian watershed. Actually, India gave them an alphabet, and their early art forms were influenced by India, while their twin religions, primarily Buddhism but including Hinduism, also sprang from the subcontinent. Historically, however, they lacked a sense of social cohesiveness, and particularly after the abandonment of the famous capital of Angkor in the fifteenth century, authority was largely wielded by regional or local leaders who were comparable to Chinese warlords and who treated the people under their sway virtually as slaves. Sihanouk tried hard to create a greater sense of unity, and to a considerable degree he succeeded; but even after he relinquished his crown to become "a working Prince" and a leader of his people, he remained a godlike figure and a man of so many contradictory parts, including playacting and playboy ones—he loved producing plays and he enjoyed women and the good life—that he never managed to identify himself with the peasants he professed to love and defend, because he was too far removed from them and knew little of the exploitation and corruption to which they were subjected. He was wise enough to realize this himself, which is why, perhaps, he also anticipated the violence of the postwar period.

As David Chandler, an Australian scholar and Cambodian expert has pointed out, this latent violence was partly the product of belief in Buddhist reincarnation, the converse of which was that "power, however ruthlessly applied, was taken as proof of meritorious behavior—in another life." Chandler went on to note "how shaky our knowledge of Cambodian rural history" was, and still is. "To understand why so many Cambodians chose revolution in the 1970s, we need to know more about patterns of land ownership, malnutrition and indebtedness in the 1950s and the 1960s, as well as the growth of personal fortunes, and corruption among the Phnom Penh elite," he wrote in a lengthy article. It was undeniably true that had it not been for French intervention in the mid-nineteenth century, Cambodia would have been dismembered by Vietnam and Thailand. It was also true that while the French treasured and helped preserve Angkor Wat and other temples, their colonial rule in Cambodia, far more than in Vietnam, was marked by contempt for the Cambodians as a people. With rare exceptions, such as André Malraux, they were simply interested in having the Cambodians produce more rubber and rice, and in nurturing what they considered a faithful and imitative Francophile elite, supported by a Vietnamese-imported bureaucracy and commercial class. Under the circumstances of the World War II upheaval, the collapse of French imperialism, and postwar chaos that brought Cambodia its formal but shaky independence in 1953, it was inevitable that a Marxist core of leaders would emerge and that the peasants in the amorphous countryside would prove ripe for revolution.

In accepting the thesis that Marxism provided the revolutionary impact and energy to overcome traditional peasant "reticence," Ponchaud pointed out in his book that after it grabbed power, the Pol Pot regime "managed to seize on the instinctive capacity of every Khmer to obey whatever authority happens to be in control and turn it to their own uses. This makes it easier to understand how four million people could walk out of their homes in the cities almost without a murmur when ordered to do so by the Khmer Rouge." Ponchaud made the further point that "the Khmer thinks by accretions or juxtapositions, but adheres strictly to the rules of his own internal logic," and that "a simple idea, intuitively perceived, was [traditionally] pushed to the limits of its internal logic, and often to the point of absurdity, without any regard for realities or any forethought for practical consequences." In this sense, he added, the Maoist doctrine that the revolution draws its strength from the peasant masses led the Cambodian Communists simply to do away with cities and towns, in the interests of "purification," without further questioning. And by the same token, since capitalism is an evil, money had to be abolished and a barter economy substituted.

Faces of the Khmer Rouge

Far less than was the case with European Communists, whose long struggles and careers were generally known before they assumed power, did the democratic West have any real information about the Communist leaders who emerged from the academic obscurity of Phnom Penh classrooms to learn their Marxist credos in France or in North Vietnam, and who then practiced the strategy and tactics of revolution in the thick, mostly unpopulated northeastern Cambodian jungles before moving into the sparse backward villages of the eastern half of the country. The galvanizing force of the Cambodian revolution, as much or more than Marxism, which simply provided the guidelines, was virulent nationalism and xenophobia. In fact, after their victory the Cambodian Communists sought to deny having obtained their inspiration from the Vietnamese Laodong (Workers) Party, but it was nevertheless the Laodong that had helped set up the Pracheachon (the People's Revolutionary

Party) in September 1951. After the war, in September 1977, when Pol Pot made an official visit to China (he had been there secretly once before, in the immediate postwar period, when he met Mao Tse-tung), the existence of the Cambodian Communist Party was "revealed" and it was said to have been formed in September 1960. (The denial of the earlier 1951 date by Pol Pot was attributed to differences with the Vietnamese Communists, who, along with the Chinese and the Russians, had persuaded the Pracheachon to postpone its revolutionary struggle and support Sihanouk in the wake of the Geneva Conference of 1954 that ended the first Indochina war.) Henceforth the Cambodians continuously sought to minimize the help the North Vietnamese gave them during the war and always claimed that they won their victory by themselves primarily with captured American arms and only "supplementary" aid from "foreign friends." One way of forgetting the past is to deny it.

In a five-hour speech at a mass meeting in Phnom Penh on September 27, 1977, commemorating the party's "seventeenth" anniversary, Pol Pot referred to the formation of a committee in 1957 "to work out the party's political line," which he said it had lacked before and had been the reason that "the revolutionary struggle of our people vanished into thin air through the 1954 Geneva agreement." It was still a time of great difficulties, he emphasized, and in 1959 "about ninety percent of our revolutionary forces in the rural areas were destroyed through arrests, killings, bribery and surrenders," while in the cities the situation was equally bad. Nevertheless, after he compiled a Marxist-Leninist draft, though one based on "the actual needs and situation in Cambodia and in Cambodian society," the first national party congress met on September 30, 1960, in a room at the railway station in Phnom Penh, and over the next three days and nights, "working round the clock," the fourteen peasant representatives and seven from the cities formalized "the basic strategic line of the national and democratic revolution, adopted the party's statute, and elected the party's Central Committee." Although Cambodia at this point was "an imperialist satellite, but in particular a satellite of United States imperialism," Pol Pot went on, there were a number of factions that thought it was already independent under Sihanouk. In fact, he added, class conflicts abounded, and the peasants, comprising 85 percent of the population, "suffered oppression by all the other classes, the landowners in particular."

Between 1964 and 1967, the peasant movement was "seething" and "powerful" and "tens of thousands of peasants staged demonstrations and insurrections in the districts, commune and provincial seats," using "knives, swords and hatchets as weapons . . . to force the ruling classes to make land reform." The landowners "kept promising to do so but could lie to and deceive the peasants only for a while," which increased "class indignation" and led the peasants "to rise up in a bloody fight against the landgrabbers," and "they stormed police stations and military barracks and exerted violence to the highest degree." The struggle reached its first climax in 1968, Pol Pot said, and between January and May of that year, attacking successively in all parts of the country, the guerrillas captured several hundred government weapons and set up movements in seventeen of Cambodia's nineteen provinces. What he described as "impregnable" support bases contained 60,000 people, while guerrilla bases, which were still subject to penetration, contained 300,000, and so-called guerrilla zones that belonged to both sides had 700,000 people who supported the revolution.

Having created this base structure, according to Pol Pot, the Communists, starting with their 4,000 "regular fighters" and their larger guerrilla force which was armed with "flintlock guns, bows and arrows, grenades and land-mines," set up revolutionary administrations throughout the country following the Lon Nol 1970 coup against Sihanouk and formed regional forces, regular forces, regiments and battalions. Striking in small groups on the flanks and in the rear of government troops, and avoiding face-to-face battles, they cut off and blocked the seven major highways and the main waterways, including the Mekong. The decision to launch a final offensive against Phnom Penh, cut the lower Mekong and attack key provincial seats still held by the government was made by the Central Committee in May 1974.

Pol Pot's account of the rise and victory of the revolutionary movement was probably more or less accurate, despite some inevitable self-serving propaganda, but what was most lacking was biographical data of the leaders of the revolution, and this particularly concerned the true identity of Pol Pot himself. His name was not known to the outside world until after the war, when he was also called Tol Saut, and said to be a former rubber worker. But both of these were believed to be aliases for Saloth Sar, who through the years, dating back to 1951, was known to have been secretary-general of the Communist Party and, in addition, chairman of the military committee of the party's Central Committee during the war, as well as head of the military department of the army.

Saloth Sar was born in May 1928 in Kompong Thom province, not far from Phnom Penh. After attending a technical school in Phnom Penh, he went to Paris in 1949, where he studied at the Ecole Française de Radio-Electricité. He failed to obtain a degree, but read and studied Marxist literature on his own and returned to Cambodia in 1953, where he became a journalist and high school teacher. In 1963, along with a small group of other Communists and non-Communist left-wing leaders, he fled to the jungle after turning down Sihanouk's blandishments to join the government, and he was not heard of again until 1971 when he and other "patriotic intellectuals" signed a declaration addressed to the Cambodian people from the "Liberation Zone." When Pol Pot went to China in the fall of 1977, and also to North Korea, a biography of him published in Pyongyang corresponded with what was known about Saloth Sar, except that the date of Pol Pot's birth was given as 1924, and no mention was made of his having visited France. Pictures that appeared of Pol Pot for the first time showed him to be a plump man of medium height, and they bore a strong likeness to photographs that had been published of Saloth Sar. Moreover, it was known that Saloth Sar had familiarly been known as

"Pot," because of his plumpness, and had been called "Comrade Pol" in the revolutionary underground in the early fifties, when the struggle for independence from the French was still going on. Saloth Sar's name had not been mentioned since just after the war, but there seemed little reason to doubt that he and Pol Pot were indeed the same man. Sihanouk subsequently corroborated it.

Khieu Samphan, who became chairman of the State Presidium, or in effect chief of state or President, replacing Sihanouk soon after the Prince returned from Peking to Phnom Penh, was considered the leader of the Khmer Rouge inside Cambodia during the war. Earlier, when Sihanouk still held power, he had been a member of the moderate group which favored supporting the Prince because of his anti-American stance and which wanted to promote the revolution from the top down, as opposed to the hard-liners such as Saloth Sar and Ieng Sary, who considered Sihanouk the enemy of the revolution and believed that it had to start with peasant organization. Samphan was a physically frail, shy youngster in his student days in Phnom Penh and later in Paris who was said to have revealed to his friends that he was permanently impotent; true or not, he was an introvert who immersed himself in books, chiefly the works of Marx, Engels and Lenin. After he wrote his doctorate in economics in France in 1959 he returned to Cambodia, where he published an obscure biweekly newspaper with pro-Communist leanings, which the Sihanouk government closed down after a year and a half. During the early sixties, when Sihanouk was flirting with the leftists in order to create a balance against the ultraright wing in his mock government, he permitted Samphan to run for the National Assembly and made him Secretary of State for Commerce, but when the mercurial prince became angry over the rambunctious activities of the left-wingers, accusing them of being subversive, Samphan took the hint and escaped to the jungle.

The most mysterious figure in the Pol Pot pantheon was Nuon Chea, the chairman of the Standing Committee of the People's Representative Assembly, who replaced Pol Pot as Prime Minister for at least several months starting in September 1976, ostensibly because Pol Pot was ill. Nuon Chea, a former plantation worker who had been active in the anti-French resistance, was still in the top job in April 1977, when refugees and other intelligence sources reported the coup attempt referred to earlier; it was mounted by some junior officers and provincial chiefs, and led to the execution of at least four of the latter as well as several hundred village, district and provincial officials. The new wave of killings that followed appears to have been directed at eliminating not only all members of the former government down to army privates and their families but also those elements in the early Khmer Rouge movement who were regarded as untrustworthy, and all those who might have pro-Vietnamese leanings. Information Minister Hu Nim and Public Works Minister Toch Phouen also disappeared from public ceremonies during this period and were later said to have been executed.

Additional testimony from refugees and others indicated that the government not only was motivated by the growing tensions along the Cambodian-Vietnamese border but was fearful of a counterrevolution inspired by ex-Sihanoukites and "reactionaries" opposed to the stringent working conditions and insufficient food rations to which all the ruralized workers who had been dispatched around the country were subjected. When Pol Pot openly re-emerged, in the fall of 1977, the government radio made frequent references to these "reactionary elements that still exist," and Pol Pot acknowledged that "between one and two percent" of such elements were still active. The purge directed against them was increased upon Pol Pot's return from China, and its newest victims included lower-ranking village officials as well as remaining Buddhist monks and anyone who, even briefly, had had any sort of attachment to or association with the old regime.

As for other members of the small group of men and women who ran Cambodia after the war, the third in rank was probably Son Sen, who since 1970 or 1971 had been chief of the general staff of the Cambodian liberation army and, after the 1975 victory, became Deputy Prime Minister for National Defense. He was born in South Vietnam of Khmer parents, and like his comrades, studied in France as a young man and then returned to Phnom Penh to join Sihanouk's government until, along with the other leftists who came to mistrust Sihanouk's plots and ploys, he took to the jungle. His wife, Yun Yat, who like himself was a former teacher, was Minister of Culture and Education in 1978. Next in line, or of equal rank, in the power structure was Ieng Sary, who, because of his travels around Southeast Asia and to the United Nations, was the best known of the Cambodian leaders. I met him in August 1976, and spoke with him briefly at the Conference of Non-Aligned Nations held in Colombo, Sri Lanka. Sary, a rotund, more approachable man than the others, was also born in South Vietnam of Khmer parents but attended primary school and high school in Phnom Penh, and then, in 1950, went to Paris, where he studied at the Institut d'Etudes Politiques and enthusiastically joined the various Marxist and leftist student groups and clubs that abounded in France. When he returned to Cambodia in 1957, he taught school for six years but was among those who vanished in 1963, when he too went to the jungle and then probably to Hanoi. In 1971 he appeared publicly in Peking, where he became a close member of Sihanouk's entourage and accompanied the Prince on his occasional trips to Hanoi and abroad, acting as his aide but in fact as overseer of the capricious Prince, who afterward called him a "Stalinist." Ieng Sary's wife, Ieng Thirith, was Minister of Social Action in 1978, and her sister was married to Pol Pot, which made the whole inner power circle both cozy and incestuous.

Waves of Killings

While the men at the top led by Pol Pot represented a strong central government and set the policy guidelines, considerable latitude and autonomy were given to regional, provincial and even local Khmer Rouge officers and officials of the new state apparatus. These faceless individuals wielded a vast power of their own, and it was they who were responsible for much of the oppression and for the deaths of scores of thousands. The initial wave of killings took place during the exodus from the cities and towns, which lasted until June 1975. To quote Ponchaud: "The liquidation of all towns and former authorities was not improvised, nor was it a reprisal or expression of wanton cruelty on the part of local cadres. The scenario for every town and village in the country was the same and followed exact instructions issued by the highest authorities. One possible explanation is that there weren't enough trained officials in the new regime, so it had to do away with all the old ones, who might have formed an intellectual or armed opposition. But this total purge was, above all, the translation into action of a particular vision of man: a person who has been spoiled by a corrupt regime cannot be reformed, he must be physically eliminated from the brotherhood of the pure."

The early victims were former officers, both commissioned and noncommissioned, of the government army; former government officials of all ranks, and teachers and intellectuals; many of the families of these various categories, including children as well as wives, were also eliminated. According to the gruesome testimony of the refugees, the killings were done in various ways: by shooting, by landmines, by clubbing with hoes and rakes, by knifing, by garroting, and by burying people alive. During the forced marches along the five highways out of Phnom Penh, the thousands of human columns pouring out of the city were ordered to keep moving, and after walking forty or fifty kilometers, were then shunted in different directions onto sideroads, split into groups of varying size and simply told at designated points to start working in the fields planting rice, and to build huts to live in or to sleep in whatever houses or buildings were available. Without any tools, most of the work, including the digging of irrigation ditches, the tilling of the soil and the building of huts out of bamboo branches and palm leaves had to be done by hand or with sticks and crudely made rock and bamboo instruments.

All those except young children, old men and women, and people who were too sick had to work from five to eleven in the morning, and from one to six in the afternoon, and sometimes, if the moon was bright enough, for several hours at night as well. If it was too dark to work, the New Villagers had to attend political lectures in the evening. During these early months there was a great shortage of food, and the average daily ration was a small evaporated-milk can of unhusked rice a day per person, or sometimes two cans, with perhaps a few pieces of vegetable but no fish or meat, except for rodents, lizards or birds caught in the fields and forests. As a result, particularly under the harsh conditions of long work hours and little sleep, thousands upon thousands suffered from malnutrition and various diseases, particularly malaria and gastrointestinal infections, typhoid fever and cholera. There were no medicines and very few doctors available, and according to estimates made by diplomats in Bangkok, the death rate in many of the New Villages during 1975 and 1976 was as high as 30 or 40 percent, and the infant mortality rate in some areas was at first 70 or 80 percent. Besides those who died from disease or starvation, the killing of "undesirable" or "useless" elements, as the Khmer Rouge put it, continued. In many instances groups of men, and some women, were piled on trucks and told they were moving to another place or were going "to meet Sihanouk." They were never seen again, but many of the refugees reported hearing shots or explosions and told stories of coming across piles of shot or clubbed bodies in ditches, or of dried skeletons.

If the outside world was shocked by the carnage in Cambodia, the new rulers of the country seemed happy to boast about it. The new national anthem contained the following lines:

> The red, red blood splatters the
> cities and plains of the Cambodian
> fatherland,
> The sublime blood of the workers
> and peasants,
> The blood of revolutionary combatants
> of both sexes.
>
> That blood spills out into great
> indignation and a resolute urge
> to fight.
> 17 April, that day under the
> revolutionary flag,
> The blood certainly liberates us
> from slavery.

Life in the New Villages, as described by the refugees I spoke with in Thailand, was an unbearable routine of drudgery, privation and misery, and it drove many who didn't want to risk trying to escape, or who were caught in the act and punished, to suicide. Punishment was meted out for the smallest infractions of any sort under a system called *kosang*, which subjected the accused person to submit to a public confession during which he promised to "construct" himself into a better person and to work solely and loyally in behalf of the Angka Loeu to create what Pol Pot described as a new form of "collective socialism." If a person was subjected to *kosang* a second time, he was in serious trouble, and a third *kosang* meant disappearance and death. Shirking of work, even if someone was obviously ill or had suffered a serious injury, was cause enough for a *kosang*, as were any breaches of discipline, such as moving about without a permit, indulging in what could be construed as unpatriotic conversation, humming, singing or playing anything but revolutionary tunes, or engaging in extramarital sex. Children of three to twelve were used as spies and informers—in Cambodian they were called "a force of fish" —and as a reward for information they received extra rations.

Despite all the hardships to which the new farmers were subjected—those of the "old population" who had not come from the cities fared somewhat better and were generally regarded as more trustworthy by the Khmer Rouge —the first harvest in the fall of 1975 was a satisfactory one, though many of the new peasants had no opportunity to share it. Between September and December of 1975, a second forced migration took place, and some half million men, women and children moved farther north and northwest, where they had to start all over again building more settlements. Once more the forced marches resulted in the death of thousands, and because people were already weaker and sick, this migration was even worse than the first. About the same time the order went out to eliminate all remaining former government servants, both civilian and military, of any rank, along with their families. Anyone suffering from what was denounced as "old dandruff," denoting military men of any rank and their families, and "memory sickness," or a tendency to cling to the past, was subject to death. The new wave of killings prompted an increase in escapees, so the army began to lay booby traps and mines along the Thai border. It was also rumored that thousands of refugees were fleeing across the border to Vietnam; by late 1976, following a third internal migration in September which was not quite as harsh, the figure of Cambodians who had fled to Vietnam was already 60,000, or almost twice the number of people who had fled to Thailand.

Once the new regime had taken over, all money was abolished, although smuggling soon became widespread and involved the exchange of gold and other valuables, and except for what personal possessions they had brought with them from the cities, such as a few clothes and sleeping mats, the New Villagers had nothing and received nothing except their meager rations. Notwithstanding the constant harping on obliterating the "old system of slavery" and "feudalism," the Angka Loeu imposed what could only be described as a new form of repression in an Orwellian sense, and in terms of primitive cruelty the regime certainly seems to have reached new limits of repression: The theme it propounded was "production power," and Pol Pot boasted in late 1977 that "more than ninety percent of the population has been completely liberated and is being nursed, fed and promoted into a seething, vigorous, vivid, grand production movement with the highest sense of ingenuity and initiative." The key words, constantly repeated, were "struggle," to obtain "mastery," especially over "water at all times."

Though Pol Pot spoke of having used "water conservation in order to maximize rice production" and of having built large reservoirs in every region, as well as more than a dozen dams on major rivers and smaller dams on streams —all of which, he maintained, had provided water for 400,000 hectares of farmland in all seasons and 312 kilograms of food per capita, as well as enough of a rice surplus to start exporting "tens of thousands of tons"—the 1977 harvest, while fairly good, had still left many areas short of food due to distribution problems. Moreover, while ranking officials, regular troops and militia were receiving improved rations, the general population was still insufficiently fed, though daily rice allotments had increased and the institution of community kitchens had provided some fish, meat and vegetables, but not for everyone. Pol Pot also claimed that "our people's health is excellent" and that malaria had been "eighty percent eradicated" (during 1976 Cambodia had imported $1.6 million worth of DDT and more than $2 million worth of medicines from Hong Kong, mostly antimalaria pills), but malaria was still said by refugees in 1977 to be widely prevalent, even among the armed forces, and dysentery and cholera remained serious problems.

With the help of the Chinese, who had sent 2,000 or 3,000 technical advisers and technicians to Cambodia, some factories, including those making textiles and cement, had been re-established. The Chinese also donated locomotives and other transportation equipment, as well as considerable machinery of various sorts. According to Pol Pot, the effort to industrialize the country would be continued, but on the basis of stimulating agricultural production first and foremost. He announced that the former illiteracy rate of 75 percent in the countryside and 60 percent among the working people in the cities had been reduced to a national total of 10 percent—much too bold a claim. For the first ten months of the new regime, the refugees reported, there was no education at all, and thereafter children from seven to twelve received three hours of schooling in the middle of the hot day, when they weren't working. After reaching twelve, the boys joined the militia. Simple literacy classes, according to the refugees, were taught by young Khmer Rouge soldiers who themselves had only received two years of education; though some teachers of the old regime had been spared, most had disappeared and were presumed to have been killed, so what was taught was pretty rudimentary and consisted largely of elementary propaganda.

From Khet to Krom

Administratively, the new Cambodia was divided into six regions, or areas, called *phumpheak,* each consisting of several provinces, or *khet,* which were gradually replaced by *damban,* or districts. The *phumpheak* and *damban* were run by veteran Khmer Rouge officers. Beneath them were sectors, called *sroks,* probably the key administrative unit under the new revolutionary system. For economic purposes primarily, the *sroks* were composed of *khums,* tantamount to cantons, and these were basically groups of villages that formed a cooperative or a commune, in line with the Chinese model. A village was called a *phum,* as before the revolution, and each village consisted of a number of family groups called *krom,* each group consisting of ten or twelve families. Each of these administrative units was run on a tripartite system, consisting of a chairman and a vice chairman and a "member," although there were sometimes several "chairmen" assigned to oversee different functions, such as supervising construction of dams and dikes, or economic and social affairs. A key person in each small community was the *chhlop,* or spy, and the larger the community, the larger the number of *chhlops.* Once a man or woman was reported by the *chhlop* to the village or canton chairman, he or she was as good as dead.

Permission to marry had to be obtained from the *krom* chief through the head of women in the *krom*. A boy choosing a girl had to apply to the chairwoman of the village, while if the girl made the first move, it went from the chairwoman to the chairman of the boys, who reported back to the chairwoman when he received the individual boy's answer. Communal weddings became the custom, in which about ten couples joined for a simple ceremony conducted by the canton chief. Then, after eating bowls of rice soup together, the couples returned to work, often continuing to be assigned to different jobs in different places and seeing each other only occasionally. The work forces were broken into groups of ten for the most part, each called a *kemlang*. Larger groups of fifty or a hundred men, usually unmarried males aged fifteen to fifty-four, were assigned to doing heavy work such as dambuilding at sites often miles from the villages where they lived, and they often stayed at the sites for days or even weeks at a time. Married men and women, if they were lucky, worked in the same or adjacent *kemlang*, planting rice or raising vegetables, while the old and infirm engaged in handicrafts, mostly weaving, and the younger children concentrated on community projects, digging small irrigation ditches or gathering straw and palm leaves.

Ironically, a month or two before the Pol Pot government was overthrown, there were signs that it was preparing to slacken the tight reins of control by moving into a second stage of its unique, cultlike, regimented form of "socialism." Plans were announced to introduce "advanced cooperatives" to consolidate the society further and replace the earlier "low-level" and "high-level" cooperatives which dated back to the liberated areas of the Vietnam war and the first three years of the postwar period. A much easier way of life was promised belatedly, including two full meals of rice and one broth meal a day, with a dessert every three days, expanded health care, improved educational opportunities, and better housing and recreational facilities. Each large community, amounting to a commune, was to grow not only rice but a great variety of other crops such as cotton, jute, kapok, corn, bamboo, sugar cane, tobacco, castor beans, rattan, bananas and other fruits, sesame, and so on, as well as "strategic vegetables," such as wax gourds and pumpkins, and "tactical vegetables," such as lettuce and eggplant. Twenty percent of total production would be for export, the rest for home consumption. New brick houses with tiled roofs were to be built, and "orchards of fruit trees are to be provided to give shade to these new cooperative villages, thus producing a pleasant scene and increasing joyful feelings among all members of the cooperative," the new edict said. By 1980, one third of all existing cooperatives would be brought to the "advanced" stage, which would also be marked by increased political indoctrination "to root out officialdom and feudalism" and create "a firm bulwark . . . for building socialism throughout Democratic Kampuchea." It all sounded too good to be true.

Concurrent with what seemed to be a policy of internal relaxation, and even earlier, the government made a pronounced effort to withdraw from its self-imposed isolation. A new diplomacy toward its Southeast Asian neighbors was marked by fresh approaches to Thailand, Malaysia, Singapore, Indonesia and Burma, and trade agreements were sought with those and other countries. Foreign journalists, notably a group from Yugoslavia and two Western correspondents, from the *Washington Post* and the *St. Louis Post-Dispatch*, were invited to Phnom Penh and taken on carefully conducted tours—the visit of the latter was unfortunately marred by the murder of a British scholar, Malcolm Caldwell, who was probably killed by Khmer Vietnamese agents representing the Samrin group that was about to take over.

Whatever was in the minds of the remote, austere leaders of Cambodia, it was apparent that in the wake of the bloodbath and the havoc of national uprooting, they had come to realize that the survival of Cambodia itself as a nation was at stake, and that pride and paranoia were poor survival weapons. Having foolishly allowed themselves to become involved in two border wars at once, against the Vietnamese and the Thais (during 1977 there had been four hundred incidents along the Thai-Cambodian border, almost all of them involving Cambodian raids into Thai territory as a result of which scores of Thai men, women and children had been killed as wantonly as in Cambodia itself), Pol Pot, Ieng Sary and their companions in carnage seemed finally to have become aware that Cambodia was in grave danger of being outflanked and outmaneuvered. But the decision to change revolutionary course had come too late. An agreement in October 1977 to relax border tensions with the Thais was welcomed in Bangkok, but Hanoi was in no mood, at this juncture, to listen to any overtures from Phnom Penh, especially after Cambodia broke off diplomatic relations. The battle plan for the Christmas Day invasion had already been drawn up by Generals Giap and Dung.

It will be a long time before the rest of the world can forget or forgive Cambodia for the postwar reign of terror it perpetrated. In his first major speech, at the end of January, President Samrin accused the Pol Pot regime of having "killed millions of our patriotic cadres and fighters," whose blood "flooded this land, almost creating new rivers" and whose bodies "have almost filled all the bomb craters, lakes and ponds of our homeland." The indictment simply echoed and corroborated what the Cambodian refugees had been saying for three and a half years. What made these earlier accounts even more graphic was the stories told by new refugees. When the Vietnamese invaders passed through the villages on their way to Phnom Penh and the other cities, the Cambodians were fearful that another wave of killings would take place, but were surprised and gratified as the Vietnamese soldiers not only behaved well but announced, through their Khmer interpreters, that the harsh measures of the past would immediately be ended. Communal kitchens were abolished and cooking pots were redistributed to individual families. The people were asked to elect new village heads and to re-establish their own communities and do their own farming. The soldiers said that they were in Cambodia only to get rid of the Pol Pot regime and that they would then return to Vietnam. But in almost all cases the soldiers only stayed a day or two, and as soon as they left, the Khmer Rouge who had fled into the jungle returned. Refugees who escaped to Thailand during late January, February and March of 1979 told frightful stories of how the Khmer Rouge soldiers again started killing villagers, especially those who had greeted the Vietnamese warmly and had agreed to become New Village officials. One such refugee typified the rest when he said, "The Vietnamese stayed two days and when they left the Khmer Rouge returned and tried to force the villagers to return to the communes. The people did not want to return to the communes, and they fled into the bush. Some followed behind the Vietnamese in order to escape to Thailand. Many were killed by the Khmer Rouge, who began to fire on the fleeing villagers. I estimate that only a thousand of the four thousand people in my village survived."

These new refugees, soon numbering tens of thousands, were perhaps the saddest of all. "There were no human rights under Pol Pot," another one of them said. "We suffered like animals. We do not know what it might be like under Heng Samrin. I never heard of him until I got to Thailand. We want to fight the Khmer Rouge, but we do not want to be controlled by either the Khmer Rouge or the Vietnamese." Several said they would stay in Thailand until they saw what developed in Cambodia, and they expressed the hope that "Sihanouk will come back." Their accounts of what was now taking place in the country corroborated what Western analysts in Thailand were concluding on the basis of reports they were receiving from other intelligence sources and from the few visitors from Communist nations who were allowed to visit Phnom Penh. It seemed apparent that the Vietnamese were having more trouble than they had anticipated, that the invaders had overextended their supply lines and were being widely attacked by the Khmer Rouge guerrillas, who were blowing up bridges and setting up roadblocks. The strength of the guerrillas was estimated to be about one-third the strength of Pol Pot's former army; they were said to be operating in groups up to battalion size, to be maintaining some communication among one another and to be depending on hidden caches of weapons and ammunition rather than on any consistent flow of fresh military supplies from the Chinese via Thailand. Most analysts agreed that whereas the Vietnamese were being subjected to unexpected heavy harassment and had been unable so far to establish either a functioning central government under Heng Samrin or any system of local governments, their continued military predominance would eventually prove too much for the Khmer Rouge and the resistance would peter out after six months or a year.

In April 1979, as the start of the rainy season approached, the Vietnamese made a determined move to put an end to the major Pol Pot resistance by mounting strong attacks in the western sectors of Cambodia. They succeeded in driving the Pol Pot guerrillas to the Thai border and in capturing what may have been the principal headquarters of the Khmer Rouge near Battambang. There were unconfirmed reports that Pol Pot had fled to Thailand as thousands of his troops sought sanctuary across the border, where the Thais allowed them to regroup and re-enter Cambodia at different points. At the same time, 30,000 to 40,000 additional civilian refugees poured across the border, further aggravating the already complicated refugee situation. The Thais tried to persuade, and in most cases forced, most of these new refugees to return to Cambodia after giving them some food and medical help. Stories of spreading famine in Cambodia were apparently true—with peasants in flight all over the country, either into the cities or toward the borders, little new rice was being planted, and stores from the previous harvest had been seized by the Vietnamese or by Pol Pot soldiers.

Predictions of what might happen in Cambodia, under such increasingly confused and chaotic circumstances, are becoming hazardous at best, and it remains to be seen how much better off the country will be, either under the Vietnamese or under whatever hybrid government emerges. If the self-destructive killing sooner or later ends, there is still no guarantee that the revolution will henceforth be peaceful, that the Pol Pot or any new guerrilla resistance can permanently be contained, with or without Chinese assistance, and that Cambodia can escape being caught up in a fresh vortex and power struggle. And even if it could, the road back to civilization would be long and painful.

Laos—
The Loose Revolution

Of the five parts of former French Indochina that became three nations, Laos in many ways remained unique and the most captivating. Saigon, Hanoi and Phnom Penh were the attractive cities; the French had taken special cosmopolitan if self-serving pains to make them so, but they always regarded Vientiane as a somewhat ugly duckling, not worth the effort of embellishment. As a source of colonial profit, Laos was never as productive as Vietnam and Cambodia anyway, and though landlocked, was always considered the backwater of the French empire in the Orient. One had the feeling, thirty years ago, that Laos was stillborn or retarded, and that it would never grow up to be a country in its own right. Nevertheless, despite its handicaps, or perhaps because of them, and because it asked so little and forgave so much, Laos won the hearts of foreigners, including the Americans, who used it poorly but loved it dearly and left it more in sorrow than in anger and with more affection than guilt, though there was a lot to be guilty about.

Laos was the last of the Indochinese countries to turn Communist, in December 1975. As befits its national character, it did so more subtly and gently than neighboring Vietnam and Cambodia, but the milder manner of its transformation did not preclude its fast becoming an avowed Marxist-Leninist state, with close ties to Hanoi and to Moscow, and lesser ones to Peking. Even so, the Lao continued to display many of the vagaries and idiosyncrasies that used to bewilder and sometimes exasperate Western officials and charm ordinary tourists. These non-Communist attributes, including an almost cavalier approach to the difficult problems of running a new nation whose population of 3 million had been badly bombed and uprooted as a result of the long war, made one wonder whether Laos could function as the "popular democratic dictatorship" its leaders proclaimed, or achieve what they grandiloquently referred to as "peace, independence, democracy, unification, prosperity and social progress." Three or four years later, with the country beset by economic woes, its limited managerial talent severely drained as a result of the escape of many old-regime experts among the 180,000 refugees who fled across the Mekong into Thailand, and the dispatch of some 40,000 others to remote internal re-education camps, and faced by sporadic and often fierce if isolated pockets of resistance and rebellion, one could still ponder these same questions. It sometimes appeared doubtful that Laos would be able to maintain its separate national identity indefinitely.

This was a matter of obvious concern not only to its most powerful neighbor and Big Brother, the Socialist Republic of Vietnam, but also to the other four nations that border Laos—China, Burma, Thailand and Cambodia—and to the Soviet Union and the United States. On a much lesser scale, but nevertheless in a manner that provoked ironic smiles and occasional scowls among the lackadaisical Lao, the Russians had replaced the Americans as the major "Western" or "European" influence in the country, and their six hundred advisers, mostly technicians of one sort or another, rode or walked around the dusty streets of Vientiane with an air of supercilious bravado comparable to that of the Americans when they were waging their not-so-secret war in the country, and savoring its many esoteric pleasures. The more reclusive Chinese, while maintaining a low profile and confining most of their activity to seemingly endless road building in the northwestern region, held to their long-range view—claiming privately that the Russians would eventually defeat themselves in Laos, just as the Americans had before them.

The Burmese, beset by their own problems, were simply watching and waiting, and as usual, smuggling. The Thais, shuttling more than 150,000 refugees from Laos in and out of their crowded camps, mostly tribal Meo, and perhaps another 30,000 or so who had not registered in the camps, maintained a tenuous relationship with the Lao aggravated by uncertain conditions along the long, loose river border and by constant arguments over trade and other matters, some of which regularly led to incidents of violence. More than the other neighboring countries, the Thais hoped that the Lao, with whom they had a close racial affinity, would somehow hold together and remain a buffer between themselves and the Vietnamese. Early in January 1979 Thailand and Laos signed an agreement pledging to turn the Mekong into a "river of peace and friendship" and to avoid any more clashes, and they also agreed not to allow each other's territory to be used as a base for subversion or aggression against one another. But it would not be that easy to guarantee peace. With 50,000 Vietnamese troops in Laos, ostensibly to help maintain security and rebuild the stricken country, the prospects of the Lao avoiding the increasing grip of Hanoi did not appear bright; and the capture of Cambodia by Vietnam in that same month of January obviously diminished the chances further.

Throughout the Vietnam war, as a result of their free use of the Ho Chi Minh Trail in eastern Laos and their seasonal movement of troops in and out of the country to support the Pathet Lao, the armed wing of the Lao People's Revolutionary Party, in their seesaw battles against the forces of the Vientiane government and the CIA-backed Meo and Thai mercenaries, the North Vietnamese had used Laos as their backyard. Some of them in fact, had already built small settlements in the areas near the border, and Vietnamese political as well as military cadres had given early indications of remaining more or less permanently in Laos, taking Lao wives and rearing "second families." There was nothing the Lao could do about this, even if they had wanted to; for thirty years virtually all the leading Lao revolutionaries, including the new Prime Minister, Kaysone Phomvihan, had been trained and guided by Hanoi (Kaysone's father was Vietnamese), and personal as well as ideological and political bonds between the two countries had always been strong, especially among the Communists. Early in 1976, while I was visiting Laos, acknowledgment of these close ties was fervently demonstrated when a large Laotian delegation headed by Kaysone journeyed to Hanoi and was ceremoniously welcomed by a group that included more high-ranking North Vietnamese than had ever before turned out to greet any visitors. At the conclusion of the gala meeting, a joint communiqué, overflowing with emotional declarations of mutual respect and admiration, promised "to consolidate and enhance . . . long-term cooperation, and mutual assistance . . . in the interest of each nation and of Southeast Asia and the world." This communiqué set the tone for future relations between the two countries.

Since the Vietnamese had their hands full unifying the two halves of their own war-torn nation and dealing with some of their own fractious elements, let alone the Cambodians already causing trouble along the southern border, they were content for the moment to encourage the Lao to follow a semi-independent, nonaligned course, as the new government in Vientiane professed to favor. But by mid-1977, whether as part of the preconceived plan to resurrect the old idea of an Indochina Federation or simply to underline their authority in Laos to the Chinese and the Russians as well as to the rest of Asia and to the United States too, the Vietnamese went a big step further. Le Duan, secretary-general of the Communist Party of Vietnam, accompanied by Prime Minister Pham Van Dong; Politburo member Pham Hung, the boss of South Vietnam; and several other ranking officials, including military men, came to Vientiane in July to cement what Le Duan described as "the special relationship evergreen, everlasting . . . a friendship deeper than the waters of the Red River and the Mekong." Kaysone took the cue, emphasizing that "the great special solidarity between Laos and Vietnam," which he described as "a lasting militant alliance," had "no precedent in history," and telling his visitors that "the birth of the powerful Socialist Republic of Vietnam has made the outpost of socialism in Southeast Asia stronger than ever, tipping the balance of forces in this region completely in favor of the revolution." As he succinctly put it, "The special internationalist combatants of Vietnam working in Laos, implementing orders from the Central Committee of the Communist Party of Vietnam and President Ho Chi Minh, have shown a high degree of proletarian internationalism. They loved the Lao people as their own parents or brothers and sisters . . . We can reaffirm that every success of the Lao revolution has been possible thanks to a direct contribution of the Vietnamese revolution on all the battlefields of our beloved fatherland . . . The assistance given by Vietnam to Laos is invaluable."

The two sides thereupon issued a joint revolutionary declaration; an agreement "delimitating" their national borders; and a seven-article Treaty of Friendship and Cooperation to run for twenty-five years. The first, aside from the usual paeans of praise for each other and for other revolutionary movements around the world, including the Cubans and a number of African nations, condemned the United States "for maintaining its troops and military bases in Southeast Asia and attempting to use ASEAN to oppose the trends for real independence, peace and neutrality in this region." The treaty significantly contained a pledge on the part of both countries "to support and assist each other wholeheartedly and carry out a close cooperation aimed at reinforcing the defense capacity, preserving independence, sovereignty and territorial integrity, and defending the people's peaceful labor, against all schemes and acts of sabotage by imperialism and foreign reactionary forces." What this seemed to spell out and certify, for as long as Hanoi saw fit, was the presence of Vietnamese troops in Laos. Both countries also agreed to increase their economic cooperation "in agriculture, forestry, industry, communications and transport, [and] the exploitation of natural resources." While the border agreement seemed superfluous, it may have been an attempt by Hanoi to emphasize the independence of Laos in the face of criticism that the Vietnamese were acting in an overweening manner. That this thought may have struck some ordinary Lao was reflected in the defensive tone of a number of radio broadcasts and newspaper editorials in Vientiane in the months that followed, including, for example, a mock dialogue between two old men named "Uncle Hak" and "Uncle Sat," in which accusations of Vietnamese "intervention" were vehemently denied and linked to "divisive schemes" by "the imperialists and their quislings to undermine and sabotage Lao-Vietnam solidarity," measures denounced as "deceitful" and as "revolutionary propaganda." These same denials and denunciations were expressed when a group of top Lao military leaders made "a friendship visit" to Hanoi in September 1977.

Uneasy New Rulers

As the Lao revolution unfolded, or in its own peculiar way unraveled, it became increasingly difficult to distinguish between rebel activity on the part of the Meo and other disaffected or remnant anti-Communist elements and internal dissension and plotting within the new regime itself. On occasion these opposition tendencies and movements seemed to blur and blend, but hard evidence was not easy to come by. It was clear, however, that resentment of the overwhelming Vietnamese presence was a considerable factor in itself. There were even reports of clashes between Vietnamese and Pathet Lao forces; in April 1977, to cite one, a Vietnamese unit was said to have killed twenty Pathet Lao soldiers near Savannakhet, in southern Laos, when the Lao troops intercepted a Vietnamese truck convoy carrying timber to Vietnam. Unconfirmed reports were heard from time to time of a conflict between

Prime Minister Kaysone and Prince Souphanouvong, who had been named President of the Lao People's Democratic Republic (LPDR) in December 1975. Both men were Hanoi-oriented—the debonair Souphanouvong had a Vietnamese wife—but he was widely regarded as more of a bona-fide Lao nationalist than the doctrinaire Kaysone, and his ties were still close with his half brother, Prince Souvanna Phouma, who had been Prime Minister of the neutralist regime that preceded the Communist takeover and had become an innocuous "adviser" to the new regime. Though French-educated, the two sophisticated Lao princes had been leaders of the underground anti-French movement during World War II; afterward Souphanouvong had thrown in his lot with the Communists while Souvanna had tried to steer a middle course, and at various times had obtained the backing of the Americans.

To all intents and purposes, Souphanouvong was only a figurehead of the LPDR, but like Sihanouk during earlier days in Cambodia, he retained considerable support among the people of Laos, whose lukewarm revolutionary pretensions over the years had not diminished their quiet devotion to the neutral and respected monarchy and its various familial offshoots, of which the Souvanna-Souphanouvong branch was one. In any event, whether a rivalry between Souphanouvong and Kaysone and power conflicts among other members of the government existed or not, it seemed apparent that the hard-line Kaysone, who had been an early member of the Laodong Party of Vietnam long before it became the Communist Party after the war, was not an altogether popular figure in the new Laos. On at least three occasions—once in December 1976 when an incipient revolt against the new regime on the first anniversary of its installation was quashed, and at least twice in 1977—attempts were made to assassinate him, and he made fewer and fewer public appearances; on one occasion, late in 1977, when he was supposed to greet some returning Lao students from abroad, his black limousine drew up to the site of the ceremony, but without Kaysone—a tape of his speech was played instead.

In November 1977, following the execution of thirteen out of twenty-six defendants charged with the three known assassination attempts, more than a hundred former soldiers and civil servants accused of "lacking revolutionary vigilance" were arrested and either imprisoned or sent to re-education camps. Both before and after that, there were constant admonitions on the radio and in the columns of *Siang Pasason,* the government newpaper, "to resolutely suppress the counterrevolutionaries." One editorial, which appeared in August 1977, in discussing "weak points in the contingents of our peace-keeping forces," cited the fact that "certain guerrilla units in certain areas have not yet been consolidated as they should be," as a result of which "the local guerrillas have failed profoundly to understand their role in suppressing the counterrevolutionaries and guaranteeing the implementation of the people's right to collective mastership. They do not yet know how to distinguish friends from foes." (The phrase "collective mastership" has been used repeatedly by the new leaders of Laos.) Such references seemed to be directed more toward internecine opponents of the regime than at the rebel Meo and other resistance groups. In April 1978 three more persons were sentenced to death, plus five in absentia, and thirty-nine others were given long prison or rehabilitation terms for carrying out "sabotage activities . . . and attempting sinister plots aimed at destroying our brilliant new regime."

No matter what happened in Laos, the chances were that the Laotian Communists, even if they succumbed completely to Vietnamese "mastership," would still be somewhat different from Communists anywhere else, and that the lotuslike quality of national life would endure. I remember, during my 1976 trip, asking a Western ambassador who had been in the country only a month what his initial reaction to conditions in Laos was. After a pause he replied, with a smile, that he felt "disoriented." That sensation, I was able to assure him, was quite natural, and he was obviously adapting himself to Laos very well. The disorientation one felt in Laos—a country that had always appealed to Westerners, from transient hippies and diplomats on two-to-four-year tours to the score or more American and European businessmen, adventurers and sometime wanderers who had settled in Vientiane for longer than most of them cared to remember (or could remember)—was akin to that induced by behavioral drugs stronger than the marijuana or opium one could still obtain around town after the war. In some ways the disorientation experienced by the visitor returning to Communist Laos was particularly acute. Many things were still the same, but many things were also different, and the mixture was confounding. At the time of my 1976 visit, there still hung in the upper lobby of the rambling, barrackslike Hotel Lane Xang a dusty glass-covered advertisement that read "Falling in Love with a Simple Country. Let It Happen to You in Laos. Laos Happens on Royal Air Lao." One could still love Laos, or at least have a platonic relationship with it in its new manifestation, but not on Royal Air Lao, which was in the process of belatedly changing its name to Air Lao, having briefly outlasted the monarchy itself.

The six-century-old monarchy was peremptorily abolished on December 2, 1975, when, at a meeting in Vientiane, the National Congress of People's Representatives, a 264-member body that had been locally elected in October and November, dissolved itself in favor of a 45-member Supreme People's Council and proclaimed the formation of the Lao People's Democratic Republic. Portly King Savang Vatthana, who announced his abdication and temporarily withdrew from his palace in the royal capital of Luang Prabang to a small farm outside the city, was, like Souvanna Phouma, listed as an "adviser" to the new government, and the old flag of the country, bearing the triple image of white elephants on a red background, was replaced by a less fanciful one, with red stripes at the top and bottom, and a broad blue band in the middle bearing a white circle; the circle represented a rising moon denoting the ascendancy of the People's Democratic Republic.

In March 1977, following an aborted plot mounted by about a hundred right-wing rebels led by the King's brother, Sisouphanh Tharangsi, and reportedly with the King's approbation, the King and eight members of his family were arrested and flown to Vieng Say, a mountain town in the northeastern part of the country which during the long war years had served as headquarters for the Communists and was now one of the main re-education centers for thousands of officers and officials of the old regime. The government made no mention of the arrests on the radio or in its newspaper, though the fact that they had taken place was discussed in special, hastily summoned indoctrination "seminars" that were being held throughout the country. In June, in an interview with a Swiss correspondent, Souphanouvong charged that "the CIA and its henchmen stealthily living in Laos or in exile in Thailand" had been behind the "dark scheme" to smuggle the former King across the Mekong to Thailand "to lead the traitors in exile." Souphanouvong added that the royal entourage, including the King's wife and son (another son had earlier fled to France), had been flown "to a safe place for a rest, with the aim of ensuring safety for his life so that he could contribute for a long time to state affairs," and that "the government continues to create specially favorable conditions for his living standards as well as his political activities." He was still there in 1979. Despite the reverence for the monarchy, there was no indication that the King's arrest had disturbed the normal passivity of the populace; but it probably did not enhance the shaky reputation of the regime, which by this time was having increasing trouble with the economy and with the administration of the country, and with the growing number of resistance groups.

All of these factors and elements must be appraised against the background of what appeared to be the almost casual takeover of Laos by the Communists and the manner in which they set about establishing their new regime. Even though the Lao revolutionary leaders did not seize power as ruthlessly and violently as did their fellow Communists in South Vietnam and Cambodia, they were by no means unprepared to consolidate their control. Throughout the long period of the American war effort, and for many years before that —as far back as the establishment of the Lao Issara (Free Lao) movement, in 1954, when Souphanouvong received his first hundred weapons from Ho Chi Minh's newly founded Vietminh—there was a hard core of dedicated Laotian Communists who were determined to overthrow the French, and then, when the Americans replaced the French in Indochina, to dispatch them too, with the help of the North Vietnamese.

Though Souphanouvong's name was heard most often, the key figure from the outset was the more elusive and mysterious Kaysone. Fifty-five years old in 1974, Kaysone's Vietnamese father had been a middle-class civil servant in the French colonial administration—his mother was Laotian. Born in Savannakhet, which is on the Mekong across from Thailand, he was sent by his parents to study medicine at the University of Hanoi. There he met Ho and other Vietnamese revolutionaries, and he may have been an early member of the old Indochina Communist Party, which Ho formed in 1930. At any rate, apparently at Ho's suggestion, he returned after World War II to Savannakhet to organize resistance against the French. He rose rapidly, becoming comman-

der in chief of the Pathet Lao forces in 1955. That same year, the man who
was to become Deputy Prime Minister, Nouhak Phoumsavan (he was also
born in Savannakhet of a poor peasant family and later became well off by
operating a bus and truck service between Laos and Vietnam), attended the
Geneva Conference as an unofficial Pathet Lao representative. Both Kaysone
and Nouhak were founding leaders of the Neo Lao Hak Sat (Lao Patriotic
Front), which was formed in 1956; more important, both were leaders of the
secret Phak Pasason Pativat Lao (Lao People's Revolutionary Party), which
was created in March 1955, but whose existence was not made public until
1975. Like Kaysone, Nouhak, a more rough-hewn and personable man, probably also joined the Laodong party of Vietnam.

From Sam Neua to Vientiane

Laos received its independence from France early in 1954, several months
before the Geneva Conference. During the next two turbulent decades, while
the country was undergoing a series of unsuccessful experiments with right-
wing and coalition governments, marked by bitter factional feuds and inter-
spersed with several coups and attempted coups, Kaysone, Nouhak and their
veteran comrades made their headquarters in a mountain fastness of Sam
Neua province, in the northeast. That area, along with much of the rest of
the country—particularly the Ho Chi Minh Trail, reaching down from North
Vietnam through eastern Laos to South Vietnam, and the Pathet Lao positions in and around the Plain of Jars, not far from Vientiane—was heavily
bombed by the Americans after the Vietnam war spread to Laos. Even in
1979, as the plain was being slowly rebuilt and resettled, buried bombs were
still exploding and killing innocent people.

Occasionally some of the other Laotian Communist leaders came to Vientiane to negotiate tentatively with the right-wing or neutralist elements. (In
mid-1959 Souphanouvong was jailed there, escaping in May 1960.) None of
these efforts resulted in any firm agreement. Despite the increasingly strong
intervention of the CIA, which financed the Meo forces and built radar
stations in northeast Laos to help the bombing of North Vietnam and of the
Trail area, the Pathet Lao, under the careful tutelage and direction of the
North Vietnamese, throughout the war maintained a hold on two thirds of
the country and controlled between a third and a half of the total population
—mostly tribal groups. The right-wing and some neutralist factions, banded
together in what was known as "the Vientiane side," controlled the western
part of Laos, including the rich Mekong Valley, but this governing group
never held together for long, and a number of wealthy families ran different
provinces as virtual fiefdoms, while the army was divided by its own feuds and
contests for power. Souvanna Phouma ultimately did his best to mold the
bickering Vientiane groups into some sort of unified government, but it
became increasingly apparent that he was engaged in a futile effort, and that
the Americans in Laos who supported him were achieving little more than

they were accomplishing in Vietnam, though Souvanna was a man of far greater distinction and character than any of the Vietnamese the United States backed.

Under the terms of the Vientiane Agreement of February 21, 1973, which formally ended hostilities between the Communists and the Vientiane side, a new coalition government was established in April 1974, but while the Pathet Lao was given control of some ministries and dominant representation on the newly formed Joint National Political Council, it was not represented in the National Assembly, which had been elected in 1972 and consisted almost entirely of right-wing partisans. The Pathet Lao, more significantly, retained military control of most of the countryside. A tenuous cease-fire line was supposed to keep the two sides apart, but sporadic fighting continued, although not on anywhere near the same scale as in Vietnam. In April 1975 the Pathet Lao persuaded the King to dissolve the old National Assembly, and he subsequently visited Pathet Lao headquarters in Sam Neua. Then, in May and June, the Communists organized demonstrations that resulted in the hasty departure of all American dependents and the closing of the American AID mission, which had long served as a cover for the CIA war effort. During this period the Pathet Lao not only stepped up its military encroachments on Vientiane but forced the withdrawal of the leading right-wing members of the coalition government, replacing them with lesser-known and more malleable representatives of the Vientiane side. Meanwhile, the Communists kept up their anti-American demonstrations and gradually took over complete control of the government. On August 23, 1975, they proclaimed the "liberation" of Vientiane.

Much of Laos is so inaccessible that it was not apparent during the summer of 1975 that the Pathet Lao (or, more specifically, the Lao Patriotic Front and the cadres of the People's Revolutionary Party) was quietly and efficiently preparing the ground for a formal takeover. The work was carried out in typical Laotian fashion, by moves not unlike those of the graceful, hand-waving traditional dance, the *lamvong*, which was still being performed in the four night clubs that were still open in Vientiane. In July and August of 1975, in thousands of villages called *tasseng*, and all over the more than one hundred districts and sixteen provinces of the country (the new regime subsequently reduced the number of provinces to twelve, plus the municipality of Vientiane), representatives of the five basic mass organizations attached to the Patriotic Front (the Lao Patriotic Youth, Patriotic Women, Patriotic Farmers, Patriotic Workers and Buddhist Federation) were setting up meetings, which in November led to elections through the provincial level. Later that month, as the Joint National Political Council held a meeting at Vieng Say and summoned the top officials of the old regime to attend re-education courses there, a big rally was held at the national stadium in Vientiane, and this was followed by several days of demonstrations demanding the abolition of the monarchy and the creation of "a new and popular democratic regime." Once the King had agreed to abdicate and to disband the coalition government, the new National Congress of People's Representatives, consisting in part of those who had been elected in the provinces and in part of carefully selected party cadres, was summoned to meet, on December 1 and 2, 1975, in the gymnasium of the former AID compound in Vientiane.

At this gathering Kaysone presented a "Political Report on the Abolition of the Monarchy and Establishment of a People's Democratic Republic," followed by a new "program of action." He reviewed the nationwide reorganization that had already taken place and promised that "the popular democratic dictatorship will be further strengthened and consolidated with every passing day." He also stressed "the military duty of youths" and said that the "organizational network of guerrillas" would be "extensively expanded." In the section of the program dealing with economic affairs, Kaysone placed special emphasis on making Laos self-sufficient in the production of food and on the protection and development of the nation's forests, with timber projected as one of the country's chief exports. He was less explicit about industrial development, referring to "new factories to produce goods from local agricultural and forest raw materials," and to developing "mineral resources and hydroelectric power sources." Laos had supplies of potash, tin and iron, but they had scarcely been developed so far, and still weren't, four years after the war. As for power, a multinational consortium had for several years been engaged in building a large hydroelectric development on a tributary of the Mekong, the Nam Ngum, north of Vientiane, which would eventually provide 100,000 kilowatts of electricity. The Americans were in charge of the first phase of the project, and after the war the Japanese took over the second. Kaysone also announced that the state would control all imports and exports as well as banking, but said that joint ventures by the state and private entrepreneurs would be permitted.

In speaking of cultural and social affairs, Kaysone made it clear that strong measures would be taken "to get rid completely of the influence of the slavish, reactionary and decadent culture; to mobilize and encourage the people to destroy all reactionary novels, books, newspapers, or pictures that arouse sexual passion in imperialist ways; and to check and get rid of various social evils, such as gambling, prostitution and robbery." (The government moved quickly to round up prostitutes, known criminals and drug addicts, and they were segregated on two islands in the Mekong, where they were subjected to re-education and "health cures." While numerous bars, mainly run by superannuated, bleary Frenchmen, were still open when I was in Vientiane in 1976, most of them soon disappeared. As for the "controlled" night clubs, I attended one of them one evening with some Laotian and Vietnamese friends. The musicians were all familiar, and most of the large crowd appeared to be the same old prerevolutionary mixture of young Laotian boys and girls and a few foreigners—the girls, however, were no longer allowed to wear miniskirts or Western-style dresses, but only blouses and the traditional long wraparound skirts called *sin.* The only dances permitted were Laotian ones, particularly the *lam-vong,* but this, too, was banned not long after my departure, and then all dancing was forbidden. Music was confined to old Laotian songs with new revolutionary lyrics.)

On the subject of religion, Kaysone said that there would be religious freedom in the new Laos. Soon, however, Catholicism began to be attacked and was accused of having brought a depraved Western lifestyle to the nation and of having had wartime associations with the CIA, and most foreign missionaries left, while virtually all Church properties were seized. Laos is basically a Buddhist country, and at the outset the new government sought to make use of the twenty thousand or so Buddhist monks by holding quasi-political meetings in wats, or temples, partly no doubt because the Buddhist organizational structure, like that of the Communists, is vertical, from the village wats up through a centralized hierarchy. However, while condoning Buddhism, the Communists slowly sought to reduce its influence, though they did not seek to eliminate it anywhere near as ruthlessly as in Cambodia or as in Vietnam. (In 1977 Kaysone, in a not-so-veiled reference to animism as well as religion, declared that "superstition, belief in the supernatural and backward tradition remain deep-rooted, thus posing a major obstacle to our production and welfare.") While the Communists accepted the "humanistic aspects of Buddhism," as another senior official put it, "we oppose the practice of merely chanting prayers without understanding what you are saying." In short, Buddhism was neither rejected nor encouraged, but efforts were made to reconcile its practices with the precepts of Communism; one way this was achieved was by establishing elected committees to run the wats and the various Buddhist organizations in place of individual bonzes, some of whom fled to Thailand.

In his important December 1975 address Kaysone made it clear that Laos would be a nonaligned country. He concluded by announcing that the government would consist of sixteen ministries, or agencies equivalent to ministries, and a Council of Ministers of thirty-nine, headed by him. From the outset the new regime made a special point of including members of the country's minority tribal groups, such as the Meo and Lao-Theung, on both the Supreme People's Council and the Council of Ministers, and some of them were present when, on the evening of December 5, the leaders of the new government held a large reception, attended by the diplomatic community, on the grounds of the royal palace in Vientiane. In the middle of the celebration, while a Pathet Lao military band played new revolutionary songs, the ten top leaders of the government, headed by Kaysone and Nouhak, arrived quietly, and standing together on the palace steps, the mystery men of the Laotian revolution dramatically made their first collective public appearance. As it turned out, it was one of their last, for the top men became increasingly reluctant to risk appearing anywhere.

Seminars and Re-education

In the months that followed, meeting and rallies were held all over Laos, in keeping with Kaysone's announced plan for promulgating the tenets of the revolution. The Lao are not easily organized, and the fragmentary reports available indicated that the initial reaction of the people in formerly government-held areas was one of bewilderment tinged with a degree of suspicion, in contrast to the solid base of support the Pathet Lao had built up over the years in the larger geographic but smaller populated areas of their control. The new situation had come about so quickly that despite their exhortation of the new mass organizations, the Communists lacked enough cadres to get their message across. Suspicion gave way to fear and uncertainty as the seminar program was set in motion and former officials began disappearing. The estimated 40,000 former officials and military men of the old regime who chose to stay in Laos rather than flee to Thailand were sent to about forty re-education centers throughout the country. Discipline and living conditions in these camps varied considerably. Lower-ranking detainees were sent to camps near Vientiane and were allowed to return home from time to time, but those of senior rank were dispatched to far-off places in the northeast around Vieng Say and in Phong Saly province, where they had to build their own huts and forage for food to supplement their small rations of rice and salt, and put in long hours on road and other construction jobs. Over the months a few were released, but the great majority was held indefinitely. Some tried, usually unsuccessfully, to escape, while others died in the camps, but conditions in general, with the exception of some camps for "incorrigibles," were not as hard as they were reported to be in similar work and reform camps in Vietnam.

Seminars for some lower-ranking administrators of the old government were also held on a continuous basis in Vientiane. While I was there one such seminar was conducted for three days in the ground-floor ballroom of the Hotel Lane Xang by an austere-looking member of the Ministry of Defense, dressed in a traditional white high-collared Laotian shirt and dark trousers. He presided over three hundred male and female Defense Ministry workers, who arrived each morning in a Russian bus, on their own motorcycles or bicycles, or on foot, some of them in dark-green military uniforms with visored caps and others in civilian clothes. As I peered through the glass doors of the ballroom I could see that they were listening with varying degrees of attentiveness to the stern man in the white shirt. According to Western diplomats I spoke with, the seminars were taking up so much of everybody's time that very little else was being accomplished, and it was difficult to obtain answers to routine questions at any of the ministries. On the other hand, government spokesmen assured me that while indocrination and ideology were being given priority, the ministries were busy preparing plans and budgets. Three years later, however, the seminars were still going on, and by the Communists' own admissions the ministries were not operating any more efficiently.

Among the best social barometers of any Asian city are its markets, and the big morning market in Vientiane seemed to me, at least in 1976, to be functioning at its normal active pace. Except for meat, there was enough food available, from rice and fish to all sorts of fruits and vegetables. After the Thais had closed the border for several months in November 1975, following the firing of shots by the Pathet Lao at a Thai patrol vessel that was said to have infringed on Laotian waters, Vientiane was deprived of much of its usual supply of food, so one of the new regime's first moves was to order all citizens, and all ministries and officials as well, to plant vegetables in their backyards, and these pleasant green gardens were soon sprouting everywhere. Meat was a problem the government was trying to solve, and it remained a difficult one. Initially there was a ration system, but the distribution of ration slips was so erratic that it had to be abandoned. New cooperative stores were then opened, where a variety of goods, including meat and other foods, was made available at fixed prices, but a flourishing black market in meat also developed.

The old official rate was 1,250 Lao kip to the dollar, but in mid-June 1976 a new "liberation kip" was issued at an official rate of 60 to the dollar, which was soon changed to 200, but the black-market rate quickly shot up to above 1,000 and then to 2,000. As the economy remained stagnant—coffee was the only sustained export item—the government's efforts to organize farmers into communal work groups according to a production points for work done and for sharing the harvest failed to engender much enthusiasm among the bulk of peasants, who owned their land and traditionally were accustomed to planting only as much as they needed to feed themselves and obtain a surplus to sell in the markets. A sliding tax on the harvest based on paddy output per family further alienated the farmers, some of whom burned their crops and even fought off the tax collectors with guns. While government subsidies had helped provide enough rice for a time, bad droughts in 1976 and 1977, especially in the south, created severe food shortages; by early 1978, as the drought struck again, near-famine conditions obtained in some areas, and international relief agencies had to be called upon to import emergency rice. Even the United States, despite the congressional ban on aid to Indochina nations, gave 10,000 tons on humanitarian grounds. Just when Laos seemed to have overcome the emergency, heavy rains caused flash floods in the mountains and inundated the whole Mekong valley, destroying 125,000 tons of rice and threatening half the population of the country with famine all over again. This time the appeal for help did not bring such generous results, and those who escaped the floods were ordered to donate two kilograms each to the victims, who were told to be "self-reliant" and to plant subsidiary crops such as corn and sweet potatoes.

At the same time the price of meat and vegetables soared so high on the free and black markets that few could afford to buy any, and many families had to subsist on a diet of rice or corn and salt. The lack of enough food and the increasing discipline imposed by the Pathet Lao, including growing restrictions on travel and constant forced attendance at nighttime study sessions and rallies, along with the mounting resentment of the heavy Vietnamese presence, were the main reasons cited by refugees in late 1977 and 1978 for their fleeing in increasing numbers across the river to camps in Thailand.

While continuing to exhort the populace, the government made no effort to hide the seriousness of the situation. In December 1977, in a second-anniversary speech, Kaysone spoke of the "unprecedented drought" that had hit the country, and called for the building of more irrigation facilities and for improvements in transportation. "We lack experience in managing an economy," he said. "This is why we have not been able to avoid the weaknesses and shortcomings affecting production and the people's welfare . . . We must recognize that we face many difficulties, including great and long-standing ones, in marching forward on the path of socialist revolution." The problems, which included the lack of specialists to build large irrigation canals, let alone dams and hydroelectric installations, were magnified by the fact, as Kaysone added, that "we face enemy sabotage and pressure." He pointed out that "we have been compelled to allocate the main part of our forces and budget to defending the country and maintaining peace and public order."

These negative and admonitory themes were not new. They had been voiced repeatedly by leaders of the regime, most notably by Kaysone in a thirty-thousand-word speech he had delivered earlier in the year, in February, to the Supreme People's Council, when he said that "our enemies are fiercely and violently opposing our new regime day and night," and severely criticized "cadres and civil servants" for their failure "to grasp the aspirations of the masses" and for "acting like bureaucrats and threatening the people." The bulk of this marathon speech would serve as the basic blueprint for the government's economic, social and political plans through 1980, with special emphasis on increasing production through gradual moves toward collective enterprise and on improving the administrative system, especially at the district level. But by the end of 1977 it had become obvious that the bold goals enunciated by Kaysone at the outset had not been met, and that his tactic of blaming "enemies of the regime" for its own failures and shortcomings in getting the revolution off the ground was a subterfuge. In mid-1978 the government started a broad campaign to mobilize the peasants into cooperatives, and within a few months about eight hundred were reported to have been started, but in many areas the peasants resented the move and cut down their orchards and killed their cattle rather than cooperate. Most of the peasants, and the cadres too, failed to understand the complicated work-point wage system initiated, and that didn't encourage compliance either. Nor did the fact that promised consumer goods in exchange for farm surpluses failed to materialize, including such simple things as soap, mosquito nets and kitchen utensils.

If the Lao lacked the means and manpower to implement and enforce their revolutionary aims, they also lacked money. Though the Vietnamese were building road and rail links between Laos and Vietnam, and had opened up the big port of Danang to the Lao to alleviate the shortage of goods caused by the sporadic closing of the Thai border, they gave little financial aid to Laos during the first two years but pledged loans and grants totaling $137 million over a three-year period starting in 1978. The new rulers of the country had aggravated their problem by treating the French almost as harshly as the Americans, closing the Banque de l'Indochine and keeping its four officers under "bank arrest" in their apartments on the top floors of the bank for two months late in 1975. The French military mission set up in 1954 was quickly terminated, and most French businessmen and technical experts left the country, with only some teachers remaining temporarily until Lao textbooks replaced French ones.

It was difficult to gauge the exact amount of aid given by the Russians, whom the Lao went out of their way to extol fulsomely in celebrations such as those marking the anniversaries of the October Revolution of 1917, but they probably either gave or loaned Laos about $75 million worth of assistance of one kind or another during 1976 and 1977. Much of this went for agricultural development, but they also donated thousands of tons of gasoline, and scores of tons of cloth, paper, medicines, powdered milk and canned goods, as well as trucks and cars and machinery for building roads and bridges, airfields, hospitals and storage facilities, sending their own experts to supervise the work and transporting 2,000 Lao students to Russia for training. Aeroflot took over internal air transport initially and part of Laos's external air service as well, and donated a dozen or more cargo and passenger planes. During 1977 ten Russian MiG-21s were sent into the country, which caused further jitters among the Thais and delayed the resumption of border trade.

Though the Russians were seen all over town, an official I spoke with at the Soviet embassy said, somewhat defensively, "We are conspicuous only because you Americans are gone." The less visible Chinese were donating or loaning money and dispensing some aid, including gasoline, but the total probably was no more than a third of what the Russians were giving, excluding what Peking was putting into the extensive road system it had been building in the northwest for nearly two decades, which was undoubtedly designed more for its own purposes than for the Lao. The new roads, when fully extended, theoretically could support the insurgency movements in Burma and Thailand, and in Cambodia as well, as a reaction to Hanoi's increasing activity in the area.

During 1978 the Chinese withdrew 10,000 of their 15,000 workers on the northern roads, including some engineer battalions, but then they sent 5,000 men back into Laos again. The Cubans were in Laos too, but in small numbers; a dozen or so specialists, mostly health workers, were there, and were said to be working on reducing malaria, which remained a major problem, particularly after a recurrent epidemic of the deadly falciparum strain. Other nations, notably Sweden and Japan, were giving assistance to a lesser extent than the Communist countries, but were slowly increasing their contributions, and early in 1978 the World Bank stepped into the picture for the first time by extending an $8.2 million credit for improving conditions among the rural poor by financing irrigation projects and donating some pork, the chief source of protein in the Lao diet. Earlier aid by the United Nations was chiefly directed at resettling the 700,000 refugees within the country who had fled the bombing and fighting over the years.

What the Lao obviously missed most, however, was direct American aid, which had been dispensed so lavishly during the war, and which had also furnished the largest amount of funds in a five-nation financial consortium that had been created to bolster the Laotian monetary system under the old regime but had been discontinued when the Communists took over. Sisana Sisan, the suave French- and English-speaking Minister of Information, told me in a long talk I had with him that the government was eager to obtain aid from the United States, "which says it wants to heal the wounds of war, but doesn't really want to help us because you think we regard you as an enemy." That somewhat seemed to beg the question. Though the Americans maintained an embassy in Laos after the war—the only Indochina country where this was the case—it had been ordered cut in half by the Lao in 1977, and the dozen or so remaining staff headed by a chargé d'affaires was virtually isolated in the small embassy compound. The former spacious holdings of the Americans, including the huge residential compound known as Silver City on the side of town, had become the headquarters of the new regime, and its seizure had created considerable bitterness between the embassy and Lao officials and become the subject of stalemated negotiations. Early in 1977 the new government received the Woodcock mission to discuss the recovery of the bodies of missing Americans. The Lao took the occasion to repeat that they wanted to "maintain normal relations with the United States and improve them," but insisted that Washington should also "honor its commitments regarding its contributions to the economic restoration and the post war reconstruction of Laos."

The advent of the new, less rigidly anti-Communist regime of Prime Minister Kriangsak Chamanan in Thailand, in October 1977, quickly created the atmosphere for improving relations between Thailand and Laos that culminated in the January 1979 visit of Kriangsak to Vientiane and the signing of the new Mekong agreement mentioned earlier. Both nations had regularly accused each other of supporting insurgents against the other—the Lao charged that right-wing Thais were instigating rebellion in Laos, and the Thais insisted that the Lao were still training insurgents for the Communist Party of Thailand. There was some evidence to support both accusations, but Bangkok and Vientiane, while accepting the fact that the porous river border could probably never be closed to the flow of agents and guns in both directions, as well as to smugglers, now seemed determined to soft-pedal these issues and to get along with each other as best they could. One of the first products of the improved relationship was the resumption of air service between the two capitals and the renewal of talks to restore joint projects of the Mekong Development Authority, including some major dam construction.

Resistance to the Regime

The continuing problem of internal resistance, which furnished the pretext for the large numbers of Vietnamese troops in the country, came to a head in the fall of 1977 and during 1978 when hostilities increased between Cambodia and Vietnam. Vientiane was forced to deny that Hanoi had sent troops into Cambodia from Laos, though this was probably the case. Until late 1978 the Lao did their best not to take sides between Vietnam and Cambodia, but they kept tilting increasingly toward the Vietnamese, no doubt under pressure, and after the capture of Cambodia by Vietnamese forces in January 1979, Laos recognized the new Heng Samrin regime, hailing its "miraculous victory" over the "dark, fascist Pol Pot–Ieng Sary clique," even before Hanoi and Moscow did so.

The Vietnamese were undeniably helping control the scattered dissidents in Laos, especially in the northern parts of the country, where about 10,000 Meo out of 235,000 still in the country (approximately 85,000 had fled to Thailand) had maintained a steady opposition since the Communist takeover. Using guns and ammunition left over from the days when they had been supported by the CIA, the Meo had managed for more than two years to blockade and cut roads, including the major artery between Vientiane and Luang Prabang, and to ambush and kill numerous Pathet Lao patrols, and some Vietnamese as well. But by early 1978, and continuing with growing violence during the year, the Vietnamese and their Pathet Lao counterparts struck back with bombers and fighters, and finally employed what appeared to be tear gas laced with something else to force the Meo out of their mountain redoubts, particularly their base in Phu Bia mountain. Even as they attacked the Meo rebels, the Lao government was trying to get them and the other tribal elements in the hills comprising nearly 40 percent of the country's population to come down to the lowlands to live, but only a relative handful did so. At one point the government accused the Chinese of supporting the Meo with guns and uniforms, which Peking denounced as "a fantastic slander," but the fact that there were nearly 3 million Meo and Yao tribesmen living in China, from where they had migrated south a century ago, offered Peking an obvious propaganda and possible insurgency advantage if it chose to capitalize on it. In the wake of the fall of Cambodia to Hanoi, it seemed perfectly possible that the Chinese might pick up the challenge, which they could carry out at very little cost as a parallel effort to maintaining a strong defensive or even offensive posture along the Sino-Vietnamese border. But whatever Peking might do in the future to support the Meo, those bearing the brunt of the fighting in 1978 were all but destroyed. The minority who managed to escape threw away their guns and fled in disarray across the river to Thailand, and only a fraction of those who tried to get away managed to make it to the already overcrowded refugee camps. The fate of the Meo was undoubtedly one of the most tragic sagas of the war and its aftermath.

The situation in northern Laos became more serious in the wake of the

Sino-Vietnamese war early in 1979. Even as the Chinese began their withdrawal of troops from Vietnam in March, they reinforced their divisions along the Sino-Laos border. The Russians promptly warned that Peking's "preparations for intervention in Laos should be stopped," while the Vietnamese accused the Chinese of "plotting to use Lao territory as a springboard for attacks on the western part of Vietnam, in coordination with attacks from the north." Peking in turn accused Vietnam and the Soviet Union of "enslaving the Lao people" and repeated its charges that Vietnam planned to take over all of Indochina. The Lao, finding it increasingly difficult to ply a neutral course, for the first time joined in the accusations against the Chinese and demanded that Peking withdraw the rest of its road-building crews in northern Laos, but the Chinese, seemingly confident of their long-time presence in the area, ignored the demands. Short of opening a new front in the expanding Indochina war, Peking seemed determined, at the very least, to keep the Vietnamese on the defensive by stepping up its shadow-boxing maneuvers in the triborder area. One result of the Chinese threat, real or imagined, was the conscription of Lao youth to serve in the army, and this led to a new flight of young refugees across the Mekong.

The situation in southern Laos was even more confusing. This area had always been a conservative stronghold, and after the war considerable natural opposition to the Communists immediately sprang up. Pathet Lao soldiers were frequently ambushed and killed, and even dragged off buses and murdered by former right-wing army elements around the southern towns of Savannakhet, Attopeu, Thakhek, Pakse and Paksane. Dissident Pathet Lao, in small units, were said to have joined rebel groups who from time to time managed to capture some villages, and early in 1976 there was at least one substantiated report of a mutiny among a group of several hundred people undergoing re-education courses said to be led by an erstwhile Pathet Lao colonel who called himself a "national Communist" and opposed the presence of the North Vietnamese in Laos. Another group, calling itself the Lao People's Revolutionary Front 21/18 (the figure "21" referred to the date of the signing of the Vientiane agreement of February 21, 1973, ending the war between the Communists and the old government, while "18" referred to the eighteen points in the political program issued by the former Joint National Political Council), favored the country's neutrality and nonalignment without interference of any kind by any foreign governments, including North Vietnam and Russia.

Using guerrilla tactics the Pathet Lao had earlier employed against the Americans, this group and other resistance elements (called *patikans*, or reactionaries, by the government) blew up bridges, conducted ambushes and assassinated people it considered antirevolutionary, including Pathet Lao soldiers and officials whose behavior was described as being "against the interests of the people." At one point both Kaysone and Nouhak paid separate emergency visits to their native Savannakhet to pacify the population and modify the stringent measures that had been taken by local authorities. When isolated attacks occurred in and around Vientiane early in 1976, including the throwing of grenades onto the grounds of the Soviet embassy, the government tightened security measures, arrested several hundred minor officials accused of "neglecting their surveillance assignments," and imprisoned some Pathet Lao soldiers whom it accused of "having done more harm than good."

By early 1978 the resistance in the south seemed to have subsided as it had in the north, but it had by no means been eliminated, as Kaysone's constant warnings and exhortations indicated. Groups of ten to sixty or seventy dissidents roamed the countryside more or less at will. Though they lacked coordination, it was entirely possible that a condition of chaos would result and that the government would not be able to rule effectively, were it not for the presence of North Vietnamese troops. If Vientiane did not relish this thought, there was no reason to suppose Hanoi objected to the circumstances that furnished an excuse for its continued heavy presence, and the outbreak of fighting against the Cambodians undoubtedly reinforced its views. And especially after the Sino-Vietnamese border war, when Hanoi accused the Chinese of threatening to invade Laos in the north, the excuse gained further credence.

Despite their disavowals and denunciations of traditional "supernatural" influences, and their orders for the people to forgo and forget them, the Communists, in their initial efforts to remold the political personality of the Lao, wisely did nothing specific to denigrate the power of the animistic spirits known as the *phi.* The immortal *phi* exist everywhere—in the jungles and forests, in air, fire and water, and in all the organs of the human body—and they constantly had to be propitiated, or sometimes, when regarded as forces of evil, be exorcised. When I asked a young man who had just come out of a long indoctrination session in the busy ballroom of my hotel whether the question of the *phi* had been raised in any of the lectures he had heard so far, he gave me a pained look and hurried away, glancing nervously around, as if to apologize to any *phi* who might have heard my indelicate inquiry. Whether the *phi* would eventually be given, or would assume, a Marxist-Leninist character and coloration of their own, remained to be determined; but in assessing the Lao People's Democratic Republic early in 1979, as it approached its fourth anniversary, it seemed more than likely that if the *phi* were to survive at all, along with Laos itself, they would in due time acquire Vietnamese names and meanings, and perhaps Russian masks and nicknames.

Thailand– The Weakest Hinge

In the days immediately after World War II, Bangkok, in more ways than one, was the most "open" city in Southeast Asia, a capacious, leisurely place interlaced with colorful but fetid canals called klongs and notable for its gold-leafed temples, its jewels and trinkets, and its tropical heat and somnolence that had inspired Noël Coward's reference to it ("In Bangkok/At twelve o'clock/They foam at the mouth and run . . .") in his mocking musical reminder that only "mad dogs and Englishmen go out in the midday sun." It was also open in the sense that since Thailand had escaped the nineteenth-century tide of European colonization, the country was not concerned with the violent revolutionary movements that were surging through the region. Rather, it was embarked, at the time of my first visit in mid-1946, on the first of its sporadic experiments in democracy, which soon gave way to a new series of military-dominated dictatorships that has governed Thailand with varying degrees of harshness and benevolence most of the time since the uprising that overthrew its ancient absolute monarchy in 1932 and replaced it with a constitutional monarchy. The Thais have always prided themselves on their three traditional pillars of king, nation and religion (meaning Buddhism). But despite their comfortable convictions and their easy ways, and perhaps because they never had to fight for freedom from Western imperialism, they have never really analyzed or defined their basic contemporary institutions of government, including the parliamentary forms they have occasionally tested but which, through their postwar history, have in practice produced more chaos and confusion than common purpose or sustained achievement.

The Thais also place special emphasis on doing things their own way in any dealings with Westerners, and this has served to make them perhaps the hardest of Asians for foreigners to understand. Nor does their peculiar traditional predilection for bending with the wind, which prompted their acceptance of Japanese hegemony in Southeast Asia during the war, as they had previously adapted themselves to conquests and developments around them, always win them the understanding or respect of their fellow Asians. During the long years of the Vietnam war they supported the United States, making seven bases available for the American war effort, and placing themselves in the position of what their critics denounced as a client state. But once the war was over, and surrounded to the north and west by the new Communist nations of Indochina, the Thais soon began bending again, and while maintaining close relations with the Americans, whose residue of 20,000 troops were asked to leave the country in March 1976, they started making new accommodations with the Vietnamese, Cambodians and Lao, and with Communist China as well.

This was not an easy procedure, particularly since the nearby Communist countries were giving sanctuary as well as moral and some material aid to Communist insurgents in the north and northeast of Thailand; at the same time the Cambodians initiated separate fights over the ill-defined five-hundred-mile border between the two countries. Meanwhile, in the southern part of Thailand, the Thais and the Malaysians were jointly trying to halt the spread of a Communist insurgency that was principally directed against Malaysia. The subtle diplomatic game of trying to maintain a delicate balance among the big powers and a position of neutrality in the region created complicated problems for the Thais and kept them in a precarious situation. By 1979, however, though their many mended fences had some holes in them, the new postwar wind to which they had adroitly bent in several directions at once was not—or at least not yet—strong enough to blow the fences down.

In trying to be all things to all people, the Thais also found themselves the recipients of at least 200,000 people they didn't want but, with mixed degrees of compassion and resentment, they accepted—refugees from Indochina. Meo, Lao, other tribal elements from Laos, Cambodians and Vietnamese poured into Thailand by all means of travel and from all directions, swimming across the Mekong under gunfire, crawling through minefields from Cambodia, and escaping by boat from the coast and inland rivers of Vietnam. The majority of these refugees rotated through some fifteen special Thai camps and were supported by the government with financial help from the United Nations High Commissioner for Refugees and a dozen or so voluntary relief agencies, mostly American. About a third eventually were resettled in the United States and France on the basis of a complicated set of rules and regulations that included their previous employment status with those two countries, their skills and language facility, and their ability to prove they had relatives already living in France or America. A number of other countries, notably Australia and Canada, took lesser numbers of the refugees, but as the influx continued, including the growing numbers from Cambodia as well as Vietnamese and Chinese from the southern half of Vietnam, many of whom also fled in their rickety boats to Malaysia or drifted about from port to port seeking asylum, it appeared likely that the Thais would have to keep at least 150,000 of the refugees indefinitely, probably permanently. It was not a prospect the Thais looked forward to, given their own problems of rural poverty and survival, though they responded, for the most part, with more humanity and sympathy than other Southeast Asian nations. But as the flow increased during the first half of 1979, even the Thais began to adopt a tougher policy, both toward the newly arriving Cambodians and also toward the Lao, many of whom were said to be fleeing more for economic than for political reasons.

The refugee tragedy in many ways dramatized more clearly than anything else the post-Vietnam situation in Southeast Asia. The stories of privation, starvation, despotism and death the various refugees told left no doubt that conditions in all three former Indochina nations were a lot worse than had been suspected, particularly in Cambodia but also, as the boat people and the fleeing Meo revealed, in Vietnam and Laos as well. Even taking into consideration the fact that many of the refugees were politically biased against the Communists or were small tradesmen whom the Communist regimes had sought to get rid of, one way or another, the stories they told of vast numbers of people being uprooted, dispatched to the countryside under slave-labor conditions, and of death by starvation or as a result of harsh conditions in prisons or re-education camps, were too real and graphic to be disbelieved. After visiting about half the camps in Thailand in 1977 and 1978, talking to a cross section of those who had fled, I came away convinced that the long revolution in Indochina was by no means over, as the Vietnamese-Cambodian border struggle that preceded Hanoi's major invasion of Cambodia demonstrated, as well as the troubles of consolidation the North Vietnamese were facing economically and politically in the South. Whatever the future course of events, including the low-key support the Vietnamese would probably continue to give to the insurgency movements in Thailand, Malaysia and elsewhere, it seemed apparent that, for the short term at least, their own difficulties of internecine struggle and reconstruction would preclude any efforts on their part to export revolution on a major scale in Southeast Asia. For the time being, they simply were not up to it, which accounted for their desire to reach some sort of accommodation with Thailand and the other four countries of the Association of Southeast Asian Nations.

Kriangsak Goes to China

As the self-styled "front-line" member of ASEAN, Thailand, under Prime Minister Kriangsak Chamanan, a congenial, unflappable, pipe-smoking man who even before he retired as Supreme Commander in October 1978, preferred business suits to uniforms and did not act as a conventional authoritarian leader, took the lead in responding to the overtures of the Communists. In March 1978 Kriangsak traveled to Peking, where he successfully cemented the diplomatic ties created in 1975 by Prime Minister Kukrit Pramoj during the period of what may have been Thailand's last experiment in nonmilitary guided democracy. As a result of Kriangsak's trip, the Chinese and the Thais drew up some thirty agreements on scientific and technical cooperation and exchange, and Peking pledged to give Bangkok 600,000 tons of crude oil and a smaller amount of high-speed diesel oil at preferential or "friendship" prices, while agreeing to buy $8 million worth of Thai products, including corn, tapioca, tobacco and gunny bags. More important than the agreements themselves was the apparent desire of the Chinese Communists, under the newly evolving pragmatic policies of Vice Premier Teng Hsiao-ping, to regard and accept Thailand as a pivotal state in Southeast Asia. If the Chinese had ulterior motives in wanting to counter the Vietnamese overtures to Thailand and the other Southeast Asian countries, and to hold back attempts by the Russians, to whom the Vietnamese had drawn increasingly closer since the end of the Vietnam war, to obtain influence in the area, Peking still seemed more sincere than either Hanoi or Moscow in its approach to the ASEAN nations; individually and collectively, the Chinese expressed the desire to deal with them as non-Communist entities with which they seriously wanted to maintain peace and broaden trade.

Kriangsak, who had made it clear when he assumed power in October 1977 that it was Thailand's intention to be on good terms "with all countries regardless of ideology," proved himself a highly skilled diplomatist whose earlier background as a military man—in fact, one of the long-time pets of the Americans—had offered little evidence of his negotiating talents in the field of foreign policy. Now assisted by an able professional Foreign Minister, Upadit Pachariangkul, Kriangsak played one card after another in subtle fashion in expanding his relations with the Communist nations. Following his visit to China he tried his best to calm down the chaotic situation along the Cambodian border, for the most part demonstrating restraint in the face of constant raids by Khmer Rouge bands, often carried out in conjunction with the Thai Communists, and on occasion responding with counterattacks and bombing of Cambodian territory to stop the incursions.

The situation along the border was aggravated by factional disputes among the Cambodian troops, by smuggling operations that often led to violence, and by Phnom Penh's gradual loss of control over its own army units, some of which were turning against the despotic government of Premier Pol Pot. In June 1978, after Upadit had visited Phnom Penh, Ieng Sary, the Foreign Minister and the No. 2 man in the murky Cambodian regime, came to Bangkok and was hosted by Kriangsak. While no firm agreements were reached, the border strife temporarily diminished, which was chiefly due to Cambodian withdrawals of soldiers to the Vietnamese-Cambodian front; though the two governments at least created the foundation for better diplomatic relations, it appeared unlikely that they would achieve much more until the border was properly defined and until a more stable regime emerged in Phnom Penh.

Kriangsak continued his delicate balancing act by playing the genial host in September to Prime Minister Pham Van Dong, of Vietnam, who followed up on visits of three of his deputies by descending on Thailand and exuding all his old revolutionary charm. He was given an audience with King Phumiphon Adulyadej, visited Bangkok's famous Buddhist temples and was hosted at dinner by Kriangsak, whose hobbies included cooking peppery Thai food for his guests. Bangkok was Dong's first stop on a tour of other ASEAN capitals, and in admitting that Vietnam had "problems," he also said that the Vietnamese would "support no activity if it is harmful to Thailand" and would "respect Thailand's independence." This was taken as a renunciation of any further aid to the insurgents, but as was quickly pointed out by some cynical Thai observers, it would be easy for the Vietnamese to continue to funnel such aid through Laos, as they had done all along. If Dong was playing his cards to counter the Chinese diplomatic offensive by declaring that Vietnam also wanted Southeast Asia to be a "zone of peace, genuine independence and neutrality"—the Vietnamese always used the ambiguous phrase "genuine independence" instead of the word "freedom," which the ASEAN countries preferred—he didn't altogether succeed in his mission. Kriangsak carefully warded off his efforts to sign a treaty of friendship and nonaggression, stating that such things had to be executed "step by step"; and an agreement to discuss the repatriation of 40,000 Vietnamese who had been living in northeast Thailand since they fled there two years after the French Indochina War ended in 1954 produced no results when it became obvious that these earlier refugees were no more willing to return to Vietnam than the newer Vietnamese refugees were, and that Hanoi didn't really want them back. If the new tone of cordiality between Hanoi and Bangkok did not last, they could serve as a convenient fifth column inside Thailand, where they had done well economically but had remained isolated, maintaining pro-Hanoi feelings, which was a safe enough position as long as they did not have to face the privations of life in Communist Vietnam.

Kriangsak wasn't yet through with his nimble diplomatic dance. Early in November 1978 Soviet Deputy Foreign Minister Nikolai Firyubin popped into Bangkok and was received cordially but without the fanfare that had attended Dong's visit, and then, two weeks later, came the climax of the diplomatic parade with the arrival of Teng Hsiao-ping. It was the first visit to Thailand of a high-ranking Chinese leader, and the Thais went all out for the occasion. By coincidence Crown Prince Vajiralongkorn, the heir to the throne, was about to be ordained into the Buddhist monkhood, and Teng, in his black Mao suit, incongruously watched the saffron-robed prince go through his ceremonial routine and then had an aide offer the young prince the traditional votive candles, a performance that millions of Thais watched incredulously on television. Teng and Kriangsak then settled down to long private talks which, in contrast to the talks between Kriangsak and Dong, did not deal with bilateral matters but concentrated on larger questions, such as the deteriorating Sino-Vietnamese relations and the struggle between Vietnam and Cambodia, in which the Chinese, with some trepidation and embarrassment, were still backing the Cambodians. The new friendship treaty between Hanoi and Moscow had just been signed the week before, and Teng also expounded on that to Kriangsak, denouncing the Russians as hegemonists and the Vietnamese as their tools. As Pham Van Dong and Teng Hsiao-ping continued their respective tours of Southeast Asia, combining blandishment with bluff, they received in return mixed doses of smiles and suspicion, plus some new trade and cultural agreements. It was too soon yet to determine what would result from all this maneuvering, which in these initial stages was more a jockeying for position than for power, but on the developing diplomatic chessboard Kriangsak played the role of a pivotal black knight. Whether he would be able to sustain his adroit movements depended not only on events in China and Indochina, which remained uncertain at best, but on what happened in Thailand too, where the political situation was, as always, anything but certain.

The subsequent Vietnamese invasion of Cambodia, and the Chinese invasion of Vietnam, caused a vast amount of consternation in Thailand and created new political challenges for Kriangsak, which he continued to handle deftly. The takeover of Cambodia by Vietnam, particularly the capture of Battambang, close to the Thai-Cambodian border, which had historically been a disputed area between the two countries, effectively ended Cambodia's traditional role as a buffer zone between Vietnam and Thailand and significantly altered the strategic situation in Southeast Asia. Thailand, along with the other ASEAN countries, reacted with expected nervousness and concern, and the organization was quick to denounce the attack and call on Vietnam to withdraw from Cambodia. Pham Van Dong was equally quick in reassuring Kriangsak that Thailand's borders would not be violated, and the Vietnamese did, in fact, make a point at first of stopping several miles short of the border, though they later occupied a number of border points. But after the Chinese invasion of Vietnam took place, Thailand demonstrated a tilt toward Peking and there was some evidence of the Pol Pot guerrillas in Cambodia receiving Chinese military supplies via islands or Chinese ships in the Gulf of Siam, from where they were apparently ferried overland through Thailand to Cambodia. Kriangsak publicly maintained Thailand's neutrality without specifically denying that such shipments took place (both Teng Hsiao-ping and Sihanouk confirmed that they did, perhaps more for propaganda reasons than anything else), but in any event, in what was a blunt warning to the Thais, the Vietnamese and their new Cambodian surrogates conducted two brief raids into Thailand. When the Chinese withdrew from Vietnam, the tension temporarily subsided, and there was a general feeling among the ASEAN nations that the Vietnamese had been administered a deserved lesson. No one, however, least of all the jittery Thais, who for the time being continued to recognize the Pol Pot regime, was willing to make any predictions about what might happen next. In the period between the two invasions, Kriangsak visited the United States—the trip had been previously scheduled—and received some reassurance when the Carter Administration increased the amount of military equipment for Thailand from $24 million to $30 million for fiscal 1979 and transferred $11.3 million worth of ammunition left over from the Vietnam war free of cost.

Throughout this difficult period Kriangsak was doing as much maneuvering domestically as diplomatically, the more so as elections set for late April drew closer. He announced that he would not be a candidate under a new constitution, the thirteenth since 1932, during which period there had been no fewer than thirteen coups in Thailand. But under the terms of the constitution, it seemed almost certain that he would be chosen to continue as Prime Minister by the appointed new Senate, since he had proven himself to be the ablest man on the scene and, many believed, Thailand's last best hope to restore some order to the often sleazy turbulence of national politics. Nevertheless, some of the right-wing military men who opposed him sought to take political advantage of the new Vietnamese threat to the country, and there was always the chance that another coup mounted by jealous general officers or by field-grade officers known as "Young Turks" would upset the applecart all over again and catapult the nation into another outright military dictatorship, or into fresh chaos.

Kriangsak demonstrated a natural flair and intuition for popular politics and mixed easily with people, whether they were rural peasants or urban slum dwellers. One of the first things he did when he took office in the fall of 1977 in his dual role as Supreme Commander and Prime Minister was to order army trucks to dispose of huge garbage dumps piled in the streets and the klongs of Bangkok, a swollen city of at least 4.5 million people which, far from being the City of Angels, as it was sometimes romantically called, had become the dirtiest, most noxious and poorly run capital in Asia. Almost a quarter of the metropolitan population lived in slum areas, which lacked sufficient drinking water, electricity and other utilities and were subject to frequent fires and floods. The city's potholed streets were constantly clogged with traffic, a seemingly insoluble problem that created pervasive noise and pollution and made it impossible for anyone moving around to maintain a planned schedule. Thirty thousand legal and almost as many illegal sidewalk vendors and hawkers added to the vehicular and pedestrian pandemonium. Despite its congestion and shoddiness, Bangkok remained one of Southeast Asia's chief tourist centers, though Singapore, with its more modern hotels and more leisurely pace, was offering stiff competition. With the departure of the American soldiers after the end of the Vietnam war, the tourists were mostly young and middle-aged Japanese and Germans, who flocked to the topless bars and massage parlors the GIs once patronized. (Taxi drivers advertised these sexual haunts by handing out cards to visitors printed in Japanese and German as well as French and English, and several thousand Thai girls were "exported" to Germany as potential brides but in reality as camouflaged prostitutes.) Slum-clearance programs, low-cost housing complexes and decentralization through the building of new satellite cities and industrial estates, as well as plans to build a large alternative port in southern Thailand, were among the solutions to Bangkok's problems Kriangsak and local officials studied, but like everything else in Thailand, except coups, things moved slowly, and it was apparent that it would be some time before these projects were completed.

In appointing some able technocrats to his somewhat unwieldy thirty-three-man cabinet of ministers and deputies, Kriangsak at least dissipated some of the lethargy in the Thai bureaucracy, but despite a wealth of natural resources, including a large reservoir of newly discovered offshore natural gas, the country's economic problems were manifold. It was doubtful that in the time limit of one year Kriangsak had set himself before the new elections, he would be able to come to grips with such fundamental broader issues as alleviating the condition of Thailand's debt-ridden farmers and reducing the nation's adverse balance of payments. Many of his potential opponents, as well as his friends, felt he made a mistake in promising to hold elections so soon, but it was his own perception that under the circumstances he had to do what he did in order to defuse the explosive political situation and seek some permanent stability.

An Abundance of Coups

There were a number of ironies that marked Kriangsak's transitional moderate regime and his calculated approach to Thailand's Communist neighbors and to China. He had assumed office as a result of the two coups that preceded the one that brought him to power, and were it not for the right-wing backlash of the second of those coups, when a reactionary civilian government supported by the generals, including Kriangsak himself, proved so unbending and rigidly anti-Communist that even they couldn't stomach it, he wouldn't have become Prime Minister. The first of the two earlier coups took place in October 1973, when as a result of a student-led uprising the country's longtime joint military dictators, Thanom Kittikachorn and Prapass Charusathiara, were overthrown and forced to leave the country. For a few exciting months, and for the first time since the period immediately after World War II, Thailand seemed about to enter a period of true democracy and to become the one country to buck the authoritarian tide that was rolling over Southeast Asia.

With the appointment of a caretaker cabinet that wrote a reform constitution and prepared the way for the new democratic government, a sense of euphoria radiated from Bangkok out into the remote countryside. Unfortunately, the reality did not live up to the dream. By the time elections were held, in January 1975, no fewer than forty-two parties were in the field. Half of these won seats in the new House of Representatives, and sixteen were represented in the subsequently formed coalition government of Prime Minister Kukrit Pramoj, a member of the old elite aristocracy of absolute-monarchy days but a "modernist" in his approach to politics as well as a talented poet, novelist, and journalist. With a few exceptions, however, the elected politicians wasted time in disputatious, factional debate and failed to carry out their legislative responsibilities with any degree of seriousness, while those in the bickering coalition ministries spent most of their time protecting their own interests and engaging in petty power struggles. The student movement grew divided and bitter; mushrooming labor unions provoked illegal strikes and growing violence; political and revenge assassinations, as well as mounting incidents of ordinary crime, occurred throughout the country, while the dangerous polarization of left- and right-wing groups, including some Communist-infiltrated factions and several Fascist-type paramilitary and hoodlum fronts and organizations, created more confusion, unrest and instability—all of which further served to weaken the nation's already shaky social fabric. As a consequence, those worthwhile reforms Kukrit had initiated, such as village self-help programs and aid to farmers, failed to make much headway in the face of poor implementation and administration, a problem that had always plagued Thailand. The economy sagged under the impact of the world-wide recession, and the country seemed more and more vulnerable to subversion after the Communist conquests of Vietnam and Cambodia and the gradual consolidation of Communist rule in Laos.

In this uncertain atmosphere, the popular and revered forty-nine-year-old King Phumiphon made a gloomy warning speech, which was partly prompted by the declining fortunes of his fellow sovereigns in Laos and Cambodia. He spoke of the "danger that is coming close" and declared, "It is now quite apparent that the Thai Nation has become a major target which hostile parties certainly aim to take over and dominate in order to exploit and appropriate our riches for their advantage and superiority." Traditionally, the monarchy had been above politics. Patterned after the British constitutional government, the Thais system accorded the king three basic prerogatives: to be consulted, to give advice and to offer encouragement. During the 1973 revolution the King had on several occasions been visited by some of the student leaders, who sought his counsel. He supported their democratic aims but admonished them to get off the streets and eschew violence. The King also advised the students to accept a belated offer by Thanom and Prapass to write a new constitution and move more gradually toward democracy while the two dictators remained in the country, but after events got out of control he told the two men that they should leave (Thanom went to Singapore and Prapass to Taipeh) but that they could return someday. As things developed, that private promise became a key factor in the complicated unfolding of events which saw the King play a much stronger role in 1976 than in 1973, a role that some veteran observers of the Thai scene believe has been tantamount to his "descending from the throne" and placing the monarchy in an entirely new and vulnerable position, to a considerable extent staking its very survival on the outcome of political events he was only partially able to control. As one astute friend of mine said, "We'll never know whether the response of the King to what took place in 1973 and then three years later was emotional, psychological, intellectual, or all three, but because he acted as he did, the monarchy may never be the same."

Although the morale and the cohesion of the military had been shattered by the revolution of 1973, it remained the major force to be reckoned with. A number of general officers had joined political parties and become members of the new government, but while the army especially, so long accustomed to

EL CAMINO COLLEGE LIBRARY

holding or influencing power, grudgingly countenanced the democratic experiment, it was by no means reconciled to the new civilian regime and was unhappy playing a secondary role. It quietly maintained its influence in conservative business and banking circles, through its connections with wealthy Thais and Chinese, and many of its members also had close ties with the monarchy. These continuing associations, secretly manipulated in many cases, enabled the army to remain stronger than any other institution in the country, including the Buddhist church—which had become a divided and somewhat spent force as the post-1973 chaos increased and many bonzes allowed themselves to be politicized by right-wing agitators. During 1976, rumors of a new military coup continued to spread in direct ratio to the increase of violence and tension on the college campuses and on the sites of labor strikes, and as the question of the final withdrawal of American troops from Thailand, which Kukrit and the students favored but the army opposed, came to a head and the troops, as well as a secret communications network for keeping tabs on the Communists all over Asia, were pulled out.

The atmosphere grew more tense as even the staunchest democrats and dedicated parliamentarians acknowledged that the new democracy wasn't working. Each time fresh coup rumors gained credence, they elicited a sharp response from left-wing agitators largely acting on their own, with support from the underground Communist Party of Thailand, and according to some subsequent evidence, from the Soviet Union; the Russians were giving considerable financial backing to a number of labor unions conducting strikes as well as flooding the college campuses with pro-Soviet books and pamphlets. Left-wing demonstrations in turn prompted right-wing vigilante groups to take to the streets or attack the campuses and bash in student heads. This sort of reaction and counterreaction went on almost rhythmically for several months, but the right-wingers were becoming stronger while the left wing grew more disorganized and divided. Particularly active were the two main vigilante groups, the Red Gauers (meaning Red Bulls), and Naverphol, an ultrareactionary front which had the financial backing of some wealthy conservative businessmen and politicians and the secret support of some important army officers. Of growing importance, too, were the Village Scouts, created five years earlier with the blessings of the royal family; ostensibly a community-service group, it began to assume a more open political role and to recruit, in addition to its original roster of young boys and girls, quite a few older men and women.

In response to the political strains and some new economic problems (a government-approved rise in the price of rice, designed to help the farmers, caused a general strike in Bangkok) Kukrit dissolved Parliament in January 1976 and called for new elections in April. There followed a fresh wave of violence, and more than fifty persons, mostly left-wingers, were killed during the campaign. As the left and left-of-center parties were demolished, centrist and right-wing Democrats, led by Kukrit's amiable but less capable seventy-two-year-old brother, Seni Pramoj, won a sweeping victory in April, particularly in the Bangkok area, the party's stronghold, and this projected Seni into the premiership, a post he had briefly held twice before. Things might have turned out differently if Kukrit had not stubbornly insisted on running for re-election to the House of Representatives in a military-dominated district in Bangkok against three other candidates. He lost, though he would undoubtedly have won in any other district and thereby remained Prime Minister.

Seni formed a four-party center-right coalition, but despite his heavy majority he had trouble from the start holding his own Democrats together, since they consisted of four major factions and some splinter elements, all of which were battling each other and were totally incapable of working harmoniously together. A number of events and circumstances conspired against Seni, who proved unable to cope with succeeding crises and became more distraught as the festering party divisions became more acrimonious, and as, at the same time, the intrigue and plotting among top-ranking army officers became more pronounced. In mid-August 1976 a number of right-wing generals engineered the sudden reappearance in Bangkok of the more important of the two old dictators, Prapass, who suddenly flew in from Taipeh. Not unexpectedly, this prompted new coup rumors and new student demonstrations. After a tense week and a quickly arranged audience for Prapass with the King, who advised him once again to leave, at least temporarily, the general flew back to Taipeh. A month later, over Seni's objections, Thanom reappeared from Singapore. He immediately donned the saffron robes of a Buddhist monk and entered a Bangkok monastery that happened to enjoy the King's particular sponsorship to pray for his nonagenarian father, who was fatally ill. His return had been calculatedly prepared by a number of generals and right-wing politicians who wanted to use it as a pretext for them to move toward power.

As Seni became more and more embroiled in and confounded by the conflicts between the liberal and conservative members of his own party and by the maneuvers of other, more reactionary politicians in his wobbly coalition, the coup wheels began turning faster than ever. Although many officers and soldiers wanted no part of a coup, at least four groups led by ambitious generals now had plots of their own in the works, and some of these plots interwove with the machinations going on within the political parties. Meanwhile the leaders of the National Student Center of Thailand (the principal student organization) were trying to mount major demonstrations against the return of Thanom, but they no longer had sufficient popular support to get ordinary citizens to take to the streets with them, let alone enough students. In a mood of frustration the left-wing students at Thammasat University, one of the country's two most prestigious, decided to take matters into their own hands. Whether they were goaded into action by the *agents provocateurs* of the right —the members of the Red Gauers, or those of Naverphol—or whether they acted spontaneously was unclear, but at any rate they knew they were taking a big risk. Bearing placards and slogans and a number of effigies, a large group of students held an anti-Thanom rally on the campus on October 4, 1976. The effigies, they claimed, were supposed to represent two labor-union organizers whom the police had admitted having lynched in northeast Thailand a few weeks earlier, but one of them bore a distinct resemblance to the King's son, the twenty-five-year-old Crown Prince Vajiralongkorn, and in published pictures of it that appeared in the papers the next morning, the resemblance was even sharper.

All through the day the right-wing vigilante groups and the Village Scouts who had been summoned to come to Bangkok by the Armoured Forces radio station, which the right wing had regularly been using, gathered at various points in the city. They demanded that Prime Minister Seni arrest the students involved on charges of *lèse-majesté;* in the evening Seni announced he would hold an investigation. But by seven o'clock the next morning, mob rule had taken over. About 50,000 right-wingers, mostly Scouts, surrounded the Thammasat campus, where between 2,000 and 3,000 students had spent the night. The right-wing mob, some of whom were armed, forced itself past the police and entered the campus. It was later claimed that shots were initially fired from the rooftops of some of the university buildings and that two policemen were killed. A few of the students had weapons, but whether or not they fired first, it was the police and special riot squads who at dusk began firing rifles, grenades and anti-tank guns into the university grounds, and fifteen minutes later the police invaded the campus, along with thousands of rampaging Scouts and other vigilantes, armed with metal bars, knives and sticks, as well as guns. Members of this mob roamed the campus, dragging students from the buildings and clubbing or stabbing or kicking them, eventually killing forty-six and wounding nearly two hundred others. For the most part the police confined themselves to forcing hundreds of students, male and female, out of their hiding places and making them strip to the waist and crawl on their stomachs on the ground of the university sports field while the right-wing mob cheered from the stands. Four students (who may already have been dead) were hanged. The fighting and killing lasted until nearly noon, by which time more than 2,000 students had been arrested; another 1,000 were jailed during the next few days.

The bloody affair at Thammasat triggered the 1976 coup, but not according to the scenario that the conspiring generals had been preparing. Late on the morning of October 6, when the killing had stopped, the mob of 50,000 right-wingers marched to Seni's office at Government House and demanded that he dismiss three members of his brother's Social Action Party he had chosen to include in his new cabinet. The rightists also wanted Seni to eliminate three liberal members of his own Democrat Party, whom the plotting generals had opposed. If Seni was the ultimate culprit because of his vacillation and his mishandling of the Thanom affair from the start, the generals had also misplayed their hand by competing for the blessing of the King. It was unclear just what role the King played at this crucial juncture, but according to the most reliable sources, he favored the retention of Seni as Prime Minister and the maintenance of a more balanced civilian government without extremists of the right or left, with a fresh emphasis to be given to anti-Communism and austerity and a greater degree of discipline, conceivably to be supervised by some sort of military collegium. But above all, the King had become thoroughly disillusioned and disturbed over the state of affairs and had reached the conclusion that a new start had to be made if the country was going to hold together.

Ironically, it was Seni who set the stage for his own downfall and the collapse of the democracy by appointing as Minister of Defense a friend who was a respected apolitical naval officer, Admiral Sangaad Chalwyoo. As Seni kept procrastinating in his selection of the rest of the cabinet, Sangaad and a group of other ranking officers from all three services and the police hurriedly met on the morning of October 6 and, in effect, pre-empted an army coup by forming what became a broader National Advisory Reform Council of eighteen members (subsequently the council was enlarged to twenty-four to placate the disappointed generals by including more of them). In the evening a series of announcements was broadcast over Radio Thailand informing the nation that the Reform Council had assumed control, declared martial law, abolished the constitution, dissolved parliament and all political parties, placed all civilian courts under military jurisdiction, banned all meetings of more than five persons, and suspended publication of all Thai and foreign-language papers until further notice. Admiral Sangaad declared, "The government cannot govern the country properly, and in order not to let Thailand become a prey to the Communists and to uphold the monarchy and the royal family, this council has seized power."

Swing to the Right

It was at this point that events took an unexpected turn and that, unwittingly, the King paved the way for Kriangsak to take over a year later. Only two days after the Reform Council's announcement, the King, acting through Admiral Sangaad, announced the appointment of a new civilian Prime Minister, a forty-nine-year-old Supreme Court justice named Thanin Kraivichien. The move to install a civilian government so quickly, which came as a surprise to most observers, was clearly in accordance with the King's wishes, and moreover, Thanin, an extremely serious, humorless and rather pedantic man who had never been a politician and was scarcely known in public life, was someone King Phumiphon and Queen Sirikit both knew and personally admired. Short and owlish-looking behind square-rimmed spectacles, he gave the impression in long speeches and occasional press conferences that he would be more at ease back in his courtroom or in a classroom than in the public limelight, but at the same time, imbued with a sense of mission, he appeared to enjoy fulfilling what he regarded as a special duty to help save his country. As a constitutional and legal scholar whose ardent anti-Communism was bolstered by vast erudition on the subject, he often seemed more attuned to the nineteen-fifties than to the contemporary challenges confronting Thailand.

Two weeks after his appointment he chose a cabinet of eighteen members who were all close friends of his, many of them academics. As a group, they were uninspiring and inexperienced. The same was true of the 340 members (later increased to 400) of a new National Reform Assembly, appointed at the end of November with a heavy preponderance of military or ex-military men. The Assembly was given virtually no powers for the next four years, described by Thanin as a "period of national rehabilitation so as to achieve economic and political stability." After this span of time Thanin said that he and his cabinet would resign, and a second four-year phase he depicted as "the embryonic period of democratic development" would begin, during which there would be two houses of parliament—an elected lower house and an appointed upper house, both with equal powers and a greater degree of legislative initiative. During a third four-year period, the powers of the lower house were to be increased, with those of the upper house confined principally to that of the veto; ultimately, "if democracy prospers to a favorable extent," Thanin envisioned a single-chamber parliament with broader powers.

The key article of the new, hastily prepared constitution gave the Prime Minister the right, with the approval of the cabinet and his advisory council of military men, "to issue any order or carry out any action that is necessary for the prevention or the stopping or suppressing of any activity which endangers the security of the Kingdom . . . or threatens peace or order or good public morals." Thanin used this article, which was severely criticized, to execute a number of criminals accused of rape and drug smuggling, and keep in prison, without trial, any political figures, including some of the rebellious Thammasat students, he regarded as dangerous. In his talks over television he made some valid criticisms of the failure of the recent three-year democratic experiment, but given Thailand's fragility and the general condition of uncertainty in the area, let alone the fact that the military was back in a predominant role, it was highly naïve and impractical to look as far ahead as twelve years or more of democracy-building. Thanin laid out his scheme as if he were preparing a legal brief in the confines of his chambers. In his almost obsessive fear of and warnings about Communism, he spoke of bringing "misled people back to the right path" and of the need to maintain martial law for at least four years so that "excessive rights and freedom" would not preclude "rectification" and "efficient suppression of economic and political harassment." When the newspapers were gradually allowed to appear again, a month after the coup, they were admonished to be careful about what they wrote, to follow the general directives laid down by the government and to avoid making "trivial comments." When schools and universities were reopened, the government at first indicated that courses on political theory would be carefully controlled and that nothing about Communism would be taught—tons of books and papers on Communism had been confiscated and burned—but then Thanin backed down and indicated that political theory, including Communist theory, would be discussed by "qualified" teachers who had "the proper psychological training as well as political knowledge." One professor at a leading university quipped, "When the question is asked during the next examination period,

'What is the only political party in Thailand?,' the answer will have to be 'The Communist Party, since, while it is illegal, all other parties are banned.' " Another professor I knew commented, "Communism and corruption are Thanin's two *idées fixes.* Get him away from that, and what's left is the legal scholar and academician. He's book-crazy—*ba nangsy,* Thais call it—and a man with an *ancien régime* mind."

Though Thanin pledged his new regime to deal with such major issues as poverty, he did very little to alleviate the condition of the poor farmers in the countryside or of the urban slum dwellers, and if anything, the tough martial-law provisions gave the police free rein to crack down on villagers they arbitrarily accused of Communist sympathies. If such actions had the approval of old-line conservative military men, they provoked opposition among many younger officers who had been trained abroad and had begun to realize that Communism had to be fought with social and economic reform measures and not just with harsh repressive tactics. These younger officers, including a number of battalion commanders, became the nucleus of the Young Turks who began using their political as well as military leverage and grew more outspoken in their criticism of the shortcomings of the rigid Thanin government.

The Young Turks attacked corruption within the military itself, and this brought them into conflict with some of the generals and intensified the continuing rifts in the military. What Thanin did do was press the drive against narcotics (there were 400,000 addicts in Thailand, which for many years had been a principal source of supply and a conduit for the distribution of opium and heroin throughout the world), and this upset a number of ranking officers and businessmen who were involved in the drug traffic. Nevertheless, Thanin cracked down, and his antidrug measures won the support of the Americans, who were putting most of their aid money into the program, but at the same time the United States became increasingly critical of his repression of human rights, which included not only the martial-law arrests of students and other political dissenters but harsh moves to restrict the influence of labor unions after the freedom they had enjoyed during the heady 1973–1976 period.

Thanin's actions were prompted by his desire to attract more foreign investment, and he offered tax advantages and eased restrictions on transmittal of profits as part of a new investment code he himself directed, but while the Thai economy enjoyed a boom year in 1977—rice exports were the highest in the world—foreign investors remained cautious because of the general political unrest and uncertainty. After a three-week period I spent in Thailand in midyear I came away with the feeling that the new government more than anything else imparted a sense of sterility, and that its proclamations and programs seemed more antiseptic than curative of Thailand's ills. Despite its hortatory claims and promises, there was nothing about it that was either very new or stimulating, and it tended to act for the most part as if it were a figment of its own imagination. In some ways Thanin reminded me of nothing so much as the Tin Woodman in *The Wizard of Oz,* who spent his days wandering about in search of a heart.

The brutality of the Thammasat killings, followed by the arrest of students and intellectuals suspected of being Communist or leftist—often just because, like Thanin himself, they owned books about Communism—had put an end to intellectual freedom after the 1976 coup and had driven hundreds of people into hiding, out of the country or into the hands of the insurgents. Over and above the 3,000 arrested, most of whom were later released (eighteen were put on trial, six of them charged with *lèse-majesté*), between 1,000 and 1,500 students simply disappeared after the coup. About half of them eventually returned to their classes, but an estimated 600 or 700 fled to the jungles of northeastern Thailand to join the Communist guerrillas, or sought refuge in Laos. About 100 went south, some even before the coup, where they underwent training by the southern-based insurgents.

Through its radio, the Voice of the People of Thailand, based in Yunnan, South China, the Communist Party of Thailand (CPT), attacked "the piratic Sangaad-Fascist clique, [who] have made themselves the enemy of the entire people" and become "the slaves of the U.S. imperialists," and welcomed these educated city-bred students to join in "the violent overthrow" of the new regime. Contrary to what many Bangkok officials expected, most of the renegade students adapted themselves to the rigors of guerrilla life in the jungle, and along with a number of socialist and other leaders of banned parties who also fled Bangkok, proved highly useful to the CPT. They blended quickly into the training and indoctrination structure of the party and its military arm, the Thai People's Liberation Army, and mixed easily with the uneducated Thai-Lao or Sino-Thai peasants who were party members or sympathizers and who admired the students for having sacrificed the comforts of cosmopolitan life to join the rural revolutionary struggle. Among them was Saeksan Prasertkul, the leader of the 1973 student rebellion, who had told me when I spoke with him in Bangkok in 1974 that while he was not a Communist, he would be forced to join the insurgents and adopt "violent means" himself if "they"— by which he meant the right-wing vigilantes—"start shooting at us or if there is another military coup."

Saeksan and several other students and labor leaders who had been working with farmers and unions had disappeared from Bangkok early in 1975 and went to France and then, probably, to China, after which they were reported to be back in northeastern Thailand, though they maintained a safe base across the Mekong in Laos. Eight of the former students and labor activists, and three leaders of the Socialist Party of Thailand, became the spearhead of a new National Democratic United Front, and helped form the subsequent Committee for the Coordination of Patriotic and Democracy-Loving Peace Forces, reminiscent of similarly named groups during the Vietnam war. They greatly increased the sophistication of the clandestine radio broadcasts and aided in the recruitment programs of the party and of the liberation army.

The Thai Communist Party, which was formed in 1932 as an adjunct of the Chinese Communist Party, adopted a policy of armed struggle in 1965 on a cue from Mao Tse-tung, to whose "thoughts" and Marxist-Leninist ideology the Thai insurgents had always been dedicated, applying the strategy of "using the rural areas to surround the towns and finally seizing the towns." This line was re-emphasized in the CPT's propaganda after the 1976 coup. Denouncing Thanin as "a man of straw in the pay of the Americans," the United Front made a fresh appeal to Thai youth in the cities and sought to act as a link between the rural and urban areas, and between the ethnic minorities in the mountains and the lowland peasants. Since 1965 the number of armed guerrillas had grown at a rate of about 10 percent a year, reaching a total of 10,000 or 12,000 by 1977, supported by about 90,000 sympathizers. About a fifth of the regulars had been trained in secret camps in Laos and in Cambodia, and armed chiefly with Vietnamese or Chinese guns, were then assigned to one of the four central CPT areas in Thailand. About fifteen provincial or regimental sub-areas were only loosely coordinated, and conducted operations more or less autonomously, maintaining liaison with each other primarily by courier.

The party central committee of twelve members headed by a "first secretary-general," a Sino-Thai named Samanan, met irregularly and disseminated its statements chiefly over the Voice of the People of Thailand. Though their aura of legitimacy was increased after the 1976 coup by the addition to their ranks of the students and intellectuals from Bangkok, the Thai Communists, despite some dramatic successes in ambushing or openly attacking government forces, had not demonstrated much imagination or flexibility. While active in half of Thailand's seventy-two provinces, where they engaged roughly half the government's combat battalions, they were still not able to sustain a major campaign capable of combining an attack southward from the triborder area of Laos, Cambodia and Thailand with a move northward by the smaller number of southern-based guerrillas; not until they could control the mountain chain of central Thailand that debouches onto the plains area north of Bangkok would the insurgents present a really serious threat.

On the other hand, the government's counterinsurgency tactics, while improving, were not adequate to cope with the steady Communist attacks mounted from the guerrillas' forest bases. Except in a few areas where they had aggressive commanders, the government troops were slow to react and reluctant to pursue the insurgents into their sanctuaries. Moreover, the Thai army remained sorely inept in gathering and evaluating intelligence, including information about the growing possibility of urban guerrilla activity, which was a tactic the new student recruits, out of their own experience and knowledge, probably encouraged, in keeping with the world-wide trend toward urban terrorism. The challenge faced by the government was made more difficult by the raids into Thailand across the poorly defined Cambodian border, which cost the Thais several hundred dead soldiers and civilians—some seven hundred Thai villagers were also kidnapped, and many of them were sent to Cambodian camps, where they were subjected to forced indoctrination and guerrilla training. There was also some degree of Vietnamese inspiration for the attacks. Thai-based Cambodian resistance movements represented another complicating factor, made more so by the encouragement given them by rightist Thai elements who had their own political axes to grind and were all along opposed to any rapprochement with the new Communist regimes in Indochina.

Aside from the fact that the Thai insurgents seemed to have enough weapons, there was no indication after the 1975 victory of the Vietnamese, Lao and Cambodian Communists that the flow of arms to the Thai insurgents had increased, though there had never been any difficulty smuggling weapons across the porous borders Thailand shared with Cambodia and Laos. What worried the Thais more, and further stimulated the anti-Communist rhetoric of Thanin and the hard-line members of his cabinet as well as some of the military, was the beefed-up presence of 40,000 or 50,000 veteran Vietnamese troops in Laos. This movement was prompted by the incapacity of the Lao to handle their internal troubles, but the Vietnamese also had their own motives, which already clearly included their desire to dominate all of Indochina, one way or another.

During the year of Thanin's reactionary and uninspiring premiership, Thailand's relations with Vietnam and Laos, let alone Cambodia, deteriorated badly. When he took office he made a number of harsh comments about the Vietnamese regime, the tone of which he later moderated on the advice of his foreign-affairs experts, but neither Hanoi nor Bangkok seemed eager at the time to resume diplomatic talks. In fact, at one point the Vietnamese denounced "the pious statements" of friendship of the Thanin government in the face of its "repeated provocations against Thailand's eastern neighbors." Though Thailand and Laos had established diplomatic relations prior to the Thanin period, these remained stalemated too as a result of continuing incidents on the Mekong, the river border between the two countries. As for Cambodia, although diplomatic talks had been held between the two countries, and one land-border point, at Poipet, just across from a large refugee camp at Aranyaprathet, had been designated for barter trade, the nasty border incidents between the two nations had led to a virtual break of formal contacts. As the situation vis-à-vis the former Indochina countries declined, Thanin's efforts to promote anti-Communist collaboration among Thailand's ASEAN partners, including greater military cooperation, were not especially successful either. Even though the other ASEAN countries were cognizant of the long-term threat posed to their security by the Vietnamese, and in different ways by the Russians and the Chinese, they were all engaged in building their own tentative bridges to Hanoi, Peking and Moscow, and they didn't particularly welcome Thanin, the zealous newcomer in their midst, stirring the anti-Communist pot.

At home Thanin was having more and more trouble because of his harsh application of martial law and his inability to reconcile the many disparate elements in the society. An atmosphere of stultification set in, mixed with fear and mockery. Friends I had known over the years told me, guardedly, that they hardly talked to each other any longer, let alone to strangers. "This government is worse than the old Thanom-Prapass regime, because the former dictators were at least proper highwaymen, while these people pretend to be one thing but act in ways that prove they can't be trusted," a young girl who had been a journalist but had quit under the tough new press restrictions told me. An elderly woman, a former language professor, said that she and her circle of academic and literary friends, mostly left-of-center liberals, existed in a state of limbo and resorted to codelike games and gestures to express their frustration and disillusion; when asked what they thought or what they planned to do, for instance, they would hold a hand close to the face in simulation of a poker player not revealing his cards, or simply drum their fingers on the table. "It helps relieve the tension and keeps us smiling," she said, "and doesn't reveal the despair we really feel."

The military was also chafing under the bit, but for different reasons, and the coup rumors were again flying. In February and March 1977, there had in fact been a coup plot mounted by an ambitious general named Chalart Hiranysiri, who was a friend of Kriangsak's (Kriangsak was not involved in the plotting). Chalart had the support of ultraright-wing members of Kukrit's shaky coalition, but his plot was aborted by other generals; Chalart was dismissed from the army and subsequently executed.

The Chalart coup, though a failure, was a clear symptom of the again tense military mood. As he watched Thanin's inept handling of the government, and the negative approach to Thailand's Communist neighbors, Kriangsak in particular nourished growing doubts and misgivings. As secretary-general of the Military Advisory Council (which had replaced the National Advisory Reform Council soon after the 1976 coup), and as Deputy Supreme Commander at the time, Kriangsak was already regarded as the most important and powerful man in Thailand, a fact of which Thanin was fully aware and which accounted for his vain efforts to keep Kriangsak from becoming Supreme Commander in the fall of 1977. Far more articulate than most senior officers, Kriangsak stressed the need for the Thais to improve their fighting capacity by building up their combat strike forces and reserves, but he placed as much or more emphasis on social and economic matters. When I saw him initially, midway through Thanin's tenure, he said, "We must prepare for the worst militarily, but we must be strong in all ways in three or four years' time, and that means narrowing the gap between the rich and the poor."

As prices of basic commodities such as rice, pork, fish and vegetables increased and the rate of inflation grew, the economy, though outwardly prosperous, left the poor worse off as the rich got richer, and then a serious drought made things still worse. The familiar rumors of another coup were stimulated by the final return to Thailand of the old dictator Prapass, whose son-in-law, General Yos Thephasdin, the former commander of the powerful First Army, stationed around Bangkok, was extremely ambitious and had the backing of some strategically located troops. Kriangsak and the more moderate generals were determined to restrain the extremists; their position grew stronger as it became apparent that despite the earlier support of the King, Thanin's time was running out and his unrealistic twelve-year program for the slow reinstitution of democracy was an illusion.

"We don't like totalitarianism," Kriangsak once told me. "We would like to have full democracy, but we can't have it now. We know the free world would like that too, but it's not practical for us. We can no longer allow the sort of polarization that existed before and let things get out of control."

The Fall of Thanin

It was Kriangsak who ultimately blew the whistle on Thanin, for just those reasons, but it was the Young Turks, including several key battalion leaders and some paratroopers, who brought matters to a head. Their opposition to Thanin covered a wide spectrum of complaints that ranged from his failure to prosecute the counterinsurgency campaign forcefully enough in the poor rural areas to the general discontent his Cold Warrior policies had caused among the people at large, and the damage this was doing to Thailand's image abroad and to the establishment of better relations with the Indochina nations. In typical Thai fashion, various elements, including the liberal newspapers as well as some of the rightist groups, spoke out against Thanin on the grounds of defending the monarchy, though they did not speak in unison. Following the Young Turks' ultimatum, a number of the top generals, including General Yos, who had become the deputy commander of the army, and who retained ambitions of his own, tried to persuade Thanin to reorganize the cabinet, but Thanin refused. Admiral Sangaad was reluctant to press the issue until he was persuaded that Thanin's stubbornness left no alternative.

Operating quietly behind the scenes, as he had the year before, Kriangsak helped convince Sangaad after he personally issued what amounted to an ultimatum to Thanin, warning that refusal to compromise would provoke another coup. Though the King was said to strongly oppose a new military move, he refused to grant the Prime Minister a private audience. Thereupon, when Thanin rejected the resignations of some of his cabinet ministers, armed delegates of the Military Advisory Council interrupted an informal meeting at Government House early on the evening of October 20, 1977, and informed Thanin and the ministers that in the name of a twenty-three-man Revolutionary Party, composed essentially of the same military men who had taken over the previous year, with Sangaad still the titular head, the civilian government was finished. It was one of Thailand's more gentle, uncomplicated coups, which Thanin had made easy by his obdurate attitude on top of his record of political failure.

As Sangaad put it, "The government has not made as much progress as it should have. The general public has been confused by the current situation, which has resulted in differences of opinion and wide disunity among the people."

It was immediately apparent that with the added title of "national peacekeeper" on top of his position as Supreme Commander, Kriangsak was the dominant figure in the government. First off, he was the secretary-general of the Revolutionary Party and then of the new National Policy Council, which, composed of the same military leaders, replaced it after the coup. With the adoption of an interim constitution and his assumption of the premiership, he quickly set about creating a fresh consensus predicated on what he declared was the need for "national reconciliation." The coming year, he said, would be the most difficult in Thailand's modern history. "I need peace to protect the peace," he added, referring to the country's "front-line" geopolitical position in Southeast Asia and to the pressures along its borders, as well as to the continuing internal insurgency; to the still unreconciled elements among the population, including some members of the military; and to the economic and social discrepancies which had led to affluence for about 10 percent of the population of 44 million but had left more than half the people with incomes close to or below the subsistence level. Thailand was the eighty-third poorest nation among nearly a hundred and fifty members of the United Nations.

Dressed in mufti and sucking at his pipe, Kriangsak visited Bangkok's slums and made arrangements for temporary improvements pending the completion of the long-delayed low-cost housing projects. He attended the opening of a new Labor Foundation he had previously helped establish, and though strikes were still banned because martial law remained in effect, he permitted unions to federate into new councils and persuaded both labor and management to adopt conciliatory policies for the general welfare and to stimulate develop-ment. A number of work stoppages did take place, however, particularly among the well-organized state enterprise unions that control essential public services. As workers chafed at continued low minimum wages and inadequate social welfare programs, the threat of more strikes loomed. Kriangsak arranged wage increases for civil servants and teachers, but as pressure mounted in the face of continuing inflation—at the rate of about 8 percent a year—he warned that "untoward events will not be tolerated."

During the honeymoon period following Kriangsak's takeover, there were other manifestations of compromise and relaxation. On the King's fiftieth birthday in December, for example, forty-four thousand prisoners, about two thirds of the total in the country, most of them ordinary criminals, were amnestied, and among them were twenty-two officers who had been sentenced for their participation in the abortive coup of March 1977, led by General Chalart. Kriangsak also reversed a Thanin decision that had aroused the ire of American and other human rights advocates and permitted the eighteen defendants on trial for the 1976 Thammasat riots to have their own legal counsel, and then, in September 1978, he amnestied them, as well as "all offenders involved in the demonstrations at Thammasat University" on Octo-ber 6, 1976. The move, prompted by Kriangsak's desire to smooth the political waters before the next election, apparently had the private support of the King. The Communists naturally hailed it as "a victory for the people."

One of the greatest anomalies in Thailand had become the role of the monarchy, which since the 1973 student coup had diminished in the public image. No longer a sacrosanct subject, in the late seventies it had become a source of gossip, and as far as the Communists were concerned, an object of derisive propaganda. In their broadcasts over the Voice of the People of Thailand, they had begun to refer to King Phumiphon as "the archfeudalist" and to Queen Sirikit as "the female feudalist." The broadcasts, as well as leaflets and pamphlets, also dealt openly and scandalously with "the power contest" akin "to dogs fighting to get the pile of bones" between "the Phumiphon group" and "the Sirikit group" in the palace, and revived the rumors that Phumiphon (who had originally declined to be King in favor of his brother) had murdered his older brother, King Ananda Mahithol, in order to ascend the throne as part of the palace conspiracy involving the Queen's family and a plot to have her marry Phumiphon. Ananda died of a gunshot wound in 1946 and a commission of inquiry never did determine whether the death was an accident, a suicide, or a murder. Reports of a rivalry between the King and the Queen also became the source of gossip in Bangkok as a result of the Queen's known attachment to her son, Crown Prince Vajiralongkorn, who in 1977 married the Queen's niece, his second cousin. His automatic right to succeed to the throne as the only son of the King and Queen was amended in 1974 when the King got the National Assembly to give their three daughters the right to take over the crown, and followed this up by giving his second oldest daughter, Sirindhorn, who was twenty-two at the time, the title of Maha Chakri, which was taken as indication of his desire to have her succeed him. The move was also said to have been prompted by the King regarding seriously the predictions made many years before by fortunetellers that there would be only nine kings of the Rama line—Phumiphon was the ninth. If Sirindhorn, who was a bright girl as well as her father's favorite, took over the throne instead of the Crown Prince, she could reign in her own right and represent the King's faction in the palace.

Anywhere else but in Thailand such matters would have been considered lightly, or as comic opera, but in Bangkok they were taken seriously, and the fact that the Communists in particular were making use of the scandals and openly denigrating the monarchy was an indication of a spreading loss of respect for traditional values. Intrigue and gossip were normally part of Thai political life, but to subject the monarchy to them was a clear case of lèse-majesté. The King was still revered by the majority of the people, but there was little doubt that the position of the monarchy, along with that of the Buddhist church, had been eroded as a result of political uncertainty and confusion about the King's purpose in overprojecting himself into the political orbit.

After the 1977 coup he was so upset that he delayed signing the interim constitution for several days and further expressed his disapproval by wearing an ordinary business suit instead of a royal uniform to an important public reception. Thereafter he accepted Kriangsak and acknowledged his ability, but his appointment of Thanin, at the Queen's urging, to the Privy Council was regarded by Kriangsak and the other generals as something of an insult to them. It was hard to judge the true significance of all this palace intrigue and scandal-mongering, but in a volatile country like Thailand, and at a time when the nation already had more than its share of troubles and uncertainties, the added factor of a monarchy subjected to its own internal struggles and rivalries did not make Kriangsak's task of fostering stability and seeking national reconciliation any easier.

The Elections of 1979

In fact, given the inherent and endemic military and political rivalries in the country, there remained some doubt that Kriangsak or anyone else could create a lasting consensus or a base of solid support. Late in 1978 the interim National Assembly, consisting mostly of active or retired military men and former political leaders such as Kukrit and Seni Pramoj, completed its draft of the new constitution. After much debate it was decided to have a bicameral assembly, with the lower house elected and the upper house appointed by the King acting on the suggestion of the outgoing Prime Minister. This meant that Kriangsak would, in effect, control the choice of senators, rather than the National Policy Council, which would be abolished following the elections. Moreover, the President of the appointed Senate would nominate the new Prime Minister. Another clause allowed "independents" to run for election to the lower house. Kriangsak had successfully outmaneuvered Admiral Sangaad and the old-guard officers and had tightened his alliance with the Young Turks, who mostly now supported him. The new constitution was criticized for disregarding political parties—the Democrat Party called the new draft "totalitarian" and threatened to campaign against it. But meanwhile Kriangsak had the choice of running for election in the lower house as an independent, joining one of the parties, or waiting to be summoned to be Prime Minister again by the appointed Senate. He chose the last alternative.

The draft pledged to restore "full democracy" in four years' time. By cementing his ties not only with the younger military elements but also with liberal middle-ground civilians who favored reforms and had also backed him, Kriangsak seemed free to become Prime Minister again, and he said that, while he wouldn't run for the lower house or join a political party, he would accept appointment to the premiership. Prior to the final draft of the constitution, he signed the annual military promotions list, which in view of the forthcoming elections was particularly important. In an obvious effort to pre-empt a new power play by his military opponents he chose a tough apolitical soldier, General Prem Tinsulananont, to be chief of the army, replacing General Serm Na Nakorn, who became Supreme Commander— Serm had expected to be given both jobs. Serm's supporters in the army, mostly right-wing and potential troublemakers, also had their wings clipped by receiving less important assignments in the military hierarchy, as did some of the more rambunctious Young Turks who were battalion commanders before. One of the generals, Amnad Damrikarn, who had headed the key First Army around Bangkok and who was shifted to a more or less powerless post as deputy chief of staff of the army, was so angry that he considered an immediate coup to oust Kriangsak, but Serm called him off, cryptically commenting that if Amnad had wanted to move on his own he should have done so instead of consulting him, Serm, who as the new Supreme Commander and the King's man in that job had no alternative but to say no. By appointing Prem, a professional conservative "soldier's soldier" with no taint of corruption, Kriangsak had cleverly outmaneuvered both Serm and Admiral Sangaad and diminished the chances of new right-wing factions to come together and prepare another coup. With equal acumen, he also managed to mollify the old Prapass-Thanom clique by giving a few important posts to its men, notably General Yos Thephasdin, a friend of Prapass', who became Deputy Minister of Defense. Prapass and Thanom, now that they were both back in Thailand, were eager to play a political role again, if not openly then from behind the scenes. Both men were also trying to recover their confiscated assets, totaling at least $20 million; Kriangsak would have to deal with this thorny problem sooner or later but he had managed to postpone doing anything about it so far.

The "dinosaurs" of the past, as the Thai press referred to them, turned out in full dress for the April election. Thanom's son, Colonel Narong, and Thanom's brother, a major general of the police, were among the hundreds of delegates who ran for the lower house, as did Kukrit Pramoj and perennials, right, left and center of earlier and reborn parties, some of which stood under their old banners, such as Seni Pramoj's Democrats, while others assumed new names and adopted new slogans. Among the new parties was one named Seritham, led by a group of technocrats and ministers which was Kriangsak's vehicle, though he remained aloof from it officially. In most respects the election seemed a rerun of past performances: the issues and platforms consisted of the same old platitudes and promises, and as usual there was more sound and fury than substance. Nothing seemed calculated to alter the alignments of power and class that had dominated Thai politics for more than three decades, and that were centered in Bangkok with scant representation in the countryside. As one observer put it, "The question is whether the interests of Thailand's poor will ever really be brought into the calculation . . . without a redistribution of power."

The results of the vote did little to answer the question. Kukrit's Social Action Party won the largest bloc of seats but not sufficient to represent a challenge to Kriangsak, who with the support of the Seritham Party and some of the independents in the 301-member lower house, and with the backing of a large majority in the 225-member appointed Senate, was chosen to continue serving as Prime Minister. The big losers were Seni Pramoj's Democrats, who were swamped in their long-time Bangkok stronghold by the right-wing Prachakorn Thai Party, led by the rabble-rousing former Interior Minister Samak Sundaravej.

If Kriangsak had proved himself the most effective leader the country had had for a long time, he had not been able "to condense six years of planning into one," which, he had told me earlier, was the almost insurmountable challenge he faced. His chief concerns, he added, were the stimulation of agriculture and small industry. He had given the drought-stricken families emergency aid and had pledged himself to deal forcefully with the problem of rural indebtedness by obtaining the support of both government and private banks for loans to farmers to replace the mortgages they had taken out with landlords and usurers. Outright distribution of land to farmers under a bolder land-reform program was required if agricultural development was to become more diversified and widespread, but except for some crown and government land, very little distribution had taken place so far, and absentee landlordism remained prevalent. In the impoverished north and northeast, where most of the farmers owned their small unproductive plots of land, the lack of development facilities, including roads, technical assistance, schools, and low interest credit programs, left them vulnerable to Communist propaganda, even though some progress on development had been made during Kukrit's earlier tenure as Prime Minister.

Most peasants suffered from a one-crop mentality, partly the product of their Buddhist passivity, but beyond that they saw no reason to work too hard, since the soil in the north and northeast was so poor and most of their meager profits were siphoned off by middlemen anyway. Peasant discontent had long been latent, and had occasionally, since the sixties, erupted through such organizations as the Peasants Federation of Thailand (PTF), which became active in the mid-seventies. The PFT's militancy had brought some results—for example, the passage by the Kukrit regime of the Agricultural Land Rent Control Act—but as the PFT became more active and radical its members were attacked, and sometimes killed, by right-wing paramilitary groups such as the Red Gauers and the Village Scouts. Kriangsak's more conciliatory policies, like his offers of amnesty to students who had fled to the jungle after the Thammasat rebellion and to farmers who had joined forces with the Communists or Communist front groups, had not dampened the spirit of rebellion, and only a handful had accepted the amnesty offers.

At the end of 1978 a confidential report of the World Bank which was leaked to the press, including the influential *Far Eastern Economic Review*, revealed that one third of all agricultural households, about nine million people, were still living under conditions of absolute poverty. The report was highly critical of the vested interests, not only rich landlords but the corrupt bureaucracy, for their failure to confront the problems of poverty in Thailand. "In recent years it has become increasingly difficult to discern a sense of direction and purpose in public sector behavior that is in any way comparable to its stated intentions and objectives," the report said. It added that "growth has been accompanied by a widening disparity of welfare among population groups and among the different geographical areas in the country." Commercialization of cash crops such as sugar and tapioca had benefited a minority, including those who could obtain credit and technological facilities, but the condition of subsistence farmers had continued to deteriorate. The wartime boom initiated by American spending, accounting for at least half the gross national product in the sixties, had brought wealth and lavish spending to Bangkok and the base cities, but had done little or nothing to help the agricultural sector. Distribution of land became increasingly fragmented, and the number of landless peasants increased. More and more unskilled rural workers flocked to Bangkok, competing for wages and lowering wage scales. To make things worse, as the World Bank report pointed out, educational opportunities benefited those who were wealthy or had moderate incomes but not the peasant poor, since the outmoded tax system increased rather than reduced income disparities, placing the highest burden of taxes on the lowest class, while the higher-income class paid lower taxes or none at all.

With an expected decline in agricultural exports, which had annually furnished three quarters of total exports, and with manufacturing exports facing increasing protectionist threats, neither the country's trade imbalances nor its chronic condition of unemployment would improve Thailand's overall economic situation. There were some bright sides to the picture. Most of the country's abundant resources, except for tin and zinc, had scarcely been tapped. The big bonanza for the future was natural gas, of which nearly four trillion thermal units were discovered in the late seventies in the Gulf of Siam by two American firms, Union National Gas and Texas Pacific. After many months of negotiations between the companies and the Thai government, a compromise was finally reached for a price of $1.04 per thousand cubic feet of gas to be sold through the Natural Gas Organization of Thailand, a government agency. Once a pipeline was built, probably by 1981, the Thais would at least be able to cut their Persian Gulf oil imports by 25 percent, which in 1977–1978 amounted to $1 billion, and the economy would receive a solid financial boost which could offer an inducement for foreign investment to start up again. During 1978 Kriangsak raised taxes on gasoline and duties on major luxury items, and promised to increase taxes on the incomes of the affluent and establish a capital-gains tax, but given the power of the vested interests, such measures would not be easy to implement. The flaunting of wealth in Bangkok, a capital whose lack of conscience remains perhaps the greatest impediment to national progress, may yet prove Thailand's ultimate undoing.

Whether this bleak outlook is justified or not will naturally depend, to a considerable extent, on what happens politically in the rest of Southeast Asia and on economic circumstances in all of Asia and the rest of the world. If not a domino, in the outworn geopolitical sense, Thailand is surely the most vulnerable pawn on the Asian chessboard, along with its Communist neighbor Cambodia, which is engaged in a separate Communist chess game. If both pawns were picked off their respective boards, the most likely victor of the matches would be the Vietnamese, unless, with their peculiar capacity to overplay their position, they defeated themselves. With the Americans out of the picture, the final contest would then take place between those two grand masters of the Communist world, China and the Soviet Union.

Burma-
Poverty and
Pride

The city in Southeast Asia that has changed the least in three decades is Rangoon, the capital of the Union of Burma, which is scarcely a union and whose 32-million population includes about two-thirds Burmans and a host of hill tribes and scattered racial groups that speak more than a hundred different languages and are variously engaged in fighting for their autonomy. The run-down, refuse-laden and rat-infested downtown area of Rangoon, composed of potholed streets and cracked sidewalks, that I first saw in the hot summer of 1946 contained, in 1978, the same gray imperial buildings, their old paint still flaking, a few outworn and ramshackle colonial hotels, sad cinemas and crumbling shops and bazaars that dealt almost exclusively in black-market goods for those who could afford to buy them. A walk along Bogyoke Street past the Open Market and desultory groups of soldiers, monks and chattering housewives, followed by a midmorning stop at the cavernous Strand Hotel, where foreigners sipped local gin or ale while they listened to shortwave radios, conjured up mixed images of Conrad, Maugham and Kipling, and one half expected to see the three authors sitting at the bar exchanging memories and gossip while that long-time Burma-lover, George Orwell, smiled and took notes.

When the military dictatorship of General U Ne Win seized power in March 1962, Burma, with an almost pathological determination, became the most isolated nation in the region, and at the same time the most badly administered, economically mismanaged and self-deprived. The Burmese were sustained in their passion for nonalignment and noninvolvement in their conviction that the "Burmese way of life"—a somewhat fanciful post–World War II blend of ardent Buddhism and fuzzy socialism—was the key to their welfare and salvation. It was, in fact, a disaster for the vast majority, affording them no blessing and leaving them impoverished and torpid, and subject to constant police harassment. Yet the Burmese, at least those who tried or pretended to run things, maintained their aloofness. "We are cautious sometimes to the extent of not doing anything," a government spokesman once told me, with as much pride as defensiveness. "Belonging to one camp or another is a luxury we can't afford."

There wasn't much of anything Burma could afford. Its aloof, hermetic attitude was partly prompted by its strategic location in the watershed zone between South and Southeast Asia, abutting India and Bangladesh on the west, China on the north and northeast, Laos on the east and Thailand on the east and southeast, and possessing a long meandering coastline on the Bay of Bengal, the Gulf of Martaban and the Andaman Sea. With a long history of invasions by the Mongols, Chinese and Siamese, as well as French and British, and with recent memories of the nation's being a bloody battleground during World War II, the Burmese certainly had good reason for wanting to be left alone. But in the raw and compelling post-Vietnam climate of the late seventies, the Americans having withdrawn militarily from the region and the latent Sino-Soviet rivalry having become the new uncertain factor, with its economy a shambles and with half the country under the control of a dozen or so insurgent movements, Burma had reached the reluctant conclusion that its doctrinaire socialist tenets and its recondite nationalist precepts were no longer a sufficient formula for survival. Like a wary snail, the country began to come out of its shell, establishing new tentative relationships with its Southeast Asian neighbors and regarding the world at large with somewhat less suspicion.

Both the neighbors and the world beyond responded sympathetically but with a degree of bemusement and a remnant suspicion of their own about the genuineness of Burma's reawakening. No one seemed unduly impressed by the fact that having made a mess of their domestic affairs for so long, the Burmese were now willing to accept more outside help and advice; indeed, some of the larger and richer nations had formed a consortium under the aegis of the World Bank to determine how serious the Burmese really were about setting their house in order. Though some aid and advice was eventually forthcoming, this was tempered by concern for the country's political future and by doubts about the ability of the Burma Socialist Programme Party (BSPP), the sole legally recognized political faction, to withstand not only the military attacks of the Chinese-supported Burma Communist Party and the scattered tribal opposition elements but also a growing amount of discontent and rebellion within the ranks of the BSPP itself. Lately this had included some plots to assassinate Ne Win and other party leaders, whose popularity had diminished in direct ratio to their growing dogmatism and tactics of repression.

Ne Win, in his mid-sixties, was an impatient and intolerant army-bred dictator who often seemed to run the country, Southeast Asia's second largest after Indonesia, more by whim than wisdom. He hired and fired subordinates just about as frequently and fecklessly as he chose new wives (in 1976 he married for the fifth time), and his political and economic philosophy, if indeed he had one, was based more on expediency and experimentation than on practicality and careful planning, or on awareness of the needs and aspirations of the Burmans and of the multilingual tribal groups that sought autonomy from the Union or at least a greater degree representation.

As with many Southeast Asian leaders whose authoritarian brands of government are uniquely their own, Ne Win's brand of patriotism and nationalism represents a strange historic metamorphosis. Was he, had he actually ever been, a true nationalist, or just a grasping opportunist; or was he, more subtly and bewilderingly, a combination of both, at least at the outset; and had he then gone astray and at the end had peculiar pangs of conscience that blended with his own fears and survival syndrome?

Aung San and the Thirty Comrades

Originally, at the start of World War II, Ne Win was one of the so-called Thirty Comrades who had formed the nucleus of the " 'We Burmans' Association," a group of ardent nationalist students who had been trained in Japan and were sent back to Burma to fight the Allies, with a Japanese promise of independence. They soon became disillusioned under mounting Japanese control and cruelties and swung their guerrilla army, part of which Ne Win led, to the Allied cause, under the leadership of a dynamic young "general" named Aung San, who formed and became head of the Anti-Fascist People's Freedom League.

In Rangoon in August 1946, I found the mood, despite many unsettled problems, one of exhilaration and hope. The AFPFL was insisting on full independence from the British, who had ruled Burma for sixty-two years, and Aung San had just begun negotiations with the new British military governor, General Sir Hubert Rance. By October, General Rance had acceded to demands for the creation of a new Burmese pro tem government dominated by the AFPFL, with the youthful Aung San head of its Council of Ministers, from which he barred the Communists, who were pressing for a full revolution.

After traveling to London to confer with the government of Prime Minister Clement Attlee in January 1947, Aung San and his comrades signed an agreement paving the way for independence starting with general elections for a Constituent Assembly in April. The AFPFL won these handily, largely as a result of Aung San's persuasive efforts to get the disparate non-Burman tribal groups—the Karens, Shans, Chins and Kachins—to support his new government and consolidate the country. By promising them considerable autonomy under the projected constitution, he initially won over all but the Karens, who still wanted a state of their own, though some of the other tribal groups also retained reservations. With patient statecraft that belied his youth, Aung San continued to negotiate with the Karens, but on July 19, two months after the first draft of the constitution had been drawn up and just before the second draft was about to be approved, Aung San and several of his followers were assassinated by a political rival, U Saw, who with a group of gunmen burst into an Executive Council meeting in Rangoon. They were later sentenced to death and executed. Aung San was one of the most inspirational nationalist leaders of postwar Southeast Asia, and his early death was a tremendous loss for Burma. He was succeeded by a gentle and serene but ineffectual scholar-statesman, the deeply religious U Nu, who concluded negotiations with the British, and on January 4, 1948, at 4:20 A.M., a time carefully chosen by local astrologers, Burma's independence was formally proclaimed.

Though U Nu, as the first Premier of the independent Union of Burma, did manage temporarily to curb some of the tribal rebellions that historically had plagued the country, he lacked Aung San's charismatic qualities and was unable for long to pacify the opposition elements, including the Communists and some of the hill tribes who opposed the defense arrangements which gave the British continued access to airfields and ports in case of emergencies. U Nu devoted most of his energies to stimulating a revival of Theravada Buddhism (the form of the religion the Burmans practice) to the neglect of economic growth and political unity. While he did create the semblance of a parliamentary democracy under the new constitution, his administrative laxities soon undermined the regime, and the country drifted into the state of disorder and rebellion which has lasted ever since. In the fall of 1958 General Ne Win, as head of the army, pushed him aside and established a "caretaker" government, ostensibly to prevent the many rival factions from starting a civil war. When Ne Win held new elections, as he had promised to do, in 1960, U Nu's Union Party was restored to power, but after two more years of chaos and confusion Ne Win staged his coup of March 2, 1962. It was typical of the unsuspecting U Nu that when he was informed of the coup his first question was "Is Ne Win safe?"

U Nu was put in jail until 1966, and then kept under surveillance. After being allowed to leave the country, in 1969, he settled in Thailand, insisting he was still de jure Premier. In October 1970 he launched a revolutionary movement against Ne Win, but he failed in a major part of his plan, which was to rally the dissident tribesmen in Upper Burma—notably the Karens and Shans, who continued to demand autonomous status. As a man of peace, U Nu was never quite at home directing a terrorist movement. Its members, numbering perhaps two or three thousand, made sporadic raids across the border from Thailand and occasionally threw grenades in Moulmein, Rangoon and other cities, killing a few civilians and soldiers. Disillusioned with politics, U Nu eventually went to the United States and then into exile in India, but his movement, known as the Parliamentary Democracy Party, continued to operate out of border sanctuaries in Thailand and conducted occasional raids into Burma, killing two or three government soldiers from time to time and serving as one of the many insurgent thorns in the Ne Win government's side.

The Burmese are generally considered a gentle, joyful people, but when I returned to Rangoon in the summer of 1973, for the first time in many years, it seemed to me that they were singularly lacking in ebullience and gaiety. The downtown atmosphere was as depressing as ever, the rats and stray mongrels as ubiquitous, and about the only difference I noted was that the streets now all had Burmese instead of British names and that there were more movie theaters than before. With nothing to do for the most part, the people endlessly sought solace from boredom in foreign films, chiefly American adventure sagas, the importation of which the government controlled and censored. What had changed as the city grew was the outskirts, which were once covered by thatch-roofed shacks but now displayed broad, well-kept avenues with modern houses, pruned trees and bushes, and clipped lawns.

The farther out one got from the old run-down part of Rangoon, the more spectacular was the sight of the famous Shwe Dagon Pagoda, which stands on a small hill there. It is the largest Buddhist temple in the world, with a bell-shaped tower, 326 feet high and covered with gold leaf, which dominates the low horizon, particularly at night, when it is brightly floodlit and looks like a great luminous gem. I visited the Shwe Dagon one day in mid-July, on the full-moon day of the month of Waso, which by the Buddhist calendar marks the start of a three-month period of special devotion and abstinence; the day is the anniversary of the Lord Buddha's First Sermon to his disciples at Sarnath, near Benares, in India, in the sixth century B.C. During this three-month period, Buddhists everywhere are supposed to heed Buddha's advice to avoid extremes of all kinds and seek insight and mental calm. Several thousand people—monks in their long robes; affluent men, women and children in their most decorative *longyis,* or skirtlike sheaths; and beggars in rags —were strolling around the circular area at the base of the tower, which is surrounded by small stupas, or domelike structures containing shrines. Though this was supposed to be a celebrative day, it seemed to me that beyond devotional obligation there was a subdued atmosphere, in keeping with the grayness of the monsoon weather. The mood, I thought, could well be attributed to the restricted lives the Burmese were leading under the unimaginative and harsh Ne Win regime.

Certainly stoicism was a quality that the Burmese had learned to cultivate as Ne Win's confining rule progressed over the years. It remained to be seen (six years later, in 1979) to what extent a new experiment in constitutional government—predicated on encouraging the apathetic, disheartened and polyglot masses to play a more active social and political role while the government slowly opened its doors to the outside world—would succeed in bringing Burma out of its miasmic isolation.

Ne Win's Autocratic Rule

Burma's self-perception of its ills began during the period of my 1973 visit when, following two years of a declining growth rate, Ne Win told an Extraordinary Congress of the BSPP that "we are not yet able to utilize the capacities, efficiency and inventiveness of all the people of the country," and declared that "it is now time for us to put things right." He had over several years nationalized almost all sectors of business and finance, in fact everything but agriculture; now he suddenly made a special appeal to "some of the opposing forces" (meaning middle-class businessmen) "to draw up a plan and start a business" so that "the unused services of workers will be utilized." Undoubtedly he was provoked by the declining production of such natural resources as tin, tungsten, lead and copper, partly because of technical difficulties and a scarcity of new mining equipment, and partly because of poor security caused by the chronic insurgencies.

Regular commercial activity had been further impeded by the growth of smuggling; and antismuggling controls were ineffective because of the long, loose border with Thailand and the fact that the streams and rivers between the two countries were easily forded, and border guards were just as easily bribed. Large amounts of textiles, watches, electronic devices, pharmaceuticals and other consumer items moved freely into the black markets in Rangoon, Mandalay and other towns. One of the principal rackets involved old automobiles. Although several hundred new small Japanese taxis were legally imported, many other taxis and buses, as well as private cars, were former ancient wrecks sold in the capital, trundled north to the Shan States, refitted with new parts smuggled in from Thailand, and then resold in Rangoon for as much as $20,000 at the black market rate in kyats, the local currency, which was usually three or four times the official rate.

Another indication that Burma was moving toward a more laissez-faire economy in the spring of 1973 was the government's decision to lift controls on the sale of rice, if only temporarily. Rice—until then bought and sold through a government agency—had always been both the country's biggest asset and its biggest problem, and as in all Asian countries it had political connotations and significance. Burma was once the world's leading exporter of rice—as much as 3 million tons were sent abroad annually before World War II, and between 1.5 million and 2 million tons in good postwar years— but this had gradually dropped off to several hundred thousand tons annually as the growing population consumed more rice and as bad weather and mismanagement caused added difficulties. The decontrol measure, which affected wheat, too, was judged necessary because the farmers were holding back most of their crop anyway, selling it on the black market for three or four times what government buyers would pay them. Moreover, many farmers preferred to grow crops they could get more money for, such as jute, beans and sesame. Administratively, agricultural policy was implemented through some sixteen thousand government cooperatives—a committee was set up in every village, but bad planning as well as bad organization had hindered their progress, and the committees had never been popular with the farmers. The new decontrol measures were at least a sign that the government had belatedly become aware of the need for better coordination, decentralization of the cumbersome bureaucracy, and long-range planning that would include foreign advice and assistance.

At the same time that Burma was making this effort to extend its economic horizons, it was already broadening its political base in what seemed a desire by the Ne Win regime to legitimize itself both at home and abroad. The process of change actually began early in 1971, when elections were held for delegates to the First Party Congress of the BSPP, which convened in June of that year. In a matter of months the party's membership was increased from an elite of 24—a Politburo, in effect—to some 60,000, and it thus ceased to be a doctrinaire "cadre party" and became a more amorphous but still doctrinaire "mass party." By 1973, there were almost 100,000 full-fledged party members, nearly 400,000 candidate members, and more than 800,000 "Friends of the Party." The new party organization extended from the top down through the 311 townships of the country, and Ne Win, in trying to build up this new civilian mass-based organization, placed special emphasis on including as many young people as possible in what appeared or pretended to be an effort to create a counterforce to the military.

These moves were followed by constitutional reform in January 1974, when the new constitution, the second, of the Socialist Republic of the Union of Burma came into force, having been approved in a referendum amid much hoopla and a government-inspired carnival atmosphere by 90 percent of the 15 million electorate. Then, two months later, on the anniversary of the 1962 coup, the Revolutionary Council, which had been almost completely dominated by active or retired military officers was dissolved, and Ne Win ostensibly doffed his military cap and became President of the new government. The BSPP, now composed of civilians as well as military men, was given the responsibility of electing delegates to the party congresses and also to submit lists of candidates for people's representatives to the new national parliament, called the Pyithu Hluttaw. The Congress remained the final authority, determining party policies and choosing the members of the Central Committee, which met between irregular Congress sessions. But real power was kept in the hands of a twenty-nine-member State Council, of which Ne Win was chairman, and which still consisted mostly of army officers or retired military men. Under the council was a cabinet headed by a Prime Minister, who was chosen by Ne Win after he relinquished the job.

Political opponents of the regime, including some who had been in jail for several years and even when released had been kept under strict surveillance, regarded these changes as purely cosmetic. Full power and control remained in Ne Win's hands alone, they said, and this indeed seemed to be the case. The BSPP was still the only recognized party, organized into ten- or fifteen-man cells and higher-echelon "sections" with roughly the same number of members; by groups of villages called "village tracts"; by towns, and then by the townships, which were composed of both village tracts and towns. Above the townships, which dated back to the days of the Burmese royal dynasties, were the traditional seven "divisions" and seven states, including the Shan and other tribal states, but the new constitution diminished their political importance as such. At the lower levels throughout the country, People's Councils and People's Courts conducted most daily business under the ever-watchful eye of the Party Central Committee, which in 1973–1974 had about a hundred and fifty members.

The Burmese tended to be as suspicious of one another as of foreigners and to look upon every new move of the government as having an ulterior motive. They regarded the first census in many years, begun in the spring of 1973—despite the fact that the insurgency situation kept the census takers from reaching at least a third of the population—as a political measure aimed at preparing electoral rolls in the urban areas and especially in the townships, where, they claimed, no one would dare vote against the government even if there were any real opposition candidates to vote for.

"Kinsmenship" with China

Charade or not, the changes that took place between 1971 and early 1974 were interpreted by Rangoon's diplomatic community as an effort by Ne Win, oblique or otherwise, to define more clearly the country's Marxist orientation and to place it more firmly in the center spectrum between the Soviet Union and China. Despite the fact that the Burmese had long been upset by the support the Chinese Communists were giving the Burmese Communist Party, formal relations between Peking and Rangoon had always been cordial, and the so-called *paukhpaw* (kinsmen) friendship between the two countries was periodically and platitudinously reiterated, through exchanges of personal visits and in endless messages of congratulation on anniversary days. But Burma's system of government, though unique in its own right, was probably closer to the Soviet Union's than to China's. Moscow was farther away and relations between the two countries were more formal and polite, though Ne Win always tried to be careful to maintain a proper balance between the two Communist giants. And despite the Vietnam war, of which Burma disapproved, relations with the United States were relatively cordial; in 1974 Washington promised Ne Win six helicopters to help track down narcotics smugglers, and when they were delivered Ne Win used them for a twofold purpose: to chase the smugglers and attack the insurgents.

Notwithstanding the country's isolationist posture, the presence of a variegated diplomatic corps brought a cosmopolitan atmosphere to otherwise drab Rangoon. The Russians maintained a huge embassy of about a hundred and twenty, and the Chinese and Americans were each represented by staffs about half as large. Both Germanys, both Koreas, and both Vietnams had diplomatic establishments, and during the war the Provisional Revolutionary Government of South Vietnam had dispatched occasional representatives. Fifteen or so non-Communist countries had small embassies that embellished the international social community, among them the Israelis. Burma-watching was always a rather difficult task because Burmese officials were so inaccessible, except informally on the golf course, so the foreign diplomats spent most of their time conducting what are known in diplomatic parlance as "third-country operations"—seeing what tidbits they were able to pick up about one another in the absence of hard facts about the host country. If this led to an inordinate amount of rumor-mongering, it sometimes produced hard intelligence and kept the cocktail circuits liquid and busy, but unlike Phnom Penh and Vientiane, which were also wartime listening posts and which retained their special charm and flavor, Rangoon never did surmount its rather dour tone and mood.

One always felt, during the period of constitutional "reform," a pervasive remoteness or unreality, an inchoate quality. At the same time one had the feeling that the slow, quiet routine of planned events and ceremonies, the stiff, formalized political activity and the repetitive round of private parties might be interrupted at any moment by something unexpected, some sudden mysterious event or happening. Much of this was due to the fact that Ne Win remained as much of an enigma to his own people as he did to outsiders, especially as he became more reclusive, leaving the daily conduct of affairs to General Sun Yu, the tough secretary-general of the BSPP and secretary of the State Council.

The elections that followed the promulgation of the new constitution, which the people were peremptorily told "expressed their long-cherished aspirations for freedom, equality and socialism," were a carefully contrived one-party affair which returned 288,681 deputies nominated by the BSPP, the great majority to ward or village councils, and lesser numbers to town, state or division councils. The new National Congress, consisting of 450 members, met for the first time on March 2, 1974, the twelfth anniversary of Ne Win's coup, and as part of the celebrations the government offered amnesty to the insurgents within a ninety-day period—nearly 1,500 of them surrendered their arms; among the 5,700 convicts pardoned were a number of prominent political rebels, including Thakin Soe, the sixty-six-year-old head of the Stalinist wing of the Burma Communist Party.

The new government soon faced its first major crisis over shortages of official supplies of rice, as the state procurement system broke down and not enough rice was available in the official stores. Workers who could not afford to pay the higher prices on the black market began a series of strikes and sit-ins in several cities, and in the ports near Rangoon they refused to load rice for export. Their demands for rice at official prices, about a third of the black-market levels, led to other demands, for improved working conditions and a lowering of the general cost of living. Demonstrations and riots in Rangoon provoked the calling out of troops, and during May and June of 1974 at least two dozen persons were killed and about a hundred were injured. The government blamed both "leftist and rightist saboteurs," but the National Congress made no effort to sort out the political or economic causes of the disturbances. However, the government did take action to meet some of the workers' demands, importing more consumer goods and providing loans for workers' welfare associations to purchase low-cost rice, as well as loans to savings cooperatives to help reduce the cost-of-living burden.

No sooner had the conditions of workers been at least partially ameliorated than the government was confronted with another crisis—student riots. These were precipitated by the death of the Secretary-General of the United Nations, U Thant, probably the best-known Burmese figure, whose body was flown from the United States for burial in Rangoon. The government intended to bury him in a simple ceremony in a cemetery near the Shwe Dagon Pagoda, but on December 6, when the burial was about to take place, a mob of twenty thousand students and monks gathered in the city, seized the body and carried it to one of the main university campuses, where the students kept it lying in state for four days, which they said befitted "a distinguished son of the soil." As both students and monks delivered round-the-clock angry speeches, it was soon apparent that they were directing their criticisms more against the "tyranny" of one-party rule than paying homage to U Thant, and large crowds of ordinary citizens came to listen.

At dawn on December 11, as government troops invaded the campus to take the body away, riots spread throughout the city and mobs attacked government and party offices, state-run shops and police stations. The government thereupon declared martial law, set a dawn-to-dusk curfew, and shut down all schools and colleges. They were reopened in May 1975, but a month later they were ordered closed again when fresh student outbreaks took place. This time the student leaders called for a boycott of examinations and a general student strike, claiming that even if they passed exams and graduated, they would not be able to find jobs. On June 11, after more than three thousand students had marched through the city to the Sule Pagoda, where they made fiery speeches demanding lower prices, the release of those arrested during the 1974 disturbances, and calling for an end of military rule (they burned effigies of Ne Win and San Yu), the government cracked down and arrested more than two hundred, most of whom were tried and sentenced to four or five years in jail. When the atmosphere calmed down, the curfew was lifted, along with the ban on assemblies, but the universities remained closed for the rest of the year and Rangoon stayed under military rule until close to the end of 1975.

The combined effect of the worker and student strikes and riots appeared to have a sobering effect on the government. It organized ten ministerial teams headed by party officials to travel around the country and hold meetings with students, workers and other citizens to seek popular reaction about how to deal with the mounting social and economic crisis. At the same time it launched drives to curb corruption, black marketeering and ordinary crime; this campaign resulted in the firing of more than five hundred officials and the arrest and trial of some fifteen hundred criminals. In the face of further economic failures, however—the growth-rate target of 6.3 percent for 1974–1975 was not even closely attained, and the final figure was only 3.5 percent—and as production of agricultural and other products continued to lag, Ne Win ordered emergency measures to forestall more popular discontent. The most important of these was an increase of 50 percent in the procurement price of rice to farmers, which brought more rice at controlled prices into the official stores. But drops in the production of other crops, including jute, sugar cane and sesame, sent the prices of these commodities soaring, forcing the imposition of new price controls. And while the government, already operating on its ninth successive deficit budget, tried to raise the spirits of the farmers and urban citizens by importing additional consumer goods, a shortage of raw materials and spare parts kept the larger industrial sector stagnant. Continued mismanagement and low worker morale did little to stimulate production, and the ever-soaring rate of inflation led more and more people to engage in smuggling, black marketeering and crime in order to survive. The country was thus caught in a vicious circle of economic problems and rising political discontent, and to make matters worse the insurgency movements, particularly the activity of the Burma Communist Party, were presenting an increasing threat to stability.

Communist Challenge

The armed strength of the BCP was variously estimated to be between 5,000 and 15,000, but a consensus of Western intelligence sources set the figure at about 8,000. Most BCP members were ethnic Chinese and the rest were minority tribesmen, recruited, armed, trained and in many instances led by the Chinese Communists. Initially, after World War II, there was a pro-Peking "White Flag" element and a pro-Russian (Stalinist) "Red Flag" group, but after the capture, in November 1970, of Thakin Soe, the "Red Flag" leader, this group began to disintegrate. Peking's influence on the BCP—the only insurgent movement in Asia it has directly and openly supported—has been constant and considerable, and Chinese weapons and ammunition have been steadily funneled into Burma over a long logistical mountain route from China. Here, as elsewhere in Southeast Asia, the Chinese always distinguished between "state relations" and "party to party" relations, and this furnished their pretext for support of the BCP. Peking has thus flagrantly had it both ways, more so in Burma than elsewhere.

During the period of the Cultural Revolution, when riots against Maoist activists took place in Rangoon and other cities, there was a rupture in relations between Burma and China, and the BCP was also torn by ideological differences and by purges, culminating in the assassination in 1968 of Thakin Than Tun, its chairman. His place was taken by Thakin Zin, and Thakin Chit became party secretary; they made their headquarters in the Irrawaddy Delta and the Pegu Yoma range north of Rangoon, establishing a separate command in the northeast headed by a one-time Kachin sergeant in the Burmese army named Naw Seng. When Thakin Zin and Thakin Chit were killed in action early in 1975 during a Burmese army attack in the Irrawaddy Delta (Naw Seng had been killed earlier, in less dignified fashion, when he fell off his horse while drunk), Thakin Ba Thein Tin, the only known survivor of the Politburo, became the party chief; he lived in Peking, where he had been for many years, frequently attending Chinese Communist functions, and has thus been cast in somewhat of a captive role.

Over the years, Ne Win made ten trips to China—he was there twice in 1977—and he tried without much success to get the Chinese to cease acting as a patron for Ba Thein Tin and to cut off or at least reduce their military support of the BCP. In January 1978 Vice Premier Teng Hsiao-ping paid an official visit to Rangoon, the most important trip out of the country by a Chinese leader since the death of Mao Tse-tung in 1976. He received a warm welcome and had the usual "friendly and full exchange of views" with Ne Win, but no details of their conversations were disclosed. There were reports that Teng may have agreed to reduce military support of the BCP if the Burmese agreed to reduce the heavy Soviet presence in Rangoon, something that would be hard for Ne Win to propose to Moscow. Peking was also interested in having Ne Win play a role in mediating the angry border war between Vietnam and Cambodia (Ne Win had recently made a state visit to Phnom Penh, the first such by a foreign leader since the Cambodian Communist takeover), but it seemed doubtful that he could do any more than the Chinese themselves had been able to do, embarrassed and upset as they were over their Cambodian allies having overplayed their hand against the Vietnamese. Ne Win, who was by then trying to build his own new bridges in Southeast Asia, had also begun to befriend the Vietnamese, and Teng undoubtedly had this in mind during the Rangoon talks. Theoretically, if the Burmese could act in China's behalf as a peacemaker, enabling Peking to improve its deteriorating relations with Hanoi, it was conceivable that the flow of Chinese arms to the BCP might be slowed down, but there were no indications that this was about to take place. In fact, as usual during and after official visits between the Burmese and the Chinese, the BCP stepped up its attacks, and it was anyone's guess whether it did so on its own or with Peking's approbation.

Although the Burmese army of 140,000 was well-disciplined and considered to be one of the best in Southeast Asia, it had its hands full over the years fighting the resourceful BCP, particularly as the Communists managed to recruit local supporters and sympathizers among the various tribal groups, notably the Shans. This was not a typical procedure for a Chinese Communist–type organization, and neither was the BCP's method of attack—often in battalion-size units, dragging its heavy weaponry, including mortars and machine guns, with it. Starting late in 1971, the BCP began an effort to widen its area of control. Its forces came down from near the Yunnan border through the Kokang and Wa states and almost captured the town of Kunlong, on the west bank of the Salween River, in the Northern Shan State. Both the Communists and the government suffered considerable casualties. In the spring of 1972, shifting their tactics to traditional small-scale guerrilla attacks and patrols, the BCP forces again moved toward Kunlong, and did capture some outposts, but then suddenly moved south to take over most of the wild no man's land of the Wa States, which are tribal sub-states of the Shan.

At this juncture the BCP created a Shan State Liberation Army, for the first time employing political cadres to recruit other tribal groups. The fighting continued at a steady pace over the next three years, and despite the government's 1975 victory in the Irrawaddy Delta the BCP maintained its base in the Salween River area below the Chinese border, stepped up its attacks, again striking west of the Salween and cutting important roads within fifty miles of Mandalay, and kept its hold on large parts of remote eastern Burma. Fighting reached its fiercest level in twenty years late in 1977, in the Wa region, when, during the month of October alone, twenty-five battles took place, and according to the Rangoon radio, more than 500 BCP troops were killed; the government admitted losing 126 soldiers. The BCP, in turn, claimed that the government lost 550 men in failing to recapture the Wa State area.

In the second half of 1978 the Communists stepped up their attacks once more, regrouping some forces in the strategic Pegu Yoma range, from which they had been ejected several years back, and pressing farther forward on the west bank of the Salween toward the Irrawaddy plain, the country's heartland, where three quarters of Burma's population lives. Rangoon, like Bangkok, was as usual full of rumors about what was really taking place. There were reports, for example, that the BCP had turned to opium smuggling to raise funds to buy arms because Peking had, after all, cut down its arms supply in the aftermath of Teng Hsiao-ping's visit, and it appeared that the BCP's alliance with the Shan Liberation Army had broken down, forcing it to depend more on its resources and strategy. While it was doubtful that the Chinese Communists would altogether cut off aid to the BCP, the practical Teng may have decided to limit the flow in the belief that increased instability in Burma would, in the long run, favor the Russians more than the Chinese, and that by relaxing the pressure on the Rangoon government, he could bring Burma closer to the Chinese camp than it already was. In any event, as both the BCP and the government moved to take the offensive, the revolution in Burma, after thirty years, showed no signs of slowing down. Although not as violent, and scarcely publicized through those years, it was as old as Vietnam's, and considerably more confusing.

Besides the BCP, the various other insurgent forces included the Kachin Independence Army, in the far northern tip of the country, consisting of 2,000 men who were said to be the best fighters of all; the Shan United Revolutionary Army, of 1,000 (separate from the Shan State Army, of 7,000); the Karen National Liberation Army of about 15,000, which operated south of the Shan states; remnants of the Parliamentary Democracy Party forces of U Nu in the far south; and the Khakweiyei, or KKY, a former local government militia that defected in the Shan area. Several additional minority groups who used to be ruled by hereditary princes before the British annexed Burma in 1886, some of whom later sided with the British against both the Japanese and the Communists, had their own small armies and controlled isolated parts of the country. Though often mutually hostile, these various armed elements were united in their opposition to the Rangoon government, and in 1976 the non-BCP insurgents formed the National Democratic Front, which held together loosely for a time but more as a political than a united fighting force. With the exception of the BCP and the Karens, and the far-southern nationalists, these various insurgent groups were over the years motivated primarily by profiteering—smuggling opium, gems, teak and elephants into Thailand, and they fought to protect their smuggling routes in the name of freedom. As a foreign diplomat in Rangoon once remarked to me, "Insurgency has simply become a way of life for tens of thousands of people here. They have no other profession."

This was especially true in the so-called Golden Triangle—the part of Burma that juts out to the east where the borders of Laos and Thailand meet. This area has for many years supplied much of the world's opium, the source of heroin. Until 1973 the Burmese government paid scant attention to the opium problem, but when it was discovered that young Burmese—and notably the sons of the rich—were beginning to use No. 4 heroin, the most select variety, Rangoon sat up and took notice. In May, government forces destroyed a large heroin refinery at Tachilek, in the Southern Shan State, and two months later Lo Hsing-han, reputedly Burma's biggest heroin trader, was captured by the Thais. He was extradited to Burma, where he was tried on charges of inciting rebellion and smuggling, and was sentenced to death. For the first time, too, the government started cooperating with American and Thai officials to cut down the drug traffic, conducting search-and-destroy operations against poppy plantations in the Golden Triangle. No one thought that the opium traffic could be stopped overnight—in fact, it probably could never be stopped altogether—but at least the regional cooperative effort to limit it began to make some progress, and an increasing number of smugglers and dealers were apprehended, while several additional border refineries were destroyed.

The Americans had delivered the earlier pledged helicopters to the Burmese to help curb the drug traffic, and they were used late in 1975 to raid the headquarters of one of the biggest smuggling groups, composed of remnants of the former Kuomintang forces that fled into Burma from Yunnan in 1949. Some of the tribal separatist elements which benefited from the opium trade found their profits, which they used to buy arms, dwindling, and as a result they were reluctantly forced into tentative alliances of convenience with the BCP. In April 1977 Bo Mya, the head of the National Democratic Front, wrote to President Carter complaining that American helicopters were being used by the Rangoon government to fight anti-Communist nationalists more than they were being utilized in the anti-opium drive. He urged the Americans to support the true nationalist minority groups, but as far as is known, there was no reply from Washington.

Early in 1978 the government faced another serious problem in the western state of Arakan, bordering on Bangladesh. Arakan has always had a large minority of Moslems, dating back to the spillover of Islam into Southeast Asia several centuries ago. Those who were later born in Arakan called themselves Rohingya, which means "native-born," and both they and the militant Buddhist majority, called Moghs, built up their own insurgent movements seeking Arakanese independence. The two religious groups also came into conflict with each other, particularly with a heavy influx of Moslems from neighboring

Bangladesh. In February 1978, when the government began an operation called Dragon King to take the first census in Arakan since 1962, antipathies exploded between the Moslem and Buddhist population which had been aggravated during World War II when the British created a Moslem force and most of the Buddhists sided with the Japanese. Government police did little to quell the disturbances; in fact, they were ruthless in their approach to the Rohingya, as a result of which 200,000 of them, classified as "illegal immigrants," fled across the border to Bangladesh, where they were settled in eleven camps under conditions described by international refugee officials as among the worst they had ever seen. Fears were expressed that both Arab extremists and the Communists would take advantage of the uprooting of the Rohingya to politicize them, but the situation improved somewhat in July when Burma and Bangladesh signed an agreement for the repatriation of the refugees. By March 1979, 80,000 had returned to Burma, and most of the remaining 120,000 were expected to return under a more benevolent government resettlement program sponsored by the United Nations High Commissioner for Refugees. Confronted with so many other insurgency sores, the government could ill afford to disregard the Rohingya problem.

Burma's Balance Game

Overall, in the light of the major power struggle, insurgencies in Burma could become as great a threat to peace in Southeast Asia as the complicated situation in Indochina. Although in 1978 it still appeared to be containable, given the strength of the Burmese army, there were a number of imponderables and potentially dangerous factors. The Vietnamese were one of them. While Hanoi was seeking to improve its relations with the ASEAN nations on a bilateral basis, and separately with Burma, the Vietnamese simultaneously were tightening their grip over Laos and Cambodia. In economic terms, even if there was potentially enough rice in Indochina to feed the growing population, the vagaries of the weather, along with bureaucratic and internal political problems, caused a permanent threat of shortages. Along with Cambodia, Burma remained an attractive source of alternative supply. Rangoon was important to Hanoi for other reasons, too, as a bridge and transit point to South Asia, especially to India. While the Burmese were unhappy about the Chinese supplying arms to the BCP, they would undoubtedly be even more upset if the Vietnamese began to give the BCP weapons, using their large reservoir of captured American arms. Peking, for its part, would look askance at Hanoi's, and by obvious implication Moscow's, rendering any such aid. For this reason, Rangoon and Peking might secretly agree on a deal whereby continued Chinese Communist support of the BCP, on a modified basis, balanced against more Chinese economic aid to the beleaguered Rangoon government, would be mutually acceptable.

Over the long term, the Burmese feared a stepped-up Communist drive southward, which the BCP might be able to sustain largely on its own initiative, or with the sometime help of the other tribal factions, and which would almost surely receive fresh Peking and perhaps rival Hanoi support in the event of a serious Sino-Soviet confrontation. Or if the Soviets simply acted to consolidate their naval position in the Indian Ocean and the Bay of Bengal, the Chinese might move quickly to raise the level of insurgency through the BCP and among the other northern tribal groups, as well as in Thailand and Malaysia and perhaps in Indonesia and the Philippines too. If the Russians should move against Bangladesh, to the west, Peking could use the Burmese rebel movements, which they might even formally recognize, as a cover to maintain a land route through Burma—east–west as well as north–south—and to outflank the Russians. The long-time road-building program the Chinese were carrying out in northwestern Laos was an important element in this strategy, and it became even more significant after the Vietnamese invaded Cambodia late in 1978 and moved some troops from Laos into Cambodia, and as Hanoi improved its relations with Thailand. The fact that the Vietnamese now posed an added threat in the region thus complicated the picture, and this undoubtedly came up during the discussions between Teng Hsiao-ping and Ne Win in Rangoon.

Though the Burmese were not expecting an attack on Rangoon, they had clear memories of their country's role as a conduit and battleground in World War II. They were also keenly aware that the Russians might want to create a counterthreat to the Chinese thrust in Southeast Asia that reached down from Laos through Burma as well as directly from China. A serious confrontation between Russia's vast army and Peking's million-strong, nuclear-supported forces on the Sino-Soviet border would obviously exacerbate the whole situation in Southeast Asia. For these various reasons, despite Ne Win's worries over Peking's continued support of the BCP, the close alliance between Burma and China remained his prime consideration, and in the long run he saw the combined threat from Moscow and Hanoi as the greater one. The alternative of drawing closer to the Russians and the Vietnamese at the expense of the Chinese was therefore too dangerous, given China's proximity. Ideally Ne Win, or whoever succeeded him, could go on trying to maintain a balance between Peking and Moscow and mollify Hanoi as well. But sooner or later, unless the government tried to come to some kind of accommodation with the rebels, the Communist sword of Damocles that hung over Rangoon's head might fall, whoever helped direct it, and Burma's ability to withstand its impact would largely depend on internal economic and political factors and on the strength and loyalty of its armed forces.

Treason Trials and Economic Temporizing

During 1976 and 1977 Burma was shaken by a number of treason and assassination plots which, with some degree of irony, had the ultimate effect of provoking Ne Win to announce that he was prepared to alter the course of his regime away from socialism to a sort of mixed economy that would permit joint ventures with foreign capital—something that the World Bank and the seven-nation Burma Aid Consultative Group, as well as his own economic advisers, had been quietly urging upon him for years. The background of the major coup plot stemmed from the long-time rivalry between the two men who were deemed most likely to succeed Ne Win—General San Yu, and General Tin Oo, who was head of the army as well as Minister of Defense. During the crisis over U Thant's burial in December 1974, and the student riots of the following June, Tin Oo had followed a course of comparative moderation, refusing to suppress the demonstrators as ruthlessly as San Yu wished—Ne Win was abroad part of that time. Tin Oo's popularity, especially among junior officers, was in sharp contrast to San Yu's unpopularity as a harsh disciplinarian who made no effort to be convivial or to hide his slavish devotion to Ne Win. In March 1976 Ne Win fired Tin Oo, ostensibly because his wife was involved in corruption, and this upset a number of the younger officers. They had already apparently been plotting a coup to alter the country's socialist course because of its economic failures, and either to press for a sustained all-out offensive against the insurgents or to try to come to terms with them. The platform of the plotters, however, was rather vague, and what was more important, they lacked enough troops clearly committed to their cause.

The leader of the group was a young captain named Ohn Kyaw Myint, who was personal staff officer to Tin Oo's successor, and with him initially were three other captains and a major. Rumors of an incipient assassination plot had been floating around the Rangoon cocktail circuit for some months. When General Tin Oo was fired, the schemers first planned to kill San Yu and Colonel Tin Oo, the chief of the National Intelligence Bureau (no relation to the general), at an Armed Forces Day dinner on March 27, but that fell through when troops that were supposed to support the coup failed to appear. A second attempt a week or so later to kill the two men during a meeting of the Central Committee of the party was abandoned because of poor astrological omens. It was never clear whether the plotters planned to assassinate Ne Win or merely replace him with General Tin Oo as the head of a new Revolutionary Council. In any event, during the first abortive attempt, Ne Win unexpectedly left town, and when he returned he was furious at the failure of his intelligence service to have found out about it and promptly fired Colonel Tin Oo (who later became his private military adviser). He was even more disturbed to discover the extent of renewed discontent, not only among students and workers but in the ranks of the army as well.

In July the government arrested fourteen persons who were accused of having planned the overthrow of the government, and they were charged with wanting to kill Ne Win as well as San Yu and Colonel Tin Oo. Only six were brought to trial in September, but then, surprisingly, two others were also charged—General Tin Oo, and a colonel who commanded Burma's northern division. All the defendants were found guilty. Captain Ohn Kyaw Myint was sentenced to death, another captain to life imprisonment, and the rest got lesser sentences. General Tin Oo was sent to jail for seven years for misprision of treason—that is, having known of the plot but not reporting it.

The jailing of the popular general only served to further fan the flames of discontent among students, workers and the ranks of the armed forces. Ne Win responded, even before the trial was over, by calling a Special Party Congress in October 1976, at which he and San Yu spoke of the need to correct "wrong policies," including the abuse of power, personality cults and corruption, in order to avoid "social antagonisms" and possible violence. It was decided to summon the Third Party Congress in February 1977, eight months ahead of schedule, in order to "arrest the country's continuing deterioration in the political, economic and social fields."

The Congress, which was held from February 21 to March 1, was remarkable for the amount of self-criticism as to how and why "things went awry," as the Central Committee report quaintly put it. "We find that the price index has risen from 100 in 1972 to 295 by October, 1976," its political report said. "For these reasons the volume of currency in circulation has increased with a proliferation of casual labor and black-market activities. Historically unprecedented deterioration in morals may now be seen among the majority of workers and servicemen. Because of these developments, some party members and party cadres have lost sight of the goal of socialism. Taking advantage of these difficulties, attempts have been made to do away with the party and the socialist system and even to assassinate leaders of the BSPP." A thorough housecleaning of party ranks took place, as a result of which, though the total number of party members increased to 181,617, 17,894 were dismissed, and of the hundred and fifty members of the new Central Committee, more than half were new faces. "Gambling, drunkenness" and the seeking of "personal gain" were cited as some of the reasons for dismissal. Significantly, however, the majority of new Central Committee members, as well as of the Council of Ministers and the new Council of State, were still active or retired military men. Reshuffles in the three bodies were basically a cosmetic redeployment of the same old faces, although the replacement of Prime Minister Sein Win and his deputy in charge of planning and finance removed two of the more liberal leaders from day-to-day supervision of the government.

In the principal speech San Yu repeatedly stressed the need of "placing the right man in the right place within the party and in the organs outside the party." Taken together with the emphasis laid by Ne Win and other speakers at the Congress on the failure of economic and other policies, it was apparent that a crisis of leadership as well as of programs and plans was felt to be at the core of Burma's problems. Citing the fact that the Second Four-Year Plan had only met 64 percent of its targets, and that the majority of the country's peasants were not earning enough to keep up with inflation and were turning more and more to black-market profiteering, San Yu said, "The main difficulty which our country is facing today is economic. Political, organizational and social deterioration and corruption are the consequences of this economic hardship." Consequently, he added, the Third Four-Year Plan, while continuing to stress agricultural development, would also require "adequate funds in foreign currency for investment purposes." Such funds could be obtained partly from increasing exports, he said, but also from "aid and loans from international organizations and friendly countries through multilateral and bilateral agreements without affecting our socialist economic principles." In order to exploit natural resources, "we must, without affecting our socialist economic system, work in joint ventures of mutual interest with foreign countries or foreign economic enterprises in areas which contribute toward further development of the socialist economic system."

If the Third Party Congress seemed to presage hope that the Burmese had faced up to their difficulties with some degree of realism, albeit mixed with an equal degree of face-saving and scapegoating, the picture was at best blurred. In September and October 1977, another major purge took place in which about a hundred government officials and party leaders, including two more cabinet ministers and three members of the four-man party secretariat as well as some members of the Central Committee, were summarily dismissed in what appeared to be a "private coup" by Ne Win to tighten his control and pave the way for his personal dictatorship to continue. The coup was engineered in his absence (he had left for London, following his second trip of the year to Peking) by a new nine-man committee of loyal supporters he had appointed, and there were indications that the move was directed at pro-Soviet elements in the party. This raised speculation that Ne Win may have ordered it in order to please his Peking hosts in his continuing efforts to get them to reduce their aid to the BCP. If this was true, the ploy didn't work, but as already noted, no one knew what might eventually be arranged between the Burmese and Chinese following Teng Hsiao-ping's subsequent trip to Rangoon.

Rumors soon spread around the capital that the real object of the purge was none other than San Yu, who had never been popular among many of his fellow military men and who was said to hold pro-Soviet views. More likely than being purged himself, at least not yet, San Yu was probably being neutralized by the wily Ne Win, who had got wind of an alleged plot to have San Yu replace him. If a power struggle of these dimensions actually was going on, Ne Win apparently nipped it in the bud, and if San Yu remained the country's No. 2 man, his chances of succeeding Ne Win were diminished. More and more, Ne Win seemed to depend on his intelligence and security aides for support, and it was said that one of them would ultimately be his successor. The political atmosphere was further charged by two additional treason trials, one of them involving a plot by two Karen nationals to kill Ne Win during a reception at his house on the shores of Lake Inya, on the outskirts of the city, and the other an armed secessionist rebellion in Arakan. At another Special Party Congress, late in 1977, Ne Win lashed out at "opportunists and schemers" anew and fired some more members of the Central Committee on charges of corruption in the purchase of cars far below the market price. He replaced them with more military men of his own choice whom he admonished to live within their means and behave like "worldly saints"—a standard he hardly set himself. The liberals in the party having been purged, the hard-line socialists now bore the brunt, and many of them were ousted, too, which appeared to leave the military in complete control. To a considerable extent, this drove Burma back into at least a temporary state of isolation and withdrawal.

The Future Seems Bleak

On the economic front, after two fairly good years of growth in 1976 and 1977, the situation again deteriorated in 1978. The earlier improvement had in large part resulted from the adoption of a tax-reform program urged by the World Bank, including the imposition of a commodities and service tax which reduced domestic borrowing for budget purposes and slowed down the money supply while lowering consumer prices. The taxes narrowed the price gap between goods sold in the state-run stores and those sold on the ubiquitous black market, but by mid-1978 the latter was again flourishing and it was estimated that three quarters of Burma's internal commerce and two thirds of its foreign trade were being conducted illegally. As the economy flattened out—a disappointing rice crop after two good years did little to help matters —Ne Win again called for the peasants and workers to stimulate production, "making up for the lost time due to disruptions," but farmers and workers were complaining about high prices more than ever, and about low levels of income.

The Burmese had been persuaded by the World Bank and the seven-nation Burma Aid Group to begin a number of feasibility studies for industrial and agricultural projects, including two to stimulate rubber, rice, cotton and groundnut production, and the government had swung a $38 million loan from a syndicate headed by the Chase Manhattan Bank to build two hundred miles of oil pipeline for speeding the distribution of onshore oil production; Burma was luckily self-sufficient in oil, but its hopes of a few years back for profitable offshore development had proved illusory when about twenty exploratory wells struck nothing, though further drilling was being contemplated if foreign funds could be obtained. In addition, the West Germans and the Japanese had agreed to lend Burma $165 million for a number of agricultural development projects. But perhaps most important, and most discouraging, a new Right of Private Enterprise Law late in 1977 seemed to have abrogated the promises of March, continuing the ban on private foreign investments and disappointing many who had hoped that Burma had meant what it said about welcoming venture capital from abroad. An American embassy report said that the lack of guidelines and incentives "combine to make Burma a rather unattractive investment prospect."

Conceivably, if the Burmese gained more confidence in themselves and tempered their stubborn self-reliance with a real willingness to cooperate more with the rest of the world, they might ultimately prove the validity of the "Burmese way," blending their own form of socialism with industrial development to complement their strong agricultural base. They were at least no longer averse to accepting foreign assistance as long as no strings were attached, and perhaps, in time, they would engage in joint private ventures they still seemed so ambivalent about. Admirers of the Burmese, including some Americans, believed that they could play a unique role in Southeast Asia and that they would eventually shape a form of government for themselves which others would emulate rather than condemn or ridicule. While the Burmese had not yet joined ASEAN, they publicly approved of many of its aims and accomplishments, and in their odd-man-out situation they could eventually act as a catalyst in the formulation of a broader regional grouping that might even include the Indochina nations. But as long as Burma remained essentially a military dictatorship, under Ne Win's despotic hand, there was not much chance for the country to play a wider effective role.

With the elections in January 1978 for a new People's Congress, Ne Win, automatically rechosen, also automatically continued as chairman of the State Council and President of the Socialist Republic of the Union of Burma. There were no signs, despite recurrent rumors, that at sixty-six he was ready to hand over the reins to anyone else. In fact, his new marriage, to a woman twenty years his junior, a great-granddaughter of the last Burmese king, seemed to have rejuvenated him. An ambulance equipped with a heart-lung machine that used to follow him around the golf course was dismissed, though the customary quartet of soldiers with cocked rifles still attended his every shot. He once loved to gamble and kept a sizable stable of horses, but a number of years ago he gave up that hobby, shut down Rangoon's popular race track (which was thereafter used for public meetings), and devoted his leisure moments to putting instead of punting. Ever since the assassination of President John F. Kennedy he had grown increasingly apprehensive, banned the possession of telescopic sights for guns and stationed soldiers on rooftops and at traffic circles throughout the city, and a bevy of black limousines and motorcycle police accompanied him wherever he went. Though he appeared in public in his own country only two or three times a year, Ne Win made frequent trips abroad, utilizing Burma's only modern jet transport and throwing off all the national airline's domestic schedules as well as its flights to Bangkok and Hong Kong.

In spite of the propaganda for new dynamic policies, the atmosphere in Rangoon late in 1978 remained repressive and depressing. Censorship of the press had increased, and editors were not only told what not to print but what to print, and to stay away from foreigners. Tourism, potentially a considerable source of foreign exchange, was still all but neglected, despite the beauties of the Buddhist temples at Pagan, north of Rangoon, which had been struck by a disastrous earthquake in the summer of 1975 but had been almost completely restored. Farther to the north lies Mandalay—the romantic road to which Kipling immortalized—whose chief attractions, however, as I discovered on a trip I took there, were the variety of its black-market goods and the colorful history of its profligate earlier kings, whose peccadilloes were eagerly recounted to visitors by shuffling guides who were not averse to interspersing their accounts by offers of bargains for jade or rubies. Despite his famous lyrics, Kipling actually never got to Mandalay, and were he to visit Burma today, it is doubtful that he would find it worth a song or a sonnet. The return of George Orwell might be more to the point.

Malaysia-
Races Against
Time

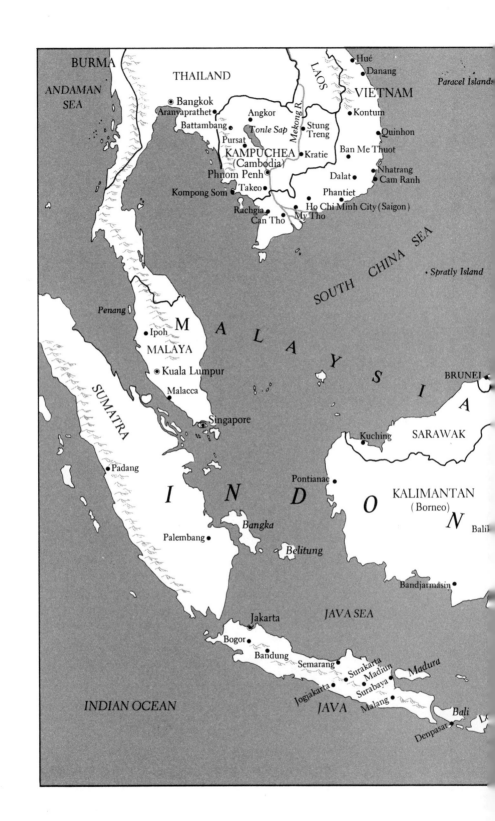

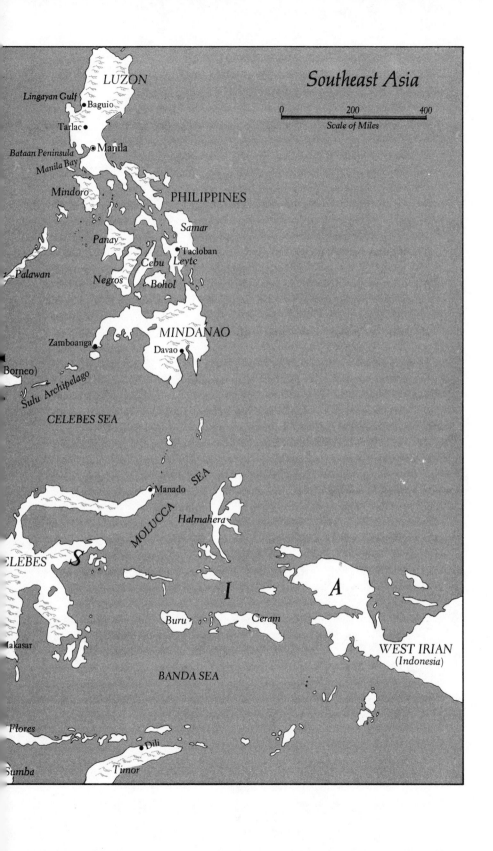

Southeast Asia

0   200   400

Scale of Miles

LUZON

Lingayan Gulf

• Baguio

Tarlac •

Bataan Peninsula

◎ Manila

Manila Bay

Mindoro

PHILIPPINES

Samar

Panay

• Tacloban

Cebu   Leyte

Palawan

Negros   Bohol

MINDANAO

Zamboanga

Davao •

Borneo)

Sulu Archipelago

CELEBES SEA

MOLUCCA SEA

• Manado

Halmahera

CELEBES   S

I

A

Buru   Ceram

WEST IRIAN
(Indonesia)

Makasar

BANDA SEA

Flores

• Dili

Sumba   Timor

Kuala Lumpur has undergone many changes over the years, acquiring some of the posh attributes and modern symbols of other Asian cities, even including a new million-dollar mosque that looks like something out of Las Vegas; but Malaysia as a whole—until one digs beneath the surface—seems to have undergone fewer changes than most Southeast Asian nations. This misleading impression of stability is partly due to the fact that it has held on to a number of British ways and customs. In Malaya, unlike other places that were under the imperialist yoke, nationalism had been watered down by circumstances going back to the manner in which the Malayans (before they became Malaysians) were accorded their freedom by the British a decade after World War II without having to fight for it. This took place, moreover, at a time when British soldiers were fighting to protect Malayan freedom against an armed Communist insurrection, known as the Emergency, which lasted all through the fifties.

There are various odd manifestations and hangovers of the British way of life that blend with the Malayan. Most weekends, for example, horse races are held in one of the three largest cities—in Kuala Lumpur, the capital, or in Penang, or in Ipoh—but no matter which track the horses are running on, during the races the stands at all three tracks are always filled with thousands of shouting people. When they are off at Ipoh, enthusiastic crowds in Kuala Lumpur and Penang stream out to the tracks, placing their bets and following the progress of the races over loudspeakers; between races they study their racing forms, evaluate the odds and discuss the pros and cons of each horse as if it were parading in front of them; then, without benefit even of closed-circuit television, they await the results, which are relayed by telephone.

A visitor who stays in the country for any length of time soon realizes that there is something symbolic, and a little scary, about this invisible horse racing. Its sense of unreality is indicative of something else that the casual visitor might tend to miss or disregard. Outwardly Malaysia is indeed a peaceful and prosperous nation, which, like Indonesia, has a tremendous wealth of natural resources, including much of the world's supplies of rubber, tin and palm oil, but beneath the bustling commercial exterior are all sorts of invisible pressures —primarily racial tensions. Because of them, highly complicated political, social and economic forces are at work almost constantly among the mixed population, chiefly Malay, but including large numbers of Chinese as well as Indians, and the tensions these pressures produce are high. In fact, they are sufficient to occupy most of the attention of the nation's leaders most of the time, and consciously or unconsciously, to preoccupy the bulk of Malaysia's 12 million people all their lives.

The country's communal problems are endemic and chronic, and they are exacerbated by poverty, which, though the government has for years made sincere efforts to ameliorate it, remains widespread—worst in the countryside but bad in the growing urban centers as well. "There may be a cure for poverty, but there is no cure for communalism," a Western diplomat with many years' experience in Malaysia once commented to me. "The search for a common Malaysian identity is an illusion that continues to be pursued. It will never become a reality."

In the years of relative racial peace that marked the seventies, the attempt to establish such an identity was pursued even more vigorously than before, through economic and social measures aimed at establishing a greater degree of equality among the various races, but the formulas, mostly designed to elevate the status of the poorer Malays, did not work as well as expected. Nor have they eliminated the causes of racial friction, and to a certain extent, they have created new animosities among the Malays themselves over issues of money and privilege.

No other country in Southeast Asia, in fact, has had to contend with such a plethora of racial problems, and they are compounded by geography. Eleven states make up West, or Peninsular, Malaysia, on the Asian mainland, which in 1978 had a population of 10.25 million, composed of 5.3 million Malays, 3.5 million Chinese, slightly over 1 million Indians, and scattered Pakistanis, Sri Lankans, aborigines and Europeans. East Malaysia, which used to be northern Borneo, occupies about a quarter of one of the world's largest islands —at its nearest point, it is four hundred miles from West Malaysia across the South China Sea—and consists of the two states of Sarawak and Sabah, the former with a population of 1.1 million, and the latter with a population of 900,000. Tribal Sea and Land Dyaks, some of them known as Ibans, are the predominant racial element in Sarawak, and then come Chinese and Malays. In Sabah the largest single group is the Kadazans, a native people also called Dusuns; there are 150,000 Chinese and a mere 30,000 Malays, and the rest of the population is a conglomeration of half a dozen different indigenous tribes and races.

Even if complete racial harmony had obtained among these disparate elements spread over 300,000 square miles of land and sea, it would have been no easy task to maintain a well-ordered government, amid endless religious, social and economic differences fanned by political rivalries. The governments in Kuala Lumpur and in the separate states of Malaysia have managed to keep going since 1957, which was when Malaya (present-day West Malaysia) obtained full independence from Britain and changed its name to the Federation of Malaya, under a parliamentary government embellished by a ceremonial monarchy and a set of sultans. The nation became Malaysia in 1963, when Sabah and Sarawak were joined to it. Singapore, the Chinese island port just to the south of West Malaysia, also became part of the larger federation in 1963, but after two tempestuous years of racial friction it broke away and became an independent republic. For two long decades, there had been a constant feeling that the whole structure—including the often contentious individual state governments, headed by chief ministers and with their own elective assemblies—hung by slender threads which could at any moment give way.

Countering the Insurgency

I saw them come close to giving way on a number of occasions. When the Federation of Malaya was born, the country was still in the throes of the Emergency. This was led by 8,000 Chinese, mostly rural residents who were armed by Peking and supported by between 250,000 and 500,000 members of a native underground network. The Emergency officially lasted twelve years, until 1960 (I covered it in 1951–1952), and 100,000 British soldiers and police were eventually needed to quell it. Because memories of this prolonged crisis remained strong, the Malaysians were concerned about a renewed insurgency that began to pick up again seriously in 1974, even though the number of armed Communists, including several hundred survivors of the Emergency, this time totaled only about 3,000 or 4,000, and only 400 or so were ever in West Malaysia at a time, the rest being gathered in sanctuaries across the border in southern Thailand. Adopting somewhat different tactics, the insurgents, who as before took their chief ideological cue from Peking, targeted top government officials instead of British planters, and managed to assassinate, among others, the nation's top police official as well as the police chief of Ipoh. Unlike in the past, too, they resorted to urban as well as rural terrorism.

By mid-1978, after working out a complicated series of joint operations with the Thais that were aimed at driving the insurgents out of their jungle sanctuaries, the Malaysians appeared to have disrupted this new Communist revolutionary effort but not to have destroyed it. They succeeded in upsetting the insurgents' lines of supply and communication, and they killed or arrested several thousand, detaining hundreds accused of being members of the new underground. They also suffered about two hundred casualties of their own, primarily soldiers killed or maimed in ambushes or as a result of cleverly placed booby-traps in the jungle.

With the continued support of the Thais (but with no help from the British this time), the Malaysians put further pressure on the insurgents, keeping them on the run. They appeared able to contain this fresh threat, but as long as it existed at all they worried because of the racial frictions behind it, and because of the possibility, depending on what happened on the still-explosive Indochina peninsula, that the Chinese and/or the Vietnamese would inject themselves into the contest. The situation was aggravated further because the Communists, spurred by the Russians, were trying, with some success, to enlist Malays as well as local Chinese, to whom they had confined their recruitment efforts during the earlier Emergency. And if the insurgency was not permanently contained or destroyed, particularly if it received outside help, the government feared not only a wider conflict but a repetition on a larger scale of communal violence such as had occurred in May 1969, when about 250 Chinese, 30 Malays and 20 Indians were killed in brutal rioting that began and was centered in Kuala Lumpur but also spread to some other cities.

In October 1975, as part of its campaign to quell the insurgency, the government issued a series of amendments to an emergency-powers ordinance that had been passed after the 1969 race riots and that was modeled on earlier legislation dating back to the Emergency. The amendments provided for virtual police-state control, and they provoked such opposition among judges and lawyers that they were revised a month later. Though this revised version was somewhat more specific—it modified the previous blanket definition of cases that involved "security," for example—the measures still were as tough a series of punitive laws as existed anywhere in non-Communist Asia. Early in 1979 there were about five or six hundred political prisoners in Malaysia, and under the regulations anyone committing a security offense was likely to be kept in jail indefinitely without being charged or tried. When he was tried, the trial took place before a special high court without a jury; the burden of proof was on the defendant rather than on the prosecutor; hooded and masked witnesses could give their evidence in camera, without the defendant or his counsel being present; secondary documentary and hearsay evidence obtained by police officers was admissible; and a defendant found guilty in a serious case could be given the death sentence, which under some circumstances was mandatory.

Privately some members of the government agreed with opposition critics that the laws were too draconian, that the internal dangers the nation faced were not severe enough to warrant them and that, in fact, rather than reducing the number of Communists, they would produce more. Others, however, including a powerful group of right-wing parliamentarians, felt that the laws should be even harsher. The issue came to a dramatic head in June 1976 with the arrests of Abdul Samad Ismael, the managing editor of the country's leading newspaper, the *New Straits Times,* and also one of its top novelists, and of a well-known editor of a Malay-language paper. Both men were accused of slanting news in such a way as to make it easier for the Communists to influence the Malays. The case, which caused an immediate sensation in Kuala Lumpur, blew sky-high in September when Samad confessed, on television, that he had been a secret agent trying to subvert the government for more than a decade on orders from foreign Communists (he did not specify whether

Chinese or Russian, but the implication was Russian) and that he had succeeded in influencing a number of important government officials. He had told the police that his targets had included a small group of insiders around Prime Minister Abdul Razak (who had died of leukemia in January 1976 and had been succeeded by Hussein Onn, the Deputy Prime Minister).

In November two of the men named by Samad, whom Hussein had kept in his cabinet, were detained under the security laws, along with the executive secretary of the Malaysian Chinese Association (MCA), a conservative group that supported the government, and three officials of opposition parties. Then, early in February 1977 those two top figures made dramatic appearances on television and confessed that they had been active Soviet propagandists for the past decade. Both men (Abdullah Majid, who had been Deputy Minister of Labor and Manpower before his arrest, and Abdullah Ahmad, Deputy Minister of Science, Technology and Environment) said they had maintained close associations with officials of "a certain foreign mission" in Kuala Lumpur since 1968—the Soviet mission was the only Communist one in the country at the time. Majid said, "I had allowed myself to be an accessory to their political designs and promoted their interests to achieve the long-term goal of international Communism," while Ahmad stated that he had been persuaded that Communists would eventually dominate Malaysia and that "the only option left for the Malays would be to accept [the Soviet] brand of Communism, which professes to allow the practice of Islam and the continuance of Malay tradition, culture and the monarchy."

Both of the accused pledged their loyalty to the Malaysian government and monarchy henceforth, but despite their confessions they were kept in jail under the emergency measures. Another of those arrested, Chan Kien Sin, the executive secretary of the MCA and a former editor in chief of the leading Chinese newspaper in the country, also confessed, but to being a pro-Chinese Communist, engaged chiefly in spreading anti-Soviet and anti-American propaganda in the country.

Security and Human Rights

These arrests and confessions not only shook the nation but brought to a sudden climax a struggle in the highest government echelons as well as in the mixed ranks of the nation's dominant political party, the United Malays National Organization (UMNO), of which Hussein became the acting head when he succeeded to the prime-ministership. The struggle actually went back several years, to when right-wing leaders of the party charged that Prime Minister Razak had allowed himself to be surrounded by men who were either Communists or pro-Communists, including the two arrested deputy ministers, who were then depicted as members of Razak's "palace guard."

While Razak was sometimes accused of being "soft" on Communism, or at least of having allowed himself to be misled, no such accusations were made against Hussein, a punctilious, rather prissy man, who had surprised most people by the firmness with which he took over after Razak's death. He had by no means the solid support of all the other UMNO leaders, who had always run the gamut from so-called ultras (or reactionary Malays), to liberals (or self-styled Islamic Socialists), to technocrats who tried to stay aloof from ideological issues but who also sometimes had become engaged in the bitter infighting that was traditionally part of UMNO politics.

The confessions of Abdul Samad, and the arrests and confessions that followed, brought out into the open some long-smoldering fights among various factions in the party, both at the national level and in several of the state organizations, some of which came into conflict with the central authority over both political and economic issues. A number of personal rivalries and animosities were also re-ignited. Accusations that right-wing leaders, including some of the most powerful people in the country, were consciously and purposely trying to conduct a witch hunt and to create a climate of McCarthyism were met with countercharges that the UMNO had, in fact, been infiltrated by Communists. Though the televised confessions seemed genuine, it was also apparent that the way they had been promoted was designed to further the political ambitions of certain UMNO leaders, particularly those of Home Affairs Minister Tan Sri Ghazali Shafie, the man in charge of security activities.

During 1976 and 1977, about fifty persons were sentenced to death for security violations, but as far as is known none were executed. Many of them received mandatory sentences of death for unlawful possession of firearms or ammunition "in a security area," which had come to embrace the whole country because of the new insurgency. In the fall of 1977 a fourteen-year-old boy (his name was never revealed) was arrested by police for illegal possession of arms—a pistol and twenty rounds of ammunition in a plastic bag, which he claimed he had been given by a "gangster" who had told him not to open the package. Since the security laws covered common criminals too, the boy was given a mandatory death sentence, and this sparked a fresh debate about the regulations being much too tough. Many groups, among them the Bar Council of Malaya, as well as civil libertarians around the world, publicly denounced the sentence as inhumane and declared that human and civil rights in Malaysia were being eroded if not destroyed. The criticism mounted, even though the death sentence was finally commuted after the boy received a royal pardon and was ordered detained in a juvenile reform school until he was twenty-one; but the government, after saying it would make a fresh review of the most stringent security amendments, decided not to make any changes, claiming that the laws had been enacted "with extreme care and caution" to deal with "the extraordinary circumstances" of the new internal threat.

During a trip to Washington about the time of the boy's arrest, Hussein had defended the security measures, saying, "It is true that the safeguards provided for in the act may not meet or satisfy the requirements of civil liberties as understood by many Western nations. This unfortunately cannot be helped, as we have had the distinct choice of either fighting the terrorists to safeguard our democratic ideals or succumbing to them by allowing them to exploit effectively inherent weaknesses in our democratic system." His arguments—which other Asian leaders, including Singapore's Prime Minister Lee Kuan Yew and Philippine President Ferdinand Marcos concurred in—served to emphasize some of the fundamental disagreements between Third World countries and the Western nations with their longer traditions of democracy and civil rights. This certainly included the United States, under President Jimmy Carter, but Asians were increasingly pointing to American shortcomings in the human rights field too and beginning to resent being lectured by a country whose improvements in that field were still only partially implemented and still far from perfect. Ironically, during Hussein's visit to America, Carter was quoted by a Malaysian official as saying that Malaysia's record on human rights was "a model for others," a comment which, if Carter indeed made it, caused some raised eyebrows in Malaysia.

The fact is that cultural and social as well as psychological and political values in Asia are so different from those in the West that what often appears to Westerners to be gross violations of human rights is not always regarded in the same light by Asians—a point that Marcos and Lee Kuan Yew have also been making. Since the value systems of the Orient and the Occident are obviously different, this has easily led to conflicts of understanding. At the same time, despite Carter's not altogether consistent approach to the human rights issue, his emphasis on it became an important factor in making a number of Asian nations, other than Communist countries, think twice about the severity of their security regulations, and Malaysia is no exception.

Throughout this difficult period Hussein managed to keep his cool and to prevent intraparty conflicts from reaching a point where they threatened the basic unity that the UMNO had always managed to maintain under pressure. While constantly stressing the dangers of the new insurgency becoming stronger and insisting that this required vigilance and firmness, Hussein also emphasized that only by redressing racial imbalances to improve economic conditions for the poor could Malaysia in the long run survive. His admonitions about creating a sounder social and economic balance—which did not appear easy to accomplish in the growing atmosphere of nervousness and tension around the country—could be traced directly to the cataclysmic riots of 1969. More than anything before or since, these outbreaks demonstrated the fragility of the new nation, and made its leaders far more aware of and sensitive to the dangers of ethnic and political instability.

The communal riots were precipitated by the national and state elections of 1969, which jolted the UMNO, until then confident that it was in firm control and that the so-called Alliance it had formed, in 1955, with the Malayan (later Malaysian) Chinese Association and with the equally conservative Malayan Indian Congress, had no serious opposition. The election proved otherwise. The results dropped the number of Alliance seats from the 1964 figure of 89 to 66 and raised the opposition number from 15 to 37. In addition, the opposition parties made significant gains in the elections for state assemblies. Not only did minority Malay parties, including an ultraconservative faction, win more seats but—what was more disturbing as far as the UMNO was concerned—new, more militant Chinese parties made strong inroads into the strength of the placid and pliable Malaysian Chinese Association. The UMNO feared that the power of the Alliance was being dangerously eroded by upstart Chinese elements, and saw its grip on the country slipping away.

Effect of 1969 Riots

Accounts of the riots still vary, but there was no dispute about the prime cause: the UMNO's inability to form a state government in Selangor, where Kuala Lumpur is situated, because the new Chinese parties had taken away its majority. The UMNO tried to persuade a predominantly Chinese middle-of-the-road party known as Gerakan (the Malaysian People's Movement) to join the Alliance and set up a new Selangor administration, but Gerakan refused to go along. On May 9, members of Gerakan and of the more leftist Chinese Democratic Action Party marched on the home of the Selangor Chief Minister, Harun Idris, and demanded that he get out. A mob of Indians and Chinese started to run through the streets, jeering at Malays and shouting such slogans as "Kuala Lumpur is Chinese now!" and "Malays, go back to your villages!" and "Malays are powerless!"

Emotional UMNO youth leaders planned to retaliate by holding a procession on the evening of May 13. The procession, for which police permission had been obtained, was to start from Harun's residence, and the preceding evening Malay youths visited seven suburban kampongs, or villages, to mobilize support. At dusk, Harun's house was surrounded by a crowd of four or five thousand, some of its members armed with sticks and knives. Harun later claimed that he tried to calm the crowd, but others said he incited it further. At any rate, shortly before seven o'clock a van was set afire near Harun's residence, and two Chinese in it were killed by Malays. The mob in front of Harun's home then took off for a market place, where most of the two hundred fifty Chinese victims were killed, after which Chinese triad, or gangster, groups responded by raiding a theater and stabbing Malays in the audience. The riots spread quickly and the list of dead grew as police and troops reacted slowly.

Amok is a Malay word, and the 1969 amok has remained sharp ever since in the memories of Malaysians, who speak of it as a national blight that seared the land. Not only did a new state of national emergency have to be declared, but more significant, the riots created a crisis of confidence among the Malays, who had badly underestimated the feelings of resentment against them among the Chinese and Indians. The solidarity of the UMNO itself was threatened when the Malay ultras questioned the leadership of Prime Minister Abdul Rahman, who was also chairman of the party, and who believed firmly in cooperating with the Chinese and the Indians to maintain a multiracial government. Rahman weathered this criticism, thanks to the support of his closest aides, including Razak, who was then Deputy Prime Minister and in many ways already the most important figure in the government. In June and July of 1970, elections were held in Sabah and Sarawak, and those results proved a pleasant surprise for the Alliance: not only did it hold its own in Sarawak, but in Sabah a local merger of racial groups supporting the Alliance swept the boards. These elections led to the termination of the national emergency the following February, and to the restoration, for the time being, of democratic rule.

Having learned a lesson and been alerted to the dangers of the new, ambitious, liberal Chinese parties, the Malay-dominated Alliance, under Razak, who took over as Prime Minister in September 1970, moved to consolidate its somewhat tattered ranks. Razak, who was emotionally more Malay-oriented than Rahman, created a broader organization, called the Barisan Nasional (National Front) in time for the 1974 elections. Starting with eight parties, it grew to ten and then eleven, including the three original Alliance members; two basically Chinese parties, one of which was Gerakan; and a mixture of other racial groups, among them the Partai Islam, a right-wing Malay party which increasingly became a thorn in the UMNO's side. Razak's strategy paid off handsomely. In the 1974 federal elections, the National Front won 135 seats in Parliament and the opposition parties only 19—defections subsequently cut their number to 10. But the 1974 results were somewhat misleading. The opposition, though its members failed to work together and apportion seats, won 37 percent of the popular vote; but the national constituencies had been flagrantly gerrymandered to favor the rural Malay voters over the urban Chinese, which was why the minority parties, mostly Chinese, did so poorly.

Razak's maneuvering had worked for the moment, but the political situation remained uncertain, both within the UMNO itself and as far as its relations with its National Front partners were concerned. During 1976 and 1977, after Hussein had succeeded to the prime-ministership following Razak's death, there were a series of party crises in the handling of which Hussein demonstrated his ability to make difficult decisions and to be a tough party leader. His performance surprised many people who, while they had respected his moderate position and his background as a good lawyer and an astute politician, had doubted his capacity for running the country with a firm hand for very long.

As Prime Minister, Rahman had been a father figure, and in 1978, when he was in his mid-seventies, he was still playing an influential behind-the-scenes political role; he also wrote a weekly newspaper column which was often critical of his fellow UMNO politicians. Razak had been an administrator primarily, and because he was suffering from his fatal illness during two of his five years as Prime Minister, he had found it increasingly hard to deal with major problems. Hussein proved a more complicated personality. A somewhat impatient and testy man, who looked and acted like a schoolmaster, he was given to private brooding; he made most decisions by himself, or only after secret consultations with a few members of his staff. He was almost completely inaccessible to the press, though his public appearances, both in Malaysia and out, were invariably impressive. A heart condition requiring him to rest as much as possible exacerbated his natural reclusiveness. His most admirable quality was undoubtedly his high sense of rectitude, and this had marked his unusual political background. His father, Onn Bin Jaafar, was founder of the UMNO and one of the leaders in the fight for independence, but in 1953 he and Hussein had quit the UMNO to start a multiracial party, which they had felt was necessary to pursue the fight for independence. Their multiracialism, which Rahman later adopted, was more tactical than ideological, however, and both father and son were regarded as strong Moslem figures. Hussein did not re-enter politics until 1968, when he rejoined the UMNO, and the following year he ran successfully for Parliament and quickly rose thereafter toward the top of the party hierarchy.

Although the sultans and the king of Malaysia, who is chosen every five years from among the various sultans, play little or no active political role, they are kept informed and are consulted about important matters, much as the sovereign traditionally is in England. Thus, when Hussein selected Mahathir Mohammed as his deputy, he went to see the King (the Yang-di-Pertuan Agong, as he is called) before announcing the appointment at a press conference, which I attended, during which Hussein demonstrated both his sharp, often acerbic wit and his basic contempt for the press. Mahathir was chosen over two other senior vice presidents of the UMNO: Ghafar Baba, the Minister of Agriculture, who immediately resigned in a huff but later became secretary-general of the party; and Razaleigh Hamzah, who was named Minister of Finance. Ghafar had been generally favored to become Hussein's deputy, but mindful of the fact that Ghafar had a number of influential enemies, and not wishing to exacerbate the divisions within the UMNO, Hussein passed him over. As for Razaleigh, at thirty-seven he was considered too young for the job, and besides, he was unmarried; among Moslems, who are allowed as many as four wives, bachelorhood is looked upon as a handicap for high office.

Despite his radical Moslem background ("radical" in this instance meaning right-wing), Mahathir was thought by Hussein to be the most "prudent choice," as he put it—in effect the lesser of three evils. Some years earlier Mahathir had written a book called *The Malay Dilemma* in which he espoused the theory that ethnocultural deficiencies among the Malays necessitated their being given special consideration. Partly because of this chauvinistic argument, and because he was opposed to Prime Minister Rahman's multiracial policies, he was banished from the UMNO for a few years (the book is still banned in Malaysia). His appointment as Hussein's deputy, particularly important in view of Hussein's poor health, was not happily received by the Chinese at first, but Mahathir soon proved a highly able administrator and served as Hussein's troubleshooter in a number of crises. And despite his rightist reputation, he adopted moderate positions on most issues. For example, he opposed the rash of arrests and the television confessions of the two deputy ministers and other alleged Communists, which led to his being criticized by some of the leaders on the right. In Malaysia, bedfellows make strange politics.

Hussein Handles the "Ultras"

Hussein had to call upon all his judicial talents to handle the conflicts that plagued the UMNO from early on in his administration. His deep hatred of corruption and his determination to keep firm control over dissidents were clearly demonstrated in 1976 and 1977 by his almost ruthless handling of the case involving Harun Idris, the Selangor Chief Minister who had been the key figure in the 1969 riots. When Harun, one of the most powerful rightists in the UMNO, permitted the UMNO youth organization, which he headed, to criticize the new government on the grounds that the UMNO had lost control over the nation's affairs and had been infiltrated by Communists, Hussein moved against Harun with a surgical precision that amazed everyone and left little doubt about his ability to handle tough situations.

First he called a meeting of the UMNO Supreme Council at his home and persuaded it to expel Harun for breach of party discipline, which thus removed him from the leadership of the UMNO youth wing. Then, when Harun got the youth group to speak up for him, Hussein called the youth leaders together and gave them a thorough and effective rebuke, after which the Selangor state assembly removed Harun as Chief Minister. He had already been on leave from that office for several months because corruption charges had been filed against him for misuse of his state office and for forgery and "abetment of criminal breach of trust" in his handling of funds for the Bank Rakyat (People's Bank), which he headed. When I spoke with him at his sumptuous private home, in the spring of 1976, he insisted that he was the victim of a political plot engineered by the Communists, but he was shortly thereafter found guilty and sentenced to a total of six years on various charges, including one that he received money from the prestigious Hong Kong and Shanghai Banking Corporation, which had sought approval to put up a large new office building in downtown Kuala Lumpur. However, while his cases were still on appeal and before the judgments and sentences were upheld, he was readmitted to the UMNO, and the conservative faction he represented had regained control of the UMNO youth group. Harun's fall from grace, while it set limits on his greater political ambitions, did not preclude him from retaining a martyrlike influence in the UMNO's right-wing ranks; in September 1978, much to Hussein's annoyance, the annual convention of the party elected him to again be a member of its twenty-man Supreme Council, even though he was languishing in his cell at Pudu Jail half a mile away.

Hussein faced a second difficult situation in the state of Sabah, where the United Sabah National Organization (USNO), headed by another powerful figure named Mustapha Harun—no relation of Harun Idris but a friend of his —was defeated in state elections held in the spring of 1976 by a new party called Berjaya. Mustapha, who had been a Godfather figure in Sabah for more than a decade, having made a fortune out of timber concessions and squandered much of it in personal pleasure seeking and lavish living, had resigned as Chief Minister of Sabah some months before the election, claiming he was tired of politics; however, he still continued to run the state from behind the scenes until the election and Berjaya's upset victory. Berjaya was headed by Mohammed Fuad Stephens, who had been a "blood brother" of Mustapha's until the latter had threatened to take Sabah out of Malaysia and form a separate Moslem nation with himself as Sultan, which would ostensibly attract the Filipino Moslem rebels in Mindanao and the Sulu archipelago to its banner. Berjaya was started with the blessings of the late Prime Minister Razak specifically to clip Mustapha's wings when he became too flagrant in his self-aggrandizement.

Berjaya's election success was soon followed by tragedy when a private plane carrying eleven passengers, including Stephens, his son and three new government ministers, crashed as it was about to land in Kota Kinabalu, the state capital of Sabah, killing all occupants. The new Chief Minister, the No. 3 Berjaya man, Harris Salleh, quickly took over and managed to form a government. It had been a wild election, full of charges and countercharges and accompanied by a few bombings, and the situation undoubtedly would have got out of hand if Hussein had not sent over a thousand extra police to keep order. Corruption in Sabah remained widespread, and its 800,000 people, especially the backward tribal groups in the rural areas, had more or less been ignored, despite the state's rich resources. After indicating an initial desire to cooperate with Berjaya, Mustapha took over the leadership of USNO again and revived it as an opposition party, but he dropped his secessionist overtures and, like Berjaya, joined it to the National Front. Previously, the UMNO leaders in Kuala Lumpur had tried to wean Mustapha away from his Sabah fiefdom by offering him the national defense portfolio, but Mustapha had declined.

In the months that followed he seemed to lose his old clout, and in April 1978, sick in a London hospital, he resigned from the presidency of the UMNO, and while no one in Sabah or Kuala Lumpur was altogether sure that he was retiring from the political scene for good, it looked as if he was finished. To add insult to injury, his son, who had argued with his father in the past over some political issues, joined Berjaya.

Hussein's political problems, over and above the other major issues he was contending with, chiefly the insurgency and the economy, did not subside with time, and in 1977 and 1978 he had to deal with a number of other state crises involving several chief ministers who were engaged in their own political battles and maneuvers. Traditionally, there was an inbuilt conflict between the central government and the various states, which not only was the result of religious differences between Islamic extremists and moderates but also concerned economics and sharing the pie of privilege that derived, for example, from such things as profitable timber and mining concessions. Too many of the states were poor in resources, and thus became pawns in the contest for both power and profit, with consequent corrupt results.

In addition to the crises involving Harun and Mustapha, Hussein had to contend with another serious situation in one of the poorest states, Kelantan, which is on the Thai border, where the Chief Minister, Mohammed Nasir, of the right-wing Partai Islam, refused to accept his ouster by the state assembly, which regarded him as being too pro-UMNO. The PI had joined the UMNO in the National Front but was widely regarded as being primarily interested in prosecuting its own political future as a possible rival to the UMNO for leadership of the Moslems. When riots took place in Kelantan, with part of the population for and part against Nasir, Hussein sent in the police to restore order. Eventually a compromise was reached and Nasir temporarily bowed out as Chief Minister (he later formed his own party in alliance with the UMNO), but the UMNO's relations with the PI had reached a point of no return; matters came to a head between Hussein and PI leader Mohammed Asri Muda, an Islamic zealot who lived handsomely and maintained that it was more important for political parties to propagate the cause of Islam than to alleviate the economic lot of the poverty-ridden Malay *bumiputras,* or sons of the soil. The issue was not only the temporary establishment of federal rule in Kelantan but the more important question of Malay unity and the PI's threat to the UMNO. After a nasty confrontation, Hussein summoned a National Front meeting and, in effect, forced out the PI, reducing the Front's membership from eleven to ten parties and paving the way for Asri and the PI openly to challenge the UMNO, not only in Kelantan but also in other states, for the Malay vote. About the same time, political and commercial rivalries over a number of issues involving nepotism, corruption and land-grabbing also came to a head in the states of Malacca, Perak, Negri Sembilan and Sarawak, and these conflicts once more demonstrated the difficulties the UMNO faced in trying to hold together in the National Front a disparate and bickering group of Malay and non-Malay parties and individual leaders with their own ambitions, racial antipathies and axes to grind.

Hussein's Election Triumph

There were many who thought that Hussein had set a trap into which he might fall himself by pushing his program for "clean, honest and efficient government" too vigorously at the expense of the old-guard Moslems and three such tough "warlord" mavericks as Harun, Mustapha and Asri. But in July 1978 Hussein met the challenge head-on by calling for national elections a year in advance of the deadline for holding them, and he won a resounding personal victory. The Front captured 131 out of the total of 154 seats, and 239 out of 276 seats in the thirteen state assemblies. The PI suffered a resounding defeat, and the number of seats it held in the federal Parliament dropped from 13 to 5. But there were some ominous signs for the Front and for the UMNO. While the Front won 94 out of 114 seats, a percentage of 82.5, in Peninsular Malaysia, it only won 55 percent of the total vote, and the leading oppositionists, the outspoken and rambunctious Democratic Action Party (DAP), which was still overwhelmingly Chinese, collected nearly 21 percent of the total 5 million ballots cast, and jumped its number of parliamentary seats from 9 to 16, while the more conservative Malaysian Chinese Association dropped from 20 to 17. Hussein undoubtedly emerged in a stronger position, but if he had reined in the Moslem extremists, at least for the time being—and there were few who thought they would remain quiescent for long—he now faced a more tense situation of racial polarization as a result of the DAP's ascendancy, which had even won its first seat ever in eastern Malaysia, in Sabah. The DAP's overall success took place despite, or perhaps because of, the troubles of its leader, Lim Kit Siang, who had been charged with violating the Official Secrets Act by disclosing information about the government's purchase of four Swedish naval craft in 1976 (Lim was later found guilty and fined). But not only Lim won at the polls—so did two of his fellow candidates who were in jail under the Internal Security Act.

Over the months that followed the election, a number of events took place that once again demonstrated the invisible strains in the body politic and emphasized anew the underlying racial tensions. Late in August 1978, four Malayans were killed by guards when they tried to vandalize a Hindu temple in the town of Kerling, just north of Kuala Lumpur. During the year there had been two dozen similar assaults on such temples, which are the halls of worship in Malaysia for about 650,000 Hindus, or about 5 percent of the population, but this was the first time any of the attacks had led to deaths. Hussein moved quickly to allay the effects of the incident, stressing racial tolerance in an address at the annual Koran Reading Championship, but the attacks had been so mysterious and eerie that no one knew when they would stop.

In September, Hussein summoned the UMNO general assembly, at which he was formally elected president of the party—despite his election victory he had still been acting president. It was a foregone conclusion that he would win the job, but what shocked everyone was the fact that while he got 898 votes, a relatively obscure former party publicist and Moslem extremist from the state of Kedah named Sulaiman Palestin, who was a supporter of Harun Idris, won 250 votes; it was the first time a candidate for president had ever been opposed in the party's thirty-two-year history. (It was also at this meeting that Harun himself was re-elected to the party's Supreme Council.) The two things together were variously interpreted as a healthy sign that the UMNO was still subject to democratic dissent within its own ranks, or that the extremists were still very much alive.

Then, as the year drew to a close, another bone of contention refused to be buried. This concerned an effort on the part of the Chinese, acting through a privately organized company, to obtain the government's consent to establish a new university named Merdeka (which means "freedom" in Malay), to be open to all but which would be attended primarily by Chinese students, who felt themselves being squeezed out of opportunities for higher education by the government's policy of enrolling more Malays. At the UMNO convention, Education Minister Musa Hitam, one of the ablest of his party's younger leaders, had rejected the demand for the proposed university on the grounds that it would be in the private sector, that it would cater chiefly to the Chinese students, and that Chinese would be the medium of instruction—the government's policy was to make Malay the medium in all schools and universities. Despite Musa's tough posture, and the failure of legal efforts of the university's sponsors to prosecute their cause, the issue, which had existed for years, was not likely to remain dormant—a government ban on a Chinese rally objecting to Musa's decision particularly aroused the Democratic Action Party, which had taken the lead in supporting Merdeka University.

Finally, and perhaps most serious, was the racial backlash that resulted from the heavy influx of refugees from Vietnam, most of whom, at the end of 1978, were of Chinese origin. Over the past several years the Malaysians had reacted prejudicially to the question of refugees, accepting Moslems from Mindanao and the Sulu area and from Cambodia, while turning back boats from Vietnam. When other foreign countries, led by the United States and France, opened their doors and promised to take in more Vietnamese and other Indochina refugees, the Malaysians relented and allowed some boats to land, as the Thais had done all along, but as the figures in the temporary camps on the Malaysian coast rose to 75,000, the government and local officials again adopted tough measures and refused to accept any more. In some cases the boats were towed out to sea while Malaysian crowds stood and watched as they capsized and scores of people drowned. The incidents assumed particularly nasty racial overtones when one ship, the *Hai Hong*, carrying 2,500 refugees (primarily Chinese who had paid Vietnamese officials and Chinese shipping brokers $3,000 or $4,000 to get out of Vietnam), anchored offshore and the Malaysian officials refused to let them land. Eventually, the United States and France agreed to take them, but not until the *Hai Hong* had become an international cause célèbre. On top of the ambivalent election results and the other racial rumblings in the country, the refugee issue did little to help Hussein in his patient efforts to promote racial tolerance and unity.

Bold Economic Plans

Having won the election and consolidated his position at the UMNO convention, Hussein had to live up to the bold pledge he had made a year earlier, in July 1977, that he would stake his political future on the success of the Third Malaysia Plan. Malaysians have always doted on planning. The country initiated five-year plans back in 1956, when it was still Malaya, and volumes of studies and statistics on every phase of the society and the economy attested to its reputation as perhaps the most thoroughly self-analyzed of all the developing nations. Rural development was the thread running through practically all the plans, though what was called the First Malaysia Plan, of 1966–1970, placed its primary emphasis on integrating the economies of Peninsular Malaysia, Sabah and Sarawak. In the Second Plan, drawn up after the 1969 race riots and running from 1971 to 1975, the stress was on national unity and on a "New Economic Policy," which together had the objective of eradicating poverty among all Malaysians, irrespective of race, and "restructuring" the nation's society to correct economic imbalances among the races, with special attention being given to the Malay *bumiputras*. The Third Malaysia Plan, running through 1980, carried these social restructuring objectives further and envisaged the redistribution of wealth as well as incomes by 1990.

In 1970, according to the statistics, Malay ownership of share capital in what are known, in British terminology, as limited companies, was only 2.4 percent of the total, while foreigners, primarily Europeans, Americans and Japanese, held 63.3 percent, and Chinese and a much smaller number of Indians held 34.3 percent. Under the New Economic Policy, as spelled out in the Industrial Coordination Act, by 1990 the Malays were to hold 30 percent ownership in all new companies and in expanded investments of already existing ones; the indigenous Chinese, Indians and other Asians 40 percent; and the foreigners 30 percent. The total volume of industrial shares held was expected to increase by 1990 to five times what it was in 1970, as the manufacturing sector became larger and the value of the gross national product increased by a projected 8 percent annually.

The government argues that if its growth goals are attained, neither the Chinese nor other foreigners will lose their equity shares and that the Malays will simply obtain a larger volume of new shares. But the Chinese, in particular, as well as foreign investors I spoke with, were highly skeptical about retaining what they regarded as their fair share of the pie. In fact, midway through the Third Plan there was little indication that the objective of share redistribution would be met, for while Malaysia was prospering in most respects, due to its large export earnings from rubber, tin, palm oil, pepper and other resources—petroleum production was averaging more than 200,000 barrels a day—private investment, both foreign and domestic, was much lower than anticipated. Instead of running at the expected rate of a 10 percent increase per year, the rate was only 3 or 4 percent by mid-1978, and while the Malaysians blamed the world-wide recession, others put as much or more of the blame on the tough Industrial Coordination Act requirements and on the equally tough Petroleum Amendment Act, which gave Petronas, the government oil company, the federal government and the state governments 83.5 percent of the profits and royalties, while the private companies, such as Shell and Exxon, only got 16.5 percent. Most of the oil to date had been found off Sarawak and Sabah, and in the South China Sea, but no one yet knew how many more offshore deposits existed and whether Petronas would relax its terms in order to attract further exploration and development. Despite the tough financial terms, the foreign concerns, chiefly Exxon, pumped in more money, and between mid-1976 and mid-1978, crude-oil output and investment in all phases of the Malaysian oil and natural-gas industry doubled, and petroleum became Malaysia's second highest foreign exchange earner, after rubber. But foreign companies expressed only sporadic interest in developing natural resources such as bauxite and copper, and it seemed unlikely that the New Economic Policy investment goal of $18 billion, of which the private sector was to supply 60 percent and the public sector 40 percent, would be met.

Inequity of income distribution remained a major problem, despite Malaysia's great wealth of resources. One study of the World Bank based on the voluminous surveys of their own economy by the Malaysians showed that in the mid-seventies, 40 percent of the population had a total household income of less than 25 Malaysian dollars ($10) a month; 87 percent of these households belonged to farmers and farm laborers, most of whom were coconut farmers and rubber "smallholders" (who grew rubber trees on a few acres), and the rest were rice farmers, fishermen and landless workers; 77 percent of the households surveyed were Malay, and only 14 percent Chinese. The World Bank and other concerned groups and individuals agreed that future planning should place the heaviest emphasis on rural development, and that the secondary goal of restructuring the ethnic shares of incomes and employment was inextricably linked with alleviating widespread rural poverty. But critics of the planning carried out so far maintained that much more work had to be done on identifying the specific problems of the various poverty groups.

Some states—such as Kelantan and Trengganu, in the north—are far more backward than others, and there are different degrees and manifestations of poverty, which require diverse solutions. Political scientists and economists at the University of Malaya, in Kuala Lumpur, were among those who stressed this point, and one of them, Stephen Chee, wrote: "Rural poverty is directly attributable to the benign neglect of a benevolent colonial government which worked on the premise that Malays were best governed if they and their socio-cultural system were left uninterfered with. Consequently, the Malays became spectators to the economic modernization of the country." Chee also denied the earlier Mahathir argument that ethnocultural deficiencies warranted special treatment for the Malays. Such "racial stereotyping" was not justified, he said in a talk I had with him, and moreover, it had dangerous communal connotations, especially in view of the fact that since the 1969 riots "communalization has gone more subterranean and is more dangerous psychologically because it has become more politicized and could be catalyzed by the new insurgency."

In a long conversation I had in 1976 with Mahathir, he cited "the extreme insecurity of the Malays" as having been responsible for the 1969 riots and insisted that "we must redress the balance." It was a misunderstanding, he said, to conclude that policies to aid the *bumiputras* would only help the Malays. He mentioned a large project under way in one area to introduce double-cropping among Malay farmers by improving agricultural techniques. "This is not just helping the Malays," he said. "The first and biggest beneficiaries are the Chinese traders, contractors, machine-shop owners, and so on, because when the Malays make more money they don't put it in the bank unless they're saving for a trip to Mecca—they spend it.

Ninety percent of the original benefits thus go to the Chinese."

This might be true in some cases, but after leaving Mahathir, I spoke with a number of Chinese and Indians and came away with the definite feeling that the *bumiputra* policy had made them seriously doubt whether, in the long run, they had any future role in the country. Unquestionably, most of the economic wealth that was not in the hands of foreigners was in the hands of the Chinese, but the non-Malays were feeling increasingly discriminated against, Mahathir's claims notwithstanding. The feeling was especially strong among Chinese professional men, and several thousand doctors and lawyers had either already left Malaysia for such places as Australia and Taiwan or were talking about doing so. One Chinese, a young businessman who was also active in politics, remarked to me, more sharply than sadly, "We feel we have a reduced commitment here."

One of the objectives of the Third Malaysia Plan, actually, was to help poor rural Chinese too—especially those who had been living in the 465 so-called New Villages that were set up to isolate the Chinese peasants during the Emergency. These villages were badly neglected after the Emergency ended, and most of the Chinese who continued to live in them because they had nowhere else to go were landless; unless they were near towns, they found it hard to obtain any regular employment. There had been talk of turning over some government-owned land around these old quarantine villages to the Chinese, just as some non-Malay smallholders had been sold small parcels of land at low prices in heretofore rented rubber areas. In addition, primarily for the Malays but also for the Chinese, new cooperatives had been formed, with the hope that they would stimulate saving and investment in industry. Undoubtedly, once the recession was surmounted, Malaysia would become more of an industrial nation, not only as production of its principal resources increased but as the number and kinds of goods that could be fabricated and manufactured in the country grew in volume. But the doubt remained that even as the corporate structure grew, the vast majority of the poor *bumiputras* would benefit very much. Even if their incomes rose with wider employment in manufacturing and commerce, they were still not likely to amass enough savings to buy heavily into business or to purchase corporate shares.

Many independent observers were afraid that the restructuring that was supposed to take place under the New Economic Policy would increase tensions not only between the various races—primarily the Chinese and Indians versus the Malays—but within the ranks of the Malays themselves. Already a new Malay elite and middle class, taking advantage of the greater opportunities afforded Malays, were improving their living standards, most notably in the urban areas, where they tended to identify themselves with the better-off Chinese. Restructuring, according to a University of Malay professor, Dr. L. Lourdesamy, might actually decrease rather than promote national unity. He pointed out that none of the races were homogeneous—nor should they be, he added—and he wondered whether the question of unity was not essentially a problem of "politics and culture" rather than of economics.

Multiracial Answers Sought

In the opinion of many, the true solution was not Malay dominance through the UMNO and the National Front, but real and effective multiracial policies, along with concentration on ameliorating poverty and on improving "the quality of life" for all races. "We haven't thought sufficiently in humanitarian terms," said another faculty member, Professor Rahim Mohkzani. "There is no mechanism to take care of individuals who are unfairly treated, regardless of what race they come from. Too much stress is laid on economic input, not enough on social considerations." The Third Malaysia Plan did take some cognizance of these considerations, and there was a fresh emphasis on setting higher health and nutritional standards, on rural resettlement schemes and urban-squatter relocation, on elevating the status of women and encouraging the growth of consumer organizations. But in all these areas, as Mohkzani pointed out, adequate research and sufficient understanding of personal factors were still lacking.

Ever since independence, and especially since the 1969 race riots, it was the government's underlying principle that the lot of the Malays had to be improved economically at the same time that their hand was strengthened politically. In accepting a secondary political position, the Chinese (or most of them, at any rate) took comfort in their far superior economic status. As an American diplomat with long experience in Malaysia put it to me, "They adopted the attitude of 'We'll make do with our Mercedes 230s and let the Malays maintain political control.' But the restructuring plans are causing increased resentment as they take effect. New horizontal rather than vertical divisions are growing up, and by internalizing politics within the National Front, the government has restricted their scope, which is the opposite of what we try to do in the United States. The problem is compounded by the fact that there aren't any outstanding Chinese political leaders."

Another source of uneasiness among the Chinese and Indians was the growing predominance of the Malays in the civil service, particularly since there had been a decline of efficiency in many departments (the police are an exception) and some increase in corruption. As a friend of mine, an Indian, said, "The Malays don't work hard because they know they don't have to in order to get ahead, and the Chinese and Indians don't, either, because they know that even if they do, they won't get promoted."

Still other sources of racial friction remained language and education, which came to a head in the campaign for the Chinese-sponsored Merdeka University. Malay had been made the nation's official language back in 1957, though every ethnic community had the right to use its own language, and Chinese elementary and secondary schools, mostly privately owned, had continued to operate. By 1970 Malay had become the only language used in government primary schools, and by the late seventies practically all teaching through the university level was in Malay, so students and professors alike had to learn it. Private schools for the Chinese still existed, but if Chinese students wanted to attend the University of Malaya or one of the seven other institutions of higher learning in West Malaysia, they had to learn Malay. English remained the second language. The Malayanization process had been extended to university enrollment. The University of Malaya was once mostly Chinese, but by 1978 its student body of 9,000 or 10,000 was more than half Malay. The quality of teaching in many faculties, such as medicine, declined as Chinese and European professors left; and approximately as many university students —around 30,000—as were enrolled in Malaysia were studying abroad.

In December 1974, student demonstrations took place at the University of Malaya and three or four other institutions which, significantly, were not interracial but involved mainly the Malays. The trouble was sparked by the government's failure to handle a poverty problem in a Malay area two hundred miles from Kuala Lumpur—in Baling, in the northern state of Kedah, where poverty was widespread. With the price of rubber depressed, local smallholders became aroused after a boy was alleged to have died of starvation and five other people died when, in desperation, they ate poisonous roots. In late November ten thousand men, women and children started a protest march from Baling but were stopped by the police with tear gas. Two weeks later, when students had just come back from their annual holidays, three or four thousand of them marched from the University of Malaya campus, on the outskirts of Kuala Lumpur, to a big downtown grassy square called the Padang. Again the police broke up the march with tear gas, and though no one was killed, a number of people were hurt and more than a thousand students were arrested (all except half a dozen, who were still detained in 1978, were released).

This incident led to the passage of amendments in April 1975 to the Universities and University Colleges Act. Under the amended act, not more than five students could hold a meeting on any university property, no boycotts of classes were allowed, no student or student group could carry on any outside activities without special permission, and strict disciplinary rules, extending even to what a student could or could not keep in his dormitory, were imposed. Full group responsibility for any breach of discipline by a single student further inhibited student action, and severe penalties were imposed for violations. These rules, far harsher than those for students in any other non-Communist nation, with the possible exception of South Korea, were regarded by students and many faculty members, not to mention opposition political leaders, as more abhorrent than the security regulations in some ways, but there seemed to be little organized effort to change them. In addition to the new amendments, the structure of the University of Malaya was altered to give the chancellor and his assistants added disciplinary powers that verged on the dictatorial—a move deeply resented by the more liberal faculty members. Not without irony, early in 1979 the faculty itself was placed by the Ministry of Education under new severe Discipline of Staff rules that barred them from political activity and curbed their freedom to publish what they wished. The faculty rebelled and threatened to strike unless the regulations were ameliorated.

Although the 1974 student rebellion was not nearly as serious as the 1969 riots, it served to focus attention anew on the poverty issue. But despite its pervasiveness in the country, poverty scarcely seemed to affect the ordinary pace of life in Kuala Lumpur, which, with a population of about 800,000, is still one of Asia's smaller capitals. But there was a growing influx from the countryside, and one had only to go as far as the outskirts to come upon squatter areas, where as much as a third of the city's population lives in huts or shacks or other ramshackle dwellings. The government had instituted a housing program, but it had not kept up with the growing numbers of squatters. They were almost all rural Malays who had come to town in search of work and were grateful to get even the most menial jobs. The Malay poor, whose religion bids them to share what little they have, don't do much begging, and about the only beggars you see on the streets are Indians who are comparatively recent arrivals and have trouble getting citizenship and work papers.

In semimodernized downtown Kuala Lumpur, the contrasts between wealthy and lower-middle-class or working-class life are far more extreme than elsewhere in the country. While the old area around the Padang and the Selangor Club, where British planters still drink their whiskey and beer under slow-turning fans, has changed relatively little, the surrounding streets provide a strange mixture of old-style colonial government structures, run-down small shops, restaurants and supermarkets, and new banks, hotels and office buildings, which are the hub of the country's busy commercial and financial life. Malays in their colorful skirts and blouses and Indians in their longer saris and robes mingle with Europeans and smartly dressed Chinese. No one appears to be in a terrible hurry, but a lot seems to get done, especially when the prices of rubber, tin and palm oil are high rather than low. Over the last several years at least half the government ministries have been moved to the fringes of the city, away from the squatter areas and the flow of traffic, but as in all Asian cities, the traffic jams get worse each year, especially in the early-morning and late-afternoon hours.

Although Kuala Lumpur is unquestionably an Asian place, with remnant overtones of colonialism, the atmosphere is becoming more cosmopolitan, and such things as entertainment, including films and television shows, are increasingly Western—specifically more American. On one of my trips to the city, a Wild West Rodeo troupe was staying at my hotel; in their wide-brimmed hats and high-heeled cowboy boots, its members looked strange among the Malays and Chinese who packed the local stadium for each noisy, galloping performance. When I asked some Malay friends about this enthusiasm for remote cultural attractions, I was told that "we Malays are cultural escapists" and "we don't have much cultural heritage of our own." Literature, for example, is parochial, most of it consisting of simple poems and short stories published in magazines and newspapers. Moreover, the Malays of West Malaysia have no indigenous heroes, in contrast to the Indonesians, many of whom are of Malay origin but whose cultural pantheon is wide and varied and full of colorful historical and mythological figures. The Malayan peninsula was cut off from this cultural heritage because of its geographical separation from Indonesia by the Strait of Malacca. Besides, in the colonial period the British sought to Anglicize much of the society of the peninsula and keep the rest fragmented.

A search for local heroes continues, but sources seem pathetically thin. In 1975–1976, for example, an official committee spent $25,000 to investigate evidence that a man said to be more than a hundred years old (in his dotage, he insisted on remaining silent) was a former Malay warrior who had fought against the British in the nineteenth century. No firm conclusion was reached. A more active and earthy centenarian named Lebai Omar, whose age was said to be one hundred and seventeen, caused a sensation late in 1977 when, having been convicted by a Moslem religious court of living in "close proximity" with his forty-year-old mistress, he mortgaged his one-acre farm to pay for her fine and bicycled twenty-seven miles to obtain her release and bring her back to his home, where he married her—it was her fourth and his eighteenth marriage. He had avoided jail because of his age and because he had pledged in court to wed the woman. The secret of his longevity, he maintained, was biking, simple food and the practice of the martial (along with the marital) arts. Although he had been in trouble with the police and with jealous villagers before for his ardent womanizing, Omar became something of an overnight folk hero.

Hussein Looks Outward

While Hussein devoted most of his attention to domestic matters, he proved himself a capable regional leader as well. Malaysia had taken the lead in ASEAN in projecting the theory of Southeast Asia being a free, neutral and peaceful zone, and more than the other ASEAN members, had also sought to establish good relations with the Indochina states, while remaining neutral in the Sino-Soviet conflict. Kuala Lumpur accepted the fact that Peking and Hanoi lent ideological support and encouragement to the Malayan Communist Party, but as long as this support did not include material aid, the Malaysians were eager to maintain good bilateral relations with the Communist countries and cooperate with them, particularly with Vietnam, economically. But because of the ticklish racial situation, Vice Premier Teng Hsiao-ping was politely but coolly received when he visited Kuala Lumpur late in 1978.

Malaysia places its greatest concentration on building up trade relations with the United States, which buys most of its rubber and tin, and with the European nations, as well as with Japan, which in 1977 pledged $158 million in loans to help the Third Malaysia Plan. In the Middle East the Malaysians maintain a pro-Arab policy and have sponsored a number of international Islamic meetings. As one foreign affairs expert told me, "We can only live with the world as it is." Overall, the country's foreign policy is as much of a balancing act as its domestic policies are. But the balances, it seems to me, are mutually dependent in an extremely delicate way, and what has happened internally, including the maintenance of economic and racial stability, is bound to have an effect externally, particularly vis-à-vis Chinese and Vietnamese reactions. If the insurgency should get worse, and if Thailand should fail to hold together under new Communist pressures, Malaysia's position would certainly become extremely precarious.

Hussein and Malaysian military and security men are acutely aware of this, and for this reason have gone out of their way to restore close cooperative relations with Thailand, following a period of near rupture. Malaysia's only land border is with Thailand, and though it is only 320 miles long, this is enough to have caused both countries constant trouble. Were it not for the fact that the insurgents were using the southern Thai jungles as sanctuaries, the insurgency problem could have been more readily contained within Malaysia. For years the Thais cooperated with the Malaysians in trying to curb smuggling, but up until early 1977 they had not been particularly eager to hunt down the insurgents, who took a live-and-let-live attitude toward the inhabitants of southern Thailand, where old-fashioned banditry also flourished. The Thais tended more or less to ignore the insurgents and concentrated on chasing down the bandits, and to cope with an armed group of several hundred Moslem separatists, whom the Thais accused, with some justification, of receiving their inspiration from Moslem extremists in the northern Malaysian states. (Nine tenths of the inhabitants of southern Thailand are Moslems, and the separatist movement there has deep historical roots.) Moreover, the Thais had a more serious insurgency problem of their own to contend with in northern and northeastern Thailand.

In April 1976 a twelve-year border agreement between Thailand and Malaysia was all but abrogated when, following some demonstrations in the Betong district of southern Thailand (which were believed to have been Communist led, since Betong was virtually controlled by the Communists), the Thais demanded that several hundred Malaysian Field Force police regularly stationed there be withdrawn. The Malaysians were furious and relations between the two countries became strained, but a year later the two governments drew up a new and much more effective agreement, which provided for regular consultation on the whole issue of insurgency, and more important, for frequent joint military and police actions.

In the ensuing months, four such major actions were mounted, including one in which 2,000 Malaysian troops operated in Thai territory with 1,500 Thais for nearly three weeks. The operations, including shelling and bombing, were designed more to flush the insurgents out of their hideouts than to kill them, and then to keep them on the run so they would be unable to rebuild their supply depots and could be isolated and tracked down. The right of "hot pursuit"—which enabled troops of both countries to follow their respective insurgents across each other's borders—was fully re-established under the new agreement, and the Malaysians were allowed to enter Thailand beyond the previous limit of five miles. In addition, Malaysian soldiers were permitted to be stationed for certain limits of time on Thai soil. Some of the Malaysian officers were so sanguine about the joint operations that they predicted the insurgency would be stamped out in a year or two, especially as they began catching more terrorists. However, the insurgents have in the past proved themselves to be highly mobile and elusive, and most officials I spoke with agreed that though their long-range plans had been severely disrupted, they would be able to rebuild their jungle hideaways and their underground network and that only by persistent and repeated attacks could the government keep them on the defensive and prevent them from entering the phase of all-out guerrilla warfare.

In 1960 (when the Emergency ended) some five hundred Communist terrorists, as the Malaysians then called them, escaped to Thailand with their leader, Chin Peng, and set up camps where they set to work reappraising their policies and slowly building up their strength. In mid-1968, responding to a new revolutionary summons issued to all Communist parties by Chairman Mao Tse-tung, the Malayan Communist Party put out a directive for resumption of "the armed struggle" and "the people's war." The following year, members of the Malayan National Liberation Army (the armed wing of the party) began infiltrating small groups of men back into Peninsular Malaysia, with the initial objectives of regaining popular support in the form of food, money and intelligence, and signing up fresh recruits. They confined their activities at first to the four northern Malaysian states of Perak, Kedah, Kelantan and Pahang, and then gradually spread south. The race riots in May 1969 inspired them to intensify their campaign. In 1978 the Malaysians doubted that the Min Yuen (the underground People's Movement) had more than three or four thousand members, but there was no sure way of knowing, except from information given by captured members, which was usually fragmentary and confined to limited areas. What also worried the Malaysian security experts was that the Communists had succeeded in recruiting several hundred Malays by touting what they call "Islamic socialism."

Over the past several years the terrorists engaged in a number of daring attacks on government installations, using both grenades and guns; one day they blew up a monument in Kuala Lumpur commemorating the end of the Emergency. Such acts, together with the assassination of top police officials, indicated that the terrorists had devised a new strategy and tactics for urban as well as rural warfare. They also reached an accommodation with veteran gangster organizations that trafficked in drugs—another problem that worried the authorities, both in itself and as a means of further subverting and weakening the society. But the Communists, too, had their problems. Since 1970, as the result of a dispute over the execution of members suspected of being government infiltrators, two separate groups have broken away from the main body of the Malayan Communist Party, one calling itself the Revolutionary Faction and the other the Marxist-Leninist Faction. Though all three branches followed the Maoist line, the dispute was a serious one, and the opposing factions fought to the death in a number of skirmishes in the Thai sanctuary areas.

Each of the factions has its own flag, its own armed force and its own political apparatus. The split was aggravated by a lack of cohesive leadership —Chin Peng, in his late fifties, was believed to be in China, though he was said to make occasional secret trips to southern Thailand—and this shortage of leaders, particularly young dedicated men, was the biggest handicap the terrorists faced. It was only partly made up for by constant broadcasts over the Communist radio, run by the main branch of the party, and probably situated in Yunnan province, in China, which include ideological directives that are often highly detailed. Malaysian security men admitted that these broadcasts are effective in helping the underground terrorists capitalize on the legitimate grievances of local villagers, which are also broadcast in detail.

On a trip to Malaysia in 1976, I went on a day's tour by car and on foot through some of the same areas where, more than two decades earlier, I had watched British and Malayan operations during the Emergency. Malaysia is a beautiful country, and as our car moved through rolling green hills, lush valleys and rubber plantations there was a pervasive calm that seemed to belie any threat to peace, in contrast to the tension I remembered from before, when British planters locked themselves in their homes at night and kept their guns beside them, and when they never drove alone or unarmed along the often ambushed roads. But despite the calm this time, there was ample evidence in some of the New Villages we visited that the Communists still had the opportunity to benefit from poverty and economic neglect. A tenth of the country's population, mostly Chinese, was still living in these villages, and those we saw were obviously living at or near the subsistence level.

As we rode deeper into the jungle along a bumpy dirt road, we passed several clusters of huts inhabited by sparsely clad aborigines, another neglected group. At a police camp we received permission to proceed seven miles farther on, to a site where the military was conducting a search operation. At the army outpost the colonel in charge, a Malay, told us that his company had been combing the area for ten days but had not yet come across any Communists or found any supply dumps. The operation was continuing, he added somewhat bleakly. It was all oddly reminiscent, I thought, of similar futile American operations in Vietnam. The colonel was polite and friendly, but he said he wasn't authorized to brief us any further. He was obviously lonely out there in the jungle, however, and seemed glad for some company. He had had some training in America and had visited New York City, where, he said, he had a fine time. "Tell me," he said, "what's it like in Times Square these days?" I felt like telling him that things were tougher in the concrete jungle than in the jungles of Malaysia, but I was prudent and said nothing.

Singapore-
The
Technocratic
State

Of all the leaders of Southeast Asia, Lee Kuan Yew, the Prime Minister of Singapore, has long been regarded as the most intellectual, astute, irascible and endurable. Though only in his mid-fifties, he has been in office for two decades and has outlasted all others in the region with the exception of Prime Minister Pham Van Dong, of the Socialist Republic of Vietnam. Although he is a man who eschews adjectives and prefers blunt nouns and tough verbs, Lee's very brusqueness invites as much criticism as praise and qualifying appraisal, for he is at once brilliant and articulate, dogmatic and domineering, withdrawn and competitive, visionary and pragmatic.

He runs his tight, some would say uptight, domain as if it were an ancient fiefdom, or principality, which he has been called upon, in his judgment, to defend against all threats and portents of doom. In so doing, and despite or because of Singapore's geopolitical vulnerability, he has over the years become increasingly authoritarian and sometimes self-righteous in ways that dismay some of his former socialist and social democratic friends, who openly denounce him for his continuing socialist pretensions. Convinced as he is that Singapore's survival and salvation as a predominantly Chinese island-city in a Malay sea depend on its being able to create and sustain its own multiracial identity and to continue to prosper economically, chiefly as a sophisticated center of technology and industry and world trade, Lee believes implacably in his own firm disciplinary measures. These include the arrest and detention without trial of persons accused of engaging in Communist or Communist-front activities, control of the press through strict licensing regulations that preclude any outspoken editorial criticism, and control of labor unions in such a way that they have become a benign and integrated part of the paternal pattern of government.

It is Lee's strong conviction, as a self-styled realist, that concepts of civil liberties and personal freedom, much as he professes to respect them, necessarily have to be circumscribed by events and "adjusted to the circumstances of the times." Western standards of human rights, he maintains, even though they might appear to have a normative value, do not always apply to Asian situations and conditions. The conditions in Singapore, as he sees them, in contrast to those in Europe, where Communist parties have been seeking peaceful partnerships with democratic governments under the banner of Euro-communism, are affected and inevitably guided by the dominant fact that the Malayan Communist Party, small as it is, wants to take over both Peninsular Malaysia just to the north of Singapore as well as Singapore itself by subversion and by force. As Lee puts it, "They want it both ways—they want the ballot and the bullet—and they want the processes that go before the ballot to aid them both internally and internationally in the use of the ballot."

Lee here referred to the Vietnam war, which he supported, partly because he felt it would "gain time" for the rest of Southeast Asia to consolidate itself against Communism, and partly because it earned Singapore a lot of money through the sale of petroleum and other products to South Vietnam. The war, he believed, was "not fought in Vietnam alone—it was fought in Washington, it was fought in the streets of Stockholm, it was fought in Sydney, in Melbourne, in Paris and London." Part of this, of course, was true, and the North Vietnamese were very adept in capitalizing on rising world opinion against the war, but in the much smaller context of Singapore, one wondered if Lee was not going too far and setting a simplistic trap for himself when he suggested that "if they can portray me as corrupt, fatuous, dictatorial, capricious, wicked, vicious, then half the battle is won because when the fight begins, I've got to get arms."

The whole question of whether Lee Kuan Yew "goes too far" is at the root of the problem in Singapore. Its record of success since it was thrown out of the Malaysian Federation in 1965 after two tempestuous years of merger, which coincidentally marked its complete independence from Great Britain, has been one of the most remarkable in Asia. In fact, between 1959, when Lee's People's Action Party (PAP) first took office with full internal self-government, and 1978, Singapore's annual gross national product grew from $643 million to more than $7 billion, and real per capita income soared to almost $3,000 a year (even higher in terms of current price valuations), which was second only to Japan's in Asia.

Success Story

The saga of economic success had unfolded slowly at first. The early years of PAP rule were marked by bitter and violent strife with the Communists, with whom Lee and the PAP broke after a period of initial cooperation. As late as 1963 (the year that merger began), a strong minority-led Communist-led opposition still existed in the Singapore Parliament. Lee and his associates finally eliminated it, mostly by jailing the top Communist leaders, and at the same time began building up the economic and social infrastructure to make the small state of 220 square miles not only self-sufficient but an attractive regional and international manufacturing and marketing emporium.

Within a short time new industrial estates sprang up, roads and factories were built, shipyards expanded, and various measures including tax incentives, special banking facilities and controlled labor costs were used to lure foreign investors. The old colonial society was transformed in less than a decade into what Lee called a "rugged" society based on free and open capitalist enterprise and initiative. The investors, starting with small firms making such things as textile products and plastics, poured into Singapore, and then came the multinationals producing a wide range of sophisticated industrial products that included machines of all kinds, electronics, transportation equipment, fabricated steel, oil rigs, and so on, all of which turned the island republic of 2.3 million people into what its Economic Development Board proudly called "a technological center."

Before the oil crisis, the annual growth had built up to 12 and 15 percent; even in 1978, although hit by the recession and concerned about the future, particularly about growing protectionist policies of the larger industrialized nations, Singapore enjoyed a growth rate of 8 percent; in typical bold fashion, it was seeking, with modest success, to expand the scope of its trade and to reach agreements, in behalf of all the ASEAN countries and itself, bilaterally with the European Market nations and with the developing Third World countries too. Small though it is, Singapore has already become the twenty-third richest nation in the world.

This phenomenal growth, in the wake of the years of violence and political turmoil, created a psychological and emotional impetus of its own, as well as a confidence and brashness not unlike that of an early American frontier town of which Lee Kuan Yew was the omnipotent sheriff. His motto has long been that no one gets anything for nothing. There is nothing egalitarian about Singapore, or in Lee's philosophy—people get what they deserve, based on what they produce, and the best and smartest do better than others. The welfare state is anathema to him, though his increasingly regimented society does enjoy some welfare benefits.

He received an elitist education, first at Raffles in Singapore, and then, after narrowly avoiding being killed by the Japanese when they captured Singapore early in 1942, in England, where he became a devotee of the radical historian Harold Laski. He has remained an acknowledged member of the elite—but as a result of ability, not wealth. Utilizing these elitist concepts, he spoke of creating a "meritocracy," a governing core of leaders consisting of no more than two hundred trained and dedicated public servants. Performance is what counts, and performance begins early, as far as Lee is concerned—in the lower school grades. The creation of a bilingual or trilingual society has always been one of Lee's paramount objectives, and in 1978 he implemented this by establishing English as the principal language of trade and commerce, making it a mandatory subject in the Chinese schools; Mandarin was to become the main Chinese language, but other Chinese dialects, as well as Malay and Tamil, could still be used. All Malays (who form 15 percent of the population —the Chinese comprise 76 percent) would have to learn English, but not necessarily Chinese. Since half of Singapore's population is under twenty years of age, the significance of these language reforms is apparent.

"If we are to modernize and industrialize, we must be bilingual," Lee declared, in enunciating his new language policy. "English cuts across all racial and linguistic groups. It provides a neutral medium, giving no one any advantage in the competition for knowledge and jobs." The monolinguist, he warned, "is more likely to be a language chauvinist and a bigot. He only sees the world through one eye." But at the same time he admitted that Singapore would never completely become a multiracial or multicultural society. "There is always an undercurrent of competition for dominance between languages and cultures," he said, but "our special circumstances lead us rationally to accept the fact that English is the working language of our society."

A decade earlier, when Chinese chauvinism was still a large factor among the different dialect groups, Lee would not have been able to impose his new language policies so easily, but by 1978 the younger Chinese, many of whom already spoke English, accepted the fact that if they were to get good jobs and succeed in life, English had to be the *lingua franca*. Consequently, there was not too much grumbling on the part of the Chinese and the minority races. "What Lee Kuan Yew really runs in Singapore is a classroom, and we're all his pupils," one of his sometime critics remarked, with grudging praise. But others were less generous, on numerous counts. They felt that over the years he had indeed gone much "too far" and had created a dust-dry, driven, overadministered, unimaginative society guided by too many unnecessarily stringent rules and regulations. One of the jokes one heard was that "Singapore is a fine city—you get fined for everything from throwing cigarette butts on the street to jaywalking, and making too much noise at parties."

A former resident, returning for a visit and noting with dismay the sterile atmosphere of the place, commented, "The only sin in Singapore is cynicism." This may have been an exaggeration, but prosperity has certainly produced a certain dullness and cultural flatness, which is due at least in part to the multiplicity of restrictions and obligations that guide people's daily lives. Young people are overprotected to the point where parents complain that they have "little chance of being adventurous." In one instance, boy scouts attending a camp slept in classrooms instead of tents, ate packaged food instead of cooking their own, and went on simulated night hikes in midafternoon wearing blindfolds. The effect overall is dehumanizing.

"It's Orwellian," said a friend of mine who had lived in Singapore for fifteen years. "People act like robots—Lee even used to call them digits! They have no stimulus in their lives. It all works smoothly, but the city lacks a soul."

If, as some say, Singapore has become a "bored" rather than a "rugged" society, there are some manifestations of the growing discontent, such as an increase in the use of drugs and in gambling, and a passion on the part of youths for motorcycle racing on the expressways (they are known as "Hell Riders"). They disrupt the flow of traffic, which, like everything else in Singapore, is controlled, confined to certain streets and areas at stated times of day. Though inconvenient, the rules work.

I went to visit Lee late in the spring of 1977, for the first time in ten years. I was astonished by the changes in the city; though I had heard about its tremendous growth and seen pictures of the place, I wasn't prepared for what I actually found: a new sparkling metropolis of tall office buildings and banks, and crowded high-rise hotels that seemed almost separate and apart from what remained of the old Singapore I remembered, which still existed below, along the waterfront and the canal. There people mingled around friendly foodstalls alongside battered sampans and barges, eating their meals and making small wagers about the flight of flies and fish or which of two chopsticks was longer. Many of the old British buildings were left too: the Cricket Club and its green mall; the cavernous but refurbished Raffles Hotel, where I had stayed twenty-five years earlier; City Hall, where Lee kept a seldom used office; and numerous nineteenth-century Gothic law courts and other government buildings. Unlike Hong Kong, which had been my home for fifteen years, and which was fast tearing down all its old landmarks on Victoria Island to make way for new tall office buildings within its narrower confines, Singapore was like two cities, with the new one superimposed on top of the old. I wondered how long it might take for someone to fashion concentric malls connecting the two, and what kind of Disneyland look that would produce.

Dinner with Lee

I had last visited Lee in his drab City Hall office, but this time he invited me to dinner at the Istana, the beautiful capacious residence of the former British Governor General on Oxford Rise, which covered several acres not far from the center of town; a few days later I saw him again in his office there. He was not living in the Istana but used it for both work and entertainment; he still resided in the same simple frame house he and his wife, who, like himself, was trained as a lawyer in England and ran Singapore's most prominent law firm, had occupied for a quarter of a century.

Lee looked somewhat younger than his age, but his handsome, mobile face betrayed the constant concern he felt for Singapore's future, and his expression was more quizzical than I had remembered it, and less vibrant. In one way he reminded me of a tragicomic actor in repose, and in another, of a classically sad, philosophic clown who no longer believed in making people laugh. Lee had always been an informal dresser, preferring open-neck shirts and easy lounge suits, and he wore such a suit on this occasion. He looked trim and fit in other respects—he has been an excellent golfer most of his adult life and regularly plays two or three times a week. As I walked over to meet him on the far side of the long room he rose to greet me, and in a manner I recalled from before, sized me up with a quick probing look that was slightly discomfiting, as if he were rendering a tentative preliminary grade prior to subjecting me to a major test or a fitness report.

In our talk I found him more mellow than before in most respects, but in some ways harsher. This was an ambivalent observation, but then again, Lee Kuan Yew is an ambivalent man. If he lacks ordinary charm, or for that matter, humor, he makes up for much of it with an incisiveness of mind, a remarkably quick perception and a consummate knowledge of the outside world, in which, in his cosmopolitan fashion, he has always felt at home—in fact, I had always sensed that Singapore in many ways is too small for him, and that part of his inner torment is due to a chronic case of political claustrophobia. His talents demand a larger historic arena; and it is part of his attraction, in lieu of gentler attributes, that one comprehends this need in his personality, which is often abrasive and intemperate but always outreaching, probing, and never dull.

Lee was born in Singapore, as was his father, but his grandfather and other forebears were Hakkas from South China. Despite his acquisition of genteel English attitudes and habits, Lee has retained his proud sense of independence, which is a racial trait. The Hakkas are a vigorous and aggressive tribal people who originally migrated, under the duress of the Tartars and Mongols, from North to South China, and many of them later drifted farther south and joined the overseas Chinese, the *hoa* people, numbering about 15 million today throughout Southeast Asia. Both Hakka men and women have retained their toughness and their sense of individuality and intrepidity; it is still a common sight, in Singapore and Hong Kong, to see Hakka women, wearing broad black cloth hats to ward off the sun or rain, doing major construction and repair work.

In our wide-ranging conversation lasting several hours, Lee expressed both his fears and his hopes for Singapore and for Southeast Asia, through ASEAN, to which he had made a much stronger commitment after the fall of Vietnam. "The shock of Vietnam and Cambodia gave ASEAN a fresh impetus," he said. "It was not taken seriously before—too many fluffy words. The problem now is to maintain the momentum and give it shape and direction, and we have made some progress." He cited five industrial projects the ASEAN countries had agreed to cooperate on and which the Japanese had agreed to help fund, but at the end of 1978 only Singapore had started work on its project—the construction of a diesel-engine plant. But Lee is too much of a realist, even a cynic, to have overabundant faith that regional cooperation among nations with competing interests and disparate attitudes and cultures could provide automatic formulas to solve economic and other conflicts. What counted first, he insisted, was what individual nations, through sound and positive leadership, did for their own people, and the best guarantees against Communism were sound local institutions with solid safeguards and prosperous economies.

The fall of Indochina to the Communists in 1975, he had said earlier during a trip to Washington, was "a lingering disaster fraught with serious consequences for the whole of Asia," but he did not believe that the North Vietnamese posed an immediate threat to the rest of Southeast Asia. The pattern he foresaw was one of the slow growth of insurgency forces in various countries; after they became more indigenous and locally led, they would try, through a mixture of propaganda, erosion of the will and endurance of local ruling groups and parties, and selective fighting in key places, to set up liberated areas as a prelude to an all-out attack, as had happened in Vietnam. But he did not see a possibility of this coming to a head for at least five or ten years. "That's about as far ahead as we can look," he told me.

Subsequently Lee was shaken by the Vietnamese attack on Cambodia, and along with other Southeast Asian leaders, regarded the Chinese attack on Vietnam as a setback for whatever further expansionist ideas Hanoi might have. But he became increasingly worried about the revolutionary pace in the region moving faster than he had anticipated. What disturbed him most, and what was obviously his greatest concern at the time of my talk with him, was the future of Thailand, for if Thailand became fragmented and the Communists took over parts of the north and northeast and the south, then Malaysia and Singapore would be directly threatened. He thought the Communists, whether Thai, Sino-Thai or Lao-Thai, would have a hard time converting the apolitical Thai peasants, and that any outside forces, particularly Vietnamese, would face a kind of reverse attrition. But at the same time he was skeptical about the ability of the Thais to mount consistent and effective counterinsurgency programs. At the time of our talk, Singapore and Thailand were trying to work out arrangements for exchanging military supplies each of them manufactured, but as Dr. Goh Keng Swee, the Deputy Prime Minister and Defense Minister, had told me, the Singaporeans were puzzled about "the Thai way of doing things," which was not nearly as direct and businesslike as the practical-minded Singaporeans would have liked.

Though Lee was in the process of consolidating a new trade relationship with Hanoi—full diplomatic relations were not yet in the offing—he obviously retained his fundamental mistrust of the Vietnamese Communists. He regarded with skepticism their blandishments and proffered olive branches to the various Southeast Asian nations while they continued to give moral support and encouragement to revolutionary movements in the area. He had expressed his dismay on this score to Phan Hien, the Deputy Foreign Minister of Vietnam, who had shortly before made a long trip through Southeast Asia, and he repeated his views to Premier Pham Van Dong when Dong had followed Hien in a swing through the region and had said that Hanoi would not seek to disrupt or overthrow any established government. When Vice Premier Teng Hsiao-ping followed Dong, Lee was even blunter in defending the independence of the ethnic Chinese in Southeast Asia, telling the equally feisty Teng that their future depended "directly on Singapore's future and not on China's future among the front rank of industrial nations," and that the overseas Chinese "cannot afford to sacrifice their national interests for China." Unlike Dong, Teng refused to declare that Peking would cease supporting insurrectionary movements, a statement that Lee, with his predominant Chinese population, took to heart.

Lee's position on aid to Vietnam was that any assistance given to Hanoi should be in small doses and should be used as a bargaining point in persuading them to restrict any support to insurgency movements. The Chinese, he thought, might continue to act as a deterrent influence on the Vietnamese for their own reasons of trying to contain the expanding Russian influence in Southeast Asia. Hanoi's already apparent tilt toward Moscow was something else that bothered Lee in the context of the larger power struggle. Earlier, at a Commonwealth Conference in Ottawa, in 1973, he had graphically expressed his fears by warning that when "elephants fight, the grass is trampled," but "when elephants flirt, the grass also suffers, and when they make love it is disastrous."

Views of America

Lee Kuan Yew viewed the major power contest in Southeast Asia with the sophistication of a man who grew up as a socialist and who personally defeated the Communists in a local contest for power, after which he either jailed them or banished them from the colony. If the word "ruthless," often applied to him, had any validity, it was in this area of dealing with those he regards as total traitors to the cause of democracy sustained by economic growth and social discipline. Again, this was all part of his admiration of strength and his abhorrence of weakness or vacillation. One of Lee's ambivalences had to do with his attitude toward America and Americans, with whom in the past he had had a number of spats over relatively minor issues. While he admired many aspects of American life, both materially and intellectually, he felt that Americans are often too permissive and fuzzy in their appraisal of others, and that they don't really understand Asians—a feeling that many of us who have lived in Asia for a long time, myself included, frequently share.

At the same time, he believed it is absolutely vital for America to maintain its role in Southeast Asia, above all economically, as a major trading partner in the region—the United States has about $1 billion invested in Singapore —but also militarily, as a naval power in the Pacific and Indian oceans. Only an American naval presence can match the growing Soviet presence, he insisted. In the spring of 1978, Lee, who had already given the Russians bunkering rights for their ships in Singapore, confirmed that American long-range reconnaissance aircraft, including Orion PC-3 antisubmarine patrol planes, were using Singapore as a staging point for flights over the Indian Ocean, thereby linking bases in the Philippines with Diego Garcia, the British-owned coral island base that lies 2,500 miles west of Singapore. This was particularly important for the United States in view of the closing down of the bases in Thailand.

Lee was not pessimistic about the future of American policy. Once President Jimmy Carter and his team "get over proving how different and how right they are, and start appreciating the objective realities, they will re-establish a presence in Asia," he told me. As he saw it, it was simply a matter of Washington sorting out its priorities, and he was fully aware that, at the moment, its attention was mainly concentrated on the Middle East, Europe and Africa. "But the new conflict in Asia has already begun," he declared, "the contest for long-term influence, and, if you like, Communization of the region, between the Soviet Union and the People's Republic of China." It was much too soon to predict the outcome of this contest, he thought, not only in the non-Communist nations of the region but in the former Indochina countries as well, particularly in sealed-off Cambodia and in Laos. As for Singapore, both ideologically and practically, in political terms, it was not only possible but advisable for it to maintain a policy of equidistance between Moscow and Peking. But "while we don't want to get engaged in superpower conflicts which do not concern us directly," it was impossible and inadvisable to adopt an equidistant posture toward the United States, or toward Western Europe, or Japan, Australia and New Zealand in the Pacific because, among other reasons, "those are the countries where our economic links are."

Lee had thoroughly approved of President Ford's Pacific Basin policy, predicated on the United States fostering a new balance of power in the Pacific through its continuing partnership with Japan, by normalizing relations with China, and by maintaining a stake in the security and economic growth of Southeast Asia. "The Americans will have to reach new definitions of what their strategic interests are in the Far East and the Indian Ocean," he said. "They will have to decide for themselves and, of course, it's not only a matter of what's important or necessary but of what can be carried in the country, that is, what Congress and the media say and do." Some months after I saw him, Lee traveled to the United States, on one of his periodic trips there, and stressed these same thoughts in talks with President Carter and Secretary of State Cyrus Vance, and others. One wonders how carefully they listened to him.

Being a patient man, and above all a Chinese, despite his British education, Lee was willing to wait for what he hoped would be a renewed American concern for Asia. But at the same time his innate self-reliance, and his determination to safeguard his own position, had already led him, as it had some other Asian leaders, both Moslems and non-Moslems, to court the Arabs as a result of the oil crisis. In Lee's case, there was a special note of irony to this, for he had long admired the Israelis, and had often compared Singapore's predicament among surrounding Malays to Israel's among surrounding Arabs. For several years, in fact, he had hired Israeli advisers to build up his small but effective army of 45,000 men, plus another 20,000 in the navy and air force —the latter was also small but efficient and it had been bolstered in 1976 by the purchase of twenty-one F5-E fighters bought from America.

With his renewed interest in ASEAN, Lee had already begun to take the lead in promoting diplomatic dialogues among the five nations of the group with Japan, Australia and New Zealand to develop more effective agreements covering trade, aid and industrial growth on a cooperative basis, thus in effect broadening ASEAN's scope and satisfying the desires of the Japanese, in particular, to play a wider and more constructive role in the area. Encouraging the Japanese to relate more to the rest of Asia assumed added importance, Lee believed, as the Americans started their troop withdrawals from South Korea in 1978, thereby raising the specter of an insecure Japan deciding at some point to rearm more strenuously. Along with other Southeast Asian leaders, Lee regarded this possibility with great trepidation, the more so since the Japanese now had a nuclear capability. In my talks with him he expressed a special concern about this, and thought there was a 45 percent chance of nuclear development within ten or fifteen years, especially as the younger generation "with no sense of guilt about the past" took over.

Lee had all along said that Singapore would be the last of the ASEAN countries to recognize Peking. At the time I saw him, Malaysia, Thailand and the Philippines had already done so, and Indonesia was expected to follow suit within two or three years. But neither Lee nor his equally articulate long-time Foreign Minister, Sinnathamby Rajaratnam, a Tamil, was in a hurry about it. It was easy enough to keep track of the twenty-eight Russians in the Soviet embassy, plus twenty-one who were working in various communications and commercial jobs, and the score or so of Russian students who annually came to Singapore to study Chinese at Nanyang University or the University of Singapore. But the Chinese would be a different kettle of fish, blending far more easily into the local racial landscape, and Lee and Rajaratnam didn't relish the task of following them about and making sure they would not sow dissension among students, workers and intellectuals, as well as among soldiers, some of whose ranks had already been infiltrated by agents of the Malayan Communist Party. "We want to avoid a confrontation between the Russians and Chinese here as long as we can," said Rajaratnam. "We don't want a spider contest."

By and large, the easily visible Russians in Singapore, half of whom were assumed to be working for the KGB or the GRU, the Russian secret services, had maintained a low profile, though Russian ships, particularly the fishing fleet, regularly passed through the port, which is the world's fourth largest, as well as third largest oil-refining center. Since they were denied access to Hong Kong, the Russians regarded Singapore as important for China-watching, and they tried to keep track of overseas Chinese who visited China as well as of foreign tourists, both Asian and European, who passed through Singapore after traveling to China. Without much diplomatic activity to occupy them, the Russians concentrated on commerce and banking, and in 1971 they established a branch of the London-based Moscow-Narodny Bank, which rapidly rose to become one of the three biggest banks in town. The bank soon got into trouble by overextending itself in making loans, mostly to Chinese developers in Singapore and elsewhere in the area, totaling more than $1 billion, about a third of which it had to write off when borrowers failed to meet their obligations. During the period when most of the loans were being extended, the Russian head of the bank gave frequent lavish parties, and there are those who believed that the blackmailing of Chinese borrowers may have been one of the bank's major objectives.

Contest with Socialist International

What worried Singapore's leaders more than what the Russians were up to, and what the Chinese might stir up after recognition, was what the Malayan Communist Party had all along been trying to achieve through infiltration and subversion. Whether Lee exaggerated this threat was arguable, and his arrest of agents, including several prominent newsmen, some of whom had made theatrical confessions of their activities on television, brought the issue to a head in 1976 and 1977 and helped provoke Singapore's forced resignation from the Socialist International, a world body composed of prominent socialist leaders. For years Lee had enjoyed his association with important European socialists, particularly with men like Hugh Gaitskell, Ernest Bevin and Clement Attlee, of Great Britain, and Willy Brandt, of West Germany, all intellectual comrades in arms. He liked to call himself an "old-fashioned socialist," though he seemed far more capitalist than socialist-oriented in most respects. His fight with the Socialist International arose when the Dutch Labor Party submitted a memorandum recommending Singapore's expulsion on the grounds that it had become a one-party state that had adopted totalitarian policies and methods in suppressing the press, free-trade unionism, students and the political opposition by indiscriminate detention of opponents who were held without trial. Singapore, the memorandum said, had become "a corporate state" dominated by Lee Kuan Yew's "elitist ideology" which was "completely alien to the principles of socialist democracy."

In a series of retaliatory broadsides led by Rajaratnam and Devan Nair, the head of the National Trades Union Congress, and by Lee himself, Singapore denied the charges, vehemently defended the twenty-year record of the People's Action Party, and attacked the Socialist International for being naïve about the nature of Asian Communism. In his lengthy reply Nair said: "If some West European socialists desire to play poker with their own Communists, we sincerely wish them good luck, for we think they will require lots of luck. But we beg to opt out. For our Communists are an altogether different breed. They do not pretend, like French or Italian Communists, to any liberal change of heart. On the contrary, with every passing day after the fall of South Vietnam, Cambodia and Laos, they mount their insurgency operations, and their campaigns of terror and assassination, in Thailand and Malaysia."

This was a valid enough point, but one still wondered if Singapore's response was more self-defeating than purely protective. When I suggested this to Lee, he bristled and vehemently maintained that he had no option but to react as he had to the Socialist International attacks. As far as he was concerned, he thought that the image of "the real Lee Kuan Yew will triumph over any other image, over a period of time," and in a rare demonstration of almost pensive humility, added, "and I think it can stand some examination." In January 1978, following a meeting of the Socialist International in Tokyo, Willy Brandt and the Malaysian and Japanese delegates argued for Singapore's reinstatement, but the French, British and Dutch opposed it; Lee mellowed somewhat and indicated that he might consider rejoining if he was asked, and if he became convinced that "non-Communist socialists are in effective charge in the main national parties"—a reference specifically directed at the French, British and Italian parties he felt had been "decimated" by the Communists as a result of united-front strategies and tactics.

There were sixty-one political prisoners under detention at the time of my 1977 visit, and three of them had been held for thirteen years; a year later, two of the three were finally released but dispatched to small nearby islands under what amounted to "island arrest." Lee's policy of holding political prisoners without trial—he had abolished the jury system in 1971—until they publicly confessed their Communist or front activities and recanted and denounced the Malayan Communist Party had lately resulted in half a dozen such performances. This had ramifications in Malaysia as well, where the confessions had led to the arrest and detention of two deputy ministers, who also confessed, "Singapore style," but "for their own safety" were kept in jail. Singapore's rejection of jury trials was based on the argument that it would be impossible to obtain witnesses because they would be subject to assassination by the Communists once they testified.

After reading a number of the lengthy confessions, I felt they were, for the most part, stultifying and unconvincing. While some of them, particularly those of two correspondents of the *Far Eastern Economic Review* who had been accused of slanting their stories to arouse support among readers for the cause of the Communists, sounded genuine and honest; the others had an unreal, almost puerile quality to them, as if these were bad boys in school who had misbehaved, and having been cracked over the knuckles, were telling their teachers that they were sorry and would be good boys from now on. I somehow doubted that they had really changed their minds, ideologically; they were simply playing a strange cat-and-mouse game, the rules of which had been laid down by the governments in Singapore and Kuala Lumpur, mainly in order, as Lee himself admitted, to warn others not to indulge in the same sort of game, which could become dangerous, especially for the mice. But what would it really prove, and wasn't it essentially spurious and self-serving?

Lee Kuan Yew said not. "Putting them on television is meant for the local audience," he said. "We've got to educate people, make the parents aware of the dangers of their sons or daughters being drawn into political groups in order, say, to make walkie-talkies for the Communists. Not that they can't go to a shop and buy them, but this is method recruitment—so they can get these chaps to the jungle to repair their walkie-talkie sets. That is what it's all about —commitment, step by step. You've got to let the students know—look, it starts off with playing games like this, and it ends up with life and death."

Subconsciously, if not consciously, Lee's precautionary reaction to the handful of Communists or Communist sympathizers in Singapore was largely based on his suspicion of the Moslem world around him. While the Communists were mostly Chinese, the Malayan Communist Party was making a concerted effort to recruit Malays, and some of the most important people he had arrested, or put the finger on in Malaysia, were Malays, among them Abdul Samad Ismael, the former managing editor of the *New Straits Times* in Kuala Lumpur. Samad was arrested there in 1976 on the basis of information supplied by the Singapore Special Branch—he had been jailed by Lee a decade earlier, and after his release, had taken refuge in Kuala Lumpur. His confession led to the arrest and jailing of two Malay deputy ministers in the Malaysian government (see Malaysia chapter). In the summer of 1977 the Malaysian Special Branch, in turn, supplied Singapore with information that led to the arrest of thirty-nine alleged members of the Malayan National Liberation Front who were accused of providing financial and logistical support for the Malayan National Liberation Army in Singapore.

It was apparent that Lee's worry about a link between the Marxist-Leninists and the Moslems was genuine. In one of my conversations with him, concerning Soviet influence in the area, he wondered aloud whether the Russians "will be more effective this time than before, when they invested a great deal in Sukarno, in Indonesia, but didn't get much out of it. It made them more cautious and circumspect, but it hasn't altered their objective. They're simply more realistic about figuring out what they can achieve. It's obvious that in Malaysia they're making a bid for the Moslem-Malay element of the population and trying to build up a Marxist-Leninist group that will be oriented against the largely Chinese-led MCP. It will be a long process but they won't give up trying." Lee had not forgotten Sukarno's confrontation with Malaysia in the sixties, when the two nations almost went to war and Singapore was caught in the middle. When I asked him what would happen if the Moslems got out of hand in Indonesia today, if the Moslem Moros in the Philippines continued their battle for autonomy, and if at the same time the Communist threat in Thailand and Malaysia, and the Moslem separatist movement in Thailand, continued to grow, he looked up with a pained expression and said, "It would be worse than it was during the days of confrontation."

Rajaratnam put it sharply when he said to me, "We trust some Moslems, others not." The Singaporeans had never really forgiven Malaysia for throwing them out of the federation in 1965, proud as they were of having made it on their own ever since. At the time that happened, Lee broke down and wept at a press conference, a rare public display of emotion for him. He wept out of anger and remorse but also because he was upset about leaving so many Chinese behind in Malaysia, and because he knew, belatedly, that he had overplayed his hand in trying to enter the broad arena of Malaysian politics too soon. Relations between Singapore and Malaysia had improved considerably over the years. "They're sound today, even though we have some perplexing conflicts of interest," Rajaratnam said. "We have inevitable economic differences, since they place so much stress on their *bumiputra* programs, where we stress open competition for all races and investors in the economy. The Malaysians also keep pressing for a zone of peace and neutrality in Southeast Asia. As an objective, that's all right, but it's impractical. Here we have the Soviet Union increasing its presence, not withdrawing. If we mount a peace and neutrality campaign, we might drive the Western powers out, especially the Americans. That would simply play into the hands of both the Russian and the Chinese Communists."

Formula for Success

Singapore's rugged society, based on discipline and hard work, is functioning well because it is such a small place—in effect, a political laboratory. There are no jungles for Communists to hide in, as elsewhere in Southeast Asia. Circumstance and geography thus enhance Lee's chances of playing a unique leadership role, and he is increasingly grasping it. Advantageously as well as precariously situated at a maritime crossroads, Singapore can be maneuvered by Lee internally, without fear of opposition, while externally he can keep an ever-watchful eye on what his neighbors are doing, utilizing his leverage in ways that suit both his temperament and style.

In some ways he is an odd mixture of a Confucian, Calvinist and Cromwellian figure. He believes that lessons have to be taught the hard way, over and over again; he once told a political opponent, "When I have a problem and find a solution, I check once, then twice, then three times, and before I do anything I check it a fourth time."

Highly analytical and methodical, Lee never could abide carelessness, and he is not one to forgive mistakes. Alex Josey, a British writer and journalist who has spent most of his life in Singapore and once was a close friend of Lee's, wrote, in a biography of him: "Lee is a finicky fusser over detail, and also a political scientist who can produce visions of broad outline and wide horizons. In between expounding a theory embracing the whole of Southeast Asia, he can grumble about the fumes from diesel-driven buses, complain that his steak is not quite right, argue that the weight of a borrowed golf club caused him to hook his shot. But Lee never confuses his priorities."

Often arrogant, Lee can also become vindictive when someone crosses him, and he is contemptuous of those, including most of his political rivals, whom he regards as intellectually inferior. He trusts relatively few people, which is one reason he has run Singapore so effectively for so many years with the same handful of loyal and able assistants, notably Rajaratnam, Dr. Goh and Toh Chin Chye, who is in charge of party affairs. In both an Asian and a Western sense, according to Josey, Lee considers himself to be the head of a collective leadership and "the first among equals." Though he doesn't always have his own way in the cabinet, he usually does "because his thinking, his arguments, have their own force of appeal."

What Lee and his cohorts have done in Singapore, undoubtedly because it is a workshop city-state rather than a large country, is to utilize its politics in behalf of economics, to make the first an engine for the second. In this sense it is a functioning technocracy, the only one of its kind in Asia if not in the world. A perceptive political scientist at the University of Singapore, Dr. Chan Heng See, in an essay on "The Political System and

Political Change," noted that Singapore "is a culture which discourages conflict, confrontation and bargaining, emphasizes stability, low risk and petition." Dr. Chan observed further that "a depoliticization has effectively taken place in the wake of the emphasis given to political stability in the interest of economic progress." One result, she added, was that "the gap between the rich and the poor remains and is in fact widening, and an inequality of sacrifice is demanded in economic development." Since "change of any sort will remain the sole initiative of the leadership or be ultimately forced by disruptive violent means," she warned that "this kind of political stability may well lead to political instability in the long run" because it "also means a loss of effective representation." There is, indeed, a threat in the overriding submissiveness; accountability is only to Lee Kuan Yew and to the PAP, and to the bureaucratic machinery they have established. In this sort of paternal socioeconomic climate, most citizens do not particularly feel the lack of more substantial political liberties, and the elections that are held every five years are like manipulated referendums. But that is a situation which conceals its own time bomb.

The problem of a lack of an effective political opposition was one that used to worry the PAP leaders in earlier years more than it did by 1978, though occasionally it stirred their consciences. "A loyal opposition?" Dr. Goh repeated when I put the question to him. "I did think of that once, yes, as a self-correcting mechanism, but the quality is so poor that one despairs. The twenty-five percent who vote for the opposition are low-income people such as taxi drivers and ordinary laborers. There are some Communist sympathizers. And some middle-class people among them too. But the good ones join the PAP and we need them, because they will take over from us. The others will simply remain resentful."

"It's not possible to create a viable constitutional opposition," Lee Kuan Yew maintained. "We've watched them over the years. They're not sufficiently spry, they don't have enough know-how. Our successors will have to come from within the PAP. If there were no Communist threat, I think a non-Communist opposition would eventually emerge. But the insurgency in Thailand, and increasing acts of terrorism in Malaysia, inhibits that now. The risk we face today is lack of political dedication. My generation didn't adopt politics as a career. We were pitchforked into it, by the compulsions of what we wanted to do. The trouble now is that the bright young men, weighing the odds, judging my breed, my generation, figure we will last another decade. So they decide to make a success in business and then, when the current leadership goes by, they'll make a bid at politics. Activists have a glandular reaction, but in a rapid-growth society most of the younger ones are busy pursuing mammon. If they can't manage economically, they'll turn back. But we have some good ones, and we're trying to expose them to a wider range of activity within the government."

One-Party State

The emasculation of the militant opposition in Singapore, whatever the validity of Lee Kuan Yew's anti-Communist position and motives, was a classic case of political castration. After 1959, when Singapore's status as a colony ended, the PAP won every election at mostly five-year intervals. Before that, in the early and mid-fifties, when Singapore enjoyed a degree of pre-independence autonomy, there were various parties, including the Labor Front, headed by an able lawyer, David Marshall, who was Chief Minister for a time (in 1978, despite his long political rivalry with Lee, he was named ambassador to France). But before the 1959 elections Marshall resigned, and the Labor Front began to disintegrate as the PAP started moving to the forefront of the political scene. Running against a hodgepodge of thirteen parties and thirty-four independent candidates, the PAP won 54 percent of the vote and 43 of 91 seats in Parliament, enough to give it power. After an unexpectedly close contest with the popular mayor of Singapore (another PAP man), named Ong Eng Guan, Lee took over as Prime Minister and began to introduce his first social and economic programs.

Within two years, as a result of the PAP's detaining left-wing political leaders and cracking down on the leftist-led Singapore Association of Trade Unions, Lee's earlier Communist or pro-Communist allies turned bitterly against him and formed their own party, the Barisan Socialis, headed by two of Lee's former political partners, Lim Chin Siong and Fong Swee Suan. Both young men, who were believed to be Communist Party members, had been imprisoned for a time by the British in the mid-fifties, at which time their attorney had been none other than their then associate, Lee Kuan Yew.

The Barisan made some early grass-roots gains and seized a number of the PAP's local committees, which prompted the PAP to fall back on its growing bureaucracy for support and to start building up the network of Community Centers which became its eyes and ears. The two parties had some major differences on the terms of merger with Malaysia which came to a head during 1962, with the PAP's views predominating. In February 1963, prior to the election that year, Lee and his PAP cohorts, using the British-inherited Internal Security Council regulations, struck climactically at the Barisan in what was known as Operation Cold Storage. A total of 107 left-wing politicians and trade unionists, including Lim Chin Siong and Fong Swee Suan, were arrested and jailed. In spite of this, the Barisan won a third of the vote and 13 of the 51 seats in the September election.

The new Malaysian government, of which Singapore had become a part, then arrested additional leaders and banned the militant Barisan unions. The party thereupon began to fall apart. Its secondary figures who were still at liberty bickered among themselves, boycotted Parliament, and ultimately the half-dozen elected members who had not already quit resigned. A number of instances of violence occurred during this period, which led to further arrests and to the virtual collapse of the party, although it continued to function as a shell of its former self and feebly contested the last election, in 1976. Although Lim Chin Siong, probably the most brilliant of the early Singapore leaders next to Lee Kuan Yew, had worked closely with him during the early days of the anticolonial struggle, he remained in jail until 1969 (after an attempted suicide), when, in a pitifully contrite letter, he finally recanted. He wrote Lee that he had "completely lost confidence in the international Communist movement," and that he was prepared "to give up politics for good." A short time later he was set free and was allowed to leave for London, where he went to work for a business house.

After the election of 1963 the PAP lost no time in establishing its one-party dominance. Five years later it swept all 58 parliamentary seats against virtually no opposition, and won by-elections in 1970 for 5 seats against one disorganized group, the United National Front, which still managed to win almost 30 percent of the vote in two of the five constituencies it contested. By 1972, four new opposition parties or fronts in addition to the United National Front had sprung up, including a right-wing Malayan-oriented party; a left-wing People's Front oriented toward the Chinese-speaking population; and a revived version of the old Workers Party of the nineteen-fifties, which emphasized human rights. But all of these parties lacked strong consistent leadership and suffered from internal differences over platforms and policies.

In the 1972 election, after only nine days of official campaigning (the maximum under the law was ninety, but the PAP consistently held to the minimum of nine), the combined opposition, including what remained of the Barisan, collected nearly 29 percent of the vote, but the PAP still won all 65 seats in Parliament. In 1976 it increased its margin to nearly 73 percent in sweeping the same 65 seats. Lee Kuan Yew exulted, especially since his record margin of victory came in the wake of the contentious issue over Singapore quitting the Socialist International. The opposition claimed that a climate of fear or intimidation had been created by the complicated ballot-marking system, based on that of the British, whereby, despite secret voting, the serial number of each voter on his ballot could be checked against the number on the polling card sent by mail several days before the election. Theoretically such a check could be made, though in practice there was no indication that this had happened. Nevertheless, the fear that it might happen, particularly on the part of middle-class voters, including professional people and civil servants, who were among the more disaffected in Singapore and who were afraid of government harassment, may well have been a factor in some of the voting.

Early in 1979 the PAP won seven by-elections (two by default) which Lee had ordered after forcing seven members of Parliament to resign in what was an apparent effort by him to bring new blood into the party and the government. He made several changes in the cabinet and the party administration, promoting younger technocrats and men with a professional background whom he regarded as potential leaders of the country. One of these was Goh Chok Tong, a former manager of the national shipping line, who was named the second assistant secretary-general of the PAP, and another was Dr. Tony Tan Keng Yam, who became Senior Minister of State for Education. Both were only thirty-eight years old and were regarded as future prime-ministerial candidates, though there was little indication that Lee was thinking of stepping down. In making a show of his move to plan ahead in this fashion, he typically showed his contempt for the opposition by announcing some of the changes before the by-elections were even held, simply assuming his chosen candidates would win. Though the opposition parties didn't capture any seats and the PAP retained all 65, they managed to obtain a slightly higher percentage of the vote than before—29 in the five contested races.

The PAP has defended its dominant political role on the grounds that it has all along been best suited to guide the destiny of Singapore, economically and socially as well as politically. As the party leaders saw it, authoritarianism could be blended with benevolent, paternal Confucianism, rendering a form of government that assured peace, material development and prosperity. As Dr. Chan Heng Shee wrote: "The entire Confucian tradition, laying great stress on the deference to authority and stressing filial piety as the basis of superior-subordinate relations, will probably stifle or curb the tendencies to display any aggressive opposition or the rejection of authority." This would last, she added, as long as the PAP could avoid "internal party decay and loss of discipline that come from the entrenchment of power," but "the real test of the system will come when the first generation of PAP leaders leave the political arena."

Planning from the Start

Political maneuvering, at which Lee Kuan Yew and his tight band of loyal supporters were magnificently adept, did not alone make Singapore an economic success story. The methodology behind the creation of the mechanism that made the system work is worth examining as a model of its kind.

With the introduction of a new constitution in 1959, the conferring of Singapore citizenship was accompanied by the registration of 325,000 new voters, bringing the total voters to about 550,000. The fact that this electorate was approximately the same as the labor force meant that economic issues from the very outset were bound to be the basis of the new republic's polity. To deal with such problems as a rapidly growing young population facing potential unemployment in what was still a colonial atmosphere marked by financial stringency and a decaying infrastructure, the PAP formulated a State Development Plan for the three-year period from 1961 to 1964. Since defense, along with foreign affairs, was still the province of the British, there were no defense expenses to be met, which was a major blessing—in fact, British armed forces remained in Singapore until 1971, after which a new defense agreement was worked out with Malaysia, Australia and New Zealand.

One of the first things the government did was to create a series of statutory boards, which, operating under the direction of cabinet ministers, took control of basic urban and economic functions. In 1960, for example, in order to develop a broad program of low-cost housing, the Housing and Development Board was created. From 23,000 units in 1960, the number of HDB flats had grown to about 300,000 units by 1978, a fourteenfold increase, and 30,000 new units were being built each year. Moreover, an increasing number of tenants were buying their own flats, partly out of government-forced savings. The flats ran from units of one to five rooms, and a two-room flat, with kitchen and bathroom, cost $10,000.

Despite certain drawbacks of people living by the thousands in high-rise housing developments, where they were subject to a variety of psychological and emotional pressures they had never experienced before, the housing program, which Singapore financed on its own and which gave a huge boost to the economy and jobs to tens of thousands of construction workers, was one of its finest accomplishments, and it became a world-famous model. It was accompanied by excellent city planning, including a "Clean and Green" campaign that converted squares into small parks, created plots of grass and small gardens wherever there was space, and generally tidied up and beautified what had before been an ugly urban sprawl spotted with slums. The high-density housing developments were carefully concentrated along the southern rim of the island, away from the heavy urban development in other areas, thereby making the most of available space and still leaving room for further industrial expansion.

Part of the rationale of this planning was that Singapore's population might nearly double, to 4 million, by the year 2000, but this might never take place because of a highly successful family-planning program, including sterilization of more women (who in 1978 comprised 40 percent of the work force) than men. As a result of abortions, sterilization, the use of pills and other contraceptives, this brought the annual birth rate down to 1.3 percent by 1978. A combination of widespread education and issuance of contraceptives plus disincentives, including greater availability of housing flats to smaller families, hastened the drop.

In 1961, a year after the creation of the housing board, the Economic Development Board was set up to promote and attract foreign investment by offering small industries financial assistance in the selection of factory sites. Land development was turned over to the Jurong Town Corporation, which built the first of several large industrial estates. A Public Utilities Board and a Port of Singapore Authority were also created. The role of the Central Provident Fund, originally formed in 1955 to collect compulsory contributions from employers and employees, was greatly expanded to cover all employees, whose contributions, along with those of employers, were used for the purchase of long-term government bonds, which were used in turn for public development and to help tenants of government-built flats purchase them. In time, a dozen or so statutory boards covered virtually every phase of developmental activity in Singapore.

After it took over, the PAP also began to mobilize and control labor in behalf of development. Having initially come to power with the help of Communist-led labor unions, headed by men like Lim Chin Siong, the party, after the bitter 1963 elections, moved to destroy what remained of the left-wing Singapore Association of Trade Unions, replacing it with the National Trades Union Congress, led by Devan Nair. A strict system of industrial arbitration was established, and under the Industrial Relations (Amendment) Act of 1968, arbitration became compulsory. This act, and the companion Employment Act, severely limited the workers' right to strike and acted as further incentives for investors, which by this time included multinationals as Singapore had made the transition from its initial strategy of encouraging import-substitution industries to luring big foreign firms to establish plants for the manufacture or assembling of products for export to the region and the world. A new Economic Incentives Act consolidated previous taxation and other incentives and added new ones for factories which exported most of their production. What amounted to an open-door immigration policy brought skilled labor and technicians to Singapore under temporary permits to help the multinationals get started. An Asian Dollar Market was introduced, and incentives were offered to foreign banks which wanted to set up branches, especially for conducting offshore business. Singapore thus became a financial as well as an industrial center.

"If a developing country is to develop, there must be social cohesion, work discipline and an order of priorities," Lee Kuan Yew said. He described Singapore as "a mixed economy," which it basically is, with the state in charge of public utilities, transport, shipping and the airlines, and at the same time cooperating in joint ventures with private industry. In a 1977 government volume somewhat misleadingly called "Socialism That *Works,*" Dr. Goh Keng Swee wrote: "Taking an overall view of Singapore's economic policy, we can see how radically it differed from the laissez-faire policies of the colonial era. These had led Singapore to a dead end, with little economic growth, massive unemployment, wretched housing, and inadequate education. We *had* to try a more activist and interventionist approach. Democratic socialist economic policies ranged from direct participation in industry to the supply of infrastructure facilities by statutory authorities, and to laying down clear guidelines to the private sector as to what they could and should do."

Socialist or Capitalist?

The fact is, Singapore had by this time become far more democratic capitalist than democratic socialist, if indeed it was democratic at all. At best it could be described as a new form of guided democracy totally geared to profit making under a carefully circumscribed and controlled free-enterprise system. While workers certainly benefited from public housing, welfare provisions remained minimal and did not go much beyond medical services. The National Trades Union Congress, which had a total of 210,000 members, only 28 percent of the working population—the rest were contract workers, including more than 100,000 a year from Malaysia—never proposed a minimum wage. Its stated reason was that full employment had virtually been attained —the unemployment rate hovered around 4 percent. A National Wages Council, in cooperation with managements that dealt with the NTUC-affiliated unions, established yearly guidelines for wage increases, which averaged about 7 percent—in 1974 they jumped to 20 percent because of the oil crisis and inflation but then dropped back to 7 percent in 1975.

Devan Nair, who played a leading role in curbing the Communist-led unions in the early days, and who became one of the staunchest supporters of multinationals, told me, "The fact that Singapore enjoys, next to Japan, the highest income levels in Asia is a cause for *worry*, and not for elation. The problem is to curb wage increases in Singapore so that our wages are not excessively high in comparison with wage levels in places like South Korea, Taiwan and Hong Kong. The chances are that if we fail to regulate our wage increases, the goods that we manufacture in Singapore may well be priced out of world markets." But wages in the places Nair mentioned are notoriously low, and in Singapore unskilled labor, and nonunionized workers, who were earning about seventy-five cents a day in 1965, by 1978 were making about $2.50. This was scarcely a living wage in an inflationary climate.

The NTUC offered its members all sorts of special incentives and benefits, such as an insurance cooperative, the profits of which were used for investment in other trade-union projects; low-cost supermarkets; a union-controlled taxi fleet called Comfort, the ultimate aim of which was to have all taxi drivers own their own cars; and a number of other cooperatives including one that provided low-cost textbooks for schoolchildren and low-cost dental treatment for workers and their families. "All these cooperatives and other undertakings are not regarded as ends in themselves," Nair said. "Rather, they are conceived as a means to larger ends, embracing the totality of interests of the working population of Singapore." Much of this was true, but one would still think that "the totality of interests" of most workers would best be served by tough collective bargaining and the right to strike for higher wages. In Lee Kuan Yew's controlled city-state, such freedom was regarded as a license or a luxury that would lead to anarchy and chaos and would play into the hands of the Communists, and thus could not be permitted in a profit-oriented community.

In building his unique integrated, multiracial and dedicated society, Lee had from the outset placed great stress on two other areas—education and communication. His 1978 language reforms, with their stress on English, was the ultimate product of his desire to create a single language for science and technology. But the trouble was, particularly with such subjects as science and mathematics, teachers in non-English schools, whose first language was not English, had to teach Chinese pupils just starting to learn English, and had to use English texts. Lee himself admitted that English-language teachers did not like to go to Chinese schools "because they have to work harder there." But he was determined to pursue his objectives. As far back as 1966 he said, "Our community lacks inbuilt reflexes—loyalty, patriotism, history or tradition," and added, "The ideal product is the student, the university graduate who is strong, robust, rugged, with tremendous qualities of stamina, endurance and at the same time with great intellectual discipline and most important of all, humility and love for his community." He had moved through the years to achieve this, often with his customary toughness, cracking down on left-wing students at both Nanyang University and the University of Singapore. All pupils had to recite a daily loyalty oath to Singapore and sing the national anthem at flag-raising ceremonies.

In his effort to create an elite society in his own image of disciplined nation-building, Lee placed increasing emphasis on separating the top students from the mediocre ones and sending the latter to vocational or technical schools rather than to universities. In addition, each student entering a university had to obtain a Suitability Certificate, which was issued to him on the basis of his own and his family's "clean" political background. (Only a relative few, in fact, were turned down.) Upon graduation from high school, all students had to enter two years of National Service and then remain in the military reserve. Most of them didn't seem to mind this, and it helped create the sense of a Singaporean identity and an *esprit de corps* that Lee so assiduously sought. There was also a paramilitary organization known as the Vigilante Corps, consisting of an estimated 15,000 members, most of them former National Servicemen. Though unarmed, they became an adjunct of the police force and were part of the grass-roots control system, working closely with such groups as Community Centers and Citizens' Consultative Committees, which, in effect, were local cells of the PAP and formed the "central nervous system" that enabled the party to maintain its hold on the whole body politic.

When I asked Lee whether he did not think he had gone too far in pushing his sense of discipline, whether it might not, as had been suggested, prove counterproductive in driving Singaporeans to the point where the nervous system of the society might break down under constant pressuring, he replied that he thought that was "an exaggeration of the actual situation." "In fact, one of the main problems is slackening of discipline," he said. "The over-thirties, the chaps who faced the problems of unemployment ten years ago, they are naturally disciplined. They know the problems of unemployment. We've got younger people in their late teens and their early twenties who have become choosy about jobs, and about eight to ten percent of jobs are being held by work-permit holders or guest workers because our own unemployed don't want these jobs."

As for such campaigns as forbidding men to wear long hair, Lee added, "We have been able to insist upon certain moral and social standards of moral conduct. We can't prevent people wanting to misbehave or do silly things to themselves. But we do object to moral standards being reduced publicly. We don't want this sort of permissive society publicly exhibited." The crime rate in Singapore is among the lowest in Asia, partly because the place is small enough to make it hard for fugitives to hide, and partly because the police force and the courts are highly efficient. Punishments, when meted out, are stiff and include mandatory caning for about thirty crimes, which is not only extremely painful but can leave lifetime scars.

Curbing the Press

Lee regards the function of the press as akin to that of schools and universities: to inculcate a proper sense of values and discipline among Singapore's citizens. He did not take lightly the criticism that was leveled against him by the Western press for the manner in which he handled his own. The matter came to a head in the spring of 1971, when he shut down three newspapers and arrested three editors of one of them, the *Nanyang Siang Pau*, which he accused of "glamorizing Communism and stirring up communal and chauvinistic sentiments over language and culture." The paper's incitement of communal strife was, Lee declared, a typical example of those who allowed themselves to be used by "outside forces" to destroy the peace and well-being of Singapore. Next he moved against an English-language paper, the *Eastern Sun*, which he charged had been financed to the tune of more than $1 million by a "black operation" mounted by Chinese Communist agents in Hong Kong. Oddly enough, the paper had adopted an anti-Communist position, but Lee said this was part of a long-range plot to subvert public opinion. "They were planning not for tomorrow, but for the next year, for ten years' time," he said. He thereupon laid out the details of the financial plot, which had been conducted so secretly that the editors of the *Eastern Sun* hadn't even known about it. Within a week, the humiliated editors and staff resigned and the paper voluntarily shut down.

In both these cases, Lee was on some solid ground. He was considerably less so in the case of the third paper, the *Singapore Herald*, a crusading publication that had been critical of Lee on such issues as national military service for high school graduates but had maintained that there should be more "social dialogue" in Singapore and that "the relationship between government and people must be modified." Lee reacted against the paper's assuming a political role for itself, which he said was the province of parties, not papers, and he objected particularly to the fact that, as had been the case with the *Eastern Sun*, its financial support ostensibly came from outside, from Donald Stephens, a rich Sabah timber merchant, and that it had received a $125,000 loan from the Chase Manhattan Bank in Singapore.

In what became a nasty contretemps involving the American embassy as well as the bank, including David Rockefeller himself, the bank's president, Lee went further and charged privately that the CIA was behind the paper. At one point a top CIA official from Washington came to Singapore to deny the charge personally and try to mollify Lee, who remained unconvinced. The *Herald* was having financial problems, and Lee eventually forced the bank to foreclose on its loan; when the paper kept publishing, he unilaterally revoked its printing and publishing license. Widely criticized abroad for his violation of the rights of a free press and for his other authoritarian actions, Lee typically flew off to an International Press Institute meeting in Helsinki, where he delivered a strenuous and bold defense. He spoke of the hidden dangers of a press with unlimited freedom, referred to the barrage of radio propaganda to which Singapore was regularly subjected from all sides, and summarized the efforts of foreign agents to "use local proxies to set up new, or buy into, newspapers, not to make money but to make political gain by shaping opinions and attitudes." Under such conditions, he added, "freedom of the press ... must be subordinate to the overriding needs of the integrity of Singapore and to the primacy of purpose of an elected government." Thereafter Lee adamantly insisted that no foreign money could support a paper in Singapore, and he made licensing provisions even more stringent. He expressed the hope that the critical Western press "will find a sufficient repose from their own libertarians" and that "they will learn that there are limits to fundamental human rights and civil liberties. Otherwise they themselves will be destroyed." But by 1978, realizing that perhaps he had gone too far, he was encouraging competition to the *New Straits Times*, though, if another paper appeared, it would obviously have to watch its step.

Lee's attitude toward the press would have pleased former Vice President Spiro Agnew, who had visited Singapore shortly after the *Herald* crisis and had listened sympathetically to Lee's views about it, so much so that he subsequently arranged for the transfer of the highly able American ambassador, Charles Cross, who had spoken out strongly in defense of the Chase Bank's role in the case and had vehemently denied any CIA or any other official American involvement in the matter. The manner in which he handled the *Herald* case certainly showed Lee in his worst cavalier and authoritarian light. In this instance he had acted vindictively, almost irrationally, whatever the merits of his argument that he wanted no foreign money backing Singapore publications. At the same time, he did allow almost all foreign magazines, with the exception of Communist and pornographic publications, including *Playboy*, to be sold, and even books that were highly critical of him were available to the public.

Power over People

There is no personality cult involving Lee Kuan Yew—few pictures of him are displayed in Singapore—yet he remains a sort of political bionic man whose presence is constantly felt. For the most part he lives a quiet, unobtrusive life, appearing as much or more on the regional and world stage than on his native arena, which again is part of his peculiar claustrophobia and his innate desire to play a larger role than Singapore can afford him. But probably more than any other Asian statesman, he epitomizes the important differences between Eastern and Western views and ideas about government, or in a larger sense, between the outlook of sophisticated developing.Third World nations and the already developed or modernized countries. Actually, late in 1977, much to Singapore's chagrin, the International Monetary Fund classified the small republic as a developed country, which meant that it would lose many of the concessions it had enjoyed as a borrower from the World Bank and the Asian Development Bank, and as a benefactor of the generalized scheme of preferences on exports. Singapore is, after all, its economic experts argued, a city-state, and its indices, of per capita income, for example, should not logically be compared to those of larger countries.

Rajaratnam, who is the closest to being an alter ego of Lee Kuan Yew, said several years ago that the basic problem of modernization in Asia and in Third World countries is one "of establishing authority and the effectiveness and legitimacy of government" in its own terms, and not in relation to larger world standards. Modernization, he added, unavoidably brings instability because it causes disruption of old traditions, beliefs and ways of life, and development per se has to be weighed against the special problems it creates rather than by statistical ratios. Furthermore, where the West thinks in terms of bills of rights, of a diffusion of authority and multiplicity of political parties and separation of powers, Rajaratnam added, the East seeks to draw a proper line between "strong disciplined government and misgovernment by the corrupt and tyrannical." Development, in this sense, is simply a by-product and not a product of the rule of law and of the economic survival of the fittest.

There is some truth to this. Nevertheless, the questions remain: Who should draw the lines and who should make the definitions? There is nothing corrupt about the hard-working, dedicated small group of men who runs the Singapore government; the big money, some of it corrupt, has been made by the several dozen wealthy Chinese who prefer to remain aloof from politics, though one has occasionally heard talk that they might, in time, when the current PAP leaders withdraw, make a political play of their own. Nor can anyone really say that Lee Kuan Yew is a tyrant. Nevertheless, he rules his tight city-state with an omnipresent authoritarian hand, and there are more reasons for this, psychological and otherwise, than the threat of Communism alone, the theme on which he constantly harps.

When I asked him toward the close of our conversation whether, looking back over the years, he would have altered any of his judgments and decisions, he replied, "I have cast my mind back from time to time to see what could and should have been done differently. I have concluded that, presented with the pressures of those various times, the decisions I took were probably the ones I would take again, given the circumstances then prevailing."

There are not many world leaders who would deny mistakes, but Lee Kuan Yew is both power-conscious and haunted by demons. He was still driven by his passion for Singapore's salvation and survival. He added, in that final answer, that he regarded his future task chiefly as one of "building up some effective institutions to help the next generation of leadership meet the more complex, even graver and more critical challenges in the nineteen-eighties than we of our generation faced." Lee meant just about everything he said, and he privately conceded that if he was pessimistic about the world, he refused to give up what he regarded as his sacred set of obligations and missions. Like all ideologues, however, or anti-ideologues who have turned coldly pragmatic, he is so programmed to his own blueprints of economic success and growth that the human emotions are obscured when he deals with such concepts as integration and multiracialism. Instead of being articulated in human terms, they have become part of his catalogue of shibboleths.

As a consequence, much of what he has said, abroad or at home, remains true and often persuasive and illuminating, but also somewhat strident and sometimes hollow. Like Nehru, he has always been split between East and West, an ambivalence which has a charm of its own and can be as intellectually appealing as it is educative. But when he became overautocratic, the charm evaporated, and left only ice and stone. This might have had something to do with the fact that he likes power more than people. And if it was not altogether Lee Kuan Yew's fault, he certainly bore some responsibility for the sterility one felt amid all the building and the boom.

Having achieved so much against so many odds, he could afford to pay more attention to people, and he could relax the tensions that overdiscipline had brought, and thereby become a finer spokesman of his time and place. What was required in Singapore was a quality of grace to match the discipline, but with all his brilliance, the fact remains that grace is seldom acquired but is a given, and it is a virtue that Lee Kuan Yew sadly lacks. But then again, in the tough contemporary world he knows so well, guts is perhaps more important than grace, and he has plenty of that.

The
Philippines–
Playing It
Both Ways

It is easy to become nostalgic when one returns to the Philippines, as I have done more than twenty times since I first landed in Leyte as a war correspondent on October 20, 1944, and then covered the recapture of Manila early the following February after two weeks of bitter street fighting and bombardment of the die-hard Japanese troops who refused to give up the southern part of the city and caused it to become the worst destroyed capital of World War II, after Warsaw. Even in the spring of 1951, when I again was there, there were still scores of shell-scarred and bullet-pocked buildings, although by then most of them were encircled by the neon glitter of the kaleidoscopic "new" Manila, and the effect was like that of a ruined university hemmed in by night clubs. By then, too, of course, the Philippines had been granted its independence—in July 1946, far sooner than many had thought possible, or even advisable—but the impact of fifty years of American colonial rule that had followed three centuries of Spanish domination was everywhere to be seen, as it still is today. What the social philosopher Thorstein Veblen called "conspicuous consumption" had remained an integral part of the emporium culture we brought to the Philippines, and our mark was indelible. The competition between postwar Filipino merchants was fierce, not only among themselves but with the American carpetbaggers who had descended like locusts. The Filipinos had made such a point of copying American merchandising ruses that they sometimes outdid themselves. I remember a local dress shop which, succumbing to the American weakness for names with a foreign flavor, had called itself Tres Chic, which led a new rival opening up nearby to call itself Quatro Chic. But then, as now, the goods piled high in the store windows were unavailable to the masses of poor Filipinos and were already creating a national frustration. The long-mimicked American way of life was essentially unattainable, and the goals were growing dimmer, the comic-book heroes more misty.

It may well be that in no other city in the world was there as much graft and conniving after the war as in Manila. The average Filipino was never very good at keeping a secret and derived an almost childish glee from telling tales on himself and on his neighbor. Almost daily one of my Filipino friends used to call me up or come see me with a fresh story of scandal, related half in shame, half in glee, and this gossip-mongering, which also went on in the flagrantly free press, developed into a sort of national self-flagellation. Under the dictatorial regime of President and Prime Minister Ferdinand E. Marcos, who was elected twice, in 1965 and in 1969, and who in September 1972 declared martial law to keep himself in power, the press became tightly controlled and run by Marcos henchmen, but the tattling and gossiping still went on, though most of it was in deadly earnest and had an ulterior or nefarious motive attached to the perpetuation of the Marcos dynasty. But Filipinos I had known for many years still came to my hotel room, and disdaining the electronic bugs that may have been hidden somewhere, whispered the latest bits of political scandal and related the bizarre details of what "really is happening" in Malacanang, the crumbling Spanish-built stucco presidential palace, where Marcos and his drivingly ambitious, handsome wife, Imelda, were consecrating something unique in the long line of oligarchies in post-colonial Hispanic countries: a working dyadic, or two-person, model.

If the Marcos tandem was new, and if things had changed politically in the Philippines under its authoritarian label, there remained much else that never seemed to change, whoever sat in Malacanang. Indeed, the country has probably retained more of its original postwar personality, flavor and quality than any other Southeast Asian nation. And this is why, each time a visitor returns, he is struck not so much by what is different but by what is still the same. If one likes the Filipinos, as I do, with all their political flaws and foibles, their predilection for theatrical, flamboyant behavior (which is known as *palabas*), it is always good to come back, even if after a time the nostalgia begins to wear a bit thin and a sense of déjà vu sets in. The scenery may change, new high-rise hotels and office buildings may alter the skyline, and whole new business districts (like architecturally striking Makati) appear to have sprung up almost overnight and proliferated; but the people, both in the barrios (villages) and in Manila seem scarcely affected. There is a peculiar vacuum to the place, the product of an odd mixture of hedonism and cynicism; despite the frenzy of activity, each crisis, each crime wave, each calamity—a volcanic eruption or a disastrous flood—becomes part of the unending pattern of Filipino life and is accepted as such. There are few surprises, perhaps because so much is predictable.

Much of this attitude of acceptance is due to the passivity of the Filipinos, which may be partly the result of their almost benign Catholicism—they are the only predominantly Catholic nation in Asia—and their religious beliefs and motivations are, in this sense, not unlike some of the fatalistic attributes of Islamic faith. This does not mean that the Filipinos are not capable of explosive emotions, especially when they feel cornered, trapped or wronged, either personally or professionally. Family feuds and personal or political vendettas are common, and often fatal, but after the shooting and shouting are over, everything settles down to a regular course again. Humor and good humor prevail. On the first evening when I was in Manila in August 1978, I rode in a battered taxi through a violent rainstorm to visit a long-time American friend in San Juan, Rizal, one of the many suburban parts of what is now called Metro Manila. The streets were as flooded as I had always remembered them, especially in the slum areas, and naked children huddled in the doorways of huts that clung to fetid canals like clusters of swollen leeches. The traffic snarl soon became impenetrable and we were stuck at one muddy intersection for half an hour, during which my driver, an elderly man with a crooked chip-toothed grin and more resignation than patience, kept inserting loud rock-and-roll cassettes into his static-ridden car radio. It was all just as it had always been—raucous, frustrating, pathetic and conscience-stirring, and yet somehow replete with so many tender and oddly joyous images and sounds that instead of getting angry, the driver and I began laughing, and the skinny, brown, dripping boys who thrust their wet two or three cigarettes or cellophane-covered slices of pineapple at us through the cracked, unworkable windows of the taxi demanding a few centavos laughed with us as they waded from car to car and enjoyed the ritual of a typical Manila monsoon dusk.

Poverty Still Prevails

I do not mean to imply that the Filipinos lack a social conscience or that their tendency to accept whatever government they have with equanimity means that the vast majority is reconciled to living in poverty and squalor while the small minority of the rich lives in blatant luxury. There is no such thing as a permanent immunity to anger. In the past few years, for example, the people living in the slums of Manila (an estimated one third of the city's 4.5 million population) have become far more socially and politically concerned than they were a few years ago. This is chiefly due to the activities of a handful of dedicated church and lay organizers. In Tondo, for example—the largest and one of the worst slums that lies alongside the harbor, which I revisited in 1978 after not having seen it for six years—the local committee was fighting the government's efforts to relocate seventeen thousand Tondoites on a nearby harbor-front strip. The battle had gone on for years, mainly because the Tondoites objected to the proposed high rate of payment plus interest for the new land, and also because they wanted to stay but not without improvements in sanitation and other facilities, which the government refused to give them. In 1976 they had signed a petition in blood and sent it to Marcos, one result of which was the arrest of their principal leader, Mrs. Trinidad Herrera, who was tortured in jail and released after the Americans made a specific human rights issue of her case; she then went into hiding because she was still accused of subversion. The morning I was in Tondo—another violent rainstorm was making a bog of the area and a heavy smell of garbage and open latrines hung over it—a city-wide meeting of eight slum groups was under way and there was talk of a new march on Malacanang, an earlier attempt having been foiled by the police before the crowd reached the palace gates.

It was hard to judge the depth of the anger of the poor, and the general level of discontent. The government had recently taken some ameliorative measures, raising the daily minimum wage in Manila to 11 pesos, or about $1.50, and was talking of a more ambitious plan to follow up on rural land reform by introducing urban land reform, limiting the amount of land any individual could own in Manila and prohibiting eviction of legitimate tenants who had lived on their property for ten years and built a home on it. As pointed out by a writer named Mil Roekaerts in a long analysis of the martial law regime in *Ichthys* (the somewhat milder successor to *The Communicator*, a Jesuit publication that was banned in 1976), the technocrats of the Marcos regime, including some able economists, "seem to have been successful in giving the masses 'satisfaction in a way which generates submission and weakens the rationality of protest' "—the quote is from Herbert Marcuse's *Reason and Revolution: Hegel and the Rise of Social Theory*. Although this rather summary comment probably applied more to the peasants in the scattered barrios of the 3,000-island archipelagic nation than to urban dwellers, there was more anger and resentment in the summer of 1978 in Manila and some other parts of the country, notably the central island of Cebu and the southern island of Mindanao, than I had seen at any other time since the inception of martial law. This was due to the fact that, after having held five rigged referendums in order to confer periodic approval upon his dictatorial rule, Marcos had opened the door for the first time, in April, to what appeared to be an effort to reintroduce some form of genuine democracy. Instead of another orchestrated political charade, he had called an election for the long-delayed Batasan Pambansa, or Interim National Assembly, that was supposed to be the first step in the creation of a parliamentary instead of presidential form of government. In Metro Manila an opposition slate of twenty-one candidates, headed by Marcos' avowed political enemy, Benigno (Ninoy) Aquino, who was then still in jail, having been arrested at the outset of martial law, won at least 7 and perhaps as many as 15 seats, according to common consensus. But through trickery and what was universally denounced as outright cheating, the Aquino slate, known by its acronym of LABAN (Fight), was deprived of any real chance to play a beginning role in the new parliamentary dispensation, and the government slate, called Kilusang Bagong Lipunan (New Society Movement), headed by Mrs. Marcos, who had been appointed by her husband to be both Governor of Metro Manila and Minister of Ecology and Human Settlements, was declared the victor of all 21 seats.

As my conservative and heretofore establishment-oriented American friend I visited that first rainy night said, "This was the worst fraud I've ever witnessed, and no wonder people are angry. I'm not a Filipino, but I'm angry myself." My old Filipino friends, including several who had so far given Marcos the benefit of the doubt and were willing to accept martial law as an inevitable antidote to revolutionary chaos, were in the darkest mood I had ever seen them. "As a moderate, I've lost what little effectiveness I've had," one of them, a novelist and editor, told me. "The young people I've been able to talk to won't listen to me anymore. Their despair is now matched by their bitterness and hatred, and more of them talk of taking to the hills and joining the Communists. If I were younger, I'd be doing the same thing."

The election campaign, during which Marcos allowed more freedom of speech than at any time since the start of martial law—Aquino had even been allowed to conduct a television interview with a press panel from a special studio set up in prison—had been an extremely volatile affair, and it took everyone, including Marcos, by surprise. If his initial intentions were at all honorable in deciding to conduct the vote, he made several bad errors of judgment. Most important, he miscalculated the genuine strength of the burgeoning opposition and failed to gauge the mood of the public. He also fell victim to his own legal bent of mind. Having invited, or allowed, an opposition to emerge, especially in Manila, which is traditionally an anti-opposition city, his biggest mistake was to let Aquino head the slate, especially since Aquino was still a martial-law prisoner awaiting a Supreme Court verdict on the validity, which he had challenged, of a military tribunal verdict of guilty on charges of subversion, murder and illegal possession of weapons.

These charges, which Aquino had not only denied but refused to meet in court because he maintained they were contrived and false, had arisen out of his alleged connections with the Communists in his native province of Tarlac, connections he privately admitted he had maintained but only in order to gather necessary intelligence about their operations. Marcos had further accused Aquino of being indirectly associated with right-wing assassination plots against him. When Marcos announced his election plans, he figured that the Liberal Party would put up a number of candidates in the various regions of the islands. The Liberals were, in fact, going to do so, but the party leaders decided to boycott the vote after Marcos announced that it would be held for party slates only and not for individuals. Given Marcos' complete control of the political situation, through the military and his own broad net of patronage, the Liberals realized they would have no reasonable chance under this block-voting scheme.

But after nearly six years of languishing in jail, Aquino decided for personal and political reasons to run his own ticket in Metro Manila, and he persuaded his fellow Liberals to support him. His slate was composed of some well-known former politicians, labor leaders and clergymen, and two activist women, Tondo's Trinidad Herrera and a lawyer named Charito Planas, who later defected to the United States. As the campaign progressed, LABAN made a growing impression on the aroused public in Manila. In the two decades following independence in 1946, elections had always been a wild, rollicking Wild West kind of performance, in which guns and goons played a major role and the press was a flagrantly reckless chorus of vaudevillian proportions. The performances entertained everyone but scarcely nurtured any awareness of what democracy was or could be all about. License to do anything and get away with it was virtually the national pastime, and it amounted to anarchy. While the level of violence in the 1978 election was less than it used to be, the mudslinging was on a par with the past. The private lives of the Marcoses were attacked by LABAN—one handbill implied that Marcos was not the real father of his eldest daughter, Imee—and the government made charges that several of the LABAN candidates were either Communists or Communist sympathizers.

Three days before the election a crowd of fifteen thousand, mostly students and workers, burned Marcos in effigy at a downtown rally, compared him to Hitler and demonstrated with torches, flags and placards for an end to martial law. The campaign reached its zenith on election eve when a tremendous noise demonstration took place in LABAN's behalf all over Manila. Cars and jeepneys (jeeps converted into taxis) honked their horns, and people everywhere poured out of their homes and offices and banged loudly on pots and cans. Church bells pealed, and in some areas fireworks, which are illegal, were set off. It may have been this spontaneous demonstration and its proof of LABAN's strength that prompted Marcos, according to some observers, to "lose his cool" and decide that nothing short of a complete victory for all twenty-one government candidates was permissible. He had already ordered all public employees to support the New Society Movement candidates or resign, and to list the addresses of the polling places where they voted. He had given them raises and housing allowances and had handed out bonuses to teachers, who had been assigned as poll watchers. Even so, it was generally felt that for foreign consumption if for no other reason, he would permit three or four LABAN candidates to win—to make it look as if the election had been fair and to provide some semblance of genuine opposition in the new Assembly. On the other hand, as others pointed out, he could not afford to let Aquino win, and Aquino was obviously the leading LABAN vote-getter.

In any event, there was no doubt that a vast amount of fraud took place, that many ballot boxes were "lost" or not counted and that others were simply stuffed. When I saw Marcos a few weeks later, he admitted that there had been "fraud on both sides but it did not affect the results," a conclusion that virtually no one else supported whom I spoke with, from jeepney and taxi drivers and hotel bellboys to clergymen, lawyers and impartial observers, including diplomats. A group of one hundred and twenty-one parents of schoolchildren typically expressed the public dismay by sending an open letter to superintendents and supervisors of the Ministry of Education in which they decried the brazen use of teachers as poll watchers as "an act of corruption." Describing the election as "the dirtiest in our whole lifetime," the parents wrote: "Many of us are products of the public school system. In spite of many defects, we had been quite proud of the fact that most of us studied in, or graduated from, the nation's public schools. But today we feel we have no right to be proud. Instead, we bow our heads in shame . . . What we now have is an acute shortage of honest, upright and courageous public school teachers. Our children should have reason to greet them 'Good morning, teacher' instead of 'Good morning, cheater.' "

Post-Election Problems

If Marcos had proved that he was congenitally incapable of holding fair elections, he lost no time in bolting the gate against further protests and demonstrations. Two days after the vote had been held, which was Bataan Day (in commemoration of the death march of American soldiers ordered by the invading Japanese early in 1942), LABAN organizers and supporters planned another march protesting the election frauds. Nearly six hundred marchers, mostly students and workers and some priests and nuns, started out from various parts of the city toward the cathedral, but before they reached it they were rounded up and arrested. Among them were a dozen or so of the top LABAN leaders, including Lorenzo Tanada, a former senator and well-known lawyer, and other defeated candidates and oppositionists. Except for Tanada and five others, they were all released two days later, and for health reasons Tanada was set free three days after that, but the remaining five were kept in prison for nearly two months. One of them was a Jesuit doctor-priest named Romeo Inteñgan, whom the government suspected of backing a military wing of a new Social Democratic Party to overthrow the regime by force. At the time of the arrest of Inteñgan, two youths who were working for him at the Loyola House of Studies were also arrested, and a week later an anonymous caller telephoned Loyola House and informed the director that one of the two, seventeen-year-old Teotimo Tantiado, had been beaten to death—but that the army claimed he had died of an acute case of hemorrhagic pancreatitis. The Jesuit fathers tried to obtain proof that Tantiado had been murdered, but despite Marcos' promise of a thorough investigation, nothing more was ever disclosed and a doctor's affidavit that the youth had died from natural causes was officially accepted.

The new Assembly consisted of 165 elected members, plus Marcos himself, ten of his cabinet members, and fourteen people from youth and labor groups to round out a total of 190 members. Having seen to it that the LABAN slate was wiped out in Manila, Marcos quickly arranged for an opposition of sorts to be elected on the island of Cebu, where, after a dispute over the counting of ballots, thirteen members of the Visayan Alliance Party in the central islands were designated victors by the Commission on Elections. Of the thirteen, however, only four were legitimate opponents of the government, along with one man elected in Mindanao. When the Assembly met, in its expensive new building on a muddy plot of land near Quezon City, Marcos relinquished his post as Speaker to a former Supreme Court justice but ran the sessions in his role as Prime Minister. He declared that the Assembly's creation marked "our formal shift to liberalism, against the trend of history which claims the irreversibility of the drift toward authoritarianism and centralism." He also said he would offer a further general amnesty to political prisoners (which he subsequently did) but made no mention of Aquino, who had formally applied for amnesty and had asked for permission to leave the country and had pledged "not to impair the image and security of the Republic"—he had already packed his bags and was momentarily awaiting release but was kept dangling on a string of legal excuses.

Obviously of two minds about what he had unleashed, Marcos warned that he would "abort any untoward development that will unmoor us from the reforms of the last six years." Any further attempts to stage demonstrations or create hysteria would be dealt with harshly, he said. As for holding local elections, which a year earlier he had promised to do, he reneged and said that the "disruptions and divisions" the Assembly vote had caused "raised doubts of the capacity of the nation to endure another election while in the midst of a crucial political transition and current economic difficulties." The Assembly passed some routine measures, including a new budget, and did little to disprove its critics, who described it as a "tame" body that would simply do Marcos' bidding and showed little initiative of its own, although two or three of the older politicians who had consented to run in the election did speak up occasionally—one of them, former Senator Arturo Tolentino, a constitutional expert, said the time had come to abandon martial law. Before adjourning its first session, a number of Assemblymen nominated Mrs. Marcos to be Deputy Prime Minister, and therefore Marcos' successor, but this performance was so flagrantly staged, in almost comic-opera fashion, that Marcos himself was forced to step in and suggest that the matter be temporarily postponed.

It was difficult at this point to tell how sincere Marcos was in his declared intentions to restore some degree of democratic freedom, and it was doubtful that he knew himself. He had used so many legal tricks, at which he is a master, to weave an intricate web in which he had enmeshed the entire legislative and judicial process that even the most ingenious spider would have had difficulty extricating itself. It seemed highly unlikely that he could undo what he had done without destroying not only the web but himself as well, thereby paving the way for the very chaos and violence he kept talking about. There are those who believe that when he declared martial law—citing lawlessness and the general disintegration of the economy and the body politic, including a left-wing rebellion and the alleged rightist plots on his life—he never intended it as a temporary measure but as the first step to keep himself in power indefinitely. Others believed him when he said the Assembly election and the establishment of parliamentary government would eventually lead to the evolution of some form of at least guided democracy. But there is no indication that even should martial law end, Marcos will relinquish his hold. As Prime Minister, ultimately under a figurehead President, he will retain the constitutional right, if he deems it necessary, to abolish the Interim Assembly or a regularly elected body, and simply issue more decrees, general orders or letters of instruction. These are the three instrumentalities by which he had run the country for six years, during which he had proclaimed 1,300 decrees, more than 600 instructions and 60 orders.

Background of Martial Law

In a speech a month before the elections, made to the faculty and students of Far Eastern University, Tanada recalled Marcos' two main reasons for declaring martial law: to save the Republic from armed rebellion and to create "a new society." "It is our submission that he has failed to achieve both objectives," Tanada said, "because instead of saving the Republic he destroyed it, and instead of reforming our society he deformed it. He destroyed our Republic by imposing upon people through his martial-law powers a government *conceived* in sin—*born* through falsification, deceit, bribery and intimidation—*existing* because of American military and economic aid, *secured* by the enlarged military forces (numbering sixty thousand at the start of martial law and now exceeding one hundred and fifty thousand), and *strengthened* by terrorism, torture, and the massive suppression of human rights."

In all likelihood, Marcos had been considering martial law a year or more prior to his re-election in 1969, when he became the first of the six Presidents of the postwar Republic to be re-elected for a second four-year term. To ensure his victory over Sergio Osmena, Jr., the lackluster son of the first President of the young Republic, he indulged in a vast overkill operation, spending $100 million to buy votes and television time; he won by 2 million ballots out of 9 million cast and would have won handily without spending anywhere near what he did. More than two hundred persons were killed during the election period, more than ever before, and with political animosities at a new high, and the economy a shambles as the government was spending far more than its income without managing to alleviate the disparities between the wealthy and the poor, it seemed to those of us covering the election that the whole society was on the verge of disintegration.

In the summer of 1970, two years before martial law, Marcos called for a special election, to be held in 1971, for a Constitutional Convention to change the form of government. Many then suspected that his intent went beyond the replacement of the chaotic presidential system with a more orderly parliamentary government. Three hundred delegates to the convention were duly elected, and amid constant bickering, began the long process of preparing a new constitution, which Marcos and his wife soon vitiated by wining and dining scores of delegates in order to obtain a draft that would allow him to remain President until an Interim National Assembly was called at his discretion.

The situation in the country meanwhile went from bad to worse. During the regular off-year congressional election campaign in August 1971, an opposition Liberal Party rally at the Plaza Miranda in Manila was hand-grenaded and all eight party candidates, led by Senator Jovito Salonga, were severely injured. It was never determined who threw the grenades—ordinary hoodlums hired by a right-wing mob, the Communists or henchmen of Marcos' Nacionalista Party. Aquino, the leading Liberal, was not running for re-election that year, since his term had not yet expired, but he was being hailed as

Marcos' successor in the next presidential election. He arrived late at the rally and escaped injury, and afterward took the lead on the Senate floor, where, repeating his earlier warnings that Marcos was trying to create "a garrison state," he delivered a number of excoriating speeches that set forth the growing plight of the country and denounced the President and his cronies as responsible for the total collapse of law and order, for reaping personal profits through extortion and corrupt deals, and for economic mismanagement which, among other things, had increased unemployment to two and a half million. Immediately after the grenade incident, Marcos suspended habeas corpus and began to talk openly of declaring martial law. The Liberals trounced the Nacionalistas in that election, winning 6 of the 8 seats up for vote, and political passions intensified further, as did violence. Several buildings, including the Manila Hilton, were bombed, demonstrations took place constantly and two dozen students and workers were killed. Wealthy citizens were kidnapped and held for high ransoms. The New People's Army of the Communists widened its area of activity and captured virtually all of Isabela province, its long-time stronghold in northern Luzon, while the Moslem rebels on the southern islands, notably Mindanao and the Sulu archipelago, stepped up their dissident attacks against Christian settlers and the ineffectual army and police. A reign of terror seemed to be spreading throughout the country, and a revolutionary uprising did indeed seem imminent.

In the Vietnam war, the two big American bases in the Philippines—the air base at Clark Field and the naval base at Subic Bay, both on Luzon—played an important part. As the war deteriorated further, Marcos, in one of his first acts after being re-elected, had pulled his 1,500-man civic-action team, mostly engineers and health workers, out of South Vietnam. One of the first things he had done when he became President in 1965 was to send it there, declaring that the American effort to halt the spread of Communism in Vietnam was a crusade in behalf of freedom throughout Southeast Asia. But things had now changed. There was talk of a New Developmental foreign policy, which bespoke the effort to break away from almost total dependence on the United States and to change the whole structure of the American-Filipino relationship, including the client reliance on the American bases to protect the Philippines. In his formal public statements Marcos continued to profess pro-American views, but it was apparent from what he was saying privately that he was responding to the new surge of nationalist and anti-American sentiment led by the students who by this time had begun to blame the Americans for just about everything that was wrong in the Philippines, including the collapse of public morale, the surging wave of crime, and the destruction of values such as belief in the family system and the sanctity of the Church.

I remember, during these days, talking to student leaders who had mounted marches on Malacanang of as many as ten thousand students and workers who hurled stones at the palace before proceeding to the American embassy to shout further deprecations such as "Yankees Go Home!" But neither they nor carping newspaper columnists and adversary academic critics had any concrete suggestions to make about what should be done to save the Philippines from internal collapse. Most of the opposition politicians were at one another's throats as well as at Marcos'. It was obvious that the postwar American-created form of government was no longer functioning, that it had become a bad Hollywood version of democracy at bay, or even a bad gangster movie. But there were no directors on the scene to rewrite the script—except Marcos.

According to Aquino, Marcos had a secret plan, code-named Sagittarius, to invoke martial law and keep himself in power. During the two months prior to martial law, Aquino said, Marcos had orchestrated a series of events to lead up to it, including a score of bombing incidents in Manila—all of them in the middle of the night, so no one was hurt. These bombings were allegedly the key part of a plot to charge the New People's Army with increasing subversive activity in the capital. On September 15, 1972, four days after some friends in the army had leaked details of Sagittarius to him, Aquino disclosed it in a Senate speech. Marcos called the account "sheer fabrication without basis in fact," but the army chief of staff, General Romeo Espino, admitted the same day that Sagittarius did in fact exist as a contingency plan to deal with the Communist revolt if it got out of hand. Thereafter, events moved quickly. On September 18 Aquino and Senator Gerardo Roxas, the president of the Liberal Party, were formally briefed by the army about Sagittarius but were told that the situation was under control and that there was no immediate cause for alarm. Nevertheless, Aquino heard from his army friends that martial law was imminent. On September 19 Marcos accused Aquino of having met two weeks before with José Ma Sison, the Communist Party leader, at a house in Makati. The following day Aquino denied in another Senate speech that any such meeting had taken place, calling the charge "sheer madness" and declaring that if it were true and if he had disclosed the meeting to Defense Secretary John Ponce Enrile, as Marcos said he had done, "instead of maligning me he should have called me to Malacanang and congratulated me." It was doubtful that Sison (who was later captured and charged with treason and subversion) would have risked venturing into Makati; but there was some evidence, according to what I later learned, that one of Sison's lieutenants, a man named Julius Fortuna, had approached Aquino to suggest an alliance between the New People's Army and the Liberal Party to get rid of Marcos one way or another, but that Aquino had turned him down.

This, then, was the background of martial law, which was declared on the evening of September 22, a few hours after Secretary Enrile's car was ambushed while he was on his way home from his office; Enrile was unhurt, and Aquino and others charged that the ambush was just another hoax to allow Marcos to assume full control.

The decree went into effect at midnight, and in the early hours of the morning hundreds of persons accused of political conspiracy were arrested. The following day Aquino was arrested while he was attending a congressional committee meeting at a Manila Hotel. Two other senators, José Diokno and

Raymond Mitra, were also thrown in jail, as were a dozen of the country's most prominent journalists, including the publisher and a top columnist of the leading national newspaper, the Manila *Times.* Marcos subsequently told a group of foreign correspondents that he had actually signed the martial-law decree on September 17 but had waited a few days to issue it "because I wanted time to commune with God and await His signal." His critics contend that he could have achieved his aims legitimately if he had simply postponed the planned plebiscite on the new constitution and asked Congress for emergency powers for a limited period so he could then issue the reform decrees he wanted and establish a new plebiscite date, but that was not Marcos' way of doing things.

Marcos as a Leader

I have known Marcos since the end of World War II and have spoken with him frequently over the years. A trim, handsome man who is now in his early sixties, he has always kept himself in good shape by exercising regularly, and he has retained his youthful dash and daring and his personal magnetism. Though he is aloof and arrogant, he is highly controlled, polite and capable of being several things at once—calculating, conciliatory and overpowering. He is a difficult opponent, and a worse enemy. Above all, he has a messianic belief in himself and his destiny, and this enables him to twist the interpretation of events to fit his own concepts, turning even apparent contradictions —including those of his own making—into a rational defense of his position. The Presidents who preceded him were a motley lot, ranging from American-sponsored figures of some stature who had acquired nationalist credentials of their own, notably Ramón Magsaysay, who took over in the early fifties, to mediocrities such as his predecessor, Elpidio Quirino, and Carlos García, his successor, both of whom played *palabas* to the hilt and winnowed their way through corruption-ridden years that solved none of the Philippines' fundamental social and economic problems. After a brief four-year interlude, during which the well-meaning but inept Diosdado Macapagal tried but failed to succeed in Magsaysay's image, along came Marcos. From Ilocano province on northern Luzon, he was a war hero during the Pacific war and became a brilliant lawyer afterward, completing his legal studies while in prison on a political-murder charge involving the killing of an enemy of his father; after successfully defending himself, he too went into politics, became a representative and then a senator and, having switched from the Liberal to the Nacionalista Party, dramatically campaigned for and won the presidency in 1965, at which point he was hailed as a potential savior of his country who had both the strength and fortitude to set things right. He enhanced his already glamorous image by marrying a Filipino beauty queen from Leyte, in the Visayan Islands, named Imelda Romualdez, thereby simultaneously broadening his political base.

I was with Marcos on that night of his big presidential-election victory, when he threw a vast party at his plush suburban home adrip with liquor and lovely ladies—they came to be called "blue ladies," all of them dressed in blue, Imelda's favorite color. It was difficult not to be caught up in the euphoria of the moment, and along with the several hundred guests who drifted through the brightly lit gardens and rooms, I felt myself transported into a Philippine setting of a Fitzgerald novel. Immaculately dressed in a cream-colored tagalog shirt with beige trousers, Marcos moved gracefully among the clusters of guests like an Asian version of Jay Gatsby, imperial and emanating a sense of almost mystic power and assurance, qualities he has always possessed. It seemed to everyone present that he was indeed the man of the hour who could become the great leader the Philippines required, a President who would make good on his promises to end the futile political bickering and bureaucratic ineptitude of the past and set the country on a true path of progress and prosperity. "This nation can be great again," he said in his inaugural address a short time later. "This I have said over and over. It is my article of faith, and Divine Providence has willed that you and I can now translate this faith into deeds . . . We must harness the wills and the hearts of all our people. We must find the secret chords which turn ordinary men into heroes, mediocre fighters into champions."

Despite these brave words, Marcos' first term as President was not an overwhelming success. He built thousands of miles of new roads and several hundred new schools, but much of the money for these projects came from the United States, and not all of it was used honestly. He also benefited from the research conducted at the International Rice Research Institute at Los Baños, south of Manila, which the Rockefeller and Ford foundations had helped finance, and which developed new miracle strains that improved rice production in the Philippines and other Asian nations. But he failed to come to grips with the fundamental problems of endemic poverty and to loosen the grip which the old oligarchic families of both Spanish and Filipino extraction held on the economy.

When I saw him at his private office in Malacanang several months after the declaration of martial law and the establishment of what he called "constitutional authoritarianism," he conceded that he was taking chances in applying emergency powers but asserted that he was not doing it "in such a way as to antagonize the people and cause worse repercussions than rebellion." He emphasized that "we have to save democracy here—that is our ultimate aim, and we don't want a new form of government." In seeking to "change the Filipino from a political animal into an economic animal," he said, he found martial law and the subsequent measures he had initiated necessary to "destroy the political power of the oligarchs" who "froze the status quo and prevented reforms by controlling the old Congress"—which he had disbanded. By means of intelligence operatives, he added, he had infiltrated both rightist and leftist groups that wanted to assassinate him and overthrow the government, and had ascertained that the two opposition elements had temporarily joined forces to attain their objectives. He had proof of such a conspiracy, he told me, and that was why he had declared martial law. "And just before martial law I saw the beginnings of a condition similar to the one in Indonesia in 1965, prior to the attempted Communist coup there, when cleavages and plots existed within the army as well as on the left."

Marcos said that by "going directly to the people" through Citizens Assemblies, or village gatherings, instead of holding the planned plebiscite to ratify the new constitution, he had managed to avoid "a very explosive situation," because, even though the plebiscite would have been favorable (this was a point that by no means everyone agreed on), old-guard politicians could have used the occasion to foment trouble which the military and the government as a whole might have had difficulty controlling. He subsequently defended his position further at a press conference at which he said that he alone would decide when the Interim National Assembly should be called, and that "meanwhile we still have a presidential form of government," adding that "we have a valid constitution. The people have voted for it; it's their will. How can this be a grab for dictatorial powers? I have not grabbed power. I was elected in 1969."

Despite Marcos' attitude of assurance, he did not seem to me nearly as confident as he pretended to be. It was true that martial law had generally been welcomed at first because it had reduced the high incidence of crime and created a far more stable state of order than had existed in the Philippines for years. Life was certainly more peaceful than it had been; the imposition of a curfew from midnight until 4 A.M. had not only slackened the crime rate but subdued the frenetic pace of life as a whole, including gambling and politicking, both of which were officially banned. People were no longer afraid to walk the streets or ride in taxis. On the other hand, they were afraid to talk in public as freely as before—rumor-mongering had been declared an offense punishable by six months' imprisonment. All the old newspapers had been shut down, and the new ones permitted were simply dull government mouthpieces.

As martial law continued, the improvements it had brought about were offset by a rigidity and stultification that were the inevitable by-products of regimentation. Despite his countless decrees, orders and imposition of more "discipline" to accomplish touted "reforms"—what Marcos called "crisis government" or, in a particularly revealing passage in his own voluminous writings, a "Cromwellian phase in our quest for a good and just society"— inefficiency, graft and corruption continued to riddle many of his programs. As time went on and discontent mounted, he demonstrated what all authoritarian rulers reveal sooner or later—a gradual loss of direction and momentum, and his attempts to generate public participation in government through the Citizens Assemblies became increasingly meaningless. The assemblies were based on the Barrio Charter Act of 1953, whereby gatherings to include all those eighteen years old and above could meet to help run village affairs, except that Marcos chose the word *barangays,* which is what the early Malayo-Polynesian settlers called their first communities, instead of the Spanish word *barrio.* He also lowered the voting age to fifteen. The first of these thirty to forty thousand assemblies met in January 1973, and were given ready-made questionnaires and prepared answers on six issues. By a vote of 90.6 percent, they did what Marcos wanted them to do—most important, approving the new constitution but rejecting the plebiscite to ratify it. The vote was completed with remarkable speed, in two days, and two and a half years later, in June 1976, the former chairman of Marcos' Media Advisory Council, Primitivo Mijares, who had defected to the United States, submitted a memorandum to the United States House of Representatives in which he said that the 1973 figures had been completely manufactured by a group that had included himself. Subsequently even the Philippine Supreme Court, which had been packed by Marcos and had ruled that martial law was constitutional, held that the 1973 ratification of the constitution had not been valid because the Citizens Assemblies had included illiterates, feeble-minded persons and ex-convicts, who were barred under the Election Code, and because "the voting . . . was done mostly by acclamation or open show of hands [and] secrecy, which is one of the essential features of the election process, was not therefore observed."

Marcos disregarded the verdict, which was rendered far too late to make any difference anyway. Two days after the first of the *barangay* gatherings, when he had declared that the new constitution, replacing the old one of 1935 before independence, had been adopted but would be temporarily suspended, he was "legally" in absolute control of the country, holding five jobs: President under the old constitution; martial-law administrator as commander in chief; acting ceremonial President under the new constitution; acting Prime Minister; and acting Speaker of the not yet summoned Interim National Assembly. In July of 1973, looking ahead to what would have been the end of his elected term in December, he again called the Citizens Assemblies together and obtained a vote of 90 percent in favor of his remaining in office and "finishing the reforms" he had initiated under martial law. In February 1975 the affirmative vote was the same—this time in answer to the question of whether the *barangay* citizens approved of the way he was exercising his powers, including the power to issue "proclamations, orders, decrees and instructions." Marcos continued the gimmickry by holding two more such referendums approving his performance—in October 1976 and April 1977—and each time his brazen solicitation of popular support became more shallow and ludicrous.

Accomplishments and Failures

When I last saw Marcos, in August 1978, in his Malacanang office, I asked him if, looking back on his declaration of martial law and on what has happened since, he would, if he had the chance, have done things differently. He said that "so many unexpected things happened that it's hard to give a rational answer, but there were probably no other options for the steps I initially took. Either I ran away to save my skin and let the country go to the dogs or organize a military junta and establish a revolutionary government.

Given my background, however, my legal training, my grounding in constitutional principles, I did what I had to do by establishing constitutional authoritarianism. If I wanted to promote a peaceful constitutional revolution, I had to start with Congress itself, which was the purpose behind calling a Constitutional Convention. And I had to assume responsibility personally. Though it's never been publicized, I also offered the opposition a coalition—they could have shared every ministry except defense, which I wanted to keep myself, and I even offered the Communists a chance to participate in a democratic dialogue and in elections. All this was before I declared martial law, but all my offers were rejected. The Liberal Party leaders with whom I met, including Aquino, turned me down, even though the only thing I wanted in return was a disavowal of the use of violence. From that you can start conjecturing what might have happened. There were two things I didn't anticipate. First, the support a foreign country [he didn't specify, but he meant Libya] gave to a secessionist movement—hundreds of millions of dollars to help the armed Moslems—and, second, I didn't anticipate that the United States would cut down on assistance to the Philippines. The Americans said they were too busy in Vietnam. I even considered invoking the Mutual Defense Pact of 1951 at one juncture, but the medicine would have been worse than the disease. A third thing I didn't anticipate was the oil crisis. These unrelated events delayed the return to normalcy."

It was true, as Marcos said, that in fiscal 1972 the United States had cut back its military assistance program to the Philippines from $16 million to just over $14 million. But in fiscal 1973 the totals were back up to $17 million, and the following year they rose to nearly $24 million, and since then have averaged about $37 million a year. Economic aid, including grants and contributions of machinery and other equipment for agrarian programs, continued throughout these years at about the same annual pace of between $75 million and $100 million. Many Filipinos, in fact, have felt all along that Marcos was *too* dependent on the United States and that he was using the military aid to build up his own power base rather than curb the insurgencies—among other things, he appointed more than fifty new generals and three hundred new colonels to ensure the army's loyal support. As opposition to the war in Vietnam increased, the Filipinos were further angered by a partially censored report issued by Senator Stuart Symington, who headed a subcommittee on United States Security Agreements and Commitments Abroad, which revealed that Washington had given the Philippines Civic Action Group of engineers and health workers Marcos had sent to Vietnam back in 1965 about $38 million worth of assistance, thus in effect making it a mercenary outfit. Other sections of the report that criticized collusion between the Americans and Filipinos in running rackets around the United States also aroused anger. If the Americans really wanted to help the Philippines, many people started to ask, why didn't they bring pressure on Marcos to institute some genuine economic and social improvements instead of just talking about reform?

The question was justified, and in many ways the situation was like Vietnam all over again, but in other respects it wasn't quite so simple. Mary Racelis Hollnsteiner, a sociologist at the highly regarded Ateneo University, in Manila, in a conversation I had with her after several years of martial law, observed, "The government has no mechanism for coping with poverty." She went on to say that the new technocrats whom Marcos depended on, despite their academic competence, were too highly specialized. "There has to be an ideology, and that's hard to develop in a society with so many rich," she said. "Marcos is trying to mix milk and water." Her point was well taken. Though by the late seventies the government was belatedly formulating a public-housing program, for example, it was not only insufficient but was concentrated on middle- rather than low-cost projects. And more revealing was the profligate spending on fourteen luxury hotels and a score of costly condominiums which were built along the harbor front and in other plush parts of the city. Though the rate of tourism was slowly rising, the new hotels were no more than half full most of the time.

Land Reform—a Plus

After instituting martial law, Marcos made land reform his No. 1 objective. Despite some omissions, flaws and anomalies, most impartial experts gave him high marks for this program and agreed that more progress was made in three and a half years than in the previous thirty. Even so, the major part of the land problem—the freeing of peasants from bondage as impoverished tenants and sharecroppers—was only partly solved because the program covered only those areas devoted to the cultivation of rice and corn. Nearly 1.5 million hectares (3.75 million acres) of these crops were bought from landlords, who received cash and government bonds, and distributed to approximately a million tenant farmers. By 1978 the program was about 70 percent completed and had been extended to embrace all landlords holding less than seven hectares (they had been excluded initially) with the stipulation that they could retain ownership but had to give their tenants firm leaseholds. One difficulty was that no provisions had been made for the peasants who acquired titles to land or obtained leaseholds to own their homes or home lots, which were often separated by considerable distances from their farm plots. This situation existed particularly among those tenants who obtained plots from landlords in the seven-and-under hectare category—57 percent of all tenants seeking leaseholds from 90 percent of all landlords. Not touched at all by the program were the large sugar and coconut plantations and the 2 or 3 million itinerant landless peasants; in mid-1978, plans were being initiated to include these categories too, necessitating a bolder set of administrative measures that would take years to implement and complete. In dealing with the sugar and coconut holdings, Marcos and his land-reform minister, Conrado Estrella, would come up against the old die-hard oligarchic landlords, who were less willing to relinquish their properties and who were determined to engage in even more legal bickering and delaying actions than the less powerful rice and corn landlords. As for the impoverished landless peasants, the government had started a plan to offer them leaseholds on public property in about forty settlements around the country. Some of these settlements, which I visited in the summer of 1978, had developed into successful cooperatives, but in most cases the land set aside was poor for cultivation and required considerable development before even marginal returns could be expected. Moreover, the administrators in charge had made mistakes, such as building feeder roads before introducing sufficient irrigation.

Not everyone hailed the land-reform programs as a boon. A study by the Institute of Philippine Culture pointed out that they had in many ways widened the economic gap between well-developed regions (like central Luzon) and poorer areas (for example, eastern Visayas), and that rural people in all regions were still suffering from "a steady erosion of their capacity to control their own lives." The study went on to say: "The forces of change have dislocated and impoverished large sections of the population, so that they have not been able to generate genuine economic growth. A substantial proportion of rural production is in fact extracted through commercial crop production for export and through the commercialization of agricultural production as a whole." Much of what is produced "goes abroad as profit remittances of multinational corporations, and is wasted through excessive consumption by the ruling elite." The result, the study concluded, had brought about "land alienation, increased tenancy, and the concentration of land holdings in fewer and fewer hands," and had caused "the erosion of community institutions and other social networks, such as the patron-client relationships of landlords and tenants, which provided a degree of security to the peasantry."

A somewhat less pessimistic prognosis was given to me by a group of five Filipino community workers involved in Program Compassion, a government effort concentrating on agricultural productivity, nutrition, the environment and family planning. Though the men I spoke with criticized the government's failure to assist peasants beyond the initial stages of land reform—by offering them production aids and incentives that the better landlords used to offer, for instance, and sufficient fertilizers and pesticides at controlled prices—the community experts felt that in general, the Green Revolution was succeeding. New highways and other roads had facilitated distribution, they said, and the barrio cooperative movement was slowly growing, even though there was still a lack of trading and marketing facilities for food products.

While Marcos' words often spoke louder than his actions, he is, as even his enemies concede, a man of imagination and ability, and combined with his innate ruthlessness, this made him the consummate politician he is today. During fourteen years of holding power, he used these attributes, and a not untypical desire to enrich himself, to make him one of the wealthiest men in Asia if not in the world. He shared an endless bounty of profits—derived from government-sponsored contracts and concessions as well as private deals, including everything from highway and nuclear energy plants to fashionable golf clubs—with his wife and relatives, and with selected friends who belonged to his inner entourage and became part of the functioning Marcos dynasty. That such a dynasty has come to exist is not altogether surprising. While he is a dictator in modern dress, his role is in keeping with the strong monarchic orientation of the Philippines, which, despite fifty years of comparatively mild colonization by the United States, retains the imprint of the previous three hundred years of Spanish rule and of the Moslem sultans and other tribal chieftains who dominated the country in the pre-Western era.

Marcos' flair for the dramatic was clearly demonstrated in a speech he made in downtown Luneta Park, in Manila, in September 1975, in celebration of the third anniversary of martial law, in which, after taking note of the gains and benefits he had achieved, he startled his audience, which included most of the ranking members of the government, by declaring that despite the popular enthusiasm for reform, "we are in fact a nation divided against itself —divided between urban and rural, rich and poor, majorities and minorities, privileged and underprivileged." He went on to speak of continuing fears that "we have liquidated an oligarchy only to set up a new oligarchy," and of the "massive opportunities for graft, corruption, and misuse of influence—opportunities which are now being exploited within the government service."

Most of Marcos' opposition not only agreed with him but singled him out as the leading new oligarch. As former Senator Salonga cogently put it, "If, indeed, drastic reforms had to be instituted to save the Republic, should it be the Chief Executive of the Old Society that should now lead the crusade for a good New Society?" The question was contained in "A Message of Hope to Filipinos Who Care," which was guardedly distributed, mostly to foreigners, a month after Marcos' Luneta speech, and which bore the signatures of one hundred and thirty prominent civilians, churchmen and academics, self-described as "a representative group of citizens devoted to the cause of truth, justice and freedom." Salonga was the principal author. In criticizing Marcos for using empty excuses to prolong martial law indefinitely and with having no "overriding ideology to which the people can make a genuine commitment," Salonga attacked "the propensity of the New Society to spend the money of the people on frivolous, unproductive projects," and he cited the $60 million spent on the 1974 Miss Universe contest and as much or more on the Muhammad Ali–Joe Frazier heavyweight championship in 1975 in Manila.

But the document reserved its strongest criticism for the government's policy of undermining "economic nationalism" by overencouraging investment of foreign capital. It noted that inducements had included "cheap labor, frozen wages, impotent unions, no strikes or demonstrations, no embarrassing investigations, tax holidays and incentives, plus firm guarantees of one hundred per cent repatriation and profit remittances." Multinational corporations operating in a poor country "invariably tend to control its economy," the document added. "They ruin or buy out local enterprises unable to compete with them, borrow working capital from local banks and financing institutions . . . corrupt the local ruling elite through all sorts of devices and pressures . . . [and] expose the native population to consumption patterns suitable only to affluent societies." While many of these allegations were true, restraints on the operations of multinationals were established in the Philippines, including, as Marcos said when I mentioned these statements to him, a maximum limit of 40 percent foreign equity in local businesses. Economic officials at the American embassy, whose role included the protection of American investments in the Philippines, maintained, somewhat defensively, that "exploitation is certainly within acceptable norms." The embassy said that multinationals had helped preserve the Philippines' financial balance by bringing in vast amounts of capital, a fact which, though true, had not kept the government from borrowing huge amounts from foreign banks and consortiums—something it was able to do because its international credit rating was high.

Opposition from the Church

Former politicians and lawyers such as Salonga and Tanada remained in the forefront of the opposition to Marcos, but almost since the start of martial law, his most consistent opponents were Catholic militants, particularly a group of nuns and Jesuit priests, and a lesser number of liberal Protestant churchmen. The National Secretariat for Social Action and the Association of Major Religious Superiors regularly issued pamphlets, reports and surveys on a variety of subjects, such as the deprivation of civil rights; the condition of the urban poor; the low status and harsh treatment of sugar workers on the island of Negros, the main sugar-producing island; and unfair treatment of such minorities as the Moslems, the Igorots, and the Kalinga and Bontok tribesmen of northern Luzon. Both the Catholics and the Protestants strongly supported the Kalingas against the government's plan to build five big hydroelectric dams that would obliterate not only some of their villages but some of their sacred burial grounds as well and would force their removal to lowland resettlement areas where there was insufficient water.

The Jesuit fathers, in particular, attacked the deprivation of human rights under martial law and the use of torture against prisoners. No one knew the exact number of prisoners arrested, but early 1973 figures varied from between 10,000 and 30,000, most of whom were ordinary petty criminals who were not held for long periods of time. According to Defense Secretary Enrile, in early 1979 there were about 500 persons in jail accused of subversion or inciting rebellion; but Enrile also told me that thirty-two military tribunals Marcos had ordered phased out still had about 1,600 criminal cases of all sorts, including subversion, to dispose of. Aside from these totals, according to Amnesty International and other private groups, unknown numbers of persons accused of crimes against the state were held in provincial or army and constabulary jails all over the country, many of them suspected or known members of the Moslem liberation movement in the southern islands or members and sympathizers of the New People's Army, which was slowly spreading its area of activity from Luzon southward.

One of the leading Jesuit activists was Father James Reuter, who had spent most of his life in the Philippines. Reuter was a stocky man of medium height who looked more like a retired prizefighter than a priest, and he spoke of his personal battles with the government as if he were recounting stories of bare-knuckles contests against street bullies back in Elizabeth, New Jersey, where he originally came from. As editor of *The Communicator,* which until it was banned in 1976 had been published irregularly by the Jesuits, along with another banned paper called *The Signs of the Times,* Reuter and twenty-three other priests, nuns and lay members of the editorial staffs were accused of libel and inciting people to sedition and violence; they had not been detained but were simply kept under investigation until, in the summer of 1978, Marcos suddenly ordered Enrile to drop the case "in the interest of national reconciliation and unity." Reuter had got into trouble for, among other reasons, writing an article about a shoemaker named Juan Adriano who had been beaten to death by the constabulary when he tried to move into a small house he had bought; he had partially rented it to a man who refused to get out and who was a cousin of one of the constabulary chiefs.

When I spoke with Father Reuter a few days after the charges against him had been dropped, he said, "Such cases take place all the time, and unless they come to our attention nothing is done about them. The situation is getting worse. Many of our priests believe that a violent solution is inevitable, that a civil war will take place—the soothsayers and faith healers that are now so popular are predicting that within a year. Since the last election, especially here in Manila, people are madder than ever. I'm hoping it will all collapse of its own weight and that the moderate element of the military will move in and take over, but I have come to expect the worst. To remain silent is unforgivable. At sixty-two, I figure that if I'm going to die I want a good way to do it—if there's nothing worth dying for, there's nothing worth living for, either. My conscience is in the marrow of my bones. I feel like an open wound."

By no means all members of the Catholic hierarchy felt as passionately as Father Reuter and his fellow Jesuits about martial law and the Marcos regime —in fact, the majority opposed intervention in secular affairs. Jaime Cardinal Sin, while far more socially conscious than the man he succeeded, adopted a moderately critical position toward the Marcos regime; he felt the Assembly election was a fraud, but while he supported several of the activist causes on moral, social and humanitarian grounds, he also believed firmly in separation of church and state. Marcos remained particularly sensitive to criticism on human rights issues, which came from varying sources, including the International Commission of Jurists and the International Law Association as well as some ranking members of the Administration of President Jimmy Carter and congressional investigators in the United States. At the same time he responded to the accusations of torture against prisoners by firing and punishing several score army and constabulary soldiers and ordering members of both the military and the police to behave better and to exercise discipline in dealing with civilians, especially in the Moslem areas, where, after seven years of bitter fighting, a total of fifty thousand persons had been killed, a majority of them civilians, and tens of thousands more were rendered homeless.

Marcos kept citing the Moslem fight for separation or autonomy and the continuing Communist insurrection as the main reasons, along with economic problems, for continuing martial law. At the end of 1978 the long-drawn-out southern war, which had its roots in racial antipathies dating back four hundred years, showed no signs of abating despite sporadic attempts to establish cease-fires and create some sort of framework for autonomy in half a dozen of the Moslem-dominated provinces. The basic fight between the Moslems and Christian settlers in the southern islands had become aggravated by factionalism within the Moslem ranks. The more radical leader of the Moro National Liberation Front, Nur Misuari, was supported by Libya, while the moderate head, Hashim Salamat, had the backing of Egypt. The various fighting units of the Front were also fragmented, and though some units surrendered to the government from time to time, the basic rebel strength remained at 20,000 armed men, who were opposed by 50,000 to 70,000 government troops. As for the Communists, the strength of the New People's Army (NPA), at the outset of 1979, was estimated to be about 2,000 armed men, with another 4,000 combat support elements, 6,000 service and support personnel, and a mass base of 30,000 to 50,000 sympathizers. This was considerably less than its predecessor, the Hukbalahaps of the early fifties, who were suppressed by President Magsaysay when he was Defense Secretary, but despite the arrest of José Ma Sison and other top Communist leaders, the movement was still active, and there were signs that the NPA was recruiting more men and reorganizing its ranks while increasing terrorist attacks.

Debate Over American Bases

The NPA was Maoist-oriented and had Peking's moral if not material support, but a new group of pro-Soviet Communists was also once again beginning to stir, seeking to regain the leadership of the party it had held in the fifties. Despite the Communist insurgency, Marcos had opened diplomatic relations with both Peking and Moscow as part of his new diplomacy of balancing his continued dependence on the United States with friendship and trade with Communist and Third World nations, and in keeping with his desire to give the Philippines a stronger independent voice in Southeast Asia. This was all a reflection of the new nationalism and the new anti-Americanism that had evolved since the debacle of the Vietnam war. Marcos wanted to retain the two American bases, Clark Field and Subic Bay, but he had purposely kept the negotiations for new agreements going at a slow pace in order to give him greater leverage in exacting continuing economic aid from Washington, and at the same time, by adopting a tough bargaining posture, to enhance his nationalist image. This enabled him to reap domestic political benefits while also elevating his role as a regional and Third World leader.

However, part of Marcos' strategy backfired. During the Ford Administration, Secretary of State Henry Kissinger offered to pay the Filipinos $1 billion over a five-year period; roughly half of it would represent economic aid and the rest would constitute rent for continued use of the bases. The Filipinos turned this down, wanting a clearer definition of outright rent, or at least "compensation," for the bases and separation of that from economic aid, which still amounted to about $100 million a year, mostly agricultural assistance of one kind or another. When the Carter Administration took over, it agreed to meet Marcos' demand to the extent that it said it would ask Congress for annual amounts of economic aid which, if turned down for budgetary or other reasons, such as opposition to martial law and human rights violations, could still be funneled to the Philippines through the World Bank or the International Monetary Fund, to which the United States was the major contributor. But at the end of December 1978, when a new agreement was finally signed, the overall package the Americans pledged was $500 million, or half of what Kissinger had offered. Marcos had previously been told by visiting American congressmen that the mood of Congress being what it was, there was little or no chance of his receiving any more than that amount. The Americans agreed to Marcos' demand that the bases be given Filipino sovereignty and that they be run by Filipino commanders, with the proviso that the United States be assured of effective command and control over American personnel, employees, equipment and facilities, and retaining unhampered control over military operations involving its own forces. It was decided that the base accords would be reviewed every five years until they expired in 1991 in order to "assure that [they] continue to serve the mutual interests of both parties." Marcos reaffirmed, as he had earlier reassured the Vietnamese, that the bases would only be used for "defensive purposes," and that they would not be used against any country or group of countries. Left to be negotiated was the question of jurisdiction in criminal cases involving the 16,000 servicemen living on the two bases with their families.

The new agreement satisfied the Pentagon, and in the wake of normalization with China, was also satisfactory to Peking, which approved of the American presence in the Philippines if not in Taiwan, but a growing body of opinion, both in the Philippines and the United States, argued against it. Labor and youth organizations—Marcos' daughter was a prominent member of the latter—campaigned for dismantling the two bases. The Civil Liberties Union of the Philippines cited the fact that no serious external threats existed to the Republic, and that even if there was a threat, the United States would probably not be disposed, after Vietnam, to come to the aid of the Philippines despite its continuing commitments under the 1951 Mutual Defense Treaty. The bases "mock our independence" and "not only contribute to the deprivation of our freedom [but] threaten our very survival as a people," the CLU said in one of its declarations, especially if there was a nuclear war, in the event of which the bases would be a magnet for attack.

They also could serve as a magnet for domestic trouble. If the Communist insurgents of the New People's Army stepped up their activities and tried to provoke an American response by threatening Clark and Subic, a likely American refusal to help quell the internal unrest under the rather vaguely defined obligations of the treaty would probably increase the tempo of rebellion and aid the rebels' cause. Another potentially dangerous condition derived from the Philippines' claim to the Reed Bank area of the Spratly Islands in the South China Sea, which because of possible offshore oil deposits were being claimed by Peking, Taipeh and Hanoi too. The Filipinos, who maintain a small garrison force in the Reed area, insisted that the Mutual Defense Treaty called upon the United States to come to their defense if hostilities broke out over the Spratlys. Washington denied this. But a refusal to help protect the Philippine claim would also heighten nationalist tensions and could lead to a demand that the Americans get out of Clark and Subic entirely, and Washington would have no alternative but to comply.

From the standpoint of global strategy, despite the obvious advantages the U.S. Air Force and Navy obtained from the use of Clark and Subic, neither base was essential to the defense of American strategic interests in the Pacific, including the defense of Japan and Korea. Though it would be more expensive, alternative air and naval facilities could be built up in Guam and the Mariana Islands to the north, or in Japan itself; to the south, access to additional facilities in Singapore could probably be obtained, and possibly in western Australia as well, and this would be sufficient to serve the Pacific fleet and counter any Russian moves in the area. The argument that Clark and Subic are absolutely necessary for the defense of air and sea lanes stretching from the northern Pacific through Southeast Asia and the Indian Ocean to the Middle East and Europe was therefore not sustainable, especially in an age of nuclear aircraft carriers and long-range bombers and cargo planes.

In sum, the two Philippine bases, especially Subic, are convenient, as was most recently demonstrated when American ships steaming out of Subic Bay patrolled the South China Sea during Sino-Vietnamese hostilities, but they are not essential; their continued usefulness could easily be impaired by embarrassing events that might embroil the United States in situations that would not make their strategic value worth the political price. This could become the case in Luzon, for example, if a Soviet-supported Cuban effort to counter the Peking-oriented New People's Army were made. Under such circumstances, the insurgency could spread to other parts of the archipelago and even beyond. And if the war in the south for Moslem independence continued indefinitely, with Egypt and Libya backing different sets of rebels, it could drag the Philippines into a new Middle East crisis in which the United States might find itself involved as a result of its support of Israel against Arab extremists seeking to foment further trouble in Southeast Asia.

An Uncertain Future

At the start of 1979, in addition to adjusting itself to its new diplomacy as it tested the international political waters, the Philippines still faced grave economic and social problems. Despite a family-planning program that had brought the rate of population growth down below 3 percent a year, the country's population would still double by the year 2000, to 90 million. This would mean an annual average of 2 million new mouths to feed over the next quarter of a century, and also the need to try to find more jobs. Rising unemployment and underemployment would not make this an easy task. Urban overcrowding had already reached unmanageable proportions, and despite Marcos' bold plans for more capital investment, too few government projects were functioning properly, largely because Marcos and his relatives and friends were too deeply engaged in trying to make money out of them.

An increase in minimum wages of two pesos a day, which along with year-end bonuses and cost-of-living increases would mean approximately a 25 percent boost in wages overall, according to the government, did little to stem the growing tide of social discontent. The govermnent itself admitted that real wages had declined 32 percent in eight years. New consumer groups protesting rises in prices became more vocal, and labor unions showed fresh signs of resisting the ban on strikes while students became more active again, declaiming against higher tuition costs. On the political front, two petitions were circulated, each seeking a million signatures—one calling for Aquino's release from jail and the other for the immediate holding of national elections. In addition, a "chain letter" was distributed, calling on the public to react against the "Marcos-Romualdez" dictatorship by, among other things, boycotting stores and restaurants owned or controlled by Mrs. Marcos, refusing or delaying to pay taxes, and engaging in work slowdowns. Marcos reacted sharply to this new dissidence by describing the leaders as "snakes" and warning once more that anyone who sought to undermine his regime would be arrested. There were indications that more marches or demonstrations were imminent in Manila, and any fresh urban show of opposition, at a time when the Communists in the rural areas and the Moslems in the South were stepping up their activities, was bound to intensify the national atmosphere of crisis.

Unless Marcos soon mitigates his arbitrary rule and holds fuller and fairer elections, including local ones, while opening the gates to greater participation by others in making decisions, an explosion of some sort and a new power struggle seems certain to take place in the Philippines. Such a struggle could involve not only Marcos and his own entourage but the whole gamut of political, military and social forces.

The Marcoses are a strange couple, often appearing to be living in more of a business partnership than a marriage. A good part of the time they have gone their separate ways and have dealt for the most part with separate constellations of favored disciples. By 1979 Mrs. Marcos had obviously gained increasing power of her own as a result of her Ministry of Human Settlement's assuming jurisdiction over a wide variety of social and economic programs under the acronymic heading of BLISS—in addition to taking care of her husband and three children, she said, she would now be tending to "a family of forty-four million Filipinos." Despite her deep involvement in the nation's affairs, however, it seems doubtful that she could survive a cross-fire contest within the military establishment, and there are those who believe that even if she were chosen by the Assembly to succeed her husband, she would soon find herself in a position similar to that of Isabella Perón, in Argentina.

Among other possible heirs in the tight Malacanang coterie, which has been showing increasing signs of being beset by jealousy and feuds and is sometimes compared to the court of the Romanoffs, are Defense Secretary Enrile; Constabulary Commander Fidel Ramos, who, although a Protestant, is a cousin of Marcos' and a widely respected intellectual officer; and Major General Fabian Ver, the head of Marcos' Presidential Security Command, who has established his own intelligence units in every government department. But probably the most important element in Philippine political life, next to Marcos and to some degree his wife, is not any one individual but the military establishment as such, including younger officers who are beginning to show their impatience and discontent over the duration and faltering administration of martial law. The growing strength and increasing participation of the military in a broad spectrum of affairs in the New Society have turned it into a powerful political instrument, though it, too, is factionalized, and there is some friction between up-and-coming younger and still-favored older officers.

Whatever happens, the Philippines is unlikely to return to its former near-anarchic way of life, "democratic" as that may have been. Not even Marcos' political opponents seek that. The new polarization that he has created in the New Society is bound to have some permanent effects. One school of thought foresees a three-way struggle between left-of-center liberals with activist Christian support; the conservative, business-oriented elements that Marcos sponsors and supports; and the Communists, who retain China's blessing. In such a conflict the military would probably hold the balance of power, and in a showdown the Communists and some of the militant churchmen would face a conservative coalition supported by the military. Under these circumstances, even Marcos' most bitter enemies look to him to move, while he is still strong and influential, toward the peaceful transition to full parliamentary democracy he has so long promised. If he fails to do so, the Philippines could undergo the same sort of prolonged political turmoil that in recent years has beset Portugal and some of the nations of Latin America. The revolutionary pendulum could swing further to the authoritarian right, or it could swing left, under some form of Communism. But it surely won't stand still, and Marcos' efforts to prolong his stay in power and to enrich his family and friends will merely postpone the day of reckoning.

Indonesia–
Rich Man,
Poor Man

Indonesia is a conundrum, a lovely country that should be able to count its blessings in peace but could instead turn out to be a classic case of arrested national development. I witnessed the nation's birth after a protracted and bitter battle for independence from the Dutch three decades ago, saw it survive the foreign adventurist and catastrophic domestic policies of a charismatic but compulsive man named Sukarno, watched it suffer the terrible mass killings that followed the failed Communist coup in 1965 (which Sukarno secretly condoned and which led to his downfall as President), and then saw Indonesia come out of shock and begin a period of dramatic economic but uninspired political recovery; by 1979 I came to the reluctant conclusion that the patient might well be on the verge of another breakdown. The tantrums and the traumas of the early years have been overcome, the aspiring youth, having surmounted the awkward period of nationalist adolescence, has approached what appears to be a promise of maturity—but something has happened along the way to hold him back. His growth is now stunted, his erratic education has failed to provide him with the necessary tools and training, and some of his profligate foreign tutors and benefactors have thoroughly spoiled him. What he needs is proper reform and vocational guidance, but instead he has been tossed into a military academy, where, to make things worse, he has become corrupt and been caught cheating. His drill masters staunchly maintain that he is on the right course, but the doctors examining his progress and development charts have every reason to be skeptical.

The trouble is compounded by the fact that the charts are so contradictory. Indonesia is tremendously wealthy in natural resources, including oil and natural gas, nickel, zinc, copper, tin, bauxite and other minerals, as well as timber and rubber, but after more than a decade under the rather plodding, colorless and rigid administration of President Suharto—a Javanese general and mystic who believes in gurus as much as in growth—the nation's riches are chiefly benefiting a minority of the privileged, although it is true that oil revenues are supporting the national budget while also boosting foreign-exchange earnings. Though oil is helping to fund the plethora of development plans which a dozen foreign nations and international organizations are supporting too, much of the planning, unfortunately, and especially its implementation, has been discordant and unrealistic. The lifestyle of those climbing up the middle-income ladder, including a surfeit of bureaucrats and burgeoning entrepreneurs, has improved considerably, and the country is being flooded with all sorts of consumer items that have come to be the status symbols of success and well-being all over the developing world—such as motorcycles, transistors and television sets. But the 40 percent of Indonesia's population of 135 million in the lower-income brackets, particularly the rural poor in overcrowded Java, are just about as bad off as ever, and in some cases, being both jobless and landless, they are worse off.

The government maintains otherwise, but some of Indonesia's own economic experts, let alone foreign ones, including members of the American aid mission in Jakarta, take issue with its assertions. Suharto proudly proclaimed, in mid-1977, that only three out of ten persons were living below the poverty line, whereas a decade earlier the figures had been nine out of ten. He explained that he was using World Bank standards of $75 a year for people in urban areas and $50 for those in rural areas. But these figures were declared to be highly unrealistic by other, independent economists. Based on 1976 consumer prices, they said, the poverty benchmark should be $273 a year, and on that basis, real per capita annual income in Indonesia was less than $200. Using those standards, they claimed that about two thirds of the country's rural population and almost half of those living in the cities and towns were still living at or below the subsistence level. "Poverty in the country remains pervasive," one of the Americans at the aid mission told me. "Suharto's figures define destitution, not poverty. If you accept them, it means that a family of four or five can barely get by with enough to eat and can perhaps afford one cheap set of clothes per person a year. Nothing would be left over for housing or for other things. That's scarcely a practical evaluation."

In traveling around Java by car in the summer of 1977, I was impressed by surface signs of improvement, by the growing number of bicycles, motorscooters and autos, and by the appearance of new or refurbished private homes alongside resurfaced roads. Most of the people I saw looked fairly well dressed and healthy. But when I moved off the main roads into the countryside, the picture began to change. The land was as lush and green as ever, and it was apparent that every arable inch was being used to plant rice or other crops, but the people and their houses looked a lot more drab, and the atmosphere seemed oddly static. I sensed an overall unfulfillment, a lack of progress, and a peculiar vacuum.

The figures compiled by the American aid experts again told the story. Of 150 million acres of arable land in Indonesia, only a little over 10 million had been irrigated—after two five-year plans. Food production, though slowly improving, remained a serious problem; despite the use of better strains of rice (which in turn had produced more motivated pests with more refined palates), Indonesia was still importing over 1.5 million tons of rice a year, more than any other country in the world. Only 6 percent of the population had access to safe drinking water. The national death rate ranged between 17 and 19 per 1,000; half the deaths were among preschool children, who continued to suffer from malnutrition and various infectious diseases, which the nation's small number of doctors (8,000) and nurses (20,000) could hardly cope with. As for education, while more primary schools were slowly being built, only 30 percent of school-age youngsters were attending schools (less than 3 percent went to universities), and the national literacy rate was only 60 percent.

A Mixed and Troubled Family

The Indonesians always spoke proudly of having achieved unity within diversity, but their unity was misleading and often more symbolic than real. During many trips to Indonesia between the early fifties and the late seventies, I was constantly astonished by the myriad contrasts of the beautiful archipelagic country, embracing more than 13,000 equatorial islands, of which only about 1,000 were inhabited. Java, the fifth largest, though highly fertile but otherwise not as richly endowed as some of the others, has two thirds of Indonesia's population, or about 85 million people (though it is only about the size of New York, this is equal to the combined population of New York, California, Texas, Pennsylvania, Illinois and Ohio, America's six most populous states). The Javanese population glut, and other attributes of glut and gluttony, including control of the most important government jobs with their attendant rewards and added perquisites of power, remained a major source of distress to the rest of Indonesia. And despite bold but lagging plans to spread people around through transmigration schemes and to hold back the soaring birth rate through family-planning programs, which had begun to make some headway, Java's continued domination of just about every phase of Indonesian life increasingly alienated what were collectively and symbolically called "the outer islands," stretching more than three thousand miles from Sumatra in the west to primitive Irian Jaya, formerly Dutch New Guinea, in the east. These islands were more and more discovering their own ethnic identities, and had become resentful of being economically and politically neglected.

The most recent member of this conglomerate and not always so congenial family (embracing several different cultures and speaking more than 250 different dialects in spite of an effort to foster a national language called *bahasa Indonesia*) was East Timor, which used to be Portuguese East Timor and which became Indonesia's twenty-seventh province in mid-1976, after Indonesian troops had intervened, somewhat clumsily and crudely, in December 1975, in a war for independence the East Timorese were waging against Portugal. The Portuguese were preoccupied at the time by their own domestic political problems and quickly renounced their hold on Timor, at which point the Timorese fight for freedom turned into a civil war fought by five factions.

The Indonesians capped their invasion with a hastily arranged plebiscite, as a result of which the East Timorese voted to become part of Indonesia, but one of the factions, the left-wing Fretelin, remained in opposition; in 1978, though most of the several guerrilla groups and the villagers they controlled had accepted the offer of amnesty extended by President Suharto and had come down from the hills, and though the government had started to build roads and develop the backward island in other respects, 150 armed Fretelin rebels were still holding out. According to neutral diplomatic observers, at least 10,000 East Timorese had been killed by Indonesian troops, who suffered 2,000 casualties of their own. An estimated 50,000 other Timorese had died of illness or starvation. Many of the Third World nations, and nearby Australia, severely criticized Indonesian brutality in East Timor, and supported Fretelin's case against Indonesian intervention in the United Nations, but having achieved their aims, the Indonesians were scarcely perturbed.

Having acquired the vast island of Irian Jaya some years earlier, in 1969, as a result of diplomatic negotiations which the Americans helped bring to a successful conclusion, the Indonesians faced difficulties there, too, in the mid-seventies, when the Free Papua Movement guerrillas and rival tribal groups clashed with army troops. As in East Timor, the Indonesian soldiers used heavy-handed methods against the rebels, but by 1979 the Jakarta government was adopting a lower profile in Irian Jaya, although it still kept some forces stationed there. Perhaps more important, the government had reversed itself on its social policy toward the local Dhani warriors, accustomed to wearing nothing but *kotekas,* or penis gourds. An earlier governor of the new province had ordered that the Dhani men wear shorts instead of *kotekas* and had sent his soldiers into the villages on a "civic mission" to enforce the measure. The warriors either pulled the shorts over their *kotekas* or simply discarded them when the soldiers left. At the end of 1978, in conjunction with his new policy of maintaining security but not pursuing the rebel fighters, the new Defense Minister Mohammed Jusuf ended the anti-*koteka* campaign. "If they still want to live in the jungles or wear their *kotekas,* let them do it," he announced.

The rich geographic and racial contrasts in Indonesia are matched by multiple contradictions in the national society, which in many ways is an artificial and strange mixture of traditional, even feudal, forms and customs and various manifestations of superimposed modernism. Even the modern sector has its share of anomalies. The nation's latest pride, for example, is its $160 million satellite communications system, which enables rapid and clear telephone calls throughout the islands (though the phones still aren't working in Jakarta) and has spread television to all the provinces. But despite this sophisticated installation, per capita consumption of electricity (except in Jakarta) is only 10 kilowatt hours per year, compared to 300 hours in the Philippines, and more than 7,000 hours in the United States; in fact, most rural areas, as well as the poorer sections of Jakarta and other cities, still have no electricity or telephones at all. The country's oil production, gushing at 1.7

million barrels a day, continues to flourish despite the serious financial scandals that rocked the government-owned but independently run Pertamina oil corporation in 1975 and 1976; the major new projects to produce liquid natural gas and to develop the country's rich mineral deposits, some of which are backed by foreign investments of as high as $1 billion, are already in production, or will be shortly; and the unbelievably rich mineral and other resources of the island of Sumatra are beginning to be tapped. Yet the broken-down rail and obsolete sea-transport systems inherited from the Dutch have scarcely been repaired and are unable to handle the expanding level of economic activity, while road development, though much improved since the end of the Sukarno era, is still highly inadequate: in 1978 Java had only a quarter of a kilometer of road per square kilometer of land, and Sulawesi, where a big nickel mine financed by an international consortium had lately gone into operation, had only seven one-hundredths per square kilometer. Garuda, the national airline, and several smaller airlines had expanded their routes so that all the provinces and most of the nation's nearly three hundred *kabupaten* (or regencies, tantamount to counties) were connected by air—many of the big foreign companies had their own helicopters, and Pertamina owned the largest private fleet in the world—but in backward rural and mountain areas of many islands, such as Sulawesi and Kalimantan, it still took two days to travel forty miles by horse or mule.

It might well be that Indonesia is simply too big and sprawling a country to be governed unitarily, and that what the Dutch penultimately tried to promote thirty years before for their own selfish purposes, a federational system, would be more feasible. Short of a series of cohesive, sustained and uncontainable separatist revolts, however (there had been some over the years, but except for one in the late fifties in Sumatra, and a Holland-based Moluccan islands independence movement that caused more trouble there than in Indonesia, they were of minor importance), it is impossible to conceive of the government and the dominant Javanese military being willing to accept the idea of a federal government.

Omens of Danger

Signs of unrest in the country were clearly manifest in 1978. In order of volatility potential, I listed them as follows: Moslem religious and political discontent; the struggle for military succession and spoils and the larger issue of military versus civilian control; social and economic imbalances, in which corruption, the lack of social justice, and the spreading rich-poor gap were major factors; renewed antigovernment student activity, which reflected all of the above conditions, and could, as happened in 1965 and 1967, act as a catalyst. These were all domestic signs and portents, and while there were no vital outside issues or pressures that threatened Indonesia, the contest for influence in Southeast Asia among the major powers, especially China and Russia, and the significant role that Communist Vietnam might eventually play in the area, were factors that had to be considered, especially if the level of internal discontent rose and a new Communist movement took root. More than the other four members of ASEAN, the Indonesians were disturbed by the Chinese attack on Vietnam, which stirred memories of their own revolutionary troubles and of Peking's role in them.

External pressures had frequently had a way of affecting or stimulating internal events in Indonesia, in some cases even triggering them. In the summer of 1965, there was ample available evidence that Peking encouraged the leaders of the Indonesian Communist Party (PKI) to launch their end-of-September coup, ill-advisedly and prematurely, as it turned out. The coup would probably have been attempted anyway, but as a result of the close ties that existed at the time between Jakarta and Peking (they included a team of Chinese doctors who were treating Sukarno for kidney and other disorders and who indicated his health was deteriorating rapidly), the Chinese influence was considerable, not only on the Communists but on a number of cabinet ministers and ranking military officers who were involved in the coup plotting and who had visited Peking shortly before the plots reached a climax. The Americans having entered the Vietnam war by sending in Marine combat troops, the Chinese may well have wanted to open a second front in Southeast Asia. Again, in January 1974, the Japanese triggered a severe riot in Jakarta that came to be known as Malari, a loose acronym for "Disaster of January 14, 1974," during which eleven people were killed, more than a hundred injured, and eight hundred arrested, about forty of whom were jailed for periods ranging from a few months to two years. The riot was inspired by the visit to Jakarta of Japanese Prime Minister Kakuei Tanaka, and its ostensible cause was the resentment against Japanese businessmen and their overweening manner of doing business in Indonesia, but it had its deeper roots in complaints that went beyond xenophobia and represented domestic grievances.

By 1978 these same grievances still existed and had become more sharply defined. For the first time they were directed specifically at Suharto himself and against his running for a third five-year term as President, which he did anyway, winning easily by stacking the elective Congress in his favor; but the mounting dissent and turbulence led many observers to believe that he might not serve the full five years, and if convinced that his *wahyu* (the magic source of light that in the Javanese mystic belief system bestows power) was failing, he would resign voluntarily, or be forced to resign by the military. The resentment against the government—as expressed chiefly by the students, Moslem politicians and a handful of dissident writers and disaffected retired generals—concentrated on the continuing corruption in high circles (including Suharto's own family), on mismanagement of the economy and the failure of national development to alleviate poverty, on social injustice, and on the restrictive political system that inhibited any real popular participation.

Most of the criticism was aimed at the army and its dominance of virtually every phase of Indonesian life, but Suharto, in his new term, displayed no sign of being willing to diminish its role—if anything, he increased it. Despite the relatively free press, or perhaps because of it and the constant fear on the part of editors and writers that they had to watch their step when criticizing (seven leading daily papers were banned for eleven days at the outset of 1978 for reporting on the opposition student movement too liberally), there remained a basic lack of communication between the government and the people. This was what students particularly complained about, so much so that two months before Suharto's re-election, in March, five hundred of them were arrested and about fifty held for investigation or trial in what was an obvious punitive action to break the back of the new campus movements.

Admonitory comments by Suharto and his fellow generals about dissent providing ammunition for subversive elements and enhancing the danger of "chaos" did little to bridge the growing communications gap. There were obvious differences within the government on this score, and a good many officers, especially younger ones, privately supported the students. So did the highly respected and revered Sultan Hamengkubuwono, who had been Suharto's Vice President but refused to run again, claiming bad eyesight, which was true, though his real reason was his disillusionment over many things the government was doing, or not doing. His place was taken by former Foreign Minister Adam Malik, who warned of the dangers of "suppressing" the students, or "brainwashing them," and suggested that the government should "invite them to talk, including those we don't like." But the predominant government view was expressed by Education and Culture Minister Joesoef; he emphatically told the students to "strengthen your power of reasoning and analysis" instead of criticizing so much and holding demonstrations. "They are still stupid and have to be educated," Joesoef declared. "Thus far the students have been glorified by the ignorant public. And now I tell them that they are actually naked."

The constant emphasis on stability had become so strong that it tended to be stultifying. In a moment of candor one of the more experienced government officials remarked to me, "Suharto puts stability ahead of everything. If there is peace and order, then the state will be prosperous, he says—it's an old Javanese adage. The trouble is, stability can become awfully boring. The country can't be ruled too long in such monolithic ways. It's been almost too quiet for our tastes the last ten years, compared to the turbulence and excitement we had before, and during the struggle for independence. Ten years ago, in 1967, we turned against statism, but now we've turned back to it, in different form, and we suffer from a degree of smugness. We need another change, though we shouldn't throw away the baby with the bath."

What the country needed most was a change in the basic political power structure, and this was important for many reasons, one of which was demographic: there was a consistent failure on the government's part to recognize that half the population of Indonesia was under nineteen years of age and that two thirds was under twenty-five, and that the majority of the unemployed and underemployed (who together made up about half of the nation's working population of 50 million) were in their twenties. One of my close Indonesian friends, Soedjatmoko, who was one of the more imaginative government planners and favored a far higher degree of involvement at the village level in development and much more rapport with the nation's youth, had warned prophetically, in a talk I had with him back in 1973, that this youth factor in itself meant: "We may be sitting on a time bomb—or maybe, more accurately, a volcano." Government spokesmen agreed, but for different, more negative and self-serving reasons.

Lack of Local Participation

Beyond the question of the government's failure to engage in a satisfactory dialogue with the nation's youth, what was required was a fundamental devolution of powers, a delegation or redistribution of responsibility in such a way that the people themselves, not just the overweighted bureaucracy dominated by the government party, Golkar, would have the opportunity for autonomous action. Under the existing system, elections every five years gave a semblance of democratic legitimacy by permitting political campaigning to take place for two months, but even then criticism of the government was monitored and restricted, and the opposition parties were limited in their approach to the people, particularly to those in the villages. Problems and issues during the five years between elections were not dealt with openly but were submerged, and the system of discussion and consensus on which Indonesia had prided itself in the past for the most part had become controlled or limited to a few matters, such as people locally deciding how they wanted to spend the 300,000 rupiah (about $570) the government regularly donated to each of the nation's sixty thousand villages.

There was no real opportunity for the vast body of the rural poor to identify for themselves the social and economic problems of development that affected them most, or to lobby or bring pressure on the provincial and national legislatures for the utilization of their own resources. The government on top determined all policies and imposed all solutions, and while the technocrats surrounding Suharto were experts in their fields and came up with all sorts of planning schemes, filling numerous huge volumes piled high in government offices, they had not succeeded in transmitting their knowledge to the middle- and low-level officials in the countryside. This gap between top-level and top-quality and low-level and low-quality bureaucrats was growing rather than narrowing as economic development became more complex. As another Indonesian friend put it, "The government doesn't dare trust the people with development tasks. There has been too much social engineering, and too little social and political vision. We have yet to make the quantum jump from manipulation at the top to participation and sharing at the bottom."

In this climate of constrained control, with the bulk of the rural population uninvolved and uncommitted, and more important, without access to social justice, there were few if any natural checks and balances, and little resiliency under the heavy bureaucratic imprint. The Indonesian sociologists who were worried about what they called "the development of development," and who were constantly aware of the Malthusian factor (despite the growing success of family planning, the population of Indonesia was expected to reach 200 million before the end of the century), were quite naturally asking the basic question, "What sort of life are we going to offer the people?" Corruption and the crass display of affluence were the visible side of the national dilemma. The invisible side adumbrated the technocrats' continuing failure to humanize their planning and to confront the perplexing moral and cultural problems that development was supposed to challenge and illuminate. "For all its blueprints, the leadership seems unable to make up its mind just what it wants to do with and for the common man," an Indonesian business friend observed. "Maybe it's simply too elitist in its own training and orientation, or too overwhelmed by the contrasts, to solve the equation."

Here again, while Suharto appeared to be aware that the ordinary people were not getting enough out of the country's economic development, his preoccupation with stability and with production charts too often led him to accept the long-standing economic disparities and to ignore the social and cultural challenges and dangers inherent in them. One long-stalled program, for instance—the effort to resettle some of Java's millions on more spacious and less populated islands—finally started moving between 1976 and 1978, but the chances of its making much of a dent did not seem great, with no more than twenty or thirty thousand families a year likely to move, though under the third five-year economic plan, starting in April 1979, the government hoped to move 500,000 families. In a talk I had with Suharto back in 1973, he brought up the practical difficulties. "We must get the land ready—it's not enough just to cut down trees on the outer islands," he said. "We need capital to fill in the swamps and introduce irrigation. We must make it possible for the people to live better—it's not our objective just to transplant misery." All this was logical, but it overlooked the fact that subsistence farmers in Java, even when they had no land of their own, were not eager to leave their ancestral homes; a great deal of political and cultural preparation and persuasion, and not just carved-out plots in a far-off wilderness, would be required to get them to move voluntarily.

Instead of spending the allotted 1 million rupiah (about $1,500 at the new rate of the devaluated rupiah set late in 1978) to move a family of four or five —and the actual cost of doing it properly was about three times that amount —economists at Gadja Mada University, in Jogjakarta, Central Java, believed it would be far more practical for the government to alleviate the plight of the growing number of landless and jobless by helping them become small entrepreneurs. Since the rural poor only spent about a quarter of their time growing and harvesting rice or alternate crops, they were forced to do whatever else they could to eke out a living. They were trying to sell local products, experiment with handicrafts, vegetable farming or animal husbandry; but the government has done little to stimulate these practical alternatives, though it promised to concentrate more on such rural enterprise in the third five-year plan. But unless there were better implementation and coordination from the level of the *camats* (subdistricts) down to the villages, and greater participation in the planning process by the farmers themselves—which called for far more training and political education than they had so far received—none of these schemes would succeed, and the rural poor would simply become further alienated. One Gadja Mada economist went so far as to say that "they are worse off today than they were in colonial times."

The Curse of Corruption

When I was back in Indonesia in 1977, the four words I heard most frequently were *"pungli,"* "planning," "poverty" and "prosperity." *Pungli* is a contraction of *pungutan liar,* which means illegal levies such as payments truck drivers are forced to make to pass police or Transportation Ministry roadblocks, but the term is used more generically to define all forms of corruption, big or small. Corruption in Indonesia is the worst in Asia, and according to businessmen with experience elsewhere, such as in Nigeria and Saudi Arabia, it is the worst in the world. The poor, simply by virtue of being poor, are by no means exempt from *pungli.* For example, all land was supposed to be registered with the Land Registration Office, and farmers needed certificates in order to apply for government loans at 18 percent interest, a surprisingly high figure to start with. In many cases, in order to get his certificate a peasant had to pay *pungli* to the local bureaucrat in charge of the land office—absentee landlordism made this increasingly difficult. If he had no certificate, the farmer had no choice but to pay 30 percent interest to a private moneylender, and even if he did deal with a government credit bank, he frequently wouldn't get the full amount of a loan because the bureaucrat running the bank pocketed part of it over and above the legal interest rate. The head of the Indonesian Farmers Association told Suharto in the fall of 1977 that more than half the average farmer's income was being absorbed one way or another in illegal levies.

Corruption, which the Indonesians call *korupsi,* adapting the Western word, is running so deep on so many levels that it has become both an institution and an art. The payment of *uang semir* (speed money) to get anything done—whether the payment consists of a pack of cigarettes to a subdistrict leader to obtain a small favor or several million rupiah to a high official in Jakarta to win a multimillion dollar contract—has reached a point where taking part in the process has come to be considered a mark of status by both the corrupters and the corrupt. From time to time, outcries by students and the press, and mounting foreign criticism, has led to the creation of various commissions and special bodies, and at one point Suharto declared, "I myself will lead the fight against corruption," but invariably very little action has been taken. In the summer of 1972 a number of top officials were brought up on charges of accepting bribes and condoning smuggling at Tandjung Priok, the big port adjacent to Jakarta, but the bribing and payoffs were soon resumed and toward the end of the seventies were as bad as ever.

The history of corruption in Indonesia goes back to the feudal system of privilege enjoyed by the early Javanese kings and their princely underlings, and to the activities of the Dutch East India Company during the early period of its hegemony, when low-paid officials routinely stole from the company and obtained trade benefits for themselves through bribery. The company's rule was superseded by that of a Dutch governor-general at the beginning of the nineteenth century, and thereafter the Javanese *priyayi* (aristocrats) paid bribes to the Dutch to maintain their expensive way of life, while local headmen maintained their positions through profiteering and extortion. The Japanese, during their occupation, did nothing to discourage such practices, and added a few touches of their own. The birth of an independent Indonesia was followed by a short puritanical period in the early fifties, but this soon petered out as the proliferation of a new bureaucracy under Sukarno invited new corruption. After Sukarno's fall, in the late sixties, the influx of large foreign-investment funds, and foreign-aid money as well, exacerbated corruption, and not only lowered the country's moral standards but helped widen the gap between the rich and the poor.

Theodore M. Smith, of the Ford Foundation, wrote a study on Indonesia in the mid-seventies indicating that "there is not a single official who can live by his income alone." His data showed that a majority of government employees required two or three times their salary to cover their basic needs for housing and food. Since only a few people in the bureaucratic hierarchy were in a position to make decisions, Smith noted, those few came to enjoy "a seller's market" and could "exact a price at each gate." Simple cheating and pocketing of funds by ordinary officials, profitable deals arranged by the military (which had its hand in a multitude of government-approved enterprises under what is known as the "dual system") and arrangements between wealthy local Chinese and important Indonesians created an intricate web of payoffs and kickbacks throughout the archipelago. A weak judiciary system and archaic taxation invited further abuses. As more money was poured into the country for investment purposes in the second half of the seventies, the rules on corruption began changing, Smith noted. "As the nuggets got bigger, coming in on top of the massive but weak bureaucracy," he said, "it was no longer a matter of everyone getting his share through a system of unspoken distribution. Now it was no holds barred, with the sky the limit."

In the summer of 1977 Suharto appointed an amiable but tough white-haired admiral named Sudomo (like many Indonesians he only had or only used one name) to take charge of what soon appeared to be the biggest and most serious anticorruption drive ever undertaken. In the first three months Sudomo, who repeatedly said he had been given carte blanche to proceed against any officials high or low, acted against a variety of low-level bureaucrats. In a series of surprise spot checks he arrested tax inspectors, immigration officers, transportation officials on major roads, public prosecutors, land speculators, one *bupati* (head of a regency, which is tantamount to a county) and a banker accused of receiving nearly half a million dollars in illicit real

estate commissions. All of the officials were accused of demanding or accepting *pungli* in carrying out their duties. But despite the arrest of the *bupati*
and the banker, and subsequently of a police general, the press and the
students and the public at large were still not convinced that Sudomo would
"get any big fish at the top." One cartoon showed him at the bottom of a rope
ladder leading to heaven and chopping off the lower appendages of an octopus
but leaving its many swirling upper tentacles untouched. In a talk I had with
Sudomo he emphasized that he was dealing with "a very complex problem"
of restoring credibility, and said that the campaign would go on for five or even
ten years. Suharto had expressed his intense desire to eradicate corruption by
choosing the embracive and ubiquitous National Command for the Restoration of Security and Order, known by the acronym of Kopkamtib, which the
admiral headed, to lead the anti-*pungli* drive. "All the ministries are now going
to have to report back to me, including the inspector generals and the director
generals and their staffs," Sudomo said, "and we'll also use the territorial
military system and obtain the full cooperation of army commanders and their
subordinates and the police." He added that he would extend his operations
down to the village level and go after the small bureaucrats who were squeezing
or cheating the peasants, just as he would crack down on foreign companies
paying big bribes and the important officials accepting them. But so far, not
much has happened to prove his point.

Most Indonesians I spoke with, including newspaper editors, said their
skepticism would be retained until they saw some firm action taken
against individuals like the former head of Pertamina, Ibnu Sutowo, who
was being investigated for violations of Indonesian law in connection with
some tanker deals and other negotiations that had contributed to Pertamina's financial collapse. The huge company owed more than $10 billion
abroad (the Bank of Indonesia, with the help of foreign banks and experts,
had been forced to step in and bail out the company by making fresh
loans and renegotiating former contracts) and Ibnu was considered personally responsible for its collapse, as well as guilty of indulging in showy ex-
travagances. But except for being held under loose house arrest for a time,
he was let off. As one former high official later said, "The only crime in
this country is political disloyalty; if you steal a million or so, you're not in
trouble, but if you're disloyal to the central power system, then you should
be ready to go to jail."

Even more important, the critics said, they would take the anti-*pungli* drive
seriously if and when Sudomo took any action against the activities of members of Suharto's own family, notably his wife, Tien, and his brother and half
brother, who were engaged in a wide variety of enterprises including real estate
development, cattle raising, cement and textile manufacturing, gambling-
casino and night-club operations, and hotel construction and management.
Many of their dealings had been carried out in cooperation with wealthy
Chinese, who in Indonesia, as elsewhere in Southeast Asia, dominate the
nation's commerce. Suharto had for many years been highly sensitive over the

issue of his family's commercial activities and had denied they were illegal, but he had lately been willing to listen to some of his top advisers who had warned him that whether they involved corruption or simply the undue use of influence, these family business operations should be curbed. An American diplomat who had his reservations about how far Sudomo would or could go said, "I doubt Sudomo will go after the family—at least not until he gets the green light from the army, which still runs this country, and that won't happen until Suharto is on his way out."

In treating the question of corruption, the press, though invited by Sudomo to cooperate and to dig out cases of *pungli,* had to be particularly careful not to implicate the President's family. Despite the leeway to criticize government policies, "it's always tiring and a strain on the conscience, trying to figure out how to be oblique and how far we can go," one editor told me. Aside from the press, however, there were other ways in which cynical criticism could be expressed, including plays and songs, and one popular song, presented by a group known as the Trio Bimbo from Bandung, was widely circulated even though it had been officially banned. The lyrics went:

> Auntie Sun, Oh Auntie Sun, a sweet auntie,
> Every day is engaged in sports,
> Goes golfing until noon,
> Then straight to the beauty parlor
> For a milk bath.
>
> Auntie Sun, Oh Auntie Sun, an active auntie,
> So active in so many different meetings and clubs,
> Morning, noon and night,
> Oh Auntie Sun, a model auntie.
>
> Emerald, diamond and crushed stone
> Gold and construction of iron bars
> Is her business.
> Tycoons, directors and brokers
> Are down on their knees submitting to Auntie Sun.
>
> Auntie Sun, Oh Auntie Sun, a stylish auntie,
> Never feels unhappy, smiling at everybody,
> Captivating the old and the young,
> Oh Auntie Sun, Oh Auntie, Auntie Sun.

The newspaper *Merdeka,* which is one of the most antigovernment papers, dared to print the lyrics with the comment "We ourselves can only judge that Tante Sun is none other than 'a new feudal symbol' which is mushrooming increasingly to form a prosperous elite in this country." Few readers, or listeners, doubted that the prototype of Auntie (Tante) Sun was Tien Suharto, and that the song had been banned for that reason.

New Waves of Unrest

The gathering student unrest of 1977 that culminated in the demonstrations early in 1978, to which the government reacted more forcibly, spread throughout Java but was strongest in the traditional university city of Bandung in West Java. Though the students lacked a core of dynamic, sophisticated leadership that had marked earlier student movements in Indonesia and were loosely organized into some forty or fifty campus groups which maintained only occasional contact with one another, a White Paper issued by the Bandung students late in 1977, which included the demand that Suharto refrain from running for President again, served briefly to unite the movement, but with the arrest and detention of the principal student leaders, and the government's new tougher line, the students as a whole subsided. However, there was little doubt that sooner or later it would gather new strength. The arrest of the well-known poet and playwright W. S. Rendra and of another revolutionary poet, Bung Tomo, for "inciting" the students caused further concern about a renewed repressive policy and about the army's apparent intention to retain its firm grip. Both men were later released.

Such control continued to be forcibly demonstrated by the territorial commanders and their subordinates, whose authority, in the person of sergeants and corporals, extended all the way down to the village level and was also pervasive throughout the bureaucracy, much of which was dominated by officers or ex-officers. As a result of the "dual system," some twenty thousand military men were executing a wide range of civilian tasks and functions as directors and managers of government or quasi-government commercial and industrial concerns. Not only did they profit personally from this arrangement, but the dual role enhanced their political power as well, and in turn served to increase the spreading popular discontent.

While soliciting popular support for the anti-*pungli* campaign, Admiral Sudomo and some of the other military leaders kept issuing warnings not to go too far in criticizing the government and becoming addicted to what was euphemistically described as an "opposition culture." This negative or defensive approach, reflecting both the military's ambivalence and a growing dissatisfaction among the public on many issues that covered the whole broad spectrum of political and economic decisions, or simply of drift, had come to characterize the Suharto administration. "The government has run out of steam and ideas," one Indonesian friend of mine commented. "The country is being carried forward by past impact, but there is no clarity about where we go from here." Certainly, beneath the malaise and dispiritedness that prevailed, the students alone appeared to be playing a preliminary role that could herald a new confrontational and possibly violent phase of the ever-unfolding Indonesian revolution. In many ways that were only beginning to be manifested, this phase might ultimately take the form of a clash between secular elements, led by the military, and the students in conjunction with religious groups, especially newly emerging members of the Moslem political parties.

On my return to Indonesia three and a half years after the Malari affair of early 1974, I was surprised to discover what a strong hangover effect it still had. And if what was taking place had the tone of a preview, a fresh rumbling of discontent which had not yet been fully orchestrated, this had to be placed in the larger context of events over the past few years. Following the fall of Vietnam, in April 1975, the Indonesians, especially the military, as was the case throughout Asia, went through a jittery period, expecting an increase of Communist insurgency, but when nothing happened they regained their confidence in authoritarian methods and in the maintenance of strict law and order. As one man who was jailed after Malari said, "Before then, and before Vietnam fell, we had relative freedom—now there are subversive undertones to everything that happens." In the late summer and fall of 1977, in an effort to pre-empt the student unrest, the government chose seven cabinet ministers to conduct a series of open dialogues with the students in several cities. But the talks worked out badly, partly because the ministers adopted a lecturing posture and were defensive, while the students assumed an adversary or confrontational role and attacked the ministers for being evasive and acting as government apologists. The discussions accordingly vitiated rather than improved the situation. As one student in Jogjakarta cynically put it, "In 1966 we took to the streets—this time the ministers did, and we ambushed them."

The Indonesians, with their fondness for acronyms, also have a predilection for categorizing their revolutionary behavior by generations. Thus, the Generation of 1920 was mostly composed of theorists and ideologues who were so deeply engaged in political debate among themselves that no predominant revolutionary leadership emerged. It was the next group of leaders, the Generation of 1945, which had experienced the brutality of the Japanese occupation, that realized independence from the Dutch could only be achieved militarily, and they proved their point after four years of prolonged and often complicated internecine fighting. The Generation of 1966, which had no colonial hangovers, was "politicized by Sukarno and by the Communist Party," as one of its student leaders said, "and as outsiders we then mounted the barricades against Sukarno and helped force him out of power after the coup by creating temporary alliances with some members of the military." He added that "we had no time, unfortunately, to develop our own philosophy or chart our own positive course— we were too busy being chased, for one thing—and once our job was accomplished, our influence flagged, as did that of the generals who backed us. Thereafter we were on a collision course with the military." Many members of the Generation of 1966 actually opted out and either joined the government, became members of Golkar, went into business or into subsidized research, and quite a few went abroad.

The new, more disparate Generation of 1977, as it has already begun to call itself, faces more diversified and complicated problems and has both a sense of inferiority toward its more dynamic predecessors and a less certain strategy. It lacks continuity of action as well, and suffers from a paucity of heroes of its own, as well as disillusionment with older heroes, not only with the 1966 generation of students, which has all but vanished, but with the older group of brilliant technocrats in their thirties and forties who graduated from the University of Indonesia and has come to be known as the "Berkeley Mafia" because some of them had done graduate work at the University of California. They thereafter joined the government and became its leading planners. Some of the remaining members of the Generation of 1966 I spoke with, who used to look upon these technocrats as their godfathers, had a sense of being forsaken and even betrayed by them, which partly accounted for the negative and even impolite reactions expressed by the Generation of 1977 students when they held their unsuccessful dialogues with the seven ministers, most of whom were of that same group of technocrats. "They lost their political souls and closed their doors on us about 1970," one of the 1966 student leaders remarked to me with some bitterness. "They became social engineers and manipulators, and now they, too, have nice cars and homes."

Some of the technocrats have, in fact, been beginning to have second thoughts about the direction in which the New Order, which is neither very new nor very orderly, is going, and like some of the younger members of the military, are privately in sympathy with the new student movement as it thrashes about in search of more positive issues. In 1966 and 1967, when the country was undergoing a serious revolutionary crisis and somewhere between 200,000 and 400,000 were killed in the bloody wake of the coup as Communist and Moslem mobs wreaked vengeance on one another, the targets of the students, notably Sukarno and the leaders of the Communist Party, were clearly defined. This was not the case in 1977 and 1978, despite the rising criticism of Suharto; ironically, a government campaign to rehabilitate Sukarno as the father of his country was widely hailed, even by some of the students. With the exception of a few notable protagonists of mismanagement and apparent corruption, such as Pertamina's Ibnu Sutowo, there were no new major ogres on the scene.

The problems the Pertamina case engendered, and newly imposed contracts for further oil exploration, extraction and profit sharing that were much less advantageous than before for foreign companies, caused these firms to lose interest, at least temporarily. Foreign investment as a whole declined, although by 1979 there were signs that it was picking up. Inflation, which had been reduced to one-digit figures, started rising again, reaching 14 percent early in 1977 and moving toward 30 percent following devaluation, which was nothing compared to the huge figures of 500 and 600 percent that had marked the end of the Sukarno era but was again ominous. All in all, the country seems to be facing a new crisis of confidence that is greater than at any time since it made its remarkable recovery, in the late sixties and early seventies, from the long years of economic disaster under Sukarno.

The 1977 Elections

Under these circumstances, the elections held in May 1977 came off surprisingly well, though many considered them a costly charade. It was obvious beforehand that Golkar, the government party (or Sebker Golkar, translated as Joint Secretariat of the Functional Groups), would win by a handy margin, and the only question was whether it would improve on its performance of 1971. Golkar was originally established in 1964 by a Sukarno edict as a body to bring together all the so-called functional groups—nationally organized bodies of civil servants, students, farmers, intellectuals, representatives of labor, women, business, and so on—that were not affiliated with any political party. Earlier in Sukarno days the various Moslem parties had enjoyed considerable influence, at one point in the fifties collecting 44 percent of the national vote, though Sukarno continued to run his virtual one-man "guided democracy" show with the help of the old Nationalist Party (PNI) and the Communists (PKI). When Suharto formally took over in 1967, and the first elections were held in 1971, Golkar's chief purpose was simply to organize them and win them. It thereafter remained primarily a bureaucratic vehicle, a kind of election bureau rather than a party as such. In talks I had with General Ali Murtopo, one of Suharto's principal military advisers and the guiding spirit of Golkar, and with a Catholic Chinese named Lim Bian Kie, the head of a think tank called the Institute for Strategic Services, which prepared analyses and instructions for the different functional groups and acted as a link between them and the government leaders, both men said they thought the army should not remain dominant in social and political affairs and that Golkar should be slowly "civilianized." But this shift did not take place, and the army's role in the 1977 elections was stronger than ever, with the Ministry of Defense and Security, known by its acronym of HANKAM, remaining in effect Golkar's politburo. As one friend of mine summed it up, "Golkar is just a big wet blanket owned and operated by the army for smothering any real political life that still exists in the country."

Back in 1973 Suharto had moved to consolidate the political opposition into two main blocs. Four of the old Moslem parties were put together under the banner of the United Development Party (PPP), while four Christian and former nationalist parties became the Indonesian Democrat Party (PDI). Having won more than 62 percent of the vote in 1971, the government fully expected to win at least 68 percent in 1977, but despite its strong-arm tactics it was somewhat disappointed. After some violent skirmishes in the villages between Golkar and Moslem groups that resulted in a dozen or so killings and in the arrests of several hundred right-wing and religious extremists (alleged right-wing plots may have been exaggerated or fabricated by the government), Golkar won just about the same percentage of votes as it had before, losing a few seats, while the Moslem parties won nearly 30 percent, gaining 5 seats, and the Democrats won 8 percent and only barely held their own. The vote was specifically for 360 members of the House of Representatives (DPR), but an additional 100 members—75 military and 25 nonmilitary members of Golkar—were then, under the law, appointed by the government to parliament. Though it is the principal legislative organ of the state, the DPR actually initiated very little legislation of its own and was hardly more than a rubber-stamp body.

In March 1978, ten months after the election, the People's Consultative Assembly (MPR) met. Twice the size of the DPR, with the added 460 members also appointed by the government, and thus overwhelmingly representing its views, the MPR promptly re-elected Suharto and then chose Adam Malik as Vice President, after Sultan Hamengkubuwono had stepped down. There was some violence during and after the MPR meeting, which resulted in the arrest of about forty Moslem activists, but the Moslem party (PPP) did not oppose Suharto's re-election, though it refused to accept parts of his new program and was unhappy about having the MPR pass a measure which acknowledged the right of the mystic sects to exist and practice their faith, though not as an organized religion. Because of the stand they took at the MPR session, Suharto refused to appoint any PPP members to his new cabinet, which had more military men in it than before, and the Moslems were thereby further alienated.

The peculiar mixture of elected and appointed members of the DPR and the MPR constituted what continued to be described as functional or guided democracy; however, with all the decisions still made by Suharto and his closest military advisers, with some help from selected technocrats, the form and shape of the government was actually more oligarchic than democratic, though it was an unwieldy and overstuffed oligarchy. It was acknowledged, after the MPR session, that something would have to be done to breathe life into Golkar if it was not eventually to disintegrate, particularly since there was considerable disunity within the party's ranks. Many of the younger officers and soldiers, being Moslems themselves, were not happy over the manner in which the Moslem candidates of the PPP had been treated by village headmen who had taken their orders from Golkar's hard-fisted organizers, and over the fact that the opposition parties had been given little chance to penetrate below the district levels and to engage in open criticism of the government. Some of the critics of Golkar were convinced that the party had to dissociate itself from the military and the "dual system," while at the same time revitalizing its ranks to recover the revolutionary spirit of 1945. But whether or not Golkar could play a more reformist role, there seemed little doubt that whoever ultimately succeeded Suharto, he would, as a top military man close to the President, assured me, "come from the same stable"—that is, the army.

If Golkar had grown complacent and stood on unfirm ground, the government had become even more conscious than before of the fact that it now faced a serious potential threat from the Moslems, even though the PPP was an unstable umbrella organization with its own problems. It was apparent that major shifts in self-perception were taking place throughout the Moslem world and that these would increasingly affect Indonesia, although the country was not overly identified with the Arab nations and their causes except through its membership in the Organization of Petroleum Exporting Countries (OPEC). It was significant, however, that several months after the election Suharto—himself a Moslem though he was more closely identified with the Javanese mystic sects known collectively as *kebatinan*—made his first trip to the Middle East, visiting seven nations on an economic and good-will tour.

"Whether fundamentalist, modernist, leftist-Marxist, or simply opportunist, the Moslem perceptions and their impact cannot be ignored," a social-scientist friend of mine said. "If I were a Moslem here or in the Middle East, I would say that Western power has peaked and that Islamic power is emerging." The nationalists, though the PDI fared badly, also felt that history was on their side, partly because the reduction of American power in Asia after Vietnam had heightened nationalist feelings everywhere, and because non-alignment had acquired its own nationalist validity.

Islamic Impact Growing

Moslem discontent in Indonesia had been slowly simmering ever since the early seventies. The majority of Moslems felt left out of the development and entrepreneurial process—quite a few, being unable to obtain loans from banks, lost their businesses. Islamic resentment rose with the introduction of a new marriage bill in the House of Representatives. The bill was an effort by the Suharto regime to "Indonesianize" four separate marriage laws that had been operative under the 1945 constitution: the Islamic law, which allows Moslems to follow their traditional marriage customs, including polygamy; a civil code for Westerners and Chinese; a separate law for Christians; and the so-called *adat* (customary law), which covers nonpracticing Moslems and those without any religion. The new law proposed that couples with different ethnic, religious or national backgrounds be given government sanction for marriage, and it discouraged polygamy. The Moslems reacted strongly—on one occasion five hundred young men and women stormed the House of Representatives, and thirteen were jailed. In response to the protests, a watered-down version of the bill was ultimately passed, allowing polygamy as long as a wife or wives consented, omitting any endorsement of interfaith marriages and maintaining separate marriage courts.

Religion was bound to be a considerable force in the 1977 election after Suharto, in seeking to defuse the opposition, in effect had helped solidify it by forcing the Moslem parties to group together; he then had made a further mistake by allowing the PPP to use the *Kaaba,* the sacred Moslem shrine, as a party symbol. Despite talk of opportunity for village debates, the party took full advantage of the thousands of mosques in the country to conduct rallies that stressed religious themes as much as political issues—this was due to the limits set against discussing politics too openly and contentiously, so the PPP instead stressed that a vote in its favor was a vote for Allah. The election also demonstrated, particularly in areas such as East Java, where mass hysteria had always been near the surface, that Moslem emotions were still running high. There were more incidents of violence there than elsewhere, including mob outbreaks and demonstrations the PPP itself was unable to control.

The growth of Moslem political forces over the next few years will bear careful watching. Like Golkar, but for different reasons, the PPP, if it is to survive, has to sort itself out, and its problems are in many ways deeper and more complex than Golkar's. The conflict between the traditionalists and the modernists in the Moslem movement is basically a generational one, with the older members of the community clinging to their Islamic tenets and to the precepts of the Nahdatul Ulama, which is still the largest and most hidebound Moslem party. The NU's major props remain the ulamas, or Moslem teachers, the strong kinship relations among them that reach down through the village mosques, and still-lingering concepts of a theocratic state. Opposed to this old-guard element are younger reformist leaders who are against the creation of any sort of theocratic rule, and who regard themselves as nationalists with Islamic beliefs but who favor a secular state with socialist tenets. They want to see the old parties, especially the NU, disbanded and a new party formed.

In 1978 I met a number of these younger leaders who were on the faculties of Islamic schools and colleges, where they continued to practice and teach Islamic cultural values. However, they opposed the older ulamas on a number of important issues, among them coeducation, which they favor, and they want schools kept open during Ramadan, the annual month-long fasting period each fall. I was particularly impressed with Abdurrachman Wahid, the assistant head of Tebuireng, one of the best-known Islamic institutions, located in Jombang, East Java. Wahid, who is one of the most prominent of the new generation of reformist Moslem intellectuals, was fully aware of the tenuous and possibly dangerous conflicts within the Moslem community that could provoke violence in its own ranks, as well as a serious confrontation with the military and with Golkar. "We cannot afford to be rash," he said, "and we must avoid a clash with the traditionalists that would create fresh trouble and give the military another excuse to tighten up on the society. We believe in democratic gradualism, but we also have to be crisis-oriented. The army and the government will do their best to keep the present three-party arrangement, and there are enough opportunists in the PPP who will go along with that, but its popular support is bound to disintegrate. So we must concentrate on developing a new mass consciousness, stressing more and better rural development and our belief in nationalism and democracy based on social justice and broader educational opportunities. The fundamental state philosophy of *pancasila*, founded on belief in God, nationalism, humanity, democracy and social justice, which our early Moslem leaders formulated and Sukarno then named and adopted, remains valid, but it has grown stale in its application and needs to be revitalized and applied in modern terms."

Other young Moslem intellectuals I spoke with in the countryside and in Jakarta agreed about the need to organize a new party which, as one of them put it, "will be less Islamic, and will be based on the advanced socialist concepts espoused by parties in Scandinavia and the Socialist Party in Germany. Indonesia is a plural society, and we have to rise above our own religion, or any other religion. But we need more political freedom to do that, and more opportunity to criticize and to investigate wrongs and shortcomings. As Moslems we must offer more secular courses in our schools, and we should make wider use of the radio and television and the newspapers and concentrate more on problems of development." Most of the Moslem leaders I met were not worried about a resurgence of right-wing extremism as represented by the Darul Islam, which played a role in the fifties and still had some supporters. Nevertheless, though it was probably true that the influence of the older ulamas and of traditionalism in general was declining, the level of political and religious emotionalism remained high in a number of communities, including some in Sumatra, and added to this were the growing factors of social unrest.

In recent years there had been an increase in the activities of the *kebatinan* sects, something that had occurred historically during times of stress and frustration. These sects, which existed all over Java in particular, were still essentially spiritual, but the orientation of some of them was becoming more political. In 1976 a former Ministry of Agriculture official named Sawito Kartowibowo, who claimed to have received a divine message from a Brawijaya-dynasty king designating him to be an instrument in persuading Suharto to resign and to "cleanse" the government, circulated a short document attacking corruption and calling for a change, and he managed to obtain the signatures of several prominent persons, including former Vice President Hatta, who, Sawito said, should succeed Suharto. Sawito then attached additional documents to his petition and ended up being arrested, along with several of his followers. He was tried and convicted and, late in 1978, sentenced to eight years in prison. Beyond the attention the case received in the press, it was symptomatic of the underlying tensions and unease in Indonesia.

Problems of Succession

What happens to Suharto and his rather sterile regime is important politically for Southeast Asia because as the largest nation in the region, Indonesia is the strongest counterforce to the new Communist nations of Indochina. Having had one President overthrown as a result of violence, most Indonesians are deeply concerned about arranging a peaceful transfer of power next time. If Suharto does step down before completing his third term, and the military moves to replace him with another general, there will almost certainly be a strong reaction from the civilian sector, including the students and the Moslem politicians, who will probably rally behind Vice President Adam Malik as the rightful successor. Although not a Javanese (he is from Sumatra) Malik is a popular political figure, and as Foreign Minister for many years, he was a widely respected negotiator on the world stage. A one-time Marxist who once headed his own small political party, and as one of the founders of Antara, the Indonesian news agency, he has a considerable domestic following, even though he has no strong political base of his own. He is, moreover, highly regarded for his concern with the welfare of the people and for his democratic philosophy, which includes a firm belief in wide-ranging political dialogue and popular participation in development.

Nevertheless, it seems highly doubtful that the military establishment will readily relinquish its power, though it has its own rivalries, particularly within the dominant Diponegoro division and between it and the other two army divisions, the Brawijaya and the elite Siliwangi. The officers mentioned most often as candidates for the presidency are General Maraden Panggabean, who has been called one of three "super ministers" in the new third-term cabinet, in charge of politics and defense; Defense Minister Yusuf; Home Minister Amir Machmud; and two of Suharto's fellow Diponegoro generals, Surono, the former Deputy Supreme Commander who is Welfare Minister in the new cabinet, and Widodo, the new army chief. Many observers think that Widodo, a politically minded officer, has the best chance. He has frequently issued statements on a variety of topics, including student unrest, and has gathered around him a highly capable group of unofficial advisers that includes some faculty members of Gadja Mada University, who have always been in the shadow of the government technocrats from the University of Indonesia, but who probably know more about conditions in the rural areas than any other specialists.

The possibilities of peasant revolts sparking another revolution in Indonesia are not to be discounted, but if they do take place, they are likely to be localized, and without any central urban intellectual direction, will quickly be smashed by the military. There is no indication that such strong urban leadership yet exists, unless some independent or Moslem leaders emerge to provide it. Nor are there any indications of a new internal Communist threat, though the leading generals, and Suharto himself, keep warning about this. The PKI was thoroughly dismembered after the 1965 coup, and whatever underground cells remain in the countryside, or in the cities, are inactive or are remaining deep underground. But this does not mean that the Communists might not again, at some time in the future and with or without outside help, make another revolutionary attempt.

Almost all the remaining 31,000 political prisoners—Communists or Communist sympathizers arrested after 1965—were to be released by the end of 1979, the government said. Only a hard core of 1,000 or 2,000 would then be kept in prison, or sequestered on small islands. It is possible that, once freed, some of the 30,000-odd may try to regain influence among the amorphous discontented peasantry, but this would not be easy, because of fear on the part of the peasants and constant military surveillance. Relatively few of the released prisoners were being allowed to return to their former homes and instead were resettled in other areas, under what Amnesty International, which claimed the total number of prisoners was much larger—between 50,000 and a 100,000—maintained were concentration-camp conditions. The government vehemently denied the Amnesty figures and said the new resettlement areas would be akin to ordinary transmigration centers, and that for the safety of the former prisoners themselves, this was the only logical solution.

There are no ranking Communist leaders left in Indonesia; the few who survived after 1965 are living in Peking, where they were stationed at the time of the coup and where they retained the blessings and support of the Chinese Communist Party. This is one of the reasons why Indonesia and Singapore were the only two Southeast Asian nations that at the start of 1979 had not yet established full diplomatic relations with Peking. Actually, Indonesia had never formally broken relations after the coup but had only suspended them. Though Peking was eager to resume a full and normal relationship, the Jakarta government was wary because of the reaction this might have among the 3 million Chinese in Indonesia, of whom 1 million were citizens of mainland China, about 800,000 were stateless, and the rest, except for a few holding Taiwan passports, were Indonesian citizens. Despite Peking's statements that the overseas Chinese should be good citizens of the countries in which they live, and notwithstanding the fact that the generally peaceful Chinese control as much as three fourths of the nation's commerce and often work in close cooperation with the military, government officials were disturbed over Peking's refusal to renounce party-to-party support for insurrectionary movements in Southeast Asia. Over recent years there have been a number of incidents between Chinese and non-Chinese, most of them the result of street accidents or local fights, and the flash points are still easily ignited.

As for the former Indochina nations, Hanoi and Jakarta concluded a trade agreement late in 1978, but the Indonesians were disturbed over Vietnam's domination of Laos and its invasion of Cambodia, with which Jakarta had established diplomatic relations, although it delayed sending an ambassador to Phnom Penh. While willing to maintain cordial relations with all the Communist countries of Asia, the Indonesians were reluctant to push things too far and too fast, especially in view of Hanoi's attack on Cambodia and China's invasion of Vietnam. And while maintaining relations with the Russians, they were disturbed over Moscow's ever-closer relationship with Hanoi and wished to avoid becoming engaged in the Sino-Soviet power struggle in any way.

Development for Whom?

Underlying all appraisals and analyses of Indonesia are the socioeconomic conditions of frustration and instability. The World Bank and the Intergovernmental Group on Indonesia (the consortium of thirteen nations led by Japan and the United States that has poured billions of dollars of financial aid into the country) have been fond of praising the multimillion-dollar industrial projects backed by foreign investment, because the GNP has kept growing at an annual rate of 7 or 8 percent; nevertheless, the nation's ability to feed an ever-growing population and provide a more equitable distribution of income remains the keys to successful development. There are other problems about the heavy influx of foreign-aid funds.

"We have to ask ourselves, How much aid can be absorbed, and how do we relate it to the uneducated poor in the nonmonetized sector of the economy?" said Emil Salim, one of the top technocrats. "More credit facilities alone are not enough. We haven't yet figured out the institutional mechanisms to handle all this."

In its annual reports on Indonesia, the World Bank has invariably been overoptimistic, placing too much emphasis on financial stability without sufficient regard for the political and social realities of the situation. It is significant that Robert McNamara, the technocratic president of the bank who once thought the Vietnam war could be computerized, belatedly declared, late in 1977, "We can and must design an effective overall development strategy that can both accelerate economic growth and channel more of the benefits of that growth toward meeting the basic human needs of the absolute poor."

If this does remain the nub of the problem, there are few signs that it is being dealt with positively and effectively. The countryside, despite the overt signs of improved prosperity, remains soaked in poverty, with farmers trying to eke out a meager living on small plots, particularly in Java. Poverty and profligacy coexist flagrantly in Jakarta, a swollen capital of nearly 5 million people which keeps drawing more and more unemployed and underemployed people to it in search of any kind of work each year. The contrasts are more pervasive, stark and naked than in the quiet rural areas. A visitor making his way through the noise and dust of the traffic to his plush hotel entrance is constantly accosted by tattered beggars, who in turn are accosted by the police. The dawn wail of Moslem prayers amplified from the ubiquitous mosques awakens the sleeping city to empty, dirty streets. Youthful soccer and volleyball players throng empty lots to enjoy an hour of relaxation and games before they start their daily grind of earning a few hundred rupiah. At dusk the prayers are heard again, and the neon lights of fancy discotheques mingle with the flickering lights of television screens in the *kompongs* of the poor below the elevated highways and high-rise office buildings and hotels. Hundreds of youngsters gather around these family-shared sets to catch a glimpse of an old Western comedy of sex or manners. One writer has described the scene as representing a transition "from subculture to cultural void," and added: "Given that Indonesia is not yet an industrialized society but is adopting the life style and leisure of Western industrialized society in spreading segments, this situation could only lead to a 'dead end.' There, puritanical and/or revolutionary reactions could manifest themselves."

The pulse of student discontent, though it is still labile and erratic, seems a major portent of what might lie ahead, as do the Moslem stirrings in the cities and the country at large, especially in such sensitive areas as East Java. Not to be discounted is the possibility that some of the younger officers with a social conscience, who are deeply if privately disturbed by the corruption and profligacy of some of their superiors, will take matters into their own hands and attempt a putsch aimed at establishing a military revolutionary government of the type that has become so prevalent in other parts of the underdeveloped world. But whether, even if they successfully seized control, they would move to set up a civilian government and restore political freedom, or would succumb to the pleasures of power themselves, as has happened in so many other countries, remains a question. What does seem inevitable is that unless the planners and promoters resolve their conflicts, and unless the country is set on the proper path of development, it will either break down or blow up again.

Korea-
In the Eye
of the Storm

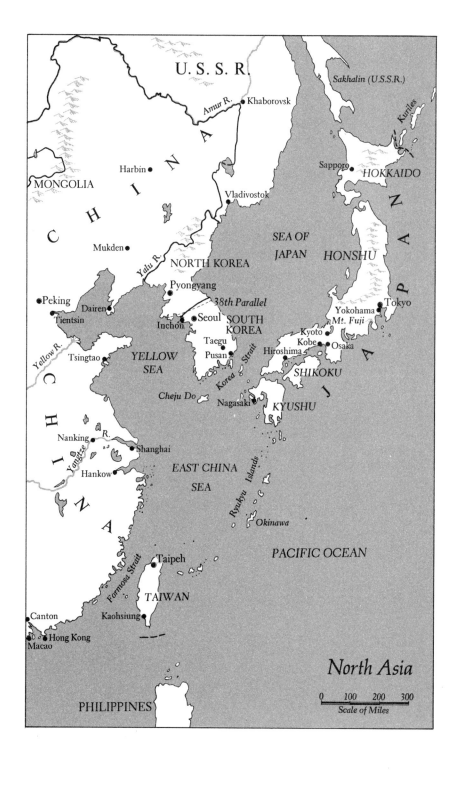

U.S.S.R.

Sakhalin (U.S.S.R.)

Amur R. • Khaborovsk

MONGOLIA

Harbin •

Sapporo •

HOKKAIDO

Kuriles

C H I N A

Mukden •

Vladivostok •

SEA OF
JAPAN

HONSHU

J A P A N

• Peking

Dairen •

Tientsin

Yalu R.

NORTH KOREA

Pyongyang •

38th Parallel

Inchon • Seoul

SOUTH
KOREA

Tokyo •

Yokohama •
Mt. Fuji

Kyoto •
Kobe •
Osaka •

Yellow R.

Tsingtao •

YELLOW
SEA

Taegu •

Pusan •

Korea Strait

Hiroshima •

SHIKOKU

C H I N A

Cheju Do

Nagasaki •

KYUSHU

Nanking •

R.

Yangtze

Shanghai •

EAST CHINA
SEA

Hankow •

Ryukyu Islands

Okinawa

PACIFIC OCEAN

Formosa Strait

Taipeh •

TAIWAN

• Canton

Kaohsiung •

• Hong Kong
Macao

North Asia

0   100   200   300

Scale of Miles

PHILIPPINES

In the spring of 1951, while I was roaming through Southeast Asia, several editors of the group of American newspapers for which I was writing a column asked me to return to North Asia, where the Korean War was reaching a two-fold climax, political and military. General Douglas MacArthur, the Commander in Chief of the United Nations Command composed of American and South Korean troops and contingents from fifteen other nations, had just been fired by President Harry Truman for disobeying orders and carrying his counteroffensive all the way north to the Manchurian border, which strained his command and supply lines and would soon bring the Chinese Communists into the war in force. I had not seen MacArthur for six years, not since I paid him a farewell visit in his Tokyo office at the start of the American occupation and then headed for China. As a correspondent in MacArthur's command during the Pacific war I had admired his island-hopping strategy and tactics, and despite his obvious imperial manner and arrogance, had come to respect him as a man of considerable intellectual stature, which had helped him succeed admirably in his postwar role as Supreme Commander of the Allied Powers (SCAP) in Japan. If he had now overreached himself in Korea, and if Truman had no alternative but to dismiss him, it was with mixed feelings that I watched his tearful and dramatic, if somewhat bathetic, departure in his silver Constellation from Haneda Air Base in Tokyo for America, where he was to make his famous "Old soldiers never die, they just fade away" speech before Congress, and then suffer the final disappointment of his long career in discovering that whatever lingering hopes he may have had to become President were not politically warranted.

After MacArthur's plane had left, I collected some cold-weather equipment and joined some of my old correspondent friends in Korea to follow the fighting, which had again become violent as a result of the new Communist offensive. For several weeks I shuttled up and down the snowy mountainous peninsula in jeeps, trucks and planes, amid a twenty-four-hour din of bombing and artillery. It was a particularly brutal war, and unlike the wars in the Pacific and in Vietnam, it remains an odd blur in my mind, perhaps because at the time it was such a seesaw, indecisive contest fought on an icy, bleak terrain. In contrast to the Vietnam wars against both the French and the Americans, which were a mixture of conventional and unconventional tactics, the Korean War of 1950–1953 was almost entirely a conventional struggle. The heavy application of fire power and ferocious, confrontational fighting between large and small units dominated the action and cost the Koreans of both sides almost a million dead, roughly the same as the total of Vietnamese who died in the fourteen years of the American involvement between 1961 and 1975. The Americans suffered 33,000 dead in Korea, 22,000 fewer than in Vietnam. The conflict ended in a stalemate. Its official resolution, the signing of a peace treaty, has not yet taken place, a quarter of a century later, nor have efforts to reunite the two still-contentious and heavily armed halves of Korea made any significant progress.

This unfortunate fact was driven home to me when, in May 1978, twenty-seven years after my wartime visit to Korea and after numerous trips since then, I was in Panmunjon, thirty miles north of Seoul, in the Demilitarized Zone separating North and South Korea. The scene was like the set for a Brecht play. Beside a long tin-roofed hut, where the Military Armistice Commission was holding its 387th meeting since the end of the war, a thirty-foot wooden boat, with an American soldier standing stiffly in the center of it, arms akimbo, was mounted on a flatbed truck. A hundred or so miscellaneous spectators, including crisply uniformed officers of European nations, on hand as neutral observers, milled about, chatting and occasionally scanning the trees for various rare species of birds, which, for some strange ornithological reason, have always made the DMZ their part-time habitat. Chinese Communist and North Korean soldiers, goose-stepping, ushered the delegates from Peking and Pyongyang into the meeting hall, where they sullenly faced the senior delegate of the United Nations Command, Rear Admiral Warren C. Hamm, Jr., a tall strong-jawed man with a crew cut who was trying to look as inscrutably expressionless as his Oriental counterparts.

Hamm sternly delivered the complaint on the day's agenda: the boat on display, disguised as a fishing vessel, had actually carried armed North Korean agents, and eight days before, had trespassed into South Korean waters, where, after refusing to heed flag signals and loudspeaker demands from South Korean navy vessels to stop, had opened fire and in turn been sunk. Eight of the seventeen-man crew were captured, and the rest drowned. From time to time over the years, such agent boats (the Americans called them "skunk boats") had been intercepted, either while engaged in seaborne espionage or during attempts to land agents on the coast. Once they got ashore, they were almost always caught and killed. This, Hamm asserted, was the first time such agents had been captured at sea. The North Korean delegates angrily denied the accusations, insisting that the vessel was simply an ordinary fishing boat that had suffered engine trouble and had accidentally drifted into South Korean waters, and they demanded the return of the eight men. Hamm refused, and said that "in view of the peculiar circumstances" they would be held "for further questioning." Two and a half weeks later, after the Americans said the eight had confessed to the intrusion and to refusing to stop when ordered, they were released "for humanitarian reasons." When they reached the North Korean side of the demarcation line, they stripped to their shorts and contemptuously threw back the clothes and shoes their South Korean captors had given them.

Troop-Withdrawal Plans

Such incidents, as well as armed clashes in the DMZ, are not uncommon. The most serious case occurred in 1976, when two American soldiers who were pruning a tree in order to improve visibility in the zone were brutally axed to death. The United States immediately put up a show of force, sending the aircraft carrier *Midway* offshore, whereupon President Kim Il Sung, of North Korea, expressed his regrets and returned the bodies. Over the years, the North Koreans have been guilty of far more violations than the South Koreans and have consistently used the Military Armistice Commission as a propaganda forum, demanding that a peace treaty formally ending the war be signed by the Americans, who had signed the armistice on behalf of South Korea and the other UN participants; that the UN Command be dissolved; and that all American troops be withdrawn from Korea. One reason Kim Il Sung is being conciliatory over recent DMZ incidents is his reluctance to throw a spanner into the Americans' troop withdrawal plans, which already are in effect, though proceeding very slowly. Under President Carter's long-range schedule, American occupation troops in South Korea—which numbered 60,000 at the end of the war but were afterward reduced to 40,000—were further cut to 34,000 by the end of 1978. Gradually, by the end of 1982, they are supposed to be reduced to 12,000, chiefly Air Force and support units, but, as of mid-1979, the withdrawals have been suspended, pending further review. The South Koreans are not happy about these planned reductions, but have reluctantly accepted them after Washington promised a "compensatory package" consisting of $800 million worth of American equipment already in the country, and $1.9 billion in credits to buy arms of all sorts in the United States. This aid, together with an anticipated step-up of South Korea's defense production under a five-year Force Improvement Plan, which would comprise more than a third of the national budget, is calculated to match the strength of the North Koreans and to make the South self-reliant.

The American military, not surprisingly, regarded its troops in Korea as a vital deterrent and was sure that the withdrawal of the ground forces of the Second Division, the only division still there, would encourage Kim Il Sung to attack rather than constrain him. In fact, a good many Americans thought that Carter had already moved too far too fast—or at least too indecisively, for in April 1978 he backtracked and announced that only one combat battalion instead of three would be withdrawn by the end of the year—the delay of additional withdrawals was announced later that year. Many also felt that Carter probably made a mistake in announcing any troop withdrawals before he had obtained some sort of concessions from the North Koreans, thereby giving away his bargaining chips without getting anything in return. The fact that Washington would not act unilaterally in Europe—that any reduction of Allied ground forces, tanks or nuclear arsenals there would have to be based on firm agreements between the Russians and the Warsaw Pact nations, on the one hand, and members of the North Atlantic Treaty Organization, on the other—was cited as an argument for moving ahead more cautiously in Korea. A number of foreign and domestic critics, among them some of the most vigorous opponents of South Korean human rights violations, believed that the United States should have normalized relations with the People's Republic of China before rather than after taking any action to withdraw the troops, a move that upset the Japanese as well as the South Koreans.

Dangerous Diplomatic Deadlock

The situation of a divided Korea has often been compared to that of Vietnam and Germany, the two other nations that were divided after World War II. But historians tend to agree that there was probably more justification for the partition of Germany than for the separation of Vietnam and Korea, since the two Asian nations were solely and arbitrarily severed for military occupation purposes that made little sense either politically or economically, let alone ethnically. In any event, the Germans in time adapted themselves to the "two Germanys" solution that now seems likely to be permanent. In fact, in December 1977, undoubtedly with the approbation of the Russians—perhaps even at their instigation—Erich Honecker, the Chairman of the Council of State of the German Democratic Republic, visited North Korea's capital, Pyongyang, and delivered a speech in which he frequently alluded to his close ties with Moscow, and in effect, suggested the "two Germanys" solution as one that might be adopted by Korea—a suggestion that others, including some Americans, have made from time to time. Honecker made this speech after Kim pre-empted him by denouncing the idea of "two Koreas" as a "splitist" tactic of the "imperialists"—a line he had always taken—and by saying, "The Korean question is fundamentally different in its nature from the case of Germany." Kim also rejected the idea of both Koreas entering the United Nations, where the Korean issue has been debated periodically and where conflicting and nonbinding resolutions backed by both Koreas and their respective friends have been passed by the General Assembly.

Kim similarly rejected the theory of "cross-recognition," supported by many diplomats, according to which the United States and Japan would recognize North Korea, and China and the Soviet Union would recognize South Korea. Both Moscow and Peking, which claim to be as eager as Washington and Tokyo to avoid another disastrous war on the Korean peninsula, might under certain circumstances have accepted cross-recognition; but as things stand, their mutual hostility precludes this, and what is more dangerous, serves as a long fuse that·could actually provoke another war. In fact, in mid-1979 the diplomatic contest that was going on between them involving both Koreas, and that was aggravated by the Sino-Vietnamese border conflict and by Sino-Soviet competition in the rest of Asia, threatened to spark the fuse.

In the past, Kim had always depended on both the Chinese and the Russians for military, economic and moral support. Immediately after the Vietnam war, the possibilities of hostilities breaking out again in Korea were regarded seriously, and there was genuine fear in South Korea, which I visited a few weeks later, that with the Americans just having suffered a major defeat in Asia and being disinclined to get involved in another conflict there or anywhere else, Kim would decide to strike while the situation was in his favor, despite restraints reportedly brought to bear on him by Russia and China. The Chinese had entertained Kim lavishly in Peking in March 1975, and on that occasion he announced that he was prepared to support a revolution in South Korea, which he always believed, or hoped, would take place simultaneously with another invasion by his powerful army. But when Kim asked the Chinese for more military aid he failed to get a definite commitment, and went back to Pyongyang disappointed. Three years later, however, in May 1978, Chairman Hua Kuo-feng, who was also Premier of the People's Republic of China, paid a return visit to Pyongyang and underlined his firm support of the position of North Korea as "the sole legal sovereign Korean state." Although no communiqué was issued, it was thought that Hua may privately have agreed to give the North Koreans some additional help. Then, in October, Vice Premier Teng Hsiao-ping attended the thirtieth anniversary of the North Korean revolution in Pyongyang, and after receiving a royal welcome, publicly promised Kim some much-needed oil to fuel his military machine. Teng did this despite the fact that North Korea had failed for several years to deliver on its trade obligations and was in default on its debts and interest payments to both Communist and non-Communist nations (notably Japan among the latter) by more than $2 billion.

If Kim was obviously tilting toward Peking—and Peking was responding—the Russians seemed to be making a slight tilt toward South Korea. Kim had long wanted to visit Moscow, and the Russians had been fending him off, though they did receive his former Prime Minister Park Sung Chul in 1977, when they may have rendered some financial assistance to help bail the North Koreans out of their debt predicament, or at least have extended the time limit for repayment. It was conceivable that, sooner or later, Moscow would receive Kim himself, if only to offset the new Chinese initiative. Kim was upset further by the new treaty of peace and friendship that was signed in October 1978 by Tokyo and Peking, and by the fact that this would prompt a formal renunciation by Peking of the all-but-dead Sino-Soviet alliance, putting him more than ever in the middle between his two rival allies. He was scarcely mollified by Moscow's sudden acknowledgment of Seoul, whose Health and Social Affairs Minister, the same month, attended a World Health Organization conference in Alma-Ata, in Soviet Kazakhstan—marking the first time a South Korean minister has ever visited the Soviet Union. It was unlikely that the Russians would go much further in wooing or placating Seoul, much as Seoul would welcome it, but it was clear that they were playing a new nettling game with Kim while also warning Peking not to overplay its Pyongyang hand.

From time to time, suggestions have been made—by former Secretary of State Henry Kissinger, among others—that the United States, China, both Koreas and Japan could reduce tensions on the Korean peninsula by calling a conference "to negotiate a more fundamental arrangement," as Kissinger once put it. The South Koreans are more than willing to make such a broad approach, to include the Russians as well as the Chinese, and over the past few years have been trying, with modest success, to establish contacts with the Communist nations of Eastern Europe as well as with the Russians. The North Koreans, on the other hand, have responded coolly to such diplomatic efforts, but they, too, have increased their contacts with the rest of the world, especially with the nonaligned nations. Having achieved diplomatic recognition from 91 countries—the figure for South Korea in 1978 was 102, and about 30 had recognized both Koreas—Kim has become increasingly eager to improve his global image. But Pyongyang is often tough, crude and inept in its diplomacy, just as Seoul is often less than subtle—in the behavior of Korean Central Intelligence operatives abroad, for instance, and in the lavish dispensation of gifts and political donations by the wealthy rice dealer Tongsun Park to American congressmen.

The diplomatic by-play over the Korean issue picked up noticeably in the spring of 1978 when President Josip Broz Tito, of Yugoslavia, and President Nicolae Ceausescu, of Rumania, both paid visits first to Pyongyang and then to Washington. Ceausescu pushed for a two-party dialogue between Pyongyang and Washington, but did so, it was said, in such a blunt, demanding way that President Carter was visibly offended. Tito suggested a three-party conference between Pyongyang, Seoul and Washington, but Kim threw cold water on that idea—much to the relief of the South Koreans, who were willing to go along with it at Washington's behest but preferred to resume the low-level dialogue with the North over trade and exchanges of family visits which was broken off after a year of fruitless discussions.

Hopes for Dialogue in 1972

This dialogue, which began in the summer of 1972, was the high point of post–Korean War relations between the two severed halves of the country. It was started by the North and South Korean Red Cross organizations to promote humanitarian exchanges, and these talks were to be followed by political discussions under the supervision of a specially established North-South Coordinating Committee created under dramatic circumstances when the intelligence chiefs of the two nations met in Pyongyang and pledged to renounce the use of force, and as a joint communiqué signed by the two top agents put it, seek to achieve "a great national unity . . . transcending differences in ideas, ideologies and systems." The two men even announced the opening of a hot-line between Seoul and Pyongyang to "prevent unexpected military incidents."

In South Korea the excitement and joy following the announcement of the communiqué were tremendous. I was in Seoul at the time and saw people literally weep in the streets. But almost immediately thereafter, as a result of go-slow signals from the government of President Park Chung Hee, a mood of caution and apprehension akin to that of the hermetically sealed North set in, and it was stressed that the road to unity would be long and difficult. The government's position was reinforced in October 1972 when Park peremptorily proclaimed martial law, dissolved the National Assembly, and announced that the constitution would be amended so as to enable the dialogues with the North to continue unencumbered by "legalities." During the year that followed, bimonthly desultory and sometimes recriminatory preparatory meetings and a score or so sessions of the Red Cross groups were held, but no progress was made either in furthering any humanitarian exchanges or in getting political talks started, and eventually the hot line was dismantled by the North Koreans. While the South tried from time to time to get serious talks started again, the North accused it of being insincere, antagonistic and bellicose, which is what the South, with greater validity but also with a degree of self-righteousness, said about the North.

Park proposed a nonaggression pact on several occasions, and in June 1978, the establishment of a new consultative body of civilian businessmen to promote trade exchanges, whereas Kim called for a confederation of the two Koreas and for a congress of Northern and Southern political leaders to discuss both unification and disarmament, and constantly repeated his demand for direct peace talks with the United States alone. But the two sides regularly denounced each other's ideas as mere propaganda maneuvers while the stalemate and invective continued. However, in his annual new-year press conference on January 19, 1979, Park called for a meeting "at any time and at any place and at any level," and surprisingly the North responded four days later by suggesting a midyear conference under the auspices of an organization originally founded in 1949 called the Democratic Front for the Unification of the Fatherland. This would ostensibly include representatives from all sectors of Korean society, including the South and North Korean governments as just two of many voices.

Not unexpectedly, the South rejected the Front idea and suggested instead that the 1972 South-North Coordinating Committee be resummoned. The North replied that the SNCC was a body "of limited scope" which "has lost reason for existence." A compromise was reached whereby, on February 17, at Panmunjon, four representatives of the North, including a high-ranking party member, appeared as representatives of the Democratic Front, while the South sent four members of the SNCC. Although the conversation, the first in six years at such a high level, was cordial, very little progress was made. The

South stuck to its plan to re-establish the SNCC, though it agreed to broaden its representation, while the North called for a "Pan-National Conference" under the aegis of its Democratic Front. What the North was after, it was later disclosed, was the creation of a "Confederate Republic of Koryo," the old name used for unified Korea during the Koryo dynasty (A.D. 935 to 1392), but Pyongyang apparently was willing to be somewhat more lenient than it had been in the past by agreeing to the retention of separately administered autonomous social and economic systems in the South and North and to the two sides sharing a single seat at the United Nations.

It was obvious that both sides were still far apart, and while it was agreed to meet again, there was very little immediate hope of any solution. What was perhaps significant, though, was that both Pyongyang and Seoul were responding in their separate ways to the changed situation in North Asia, and particularly to the new relationships between the United States and China, and between China and Japan. Like China, North Korea was eager to establish closer contact with the West in search of economic and technological guidance and assistance, while South Korea was anxious to pursue its efforts to trade with the Communist nations. Over and above their separate propaganda motives, some hope could be obtained from this new global outlook both parts of Korea were adopting, and, meanwhile, on a much smaller but symbolic level, plans were made for a group of Ping-Pong players from South Korea to play in a world tournament in Pyongyang. But, as it turned out, the Ping-Pong contest took place in April 1979 without the participation of the South Koreans, although a team from the United States did take part in the tournament, and a number of American newsmen and television crews covered it. At about the same time, United Nations Secretary General Kurt Waldheim visited both Pyongyang and Seoul in an effort to promote a more serious dialogue.

South Far Ahead Economically

One of the reasons the 1972 talks broke down a year later was that the Northern delegates were overwhelmed by the sight of the South's growing economic prosperity. In the years that followed, the growth was even more remarkable, and Seoul became Asia's biggest boom town: a throbbing metropolis of 7.5 million (a fifth of the South's population) and the hub of what was probably the fastest-developing nation in the world except for the petroleum powers. Though there was talk of getting people to spread into satellite suburbs and of eventually building a new capital farther south, near a cluster of industrial centers, in Seoul lush high-rise office buildings and apartment buildings were topped off each month, and four or five new subway lines were planned to supplement one already completed. Hotels, old and new, were jam-packed, largely with overseas buyers—mostly Americans with orders for everything from textiles and toys to electronics. It became impossible to find an empty taxicab, and it was necessary to fight other passengers in an effort to share one. Though a good meal for two cost $30, restaurants were crowded each night until ten o'clock, and the country's growing affluence, which affected a rising new middle class as well as the rich, kept people out on the streets until close to the midnight curfew, shopping before and after they ate. A $44 million Cultural Center that was opened in Seoul in the spring of 1978 drew capacity crowds to concerts and performances by famous orchestras, singers and ballet troupes brought from abroad. Golf and tennis were the rage, and money was the chief topic of conversation.

Development and more development became the national theme song, emphasizing both light and heavy industry. The growth rate of the gross national product in 1978 approached 15 percent—about what it was in 1976, before it dropped to a healthy enough 10 percent in 1977—and the per capita annual income, which was $650, or nearly four times what it had been ten years before, was rising at the rate of about 20 percent a year. In fact, the economy was somewhat overheated, with too much money in circulation, forcing the government to adopt a tight-money policy and restrict domestic credit in an effort to get the inflation rate below 20 percent (in late 1978 it was unofficially about 27 percent). But exports, on which South Korea prided itself, kept soaring. In 1977 the country exported more than $10 billion worth of commodities—chiefly heavy-industrial and chemical products. In 1978 the figure was $12.5 billion, and the goal was $20 billion by 1981, $50 billion by 1986, and $100 billion by 1991.

Vast new industrial complexes—steel mills, cement works, shipyards and machine plants—were springing up all over the South. One nuclear power plant had been completed, two were being constructed, and eventually there were to be seven, which would do much to reduce the $2 billion annual oil bill the country had to pay—a bill that would, of course, grow if no alternative sources of energy were developed. Forty-three atomic power stations were also planned, to be completed by the year 2000, which would give the country a nuclear generating capacity equal to that of the United States in 1978. South Korea had also begun making its own automobiles; the rate of production in 1978 was 40,000 a year, but by 1990 nearly 1 million would be rolling out annually, a hefty proportion of them for export. Another major export was labor; there were almost 100,000 South Korean workers abroad, most of them in the Middle East, where they were famous for their round-the-clock work on construction projects and where they earned as much as $500 or $1,000 a month—much more than they could make back home.

The pattern of development in South Korea was astonishingly similar in many respects to what it was in Japan in the late fifties and sixties, but South Korea didn't really take off until the seventies, and the rate of growth proved much faster. As in Japan, with which Korea was becoming increasingly competitive, especially in such major areas as shipping, a dozen or so major conglomerates had their own trading concerns, which dominated the export markets. Most of South Korea's big new multimillion-dollar companies, such as Hyundai, Samsung and Lucky, had been formed before, during or just after the Korean War as small trading shops dealing in noodles, rice, textiles and sugar; their wealthy owners were now Horatio Alger rags-to-riches figures. As one of my Korean friends put it, "We're moving so fast it makes me dizzy, but it's exciting." But although the country prided itself on achieving a better distribution of income than other fast-developing nations, wages were still low by Western standards, and lower than in many other parts of Asia—a situation that helped give Korea a competitive advantage pleasing to the manufacturers, but one that was causing increasing social and labor unrest. Moreover, the concentration on accelerated growth threatened to deepen the division between the modern and traditional sectors of the economy, and to create an overdependence on foreign markets similar to the crisis the Japanese were already facing.

The Temptations of Kim

The tension and anxiety that were felt shortly after the end of the Vietnam war had diminished by 1978, but beneath the surface the exuberant confidence in a rosy economic future was tempered by continuing worries about the permanence of peace. The very boom in South Korea, it was thought, might cause Pyongyang to feel that the prosperous South of 37 million people would ultimately prevail by virtue of sheer manpower and will power over the less than half as populous and prosperous North. Hence, the fear in Seoul was that this might give Kim Il Sung another reason to strike before the economic imbalance became still greater. The psychological factors involved in this deadly game were as important as the military and economic statistics, particularly since, with the possible exceptions of Cambodia and Albania, North Korea remained the most closed society in the world.

Besides severe economic problems, Kim Il Sung was facing internal political divisions, which derived partly from the fact that his son and supposed heir, Kim Chong Il, thirty-eight, had dropped out of sight after being seriously hurt late in 1977 in an automobile crash (which was rumored to have been an assassination attempt), and partly from competition between the technocrats and the old political stalwarts, with the military in the middle. As Kim, sixty-six years old in 1978 and in poor health, realized that time was no longer on his side, he conceivably could become more desperate. This personal equation could be tempered, however, by his still-limited awareness of the outside world —particularly of the non-Communist world, but also the Third World. In the latter he clearly had come to regard himself as a vanguard revolutionary leader, for he was offering guerrilla training both at home and abroad to a number of African and Latin-American nations. There were also reports that at China's behest he had sent military instructors to Cambodia to help the Cambodians in their bitter border fights against the Vietnamese.

One could hear various forecasts in Seoul, where most people were obsessed with the pursuit of economic gain, but where the prospects of war weighed heavily on the minds of the policy makers in the presidential palace, known as the Blue House (named after a peculiar blue Korean tile); on the minds of the military men; and on the minds of some of the academics and the more thoughtful politicians. In the course of interviewing nearly a hundred such people, I found some who believed that notwithstanding China's desire to cement relations with Washington and to include Tokyo in a trilateral scheme of cooperation, Peking might have gone so far as to make a secret pledge to help Pyongyang in another revolutionary struggle—perhaps even employing troops, as before. Other experts felt—more plausibly, it seemed to me—that Moscow might conceivably support a quick strike south by Kim if the Russians believed that a Washington-Peking-Tokyo alliance was in effect being directed against them, and if they felt that such a strike would benefit their strategic position as a growing naval power in the Pacific and thus strengthen them against China. Moscow, which had to maintain freedom of movement for its big Pacific fleet in the Tsushima Strait, between Korea and Japan, could not afford to let Peking get the upper hand on the Korean peninsula. For its part, Peking could not countenance a Soviet-controlled Korea, which would provide a Pacific flank for Moscow if war broke out on the Sino-Soviet border. Korea, therefore, remained a linchpin—not only in the strategic contest between the Communists and the non-Communists in North Asia but also in the narrower but equally volatile struggle within the Communist world. In a crunch, Kim Il Sung still believed that neither Communist power could refuse to help him, and in this sense, despite his new bias toward Peking, he continued to hold a blackmail leverage over both Communist powers.

For this reason, and because of the overriding fact that North Korea's steady military build-up, which reached a peak in the mid-seventies, continued to make Korea one of the primary danger zones of the world, some experts favored a direct American approach to Pyongyang, accompanied by simultaneous (though naturally separate) consultations with Moscow and Peking about the Korean question. This could best be achieved, it was suggested, either through private channels (as when efforts of that nature were made on several occasions to settle the Vietnam war, which might have succeeded if they had been seriously pursued), or by the establishment of contact with the North Koreans in a third country, or at the United Nations. If this was done judiciously, the South Koreans would not need to be unduly upset, especially if they were convinced of three conditions: that the American troop withdrawals would be carried out more slowly, as projected; that Congress would not throw blocks in the way of sufficient military aid being continued; and that the United States would continue to honor the 1954 Mutual Defense Treaty, whereby it was pledged to support South Korea in any new military crisis. Moreover, if Kim Il Sung should be thinking of making another attack on the South, even an exploratory approach to him would give him pause. In such a situation, deterrent diplomacy surely seemed as important as military deterrence.

President Carter, however, showed no signs of being willing to deal with Pyongyang on a bilateral basis, or of using the Japanese, who were in a unique position as a result of having trade relations with both Koreas and serving as a useful funnel for what little news trickled out of North Korea, to facilitate a dialogue. Because of their vulnerable role in strategic northeastern Asia as a result of their proximity to the two Koreas as well as to China and Russia, the Japanese were worried about becoming the eye of a new tornado and would have welcomed a common effort to resolve the Korean issue and then be able to go about their business—which was mainly business. Though they had not been consulted in advance about the American troop withdrawals, as they had assumed they would be, they had been mollified by Carter's promise to keep them informed of each move henceforth.

Strains between Seoul and Washington

While the American and South Korean military seemed to have come to terms on future plans, holding regular joint exercises at sea and on land to prove their readiness to meet an emergency, this was not true of the civilian branches of the two governments. For several years so many conflicting and confusing issues had been injected into the tortuous relationship between the United States and South Korea, including the human rights question, the Tongsun Park bribery case, and million-dollar kickbacks by American corporations seeking to do business in Korea, that while both countries insisted their relations remained substantially sound, a good number of American and Korean officials were growing increasingly wary of each other. Given the historical background of the relationship, and its many anomalies, which started with the illogical separation of the Korean peninsula at the thirty-eighth parallel after World War II—a move that was hastily engineered by the Soviet Union and the United States and was followed only five years later by the Korean War—it was not surprising that over the years there had been as many disagreements as agreements. These had been exacerbated by what had all along been the principal American policy objective in North Asia: to strengthen Washington's alliance with Tokyo, and to make the alliance with South Korea, important though it also was, subservient to it. Largely at the Americans' instigation, the Koreans and the Japanese, who had never had much fondness for one another, and who for years had assumed the role of colony and overseas ruler, respectively, signed a treaty of peace and friendship in 1965, which led to highly profitable—if often questionable—business transactions, including the construction of Seoul's new subway, that had benefited wealthy entrepreneurs and politicians of both countries.

Going even further back, the Koreans had a considerable basis in fact for being suspicious about the reliability of the United States. At the turn of the century, Theodore Roosevelt had in effect tossed them into the lap of the Japanese with the Taft-Katsura agreement, which William Howard Taft, his Secretary of War, negotiated after the Russo-Japanese War. Then, after World War I, Woodrow Wilson's Fourteen Points, which gave the Koreans great hopes for independence, proved illusory, and no one listened to their pleas at Versailles. Further, in 1950, six months before the Korean War started, Secretary of State Dean Acheson made a historic speech in effect placing Korea outside the American defense perimeter; this, following as it did the withdrawal of American troops from Korea the year before, certainly was a factor in encouraging the invasion from the North. Lastly, after the Korean War the United States allowed the thirty-eighth parallel to become a permanent political barrier.

There was another historical fact that was often forgotten or obscured, just as it was, to a different degree, in Vietnam: the United States, despite all its pretensions, had never really concerned itself much with the question of Korean nationalism. Partly for this reason, the Americans too readily accepted the concept of two Koreas as a more or less unavoidable circumstance—and perhaps even as a condition which, over the short or long term, served Washington's security interests in Asia and the Pacific. As a consequence, the United States did relatively little over the years to promote the possibility of unification, and continued to favor the existence of two Koreas as at least a convenient semipermanent solution, just as it favored two Germanys in Europe. Selig S. Harrison, a former foreign correspondent who had become a Senior Associate of the Carnegie Endowment for International Peace, pointed out in a provocative book published in 1978 entitled *The Widening Gulf: Asian Nationalism and American Policy* that in Korea, in contrast to Vietnam, "where the Communist side had the political and military strength to pursue a successful unification strategy, neither the North nor the South is able to claim a position of preeminent national leadership"; as a result, "nationalism has now been neutralized in the Korean equation."

The Koreans, like the Japanese, are a homogeneous people, with strong patriotic feelings, yet the unrealistic bisection of the peninsula prevents either side from penetrating the other politically or influencing it nationalistically. In the thirties a strong nationalist movement did exist in Korea, which the Japanese overlords weakened by divide-and-conquer tactics, and which the Comintern subsequently torpedoed because the Communists couldn't seize control of it. After 1945, when there was again an opportunity for a non-Communist nationalist movement to grow up in the South, and at least a possibility that an authentic coalition government might be formed, the United States helped perpetuate the partition by supporting the austere Syngman Rhee; under his regime the non-Communist nationalists in the South were fragmented and dispersed, and the Communist leaders there fled to the North, where they were eventually purged by Kim Il Sung. Thereafter there was no opportunity to create a common nationalist front. Kim, originally a Soviet puppet whose nationalist credentials were somewhat dubious, gradually evolved an independent policy of *juche*, or self-reliance, while in the South, Park Chung Hee, the diminutive, bland but tough professional soldier, who was propelled to power in 1961 by a military coup after a period of democratic chaos and a student revolt (which Kim Il Sung, to his lasting regret, failed to take advantage of), started out by establishing law and order, and turned to total dictatorship a decade later, when an American-inspired effort to create and sustain a democratic system based on free elections had come to nothing. Though both Kim and Park sought to project themselves as nationalist figures, neither could lay claim to a true nationalist ideology, such as was formulated by Ho Chi Minh, in Vietnam. Both men were messianic zealots, but they rode different horses—Kim seeking national unification through military conquest or revolution, and Park seeking the same end through superior economic development and the ultimate weakening of the North.

Kim Il Sung was born in the village of Mangyondao, near Pyongyang, in 1912, five years before the birth of Park. His real name was Kim Song Choo, but when he was fourteen and fled with his family to Manchuria he renamed himself Kim Il Sung, after a legendary hero of the Korean resistance movement there. Despite his youth, according to Communist Party accounts, he organized a Down with Imperialism Union and a Young Communist League in Manchuria, and by the time he was twenty he had set up anti-Japanese guerrilla bases and an alleged underground "revolutionary government." Non-Korean versions of Kim's life, mostly Russian and Chinese, indicate that his guerrilla band merely made a few ineffectual raids at the outset of the Japanese occupation of Manchuria and was actually one of the smallest guerrilla groups. Furthermore, Kim was not particularly well known for his ideological abilities, though it was recognized that he possessed strategic and tactical skills. In the early forties he spent several years in the Soviet Union, but by the time Soviet troops moved into North Korea at the end of the war in 1945, he had gone back to Manchuria and was ready to return to Korea himself.

In addition to a group of domestic Communists, there were at that time three other Communist groups in Korea: returnees from China, known as the Yenan group, and two comparatively weak Soviet groups—Soviet Koreans who had lived for years in the Soviet Union and who retained Soviet citizenship, and the so-called Kapstan faction, whose members had fought in Manchuria against the Japanese in the thirties and forties. Kim Il Sung belonged to this faction, but he had no official Communist Party position and was still a fairly obscure figure when he went back to Korea under Russian sponsorship in September 1945.

He appeared publicly for the first time at a rally in Pyongyang a month later. Though projected as a national hero, he was short and pudgy, hardly a dynamic figure, and his official introduction to political life was a colorless performance. For one thing, many of his fellow Communists felt he was too young for leadership and would have preferred any one of several more veteran figures of the party and the movement whose credentials were far better than his. However, he was made the first head of the North Korean Central Bureau of the Korean Communist Party and it later became known that he was the personal choice of Josef Stalin—precisely because, as one Communist historian put it, "he was a limited man, a guerrilla rather than a political animal," and thus was regarded by Stalin as someone he could trust.

The Russians quickly made apparent their intention to take complete political control of North Korea, and by the end of 1948 Kim, with the encouragement of Moscow, had eliminated his chief rivals of the Yenan group. In September of that year he became President of the Democratic People's Republic of North Korea. When the Soviets withdrew their troops at year's end, they recognized his new government and maintained a firm rein on it, not only through Kim but through trusted Soviet Koreans who had been installed in key government posts and in the top hierarchy of the Communist Party. North Korea thus became a complete Soviet satellite, and its status was underlined in a mutual economic-and-cultural-cooperation agreement between Stalin and Kim, signed in March 1949, in which Kim acknowledged the superiority of Russian accomplishments and tutelage.

The Korean War enhanced the power of Kim Il Sung, enabling him to eliminate most of his remaining rivals, both Soviet Koreans and pro-Chinese Koreans. He resented the fact that he had to defend his country with the help of huge numbers of Chinese troops, while he was annoyed at the Russians for the opposite reason: after their initial build-up of his army, they failed to give him the additional logistic support he wanted. When the war was over, he decided he would emulate both the Chinese and Soviet systems as he saw fit without committing himself completely to either, though he required the economic and military help of both. However, he was unable to avoid being caught in the middle of the Sino-Soviet ideological split when it took place. Late in 1962, partly to extricate himself from this predicament, and to supplement his *juche* policy, he propounded the theory of "walking on two legs" (a phrase he adopted from the Chinese), which meant placing equal emphasis on developing both North Korea's economy and military power. By 1968 he had built up a regular army of about 400,000 men, armed mostly with Russian weapons, and a people's militia of 1.3 million men. North Korea had become a virtual fortress and Kim was probably the strongest dictator in the world at the time, deified in the personality cult that he built up around himself as "the peerless patriot," "the ever victorious iron-willed brilliant commander," and so on. To enhance his personal image, he formulated a vague mixture of hortatory "thoughts" and fiery statements that he called Kim Il Sungism.

Rise of Park Chung Hee

There are some interesting comparisons as well as obvious differences in the backgrounds of Kim Il Sung and Park Chung Hee. The son of a poor peasant family in the southern part of South Korea, Park, after attending normal school, went to the Manchukuo Military Academy (Manchukuo is what the Japanese called Manchuria), after which he was admitted to the highly regarded Japanese Military Academy. As a youth, before going to Manchuria, he and an older brother were associated with left-wing elements seeking independence from the Japanese, and when he returned to Manchuria in 1944, left-wing groups again tried to contact him, even though he had been subjected to intensive anti-Communist indoctrination in Japan and had be-

come a first lieutenant in the Japanese army. After V-J Day and the partition-
ing of Korea, there were two left-wing uprisings in the South, which were put
down by the police, backed by the Americans. Park's older brother, who had
a more direct association with the Communists, was killed during the 1946
rebellion in Taegu, in the South; and during the so-called Yosu rebellion, in
1948, which was also led by the left wing, Park was arrested. He promptly sent
word to officers of the Korean army that if he was set free, he would identify
the leaders of the Yosu rebellion. He was thereupon let out of jail, and joined
search parties tracking down and killing or arresting the rebels.

After working for a year as a civilian intelligence officer, during which time
he also taught school for a while, Park returned to military status at the
outbreak of the Korean War, as a captain in army intelligence. Over the years
following the war, he was frequently transferred, and as one historian has
noted, remained "outside the main political traffic in the army." Though he
eventually became a general, his resentment against the faction-ridden military establishment undoubtedly helped rekindle his revolutionary energies.
When two hundred and fifty or so officers organized the May 1961 coup that
overthrew the well-intentioned but inefficient and chaotic regime of Premier
John M. Chang, who had taken over when President Syngman Rhee was
forced out of office in April 1960, Park was chosen to be the leader as the senior
officer of the group, even though the coup was engineered by Kim Jong Pil,
who later became Park's Prime Minister. At the time of the coup, Park was
forty-three years old. Having grabbed power, the military promised to turn it
over as soon as possible to "new and conscientious politicians," but following
the passage in 1962 of a new constitution, which prescribed a strong form of
presidential rule, Park himself, after considerable political infighting, became
the candidate of the Democratic Republican Party, which Kim Jong Pil had
created. In a surprisingly free and close election in October 1963, he defeated
President Yun Po Son, who had been a ceremonial President during the
Chang regime.

Though Park's picture was already on display in South Korea in the mid-
sixties almost as much as Kim's was in the North, he did not emphasize his
own image and personality to the degree that Kim did; instead he sought to
project himself as a man of Spartan discipline and simple ways who had his
private roots in the countryside. He spoke often of his rural background and
identified himself with the simple peasants of the South rather than with the
urban rich or merchant class, whom he instinctively distrusted, just as he
looked askance at the intellectuals and educated dissidents who complained
the most about his regimented regime.

Tracing the course of alternating repression and relaxation that Park afterward pursued provides a case history of political pathology that, puzzling and
disturbing as it is to many Westerners, must be regarded in the context of
South Korea's semiconfined society set against the threat of Kim Il Sung's total
dictatorship in the North. A starting point can be said to have been the passage
in 1969 of a constitutional amendment that permitted Park to run for a third

term, which he did, in 1971, when he won by a narrow margin over Kim Dae Jung, the leader of the opposition New Democratic Party. Kim subsequently exiled himself in Japan, where he increased his criticism of Park, but in August 1973 he was kidnapped from a Tokyo hotel by the South Korean CIA. The agents put him aboard a ship bound for Korea, with the apparent intention of throwing him overboard en route, but wide publicity given to the incident in Japan, the United States and other nations deterred the kidnappers, and Kim was brought back to Seoul and placed under house arrest.

(Late in 1975 Kim was tried and found guilty of violating the election laws in 1967 and 1971, and sentenced to a year in jail. In August 1976 he was found guilty again as one of eighteen dissidents on trial for demanding that Park step down as President and reinstate full democracy by abolishing the new so-called Yushin—the word means "Revitalizing Reforms"—constitution. Like former President Yun Po Sun, Kim received a five-year sentence, which he started serving early in 1977. Because of his age, Yun Po Sun's sentence was suspended, and the other sixteen dissidents were later released. Late in 1978 Park released Kim from the prison hospital where he was receiving treatment for a nervous disorder, and placed him on parole. A broad amnesty freed about 5,000 prisoners in all, of whom 106 were political prisoners. Kim was the best known of them, along with Kim Chi Ha, one of Korea's leading poets, whose life sentence was commuted to twenty years. One of the charges against him was that he had aided the cause of the People's Revolutionary Party. This was allegedly a North Korean spy organization, which most neutral observers believed was a total fabrication, although twenty-one persons had been found guilty in the case and eight of them had been hanged, an event that failed to arouse much attention in Washington or elsewhere because the trial took place just as South Vietnam was falling. The release of the political prisoners, which left about two hundred, most of them student dissidents, and a few clergymen, lawyers, editors, labor organizers and writers still in jail, was an obvious effort by Park to improve his human rights profile and to pave the way for a summit meeting with President Carter which he had long sought, and which was scheduled to take place in June 1979 in Seoul. Upon his release, Kim Dae Jung risked being jailed again by immediately assailing Park's Yushin constitution as "illegal." He claimed that its enforcement "suppresses the opposition parties" and said that "unless democracy is fully and quickly restored, South Korea will go the way of South Vietnam and now Iran.")

Park's moves toward complete authoritarianism, after his third-term victory, came to their first climax in December 1971 when, after having called out troops a few months before to quell antigovernment demonstrations on university campuses in Seoul, he declared a state of emergency; this gave him complete control over the nation's economic life, the press and labor, and the movement and mobilization of the population in any part of the country. At the same time he rammed a law through the National Assembly granting him special presidential powers. After the Yushin constitution had been approved by 91 percent of the voters in a national referendum at the end of 1972, martial law was lifted. Since any opposition to the new constitution had been forbidden, the vote was simply a convenient gimmick for Park to get what he wanted. The Yushin constitution was a strange document that promised all sorts of freedoms with one hand and took them away with the other by regularly invoking the phrase "except as provided by law." (One of the few unhedged provisions was "No person shall be tortured nor be compelled to testify against himself in criminal cases"—a pledge that was regularly and systematically violated by the KCIA.)

Yushin Ensures Park's Rule

One of the main objectives of the new constitution was to ensure Park's re-election for as many six-year terms as he desired; until its passage, the presidential term had been four years. Yushin provided for the establishment of a new political body, the National Conference for Unification, whose members were to be elected locally throughout the country after careful preselection of candidates—most of them farmers and small entrepreneurs. The NCU's sole tasks were to elect the President by secret ballot, and to give its routine approval of the President's appointment of a third of the members of the National Assembly, who were automatically designated as a separate party and thus, in alliance with Park's Democratic Republican Party, helped form a permanent majority that successfully emasculated the opposition New Democrats. Despite being badly factionalized, in the first parliamentary elections under the Yushin system the New Democrats won 52 out of 146 seats. (Even more surprisingly, in the second election, held in December 1978, they captured 61 seats to the ruling party's 68, and actually won a larger percentage of the popular vote, 33 to 32 percent. By appointing the remaining 77 members of the Assembly, Park easily held on to power, but as a result of their strong showing, especially in the two major cities of Seoul and Pusan, the New Democrats served notice that the opposition was latently a force to be reckoned with, even if its hands were tied by the constitution. With Kim Dae Jung out of jail, though he had quit the party, at least temporarily, Park's opponents seemed in a better position to challenge him than they had been for several years.)

Criticism of the Yushin constitution had begun at the outset, but it was held in check by a series of tough supplementary decrees under which Park was able to maintain full control of the government and to keep the dissident movement on the defensive. Nine such basic decrees were issued in all, but with the exception of one economic decree, each was canceled and superseded by the next, and the operative dictate became Decree Number Nine, issued in May 1975. This was an omnibus edict that prescribed imprisonment of not less than a year for virtually every phase of public or private activity the government deemed dangerous, and made the head of any organization, school or company responsible for the behavior and activities of his subordinates.

Park adroitly followed a zigzag course, relaxing when he felt he could afford to and then tightening the reins again, often unpredictably. For example, after his wife was killed in an attack on his life, in August 1974, he surprised his critics by issuing two temporizing decrees; this led to a period of active opposition to the government on the part of university students and church leaders which lasted several months and built up to a new level of violence before Park changed course and struck back with a fresh campaign of repression. Demonstrations were then broken up, a number of protesters were arrested, and about twenty universities were closed down temporarily. Religious groups mounted more protests and staged rallies attended by as many as five thousand people, and on a number of occasions student demonstrators ventured out beyond the traditional high university walls and carried their campaign to the streets, where they threw rocks until the police used tear gas to disperse them. High school students also joined in, and newspaper reporters, led by those of Seoul's respected *Dong-A Ilbo,* met to protest the new press restrictions. A National Council for the Restoration of Democracy, listing on its roster seventy-one of the country's most prominent churchmen, intellectuals and opposition politicians, was formed in November 1974. It became apparent that Park and his government were under attack on the broadest front to date, and the foreign press started predicting his downfall.

Park responded with another gimmick, a new national referendum, held in February 1975, on one question: whether or not the people approved of his policies. The strategem nearly backfired when he won a modest 73 percent affirmative vote. Park cited the results as proof that the ordinary people of the countryside, his chief "constituency," were completely behind him, even if the maverick urban intellectuals were not. A few days after the referendum he freed approximately a hundred and fifty opposition leaders, including Bishop Daniel Chi Hak Sun, the Roman Catholic Bishop of Wonju, and, temporarily, the poet Kim Chi Ha. Within days after the release of these prisoners, a score of them issued statements about tortures they had been subjected to in jail, and the newspapers daringly printed some of these stories, including graphic descriptions of how the victims—mostly students, intellectuals and some former members of the National Assembly—had been severely beaten, had had water poured into their mouths and nostrils, and had been subjected to electric shocks and injections of drugs to make them sign confessions.

The government unconvincingly denied the torture stories and responded by passing a tougher revision of the criminal code. It also announced that the released professors and students would not be allowed to return to their classes until they were granted official amnesty—something that in most cases never did take place. The issue of press freedom momentarily took the limelight, and after the government forced big commercial advertisers to withdraw their advertisements from the *Dong-A Ilbo* and brought pressure that led to the firing of some reporters and editors, other staff members went out on strike or conducted sit-ins, on occasion delaying publication. Park thereupon intensified his pressure on advertisers, but the *Dong-A Ilbo* retaliated by running small ads placed by individuals and groups, mostly of a few lines each, such as "To Korea with love—Sunny and Steve," "We would rather die standing than live kneeling—Nine Women Textile Workers," and "I am thirteen years old and have lived under only one President—A Magpie." The newspaper survived, but a shuffle of its top editors and staff shortly turned it into a pale carbon copy of its former self—if not totally a government mouthpiece, a malleable and no longer outspoken publication.

The pattern of repression continued, as well as fresh confrontations between the government and university students, and some of the largest universities were once more shut down and a new wave of arrests took place, including the rearrest of Kim Chi Ha on the charge of having helped the alleged People's Revolutionary Party. In a long passionate defense of his own beliefs and protests against Park's tactics that he managed to smuggle out of jail (in which he claimed that a "confession" the KCIA had published had been obtained under duress), Kim wrote in part: "The government constantly asserts that the threat from North Korea is so serious that civil rights are an impermissible luxury. But a corrupt, immoral dictatorship is the greatest spur to Communism. What greater argument do the Communists have than the Park regime? Dictatorial rule will never make South Korea secure."

Despite the obvious truth of such statements, time and events were running in Park's behalf. On April 29, 1975, the day before Saigon fell, Park issued a declaration of his own: "It becomes evident to us all that there can be no such thing as opposition forces among our ranks in the face of constant Communist threats." The debacle in Vietnam changed the temper of the nation decisively, and the discontent subsided. Huge patriotic rallies were held, and there were meetings in the churches and on university campuses in support of the government. Whereupon, in mid-May, realizing the tide was once again in his favor, Park took advantage of the new atmosphere of patriotism and issued the omnibus Decree Number Nine. This strategy of moving when he was strong and his enemies were weak always kept the opposition off balance, and enabled Park to confuse and divide it, though not destroy it.

How Strong Is the South?

As an extremely astute politician who, despite his remoteness and his inclination to isolate himself (after his wife was killed he seldom appeared in public), Park understands the character of his fellow Koreans and knows how to orchestrate their responses. While the manner in which he has maneuvered has proved self-serving, and could prove self-defeating in the long run, particularly if and when the threat from the North diminishes, he has benefited from the actions of Kim Il Sung, who has frequently provided him with fresh evidence of bellicosity and danger just when Park required it in order to crack down on his opposition again. Thus, for example, the discovery in 1974–1975 of two ingeniously built tunnels under the Demilitarized Zone served his purposes. (A third one was discovered in the fall of 1978, and South Korean and American military experts suspected there were a dozen more.) The North Koreans variously claimed that the tunnels were fabrications, that they were only for irrigation, and that they were for the evacuation of Southerners sympathetic to the North Koreans. But an exploration of the second tunnel, a large one reaching about 500 yards south of the DMZ and capable of enabling a division of troops to pass through it in an hour or two, convinced me that it was definitely suitable for transport of heavy equipment and was indeed a secret invasion route. Such examples of the North's continuing hostility—the ax killing of the two American soldiers in 1976 was another case in point—prompted one American diplomat who has watched the dangerous Korean interplay for many years to comment, "It almost looks as if Kim Il Sung operates with Park on an annual contract basis."

Park's more positive strength is the booming South Korean economy. But while the phenomenal development of modern Seoul (which has become the eleventh largest city in the world) brought vast benefits to the nation as a whole, it also created problems endemic to all overpopulated and overactive cities, such as air, water and noise pollution. The contrasts visible in Seoul, a drab, concrete slab of a city, were manifold. Despite its score of golf courses, modern freeways and abundance of tall office buildings, hotels and banks, to say nothing of its proliferating new factories and shopping arcades, admiration of such modern improvements was tempered if one explored the outer reaches of the city. For example, the poor area of Yung Dung Po was predominantly made up of small textile, machine and other plants employing from ten to fifty workers each, who lived in houses only slightly above the quality of those in the city's slums. Nearly a third of the city's population lived in such areas, and thousands of others had no homes at all and slept on the streets, in momentarily dry sewers or pedestrian tunnels beneath busy intersections.

In spite of its dictatorial ways, the government showed signs of awareness in 1977 that it should do something to contain the pressure-cooker effect of social discontent. An excellent group of foreign-educated economic planners submitted a new five-year plan, South Korea's fourth, which for the first time stressed welfare and social development equally with sustained growth. The plan envisaged a per capita annual income of $1,200 or more by 1981, about double what it was in 1975, and included programs to aid the urban poor through low-cost housing projects or by moving people out of the slums and congested areas into the suburbs or the countryside; to build up new industrial regions as a means of increasing employment opportunities; and to improve the quality of education, health and social insurance schemes. The plan was a plausible one, but even its most ardent supporters admitted that it would not easily be implemented so long as a third of the national budget was being allocated for defense. Balancing the goals of more industrial growth against these welfare objectives could, in fact, heighten social tensions, and one wondered whether any welfare plan could succeed in an atmosphere of supression of human rights. As one American scholar put it, "In order to get a social revolution started, you need a group of turned-off intellectuals, which you have now, and a seething mass, which existed in 1960 before Park took over the country, but which you don't have as yet. There's no denying that despite the inflation and other economic problems typical of the mid-seventies, the man on the street never had it so good. As long as the country can maintain a rapid pace of economic development, and as long as the distribution of income is reasonably good, authoritarianism won't worry a great many people. But if there are real economic and social problems, things will change."

It was a matter of speculation how much Park Chung Hee was aware of all this. Some of his advisers in the inner secretariat of the Blue House, whose status symbol was an open-collared white shirt worn beneath a dark-blue suit, were privately worried about the possibilities of a social explosion but were wary about expressing their views. For one thing, they were all convinced, along with Park, that South Korea remained under constant threat from the North and were defensive about what others, outside the government and abroad, described as his "siege mentality." Those on the outside, on the other hand, including academics and churchmen who were in the vanguard of the opposition, were not so charitable or willing to condone Park's excesses. They felt that the reasons for Park's tactics lay primarily in his peculiarly messianic vision of his role, and in the fact that, as an American priest who had lived in Korea for many years remarked to me, "In the past fifteen years we have watched a feudal country become an industrial one, but it hasn't lost its feudal outlook." Another man, a Korean clergyman who had been imprisoned for several months, and who felt that social discontent and cynicism were growing in ratio to the increase of corruption, made the point that Park is bound to be essentially autocratic and pedagogic, the victim of "his own narrow, simplistic approach to social problems."

Compromise and Stability

A Korean social scientist I met felt that the society has become so competitive, with so much concentration on simply earning a living, that the majority of people, including poorly paid workers, are too busy to take much interest in politics or to react in political ways to social unrest. "Most people don't like the sledgehammer tactics the government employs," he said, "yet they want stability. The fact that the poor were so much poorer ten years ago puts a damper on social activism. People wish that Park would relax his unnecessary repressive actions, and they wonder why he has gone so far, but they accept the fact that he has done a great deal for the country. What they don't comprehend is the fact that he can't stop acting the way he does because he's intoxicated by the sweet smell of power."

Except for the student activists, most youths and almost all adults simply go about their daily business without any concern for politics. City adolescents always seem to have enough money and time to frequent tea and coffee shops that are also often discotheques, and they sit and listen for hours to modern recordings, mostly American jazz or sad Korean love songs. Younger boys and girls go to small and dimly lit comic-book libraries, where for a few won (the local currency) they can read their favorite strips in paper booklets. Long hair for boys is officially disapproved, but girls wear miniskirts, even though these also are officially taboo. Older people sit around the cafés and drink *makkoli,* a traditional liquor made from barley and rice, or *chung-jong,* a rice wine of better quality. If they can afford it, businessmen visit *kisaeng* houses, the Korean version of Japanese geisha houses, where many of them have regular or part-time mistresses. Thus, life for most people is not especially affected or limited by the authoritarian measures of the Park regime.

Yet, notwithstanding the impact of traditional Buddhist values and more recent Christian influence, there is a strange spiritual void and even a sense of malaise amid the bustling prosperity and benign acceptance of the pervasive military influence in national life. In many respects this denotes not only Korean traditions, including a rediscovery of old folk values, but a basic conservatism whose bedrock is as much Confucian as Buddhist, with its stress on filial piety and dependence. On top of this a new national psychology of materialism has been planted, with its prime emphasis on economic growth as an end in itself and a bastion against the Communist threat from the North. The condition was aptly summed up by a young American friend of mine: "The thought processes of the Koreans haven't really changed very much over the years, and the impact of Westernization is still largely superficial. The economic improvements that have taken place both in the countryside and in the cities have created a stronger sense of Korean identity—of *uri nara saram,* or 'we Koreans'—and the government makes the most of this in its campaigns to stir national fervor. It's not surprising, therefore, that there is a lot of moral confusion on the human rights issue. The repressions may eventually build up to a breaking point, but whether the government exaggerates the danger of war or not, most people seem willing to go along with what they're told to do or not to do."

American diplomatic pressure during 1978 was largely responsible for the government's more relaxed policy on human rights and the dissident movement. Prior to the release of Kim Dae Jung, thirty-five leading opposition figures were set free, including those clergymen, political activists, lawyers and labor leaders who, on March 1, 1976, were among the original signers of the Declaration for the Democratic Salvation of the Nation. This had been read in Seoul's Myongdong Cathedral and called for the full restoration of democracy, for a more active effort to promote the unification of the North and the South, and for an economic policy that would make South Korea less dependent on foreign capital. But when the students resumed their demonstrations in 1978 on a number of campuses, the riot police again intervened with some degree of brutality, arresting more than a hundred and holding a dozen or so for possible indictment.

By and large, however, the society became a more subtly controlled restrictive one; the line between what was allowed and what was not was very narrow and was drawn according to the whim of the authorities, at both the central and local government levels. As a result, although the anti-Park dissidents could often get away with more than before (they could hold meetings and issue declarations and statements that were critical of the government up to a point—that is, there could be some criticism of the Yushin constitution but not of Park Chung Hee), they were for the most part in a state of perpetual frustration because of the government's Orwellian tactics. Forbidden to engage in open political action and having no outlets in the press, the opposition was forced to distribute clandestine mimeographed statements, of which the government was always aware, and which it either countenanced or took action against, as it saw fit, in what amounted to a debilitating cat-and-mouse game.

Since the tight system of surveillance and control—with the 30,000 members of the KCIA and the local police serving as the ubiquitous eyes and ears of the government—runs across every seam of the society, from the administration of the village-improvement program known as the Saemaul (New Community) Movement to the growing but supervised and restricted labor movement, there remained a serious question whether in the long run the system would enable the government to survive or would in time lead to increased underground turbulence and ferment. There was a question, too, of whether industrial growth, accompanied by upward social and economic mobility—a combination that the Americans officially commended and privately profited from—would automatically suffice to provide a national will that could prevail against another invasion from the North, or against organized national discontent. Such internal opposition, primarily labor- and farmer-based but with a political motivation covering a spectrum that would conceivably include members of the emerging middle class, would not be a new phenomenon in a rapidly developing nation. There were many Koreans, including academics and some Blue House intellectuals, who believed that the emergence of this kind of opposition would be a healthy long-term development. But there were just as many who warned that a heterogeneous mixture of dissatisfied farmers, workers, civil servants and even young military officers could create new cleavages in the society which might lead to more volatility, and if allowed to get out of hand, could benefit the Communists. It was this school of thought that defended Park Chung Hee as an indispensable leader.

Under these circumstances, the dissidents believed that the new period of relative relaxation was creating "a quiet state of suspension underneath which there was still a deep anxiety and uneasiness about the predicament of the people," as Kim Kwan Suk, the general secretary of the Korean National Council of Churches—a group that has been among the government's strongest critics—put it to me. He went on, "In spite of the highly sophisticated mixture of regimentation and appeasement which the government has developed, and the internalized sense of fear this has produced, which has mesmerized and narcotized so many people, our human rights struggle has come a long way since 1973. Where it was once ignored because of so many threatening elements, we now have far wider support; in fact, human rights have acquired a new meaning because of economic progress." Kim was one of the leaders of a new Coalition for Human Rights Movement in Korea, which the government disapproved of because it represented the first effort to bring all the opposition groups together and thus was a potential political threat. The coalition and half a dozen other dissident groups operated out of the Christian Building, which was an inconspicuous structure in one of Seoul's busy commercial districts, and which was kept under government surveillance; the police raided it in October 1978 and arrested thirty persons who had conducted a demonstration against Park.

Varieties of Dissidence

Overall, the dissident movement continued to suffer not only from being small but from the inability of its components to cooperate. There were considerable differences even within the church groups alone, which included activists, moderates and conservatives. On occasion they got together with students, workers and academics, such as when they put out an Open Letter to President Carter in February 1978 in which they took issue with a State Department Report on Human Rights that had cited improvements in Korea. The letter said the report had overlooked the question of political stability, which would "become possible only when human rights are respected and a democratic system is firmly established allowing the full expression of the will of the people. It is our view that until such a time, military strength, no matter how powerful, will become merely a power for self-destruction."

More often, the various dissident groups acted alone in their own special fields of interest. One of these was the Urban Industrial Mission, a group of about a hundred Protestants that was working with labor, organizing unions and concentrating on the social education of workers and community development programs. There were about a million organized workers in the country —only a small minority of the total labor force—and most of them belonged to seventeen industrial unions under the aegis of the Federation of Korean Trade Unions. All of them, organized on a company basis, had to be registered with the government; they were allowed to bargain collectively on wages, bonuses and pension schemes, and so on, but the government supervised the negotiations and as a rule favored management. No strikes were allowed, though some illegal ones and slowdowns occasionally took place. As the economy grew, wages went up between 30 and 40 percent a year, and bonuses were doubled, but the minimum wage scale of $63 a month was not always followed by employers, and women were especially discriminated against. In mid-1978 the Urban Industrial Mission was in trouble because it had supported a strike of women textile workers whom the KCIA accused of being influenced by the Communists, and the Mission's Credit Union was accused of illegal financial dealings, a tactic the government had begun to use in attacking or destroying other opposition groups too, including a farmers cooperative in the southern province of Cholla that went on a hunger strike in an effort to collect several million won it claimed the government owed them for being ordered to grow potatoes instead of rice, and had reneged on paying. The most interesting aspect of this case was that it was the first time a farmers' revolt had occurred, despite the well-organized Saemaul Movement in the rural areas.

A number of American missionaries and teachers in Korea told me they were disturbed about the ever-increasing controls the government was imposing on foreigners as well as on Koreans. "There are now identity cards for all, including us," said Ed Poitras, a Presbyterian missionary. "The cards bear fingerprints, photographs and numbers, and are laminated and computerized, so that any person's record is available to the police at a moment's notice. The screening process is complete. Everyone is on a short string." Horace Underwood, who was born in Korea and was the administrative head of Yonsei University, a Presbyterian institution, agreed, and noted that the Ministry of Culture and Information had slowly extended a more pervasive and obstructive control over the work of foreign missionaries and teachers. "The juridicial language with regard to the founding of our church entitles us to engage in 'evangelical, educational, medical, and social work,' " he said, "but now, as chairman of Yonsei, I've been told by the ministry that we must confine ourselves to evangelical activities. We've said no, and nothing has happened yet, but I'm worried because they can exert all sorts of pressures on us, including taxation, residence permits, and so on." Underwood also felt that the government's tactic of alternately cracking down and relaxing constraints on all forms of dissident activity, including student activity, was creating "a vicious circle," and that "it can't go on forever." He added, "Humanly speaking, I see no solution."

One of the strongest indictments of the lack of human rights in South Korea that I heard came from Mrs. Lee Tai Young, who was the director of a legal-aid society and the leader of the country's women's-rights movement. She had succeeded in getting the National Assembly to pass several liberalizing laws, including a suspension for a year of the traditional ban on marriages between persons of the same clan and place of origin, but since more than 50 percent of all Koreans are named Kim, Park or Lee, and many of each name come from the same area, the proscription discriminated particularly against women, who had far fewer legal rights than men did. In an article for *Voice of the People,* one of the few underground papers the government allowed to appear from time to time, she wrote: "We are living in an era of false prosperity, but it will all lead to nothing. People can say they look better, and live better, and they may be fatter, but inside them is a bad disease. As human beings, we are made to do more than eat. A mouth is made to speak as well as to eat with. A dog may be satisfied with a nice house and enough food, but a person is more than a dog. He has a spirit, but we don't live as human beings here, because we cannot talk freely and we cannot live fully. Our arms and legs are tied, our eyes don't see what they should see and our ears don't hear what they should hear. Our characters are handicapped. For eighteen years now, we have lived like automatons, and we have become dehumanized. The economic miracle has made us fat, handicapped fools, people without souls."

If this emotional indictment was somewhat overdrawn, and if there were millions of Koreans who were not only living better than they ever had but leading daily lives that were virtually unaffected by Decree Number Nine and the restraints of the Yushin constitution, it remained for people like Mrs. Lee, Kim Kwan Suk and the rest of the small but dedicated band of dissidents, including the silenced press and those students who were less interested in comfortable corporate jobs when they graduated than in the political future of Korea, to continue to represent the national conscience. They believed that their task was to keep the idea of democracy alive long enough to nurture new forces, which they felt were bound to develop in the nation if another war could be avoided.

Amid the many worrisome aspects of the controlled society, there were some encouraging signs. They included a new assertiveness on the part of people in rural areas who, holding themselves aloof from the Saemaul Movement, were beginning to make their own decisions about what they wanted for themselves and how they intended to achieve these goals. A similar assertiveness was being demonstrated by the increasingly active if still controlled labor movement, in fact, some labor-management schemes had already been adopted and some profit sharing had begun—portents, one hoped, of the role that workers might someday play in the evolving consensus system that would be akin to Japan's but would also be specially Korean. This would become more marked as labor became more skilled, under manpower-training programs that the government and business had begun. Although the government had given both big corporations and small concerns their head in formulating investment policies and putting them into practice, it was beginning to offer them some degree of what the Japanese called administrative guidance. The Korean bureaucracy was also strong and generally able and was growing rapidly—some academic experts believed too rapidly. One of them said to me, only half facetiously, "The bureaucracy could become more of a problem than the KCIA."

Political Options

There was a danger that even if the Koreans evolved their own consensus system with its own proportions and dimensions, a continuing political void would stultify and inhibit the process. As it is constituted, the National Assembly is essentially a rubber-stamp body, although occasionally it has asserted itself, as in budget and education debates. However, the political parties remained vapid and lacked any real substance or ideology. The point that a number of academic friends of mine stressed was that there was vital need for new political movements to emerge from new directions—from the enlightened sector of the business world, for example, or from among the younger university graduates trained in the social sciences, or from farm and labor groups. At the same time, the bureaucracy would inevitably be called upon to play an increasing political role of its own, and the question was whether it could contain and guide the rapid rate of growth in ways that would give more social meaning and content to people's lives and thus promote an atmosphere in which political dialogue could flourish. A dialogue and a contest between a conservative party, resembling the Liberal Democratic Party in Japan, and a Socialist or Social Democratic Party were what a lot of people wanted to see, but the chances of that happening under the Yushin system were slight, which was one of the main reasons the dissidents wanted it abolished.

It is dubious whether Park Chung Hee, who is young and healthy enough to stay in power for another five or ten years, will allow the development of independently motivated political parties that are more than sycophantic pets, especially as long as he is obsessed by the fear of another invasion from the North. Another big question is that of succession. It is unlikely that whoever ultimately succeeds Park will wield the same power. Temporarily, at least, a military consortium will probably take over the country and choose another officer or an experienced technocrat to run it. Some observers believe that the most likely candidate to succeed Park, despite a series of political ups and downs he has suffered over the years, is former Prime Minister Kim Jong Pil, the organizer of the 1961 coup.

In mid-1978 I spent three hours with Kim discussing a wide range of subjects, and I found him not only blunt and frank, as he had been before, but more expansive and willing to talk analytically and philosophically about the past, present and future. When I asked about the evolution of a Korean consensus system, he said, "Yes, we have followed the Japanese model to some extent, but we're still a fledgling nation when it comes to development. As we continue to grow, and trade with the rest of the world, we not only will discover more about other countries and their ways, but will also be able to define our own identity more clearly, and this will help us find a system of government that will be adaptable to our needs and character. But as long as Korea is divided into two parts, and we face the threat of another invasion from the North, I think we are limited by fate in our efforts to move toward total freedom and the creation of new political parties. Yet I can tell you that we are approaching the day when we will have a truly open society. We have to grow into it, though, and cannot just try to copy the Western system, as we did in 1963. What we tried to do then may have looked democratic and open, but it wasn't really. We were simply imitating the Americans without being ready, and then we realized that it wasn't the right course for us—that we needed something stronger. Now, because we have a good bureaucracy and our own ways of communication, down to the grass-roots level, we are beginning to develop our own ways of consensus and decision making as well, and this will lead to democracy from the lowest level up to the top."

If Kim Jong Pil was right, there may be more hope for South Korea than many Americans are willing to believe. The relationship between the two countries has grown so complicated, and the complexity was so aggravated by the events of the late seventies, that fundamental perceptions became blurred and criticism led to increased suspicion and acrimony. The activities of Tongsun Park and the KCIA, and of the South Korean evangelist Sun Myung Moon, who sought to set up an "automatic theocracy to rule the world," have been thoroughly reviewed by various congressional committees, including the Select Committee on Ethics of the Senate and the Subcommittee on International Organizations of the House of Representatives. The lavish bestowal of gifts to selected congressmen by the profligate Tongsun Park, who testified under immunity from prosecution, left a bad taste all around. Although Park claimed to have operated on his own, as a private businessman (he was also said to have engaged in efforts, as did Moon, to sell Korean-made arms abroad), there was little doubt that his lobbying activities in Washington had been conducted with at least the support and perhaps the direct cooperation of the KCIA, two members of which had defected in America and given testimony about violations of human rights, including the intimidation of hundreds of Koreans in the United States as well as in South Korea.

If the military confrontation on the peninsula were not diffused—that is, if another war led to the killing of more hundreds of thousands of Koreans—there would be no rights to be defended or preserved. One of the most difficult factors to be gauged remains the perceptions that Kim Il Sung has of the situation, including the military balance on the Korean peninsula; his complicated relations with Moscow and Peking, and how these in turn affect his judgment (or misjudgment) of the security picture in the Far East and of American concerns or intentions; and the many ramifications of the convoluted relationship between the Americans and the South Koreans.

The Military Balance

Despite the growing military strength of the South, the North continues to possess heavy superiority in tanks, armored personnel carriers, mobile field artillery, and truck-mounted-and-towed multiple-rocket launchers—all vital factors in any sudden attack. Between 1976 and 1978, the forward strength of the North Koreans increased, and artillery emplacements and other military installations above the DMZ were hardened or placed underground, while there was a vast build-up of weapons farther north ready to be rolled forward. Early in January 1979, American intelligence data indicated that the strength of the North Korean army was 600,000, about one-fourth greater than had previously been estimated and larger by about 40,000 men than the South Korean army. North Korea's superior tank force, previously estimated to total 2,000, was now said to be 2,600. According to these revised figures, North Korea was said to have the fifth largest army in the world—after China, the Soviet Union, India and the United States—and the caliber of its forces was ranked only behind that of the Americans and the Russians. While neither the Russians nor the Chinese had equipped the North Koreans with advanced weapons or planes for more than five years, and while the South Koreans were engaged in a rapid military modernization plan backed by the Americans, the Pyongyang regime was said to have advanced to the point where it was able to build modern tanks, ships, artillery weapons, submarines and just about everything except advanced aircraft, surface-to-air missiles and other electronic equipment on its own.

As a result of these disclosures, which may have been self-serving as far as the Pentagon was concerned, the Administration and Congress debated a further slowdown in the removal of United States ground forces from South Korea. It was decided that a second contingent of 2,400 troops scheduled to be withdrawn during the year would be kept in Korea for the time being, on top of the already delayed withdrawal of a similar number, even though President Carter was still on record saying he would reduce the total number of ground troops and Air Force personnel to 12,000 by the mid-eighties. American military men welcomed the move to postpone the withdrawals. General John W. Vessey, Jr., the Supreme Commander of the United Nations Forces in Korea, who had accepted with reluctance the initial Carter announcement, told me in mid-1978, "I lose a lot of sleep over Kim Il Sung. North Korea has more men under arms than ever, and has more modern weapons, and more attack preparations under way. One has only to look at the intelligence to conclude that that the North Koreans are making plans to attack. If it's saber-rattling, it's a real saber and a real rattle. Kim Il Sung may run out of options to attack, and the real danger is that he may say that though the time is not propitious, especially with American troops that are scheduled to go still here, it will never get any better."

South Korean forward troops and the American Second Division felt themselves in a state of readiness to meet an assault, but it would take up to a week to mobilize and reinforce the whole South Korean army and reserves, move the troops into position, distribute ammunition, lay mines, and so forth. A North Korean attack aimed at Seoul, as it was in 1950, could move so fast that it would all be over by then, and the North might sue for peace, even accepting a return to the status quo, and relish the fact that the South would be set back a decade economically. Two big questions remain unanswerable: If an attack should take place, would President Carter, or any other President, respond rapidly by invoking the executive right under the War Powers Resolution, passed by Congress in 1973? This resolution allows the United States to come to the defense of the South Koreans with full naval and air support and the possible infusion of more troops, chiefly Marines—a defensive action the President could carry on for sixty days, with a possible thirty-day extension subject to congressional approval. Secondly, would he, if it seemed necessary, elect to employ the tactical nuclear bombs still hidden away in South Korea? Nearly a thousand such weapons are said to have been stored in the country, half of which have been removed, and the rest of which, if Carter lives up to his campaign pledges, will be withdrawn over the next few years. But the bombs could still be employed from offshore, along with submarine-fired missiles and rockets, virtually as easily as if they were on land. However, it is by no means certain that Carter, or any other President, in the light of the post-Vietnam feelings of the American people, would choose to intervene on such a large scale—or even on a lesser one, despite the standing pledge made in the 1954 Mutual Defense Treaty.

In early 1979, diplomacy that might avert another Korean catastrophe appeared to have been impeded, perhaps to the point of atrophy, by the Korean-American scandals and by undue concentration on military and economic details, on missiles and markets, and on growth for growth's sake in South Korea. An American friend of mine who has worked in an official capacity in the country on and off for two decades summed it up cogently: "The trouble in Korea today is that the economic-miracle idea has been brought to the point where nothing else is considered by anyone. We, as Americans, are partly responsible for this, and in the process we have lost our credentials, among even the Korean nationalists. That includes Park Chung Hee, who has never liked us much anyway and admits he doesn't understand us. Twenty-five years ago we allowed Syngman Rhee to handle us—though we thought we were handling him—and that was disastrous. Now we've wedded ourselves to Park, but there are other voices we should listen to, and they include the voices of some of the dissidents. We should stand up on principle for the Korean people—not just for one man or one group. The Koreans in the North are quite as nationalistic as those in the South; two million of them came South after the Korean War but those who stayed up there are quite as independent-minded as those down here. After Kim Il Sung dies, there will be a scramble for power, and the Soviets or the Chinese will probably control that situation. If we aren't careful, either of them might outmaneuver or outbluff us, all over the Korean peninsula. But if we take our stand now in favor of nationalism, we can avoid such an eventuality."

More clearly than ever, the solution in Korea, difficult as it may be to achieve, remains unity, not two Koreas. Both Kim Il Sung and Park Chung Hee are right—though unfortunately each wants to achieve unity in his way. Short of war, this appears to be impossible. The only alternative, accordingly, is to get a serious dialogue started, which would ultimately include Pyongyang, Seoul, Peking, Moscow, Tokyo and Washington. This may not be easy to do, and it surely cannot be done at once, if only because of the Moscow-Peking confrontation. But it could be approached step by step, segment by segment. What such a move calls for is the rarest form of diplomacy, combining imagination with tact, and this has to be pursued with patience and persistence, probably secretly as well as openly.

To do nothing about the situation as both parts of Korea become stronger militarily and glare down each other's throats is to court disaster. One can only hope that the United States, having been involved in Korea for so long, for better or for worse, will take the lead in seeking a resolution of the Korean problem while it is still possible. One way to do it is to encourage the recent resumption of bilateral talks between South and North Korea, even at the risk of affording to the Pyongyang regime what appears to be an initial political advantage. Washington should also open the door to a dialogue of its own with Pyongyang and, with Peking's support, then move to widen negotiations, perhaps under United Nations auspices, to include Seoul as well as Tokyo. Moscow's participation would undoubtedly depend on the separate progress of détente with Washington, embracing the Pacific and Indian oceans as well as SALT and Europe, but if the parameters of peace and unification in Korea are first defined—above all, between the two Koreas themselves—the Russians would be diplomatically outflanked and would have no alternative but to go along with the process. The sooner the process starts, the better it will be for all of Asia—indeed, for the West as well.

Japan–
Miracle or
Myth

1-At the End of the War

My first "view" of Japan was an awesome and frightening one I shall never forget. On the night of August 9, 1945, I was aboard a B-24 Liberator bomber flying south of Nagasaki, which is on the western tip of the island of Kyushu. The plane was making a shipping-reconnaissance run, and I went along as a correspondent. At 11:01 that morning, about five hours before we had taken off from Okinawa, an atomic bomb had been dropped on Nagasaki, three days after the first such weapon ever used in war had devastated Hiroshima.

After the Hiroshima bomb, which according to official Japanese statistics killed 87,150 people outright and subsequently caused the deaths of about the same number from wounds and radiation sickness, we all thought the surrender of Japan could not be far off. My reaction upon hearing of the attack on Nagasaki was one of profound shock because, while the painful decision made by President Harry S. Truman to drop the bomb on Hiroshima could perhaps be militarily condoned, dropping a second bomb seemed to most of us to be inhumane and unnecessary.

As we drew closer to Nagasaki, we had the eerie sensation of being on the edge of doom as a red glare rose higher and higher on the horizon. The mushroom cloud had disappeared hours before, but the city, or what was left of it, was still blazing. We turned back to Okinawa in silence. Five days later, when the Japanese surrender was announced, I was still there, and watched with wonder, and a certain trepidation and foreboding, the wild nighttime firing of hundreds of rounds of glowing anti-aircraft tracer bullets across the ostensibly peaceful postwar sky.

Thirty years later, in the spring of 1974, I visited Nagasaki. While not among the thriving cities of contemporary Japan, it afforded impressive evidence, in its reconstruction, of the remarkable recovery of the country from the complete prostration of 1945 to accepted status as one of the world's economic superpowers. The city was one of ninety Japanese cities that were heavily bombed during the war—about twenty, including Tokyo, were more than half destroyed. At the time of the bomb attack, Nagasaki's population was about 200,000, and according to local casualty statistics (which the American military still disputes, as it does the casualty figures for Hiroshima), 73,884 people had been killed immediately by the bomb, and about as many initially listed as missing or injured were afterward reported as dead. Of the current population of 400,000, roughly a fourth still received periodic medical tests for an increase of white blood corpuscles, for malignant growths, and for kidney and liver damage. Eight hundred people were officially registered as suffering from chronic radiation ailments.

I spoke with a number of the bomb victims who were among those receiving regular hospital treatment, as well as with others who routinely got semiannual check-ups. They expressed virtually no resentment about the atomic attack but only a resolute determination—which the citizens of Nagasaki shared with those of Hiroshima, and indeed with most Japanese—to maintain a constant public campaign to outlaw the use of atomic bombs in the future. Nevertheless, there was a growing belief, as revealed in public opinion polls, that in a world of proliferating nuclear arsenals Japan might be forced to develop its own bomb sooner or later, even though there was little doubt that the country would be destroyed almost overnight in a new atomic war. As a deterrent, a Japanese nuclear capability was therefore all but meaningless, but in a tenuous and often jittery world, the psychological and political connotations even of non-nuclear rearmament were as significant as the purely military aspects.

Arrival at Atsugi

On August 28, 1945, with that staining red glow in the sky over Nagasaki still sharp in my mind, I landed with some of the initial American occupation troops at Atsugi Air Field, near Tokyo. That first day on the ground in Japan offered me another view I shall always remember. With two fellow correspondents I drove through the countryside and then through the streets and squares of the heavily populated port city of Yokohama, where the three of us experienced an unanticipated negative shock about Asian, specifically Japanese, responses to Americans. Here, of course, we were the victors, and in contrast to our status quo upon our joyous return to the Philippines we came as conquerors, not as liberators. Even so, we were not prepared for the reception we received. It was, in fact, a nonreception—simply a bland if not sullen ignoring of our arrival and presence. The sensation of riding and walking through the teeming main square of Yokohama, and of looking at thousands of Japanese rushing all about us but paying absolutely no attention to us, not even looking at us, was as eerie as and more directly disconcerting than watching Nagasaki burn from the cockpit of a plane sixty miles or so away. To be sure, this was not a condition that obtained for long. A few days later, after basing myself temporarily in a room in the catacomblike old Imperial Hotel in Tokyo, I visited the former imperial capital of Kyoto, which had been spared except for one bit of accidental bombing. Here we were welcomed by gushing guides and geishas, but in general, at the outset, the orders had apparently gone out to accept our arrival passively—to cause us no trouble but to pay us no heed, as if, in effect, we weren't really there.

This initial Japanese reaction, beyond orders, was the product more of isolation, shock and pride than shame or remorse. Japanese scholars, such as Masataka Kosaka, of Kyoto University, have commented on the fact that in general "the Japanese felt no deep sense of guilt about the wrong they had committed during the war." It was probably for this reason that, as a practical people endowed with an amazing energy, they were able so quickly to set about doing what they could with their meager means to re-establish some semblance of their former existence—even before most of them began to realize that a whole new system of government was about to be imposed on them by the occupation.

"The modern Japanese way of life, both for good and bad, had been shaped during the hectic eighty years since the Meiji Restoration," Kosaka later wrote. "Never, since the time Japan opened her doors to the West, had her people had time to consider good and evil, right and wrong, from any consistent point of view. Confronted with wave after wave of foreign influence, the Japanese were forced to adapt their ethics, as far as they were able, to constantly changing situations."

Many years later Henry Kissinger, shortly before he became Secretary of State, had much the same thing in mind when he privately complained that the Japanese "don't think conceptually." The Japanese themselves have admitted this, and some of them, particularly in recent years of fresh crises such as the oil shock, economic recession and the need to adjust themselves to a growing degree of political and social change, have sought to overcome this deficiency—still without notable success, especially as regards their relations with the rest of the world. They could surely have been pardoned, however, for not having any conception of what was about to happen to them when, at noon on August 15, 1945, for the first time ever, they heard over their battered radios the static-ridden, whiny voice of Emperor Hirohito, who told them that the war had indeed been lost and that "we have resolved to pave the way for a grand peace for all the generations to come by enduring the unendurable and suffering what is insufferable."

This was the first defeat Japan had ever experienced, and the shock was naturally profound. About 1.5 million men had been lost in action. More than 8 million people on the main islands had been killed or wounded, and 2.5 million homes had been destroyed or badly damaged. The population of Tokyo had declined from 6.75 million to about 3 million, and most of those left were living in huts or in sheer rubble. On one day alone, March 10, 1945, as a result of the biggest of many B-29 raids on Tokyo, 100,000 people had been killed, and 125,000 homes had been destroyed when 1,700 tons of incendiary bombs turned the low-lying areas of the city into an inferno.

Strange as it may seem, by the time General of the Army Douglas MacArthur alighted from his plane at Atsugi, at the end of August, tieless and nonchalantly brandishing his corncob pipe, an odd involuntary admiration for the Americans had surfaced, despite the initial silence that greeted us. Such admiration, in Kosaka's opinion, was inspired by the "technological perfection" of those huge fleets of silver B-29 bombers which the weary population had seen overhead for so many dreadful months, symbolizing "the superior strength and higher civilization of the United States."

The imperious MacArthur would have been the last to deny this gratuitous appraisal of American supremacy. On September 3 I went aboard the American battleship *Missouri* off Yokohama in Tokyo Bay to watch the formal surrender ceremony. This was MacArthur's most triumphant moment. As Mamoru Shigemitsu, the crippled former Japanese Foreign Minister who had privately opposed the war but would be jailed by the Americans for several years anyway, climbed painfully up the ladder and limped to the long table where the papers of surrender had been laid out, MacArthur paid him about as much attention as the people of Yokohama had paid to us, brusquely ordering him to sign the designated documents and then take his leave. Squadrons of American fighter planes roared overhead—I can still hear Admiral William (Bull) Halsey, the blunt, outspoken Navy commander in the South Pacific during the war, who bore no love for MacArthur, snarling, as he looked up at the flight of Navy planes that had followed the B-29s, "Those are mine." The war was indeed over, though the "war" between the services continued, as it has through the years, for money, power and prestige. But that did not detract from the splendor of that *Missouri* moment, and we all felt that a new era of peace was at hand. How wrong we were would soon be demonstrated all the way from Manchuria and Korea to Indochina and Indonesia.

Neither Fish nor Fowl

The first month of the occupation—as the Japanese and Americans, over and above their roles as vanquished and victors, went through a mutual culture shock—had strange, phantasmagoric qualities that, as I look back on it, were akin to those one discovers in the plays of Pirandello and Harold Pinter. At the outset, though plans galore had been made, no one was at all certain what was going to happen. How long were we going to stay in Japan; what would our relationship really be like with the Japanese; and more important, what would their new relationship to each other be like in defeat, including, among other things, their relation to their Emperor?

I remember going on a tour of the Diet building in Tokyo one day during the first week and being haughtily told by our guide, in his dark well-tailored suit, that we could not see the room where the Emperor "retired" on one of his rare visits to the Diet because "no one is allowed to see this room." It was all Mikado-like, and also mystifying and even macabre. The sheer experience of actually being in Japan, after three and a half long years of exhausting and bitter jungle fighting, and of now wandering through Tokyo's department stores to see what was left to buy, or of trying to elicit some early responses from the reticent Japanese, was matched by an overriding sense of unreality. In some ways, despite the obvious impact of ruin and destruction, it almost seemed as if the war had never taken place, and that we had just simply dropped in on a visit, en route somewhere else, perhaps to another unknown beachhead.

Once the initial shock of our arrival was over, the Japanese quickly regained their self-discipline. Within ten days they had obeyed American orders to disband their armed forces, although a few groups of die-hard military extremists, including some kamikazi pilots, had to be forcibly persuaded to abandon their weapons and surrender. But if there was no trouble, there was a gathering feeling most of us had—beyond the exciting adventure of simply being there —that we were up against the sort of challenge the United States, and no nation or civilization, had ever faced before, not even the Romans, the Mongols, the Huns, the Turks or the Christian Crusaders. In this case, we were not engaged in expanding our empire or in a campaign of religious salvation. We were opening an American laboratory in a country we knew very little about, and our democratically honed instruments had never before been tested in such an altogether strange place, or in relation to such unknown specimens of humanity. Would the instruments work? And how would the patient or the subject, let alone the physician and psychiatrist—or whatever we were— respond and react?

I am not sure, even now, more than three decades later, that we found the answers to all those questions. During many trips to Japan through the years, and particularly on several extended visits between 1974 and 1978, I had the constant feeling of dealing with a people whose whole postwar experience had been so extraordinary that in some ways it was still impossible for them, let alone for us, to grasp its real meaning. Certainly, over the past decades of tremendous economic growth the Japanese have scarcely had time to do anything but compose more progress reports, which they have done assiduously, with obvious pride and a degree of smugness. Once the tomorrows no longer loomed quite so promising, the Japanese were for the first time engaged in a process of true self-analysis, which they were finding both pleasurable and painful, and which somehow suited their character, compounded as it was of as much romanticism and optimism and naïveté as practicality and pessimism.

Invariably, during countless hours of interviews with politicians, officials, social scientists, historians, critics, journalists and others, in my efforts to determine how and why Japan had succeeded so astonishingly in becoming an economic giant, and in trying to fathom the very special nature of Japanese society and of the changes that were taking place in it, I kept harking back to the days when the occupation began and to the feeling all of us had then that we had landed on another planet—one that had undergone some sort of cosmic convulsion. And even after I had begun to know the country somewhat better, I retained this odd feeling that the Japanese were other-planetary.

Certainly they were vastly different, not only from Westerners but from all other peoples of Asia as well. The qualities that made them unique were among those that had enabled them to survive and prosper so spectacularly. In their darker moments, when they were beset by rampant inflation and by the threat of economic chaos initiated by the oil crisis, and thereafter by such challenges as protectionism and economic greed, their sense of doom, which they liked to write and talk about, was tempered by their stubborn confidence in their ability to deal, however awkwardly at times, with whatever dire circumstances confronted them. Despite their pragmatism, beneath their sphinxlike surface they were highly emotional; this was periodically evidenced in their political and economic conduct when their customary wall of discipline was broken by sudden jolts and shocks. The foreigner, or *gaijin*, who remained an object of suspicion and constant, cautious scrutiny, quickly became aware that the Japanese were scrutinizing themselves in their own private way, scanning themselves as if through either end of one of their excellent telescopes, trying to decide, in the sort of cinematic or theatrical game they so enjoyed playing, whether they looked big or small.

Whatever the economic climate of the moment, one could always hear any number of guesses, speculations and prognoses concerning their future, ranging from ultrapessimistic to ultraoptimistic. All of these were dependent on what, at least until recently, was their near-obsession with their gross national product, or GNP—initials that might just as well have stood for "great national pastime"—and all somewhat like an endless Kabuki drama in modern economic dress.

Painful Reassessments

Despite prior centuries of isolation and passivity, the Japanese could no longer ignore the rest of the world, as they belatedly were beginning to realize after the series of economic jolts, dominated by the energy crisis, inflation and recession during the period from 1973 to 1978. But though excellent adaptors and modernizers at home, the Japanese were not good diplomatic innovators. Their sense of frustration and inferiority in dealing with Westerners, and a feeling of superiority if not remnant contempt for Asians other than the Chinese, on top of a basic incapacity to identify with any other people, encouraged their determination to do things very much their own way, often bluntly and obtusely, as a defense mechanism. Traditional forms and habits provoked odd mixtures of tactlessness and stiff politeness in their diplomatic forays, and frequently masked a fundamental uncertainty and lack of consistency about their goals. Part of this was due to the fact that, though Asians themselves, they felt closer in many respects to the West, and particularly to the United States, on whom they had been dependent for so long but against whom they now found themselves cast in an adversary role concerning such mundane matters as trade and tariffs.

The readjustment of their role in Asia alone, about which they were so unsure over the years, could not help but affect big-power relationships in the whole Eastern hemisphere, and this in turn was bound to influence their relations with Europe and America in ways which were only beginning to be redefined and comprehended. Having failed militarily in Asia during the Pacific war, the Japanese did not seem to have quite learned the lessons of humility. Their economic relations with the Southeast Asian nations, while highly profitable for them, were less than satisfactory for the other Asian nations with clear memories of the brutalities and self-aggrandizements of the past. Only recently, individually and collectively, had these nations begun to assert themselves and let the Japanese know what their own goals and aspirations were and that they could no longer be dealt with cavalierly, with Japan reaping the rewards of their valuable natural resources and offering primarily cheap manufactured goods and voracious tourists in return. There were some tentative signs that the Japanese were beginning to get this message and learning how to mix aid and trade more efficaciously, but it would take time to determine how successful their new forays into still alien Asian cultures would be, over and above their compulsive profit motivations.

Some, though a diminishing number, of Japanese scholars regarded with skepticism the possibility of Japan's playing a more powerful world role. Chie Nakane, an eminent anthropologist and sociologist, made the point that in contradistinction to the Chinese, the Japanese "way of thinking depends on the situation rather than the principle," and she added that "we Japanese have no principles." Her comment was more a historical than a moral one, but it included the observation that the Japanese lacked what she described as a "checking mechanism" and that therefore it was better for them "not to do anything . . . to remain just as we are."

Others, however, such as political scientist and writer Kei Wakaizumi, in taking note of the continuing debate between the "passivists" and the "positivists" in Japan, came out clearly on the side of the latter. In advocating "strength without arrogance, international co-operation, particularly in Asia, without domination," Wakaizume maintained that "Japan must go beyond the old-fashioned and conventional framework of power politics in search of new ideals aimed at creating a 'world community.' " In order to do this, he added, the Japanese "must exercise effective control over our tendency to become too single-minded."

As the country began to recover from the recession it moved ahead into what was projected as a period of lower growth, at a pace of 5 to 7 or 8 percent a year in contrast to the annual growth rate of 10 to 12 percent that marked the halcyon years of the sixties and early seventies. Most Japanese, including prominent politicians and bureaucrats, were aware that they would find it harder to cope with their domestic predicaments and with such complex international problems as obtaining enough of the raw materials upon which they were so dependent and simultaneously maintaining good relations with regions such as the Middle East and Africa, with which they had had little experience, let alone with the Western nations and the rest of Asia. One prominent bureaucrat, a ranking member of the Foreign Ministry, put it succinctly when he told me, "Internally and externally, we are faced with a psychological wall. How are we going to climb over it?" He, as did others who took a positive approach, felt that the crises of the past few years could prove salutary if the Japanese stopped "working breathless" long enough to reorient both their internal and external outlooks and aspirations.

In 1979 there were some indications that this was beginning to take place. The Japanese at least were finally trying to adjust their trade imbalances with the United States and Europe. Their delicate domestic balance was becoming increasingly influenced by what was happening elsewhere. It also seemed that they would be unable to avoid permanent alterations in their intricately woven society. Whether this would occur without bringing about drastic internal political shifts, or even destructive clashes between opposing forces on the left and the right, was of paramount concern to them, and a source of worry to others. The political landscape, having already undergone shocks and fissures as a result of the slow decline over recent years of the popularity of the Liberal Democratic Party (LDP) after more than two decades of uninterrupted rule, seemed likely to change further as a result of a number of factors, including the Lockheed bribery case. Initially the Japanese were disturbed and angered by the fact that this scandal was initiated, without much warning, by Senate hearings held in the United States. Once again, as happened twice in 1971 when President Richard Nixon went to China without first telling them and then suddenly devaluated the dollar while raising surcharges on imports, the Japanese felt that their big American partner had failed to realize the impact in Japan. By the same token, the Americans felt that the Japanese were selfishly unaware of the adverse effect their compulsive desire to increase their exports was having on the rest of the world.

As things turned out, the Americans cooperated in turning over vast amounts of Lockheed evidence and testimony to Japanese prosecutors. This material was used during the trials of former Prime Minister Kakuei Tanaka, accused of accepting a bribe of $1.6 million from Lockheed to help sell its planes in Japan, and of fifteen other defendants brought to court on various charges in connection with the case. In many ways, Lockheed was to Japan what Watergate was to America. It clearly revealed the close ties between corporate business and conservative politics, as represented by the LDP, and put a spotlight on the extent of corruption and behind-the-scenes manipulation and chicanery in Japanese society as well as in politics. Though the fiber and mood of the nation remained conservative and were likely to stay that way, it had become apparent that the one-party rule of the LDP was being challenged and that alternatives of two conservative parties, or of one conservative and one middle-of-the-road party, or of a coalition of some sort, had to be seriously considered. In this sense the Lockheed case, coming at a time when serious economic problems were also coming to a head, was an important turning point.

All of these developments, above all the potential changes in Japan—social as well as economic and political—called for appraisal in the light of what had happened in the more than thirty years since the occupation began in 1945, a relatively short historic time span during which Japan had got where it was in the late seventies through an extraordinary combination of luck, pluck and perseverance.

2-The Occupation, and the Road to Success

Early in 1945, several months before the war ended, a small group of half a dozen Japanese economists of various political persuasions began meeting secretly in Tokyo, carefully avoiding the scrutiny of the military police, to discuss what would happen to Japan after the war was lost, as they all assumed it would be. One of the leaders of the group was Saburo Okita, who would become a prominent government planner throughout the postwar period and later, in his sixties, would try, unsuccessfully, to enter politics. In 1945 Okita was only thirty years old and was on the staff of the Greater East Asian Ministry. "We didn't know when and in what way the war would end, or whether Japan would be partially or completely destroyed," he began as he related the story to me, "so we used our lowest projection, figuring our imports would be cut off entirely and we would have nothing at first but our domestic and human resources. We felt that the initial stress had to be put on agricultural production, on just feeding the people, but we also recognized the need for industrial rebuilding.

"As we continued to meet in the months after the war ended, we used the years 1933–1936 as a guideline for the first level of Japan's recovery. We figured on a population of some seventy million, including six million repatriated soldiers and civilians. We knew we would have to build up some export industries in order to obtain raw materials, and we thought, naturally, of textiles—we had a large silk-and-cotton-producing industry before the war—but we also felt we could rebuild our steel industry and turn it to useful purposes."

As it turned out, the objectives set up by Okita's secret group were amazingly close to the mark, although its predictions took some time to prove out. Economic activity at the end of the war was practically at a standstill. Food was very scarce. Japan proper had not been self-sufficient in food since about 1900, and the demands of the war and the damage and dislocation caused by the bombings had made things worse; urban workers were averaging 1,600 calories a day, of which 2 ounces were protein. Not only was there a serious lack of fertilizers and farm implements, but the rural population had swollen because of lack of work in the urban centers and the greater danger of living in them during the bombing. Those who had stayed in the cities now wrapped up what was left of their possessions, jammed themselves into the few trains that were still running, and trudged dusty roads to far-off villages to trade their belongings for rice, in what came to be known as the "onion-skin" economy. They also bartered for such commodities as sugar, sake and shoes, which they brought back to the cities and sold illegally on the black market. The black marketeers and the "pan-pan" girls (the prostitutes the Japanese government made available to the occupation troops—there were some seventy thousand such girls by 1952 and they were collectively earning about $200 million a year) were actually the first big groups of postwar entrepreneurs.

If the Japanese, driven by day-to-day survival, had little or no idea in those early postwar days of what direction they were going, the Americans, despite their many blueprints and plans to democratize Japan, were not very sure themselves of how it was all going to work out. As Supreme Commander for the Allied Powers for the Occupation and Control of Japan, General MacArthur operated under a broad yet peculiarly ambiguous set of instructions from Washington. SCAP (a term that designated both MacArthur personally and the whole American bureaucracy in Japan) was to encourage "changes in the form of government initiated by the Japanese people or government in the direction of modifying its feudal and authoritarian tendencies"—even if such changes involved the use of force. The orders directed MacArthur not to "assume any responsibility for the economic rehabilitation of Japan or the strengthening of the Japanese economy," and stipulated: "The standard of living will depend upon the thoroughness with which Japan rids itself of all militaristic ambitions, redirects the use of its human and natural resources wholly and solely for the purpose of peaceful living, administers adequate economic and financial controls, and co-operates with the occupying forces and the governments they represent."

MacArthur, whose arrogance and strong will did not diminish his undoubted intellectual brilliance—which was largely focused, however, on nineteenth-century politico-economic theories—interpreted his directives pretty much as he saw fit. After imposing an American-style "peace constitution" in March 1946, which made a figurehead of the Emperor, abolishing the old Privy Council and the House of Peers, establishing universal suffrage and setting up a parliamentary system, he and his staff set out to reshape Japanese life with sweeping reforms. The goal was to create an independent labor movement, shape a broader and more liberal educational system, disestablish Shinto as the state religion, give the vote to women, introduce a successful land-reform program and dissolve the major family-owned holding companies, known as *zaibatsu*. But probably most important was the manner in which the Japanese implemented, or evaded, some of these measures.

Purges and Comebacks

The evasions were made easier by a sharp division between liberals and conservatives in the ranks of SCAP policy makers, of which the Japanese took full advantage. By 1947–1948, SCAP's shifting policies had resulted in the reformist elements losing out to the more conservative bureaucrats, politicians, financiers and military men. As the Cold War intensified, this shift, which became known as the "reverse course," gave the Japanese more leeway to develop economically in their own fashion, as a potential American ally against Communism. The revised policies also made possible the mechanisms by which the diligent and perservering new Japanese entrepreneurs began to prosper and the modern Japanese capitalist system would soon flourish.

One of the issues that caused widespread debate was the SCAP purges of military, political and business leaders, as well as of intellectuals deemed guilty of having supported the war. This process involved elaborate screening procedures—carried out with the help of the Japanese government—which took about two years. A total of 717,000 persons were screened, and 210,000 were purged from public life—115,000 of them military career men. Twenty-eight officials of the wartime regime, including its top military leaders, were indicted as war criminals. Of these seven, including General Hideki Tojo, the wartime Prime Minister, were put to death. Though questions of guilt and responsibility were debated, as they were to a greater degree at the Nuremberg Trials in Germany, the majority of Japanese shed no tears for the demise of the men who had led them down such a disastrous path.

Most of the 210,000 on the final purge list reappeared after the occupation ended in 1952 and regained their former status or assumed new roles. Three of the purged politicians, including one who had been jailed, Nobosuke Kishi, became prime ministers. Largely unaffected by the purges were the civil servants in the national government, of whom only 145 ranking officials, out of 4,000, were discharged. Many of these bureaucrats went into politics and became national leaders, and others served effectively in the new ministries. The survival of the bureaucrats, who in many respects were to run the new Japan, must be placed high on the list of factors facilitating the country's rapid recovery from the war and its subsequent astonishing growth and progress.

One of every four top business executives was purged, but the Japanese responsible for this part of the program adroitly interpreted the SCAP directives to include only the heads of the *zaibatsu* and other big concerns, down through the top-executive levels, which left those below them untouched. Many of these so-called third-rank executives took over and subsequently assumed important roles in managing the reorganized and newly prosperous companies after the mid-fifties. Mergers of some of the earlier components of the big *zaibatsu* were permitted, but the centralized, family-owned holding companies, as such, remained barred. In 1978, for example, there were twenty-seven separate, though closely related, firms under the banner of Mitsubishi, the largest of the new industrial trading conglomerates. Demonstrating the wide disparity of opinion within SCAP, William Sebald, a State Department man who was one of MacArthur's top advisers, took issue with those who wanted the *zaibatsu* broken up and felt that "the occupation tinkered too deeply and often needlessly with Japan's social and institutional life"; he said, in retrospect, that "the attempt to destroy the so-called *zaibatsu* was foredoomed, for, as was later demonstrated, the Japanese preferred economic centralization and cartelization and quickly restored them."

One of the occupation's principal accomplishments and one that has had a lasting effect on Japanese life is the land-reform program. The Japanese had long talked of reforming the country's feudal land-tenure system. Soon after Hirohito succeeded to the throne, in 1926, ushering in the Showa (Enlightened Peace) period—each emperor gives a name to his reign—both farmers and bureaucrats recognized the need for improving outmoded farming techniques, and a movement to untie the feudal bonds of the landlord-tenant relationship arose. But before long the militarists put an end to such talk of reform. Now, at SCAP's urging, the Japanese passed a reform measure—in December 1945—but it allowed a landlord to retain 12 1/3 acres of his property, which didn't satisfy SCAP's reformers. In October 1946 they forced the passage of a new bill, under which all land owned by absentee landlords, as well as that leased out by village landlords in excess of 2 1/2 acres, was to be bought by the government and resold to tenants at controlled prices. Within two years, 5 million acres formerly owned by 2 million landlords or their families, were sold to 4.75 million tenant cultivators. Some landlords fought to keep as much land as they could by various subterfuges—taking advantage, for instance, of their long-time relationships with tenants to persuade them to return some acreage. But local land committees set up to supervise the land-reform program, though they often became centers of dispute, for the most part supported the claims of the new landholders.

Land reform was instrumental in building up rural homogeneity and solidarity by reducing class differences. Inevitably, however, new political and economic power bases arose, and a new class of local farm officials slowly emerged to take over the leading village and prefectural posts. They worked with Nokyo (the Union of Agricultural Cooperatives), which, despite a dwindling number of farmers, became one of Japan's most powerful pressure-groups. It included almost all of the country's 7 million farm families, about 15 percent of the population. Nokyo was sometimes called a "mammoth agricultural *zaibatsu*" —a by no means far-fetched comparison, since it operated a business organization of its own that rated favorably in total yen volume with the top industrial conglomerates. In addition to dealing in agricultural products and machinery, Nokyo ran, among other things, a huge insurance business, a travel agency, chains of hotels and supermarkets, and a publishing business. It acted as a lobbyist and spokesman for the farmers, and though it cut across party lines, it was closest to the Liberal Democratic Party and to the main conservative stream of Japanese politics. Farmers became among the richest people in Japan as a result of soaring land prices. None of the early reformers in SCAP could possibly have foreseen that the land-reform program was to create a rich rural society which would become the bulwark of conservative strength as well as a foundation stone of the social and political stability that facilitated Japan's postwar growth.

Crisis in Labor

As important as land reform was in the reshaping of postwar Japan, the creation of a free labor-union movement, which gave new impetus to the traditional Japanese work ethic but pointed it in a fresh direction, was perhaps even more important. Before the Pacific war, fewer than half a million workers were organized; during the war, unions ceased to function entirely. In December 1945, urged by SCAP, the Diet passed a trade-union law modeled on the United States National Labor Relations Act of 1935. A year later there were more than 17,000 unions, with a membership of nearly 4.5 million—about half the nonagricultural wage earners of Japan. The Communists played an important role in early union organization—they had been among the thousands of political prisoners released from jail shortly after the occupation began. They controlled the Congress of Industrial Labor Unions of Japan, while the Socialists backed the Japan Federation of Labor, the forerunner of today's largest labor federation, the General Council of Japanese Trade Unions, known as Sohyo. As uncontrollable inflation convulsed the country in the immediate postwar period—prices more than doubled in the first six occupation months—a series of strikes and slowdowns took place, and Japanese workers developed a special tactic called "production control," whereby, rather than strike, they simply took over a plant or a railway line and ran it until their demands were met or a compromise was reached.

Increasing strikes and demonstrations in the spring of 1946 caused the same divisions about labor in SCAP that had marked other reform measures, especially on the issue of production control. Early in May 1946, a week before the formation of the third postwar Japanese cabinet, headed by Shigeru Yoshida, who was eventually to rule as Prime Minister for fifty-three of the seventy-nine months of the occupation, a large demonstration took place in front of the Imperial Palace, followed by a series of smaller ones at food-rationing centers in Tokyo, where workers and housewives demanded rice and complained about the breakdown of the rationing machinery throughout the country. On May 19 a quarter of a million people again demonstrated at the Imperial Palace and elsewhere in Tokyo. The next day MacArthur issued a tough warning against "the growing tendency toward mass violence and physical processes of intimidation." Many SCAP members thought MacArthur had exaggerated the situation, and the warning caused confusion and consternation among the unions. In August, after two months of relative quiet, the strikes and demonstrations were renewed, and at the end of the month MacArthur banned all "strikes, walk-outs or other work stoppages which are inimical to the occupation." SCAP thereafter got tougher, as did Yoshida, who denounced those who struck as "lawbreakers."

The climax came in late January 1947, when, in protest against Yoshida, a general strike was planned for February 1 by a united front representing 4 million workers. SCAP was unable to work out a compromise, and on the afternoon of January 31, nine and a half hours before the strike was due to start, MacArthur issued a blunt order forbidding it. This, too, was a milestone in Japan's postwar history, because while it jolted the unions, it eventually led to the emergence of a more moderate and disciplined labor movement, without which industry would never have achieved its remarkable production records. As it developed, workers would not have benefited as much either.

By the spring of 1947, after Yoshida had resigned and two weak coalition governments headed by the socialists and the Democratic Party failed to bring political peace or improve the dismal state of the economy, the contest for power among liberal and conservative Japanese politicians had intensified and had also become thoroughly intertwined with the bitter battle among similar factions within SCAP. These issues exacerbated the already angry differences within the Allied Council for Japan, which was composed of representatives of the United States, the Soviet Union, Great Britain and Nationalist China, and also within the more moribund Far Eastern Commission, representing eleven nations, including the major powers. Despite the existence of these two bodies, MacArthur had continued to run Japan on his own as personal SCAP, though his decisions had reflected the divisions in the SCAP organization. In the spring of 1947, however, the basic course of American policy was changing. In March, President Truman proclaimed his famous doctrine espousing opposition to Communism in Turkey and Greece. Over a period of months, various top American officials, including Undersecretary of State Dean Acheson and Secretary of the Army Kenneth C. Royall began referring to Japan as a coming industrial and political bulwark against Communism in the Far East, and a number of visiting American missions led by businessmen and bankers called for a halt to the breakup of the old companies in the interest of spurring economic recovery.

Despite these encouraging declarations, the economy failed to improve, and in October 1948 Yoshida returned to power as Prime Minister, vowing "to break the vicious circle of wages and prices and to promote economic stability and reconstruction." The earlier coalition government of Hitoshi Ashida had cracked down further on labor, forbidding collective bargaining as well as the right to strike. Now, as a result of new MacArthur-inspired directives, 11,000 leftist labor leaders were fired from their jobs, as were 3,000 government employees, newspaper editors and writers, in what became known as the "Red Purge." In one year, total union membership declined by nearly 1 million, and it was not until 1951 that the labor movement would recover under Socialist leadership.

As Japan slid further into economic chaos, Washington took drastic action early in 1949 by appointing a tough, conservative Detroit banker named Joseph Dodge to take over the economy. Many Japanese still speak of the stringent Dodge measures as the major occupation turning point; but just as many add that if it had not been for the outbreak of the Korean War in June 1950, Dodge's tough deflationary policies would have ended in total collapse. He quickly established himself as the virtual economic dictator of Japan, insisting that "before anything else, the Japanese budget must be balanced." He reorganized the program of American economic assistance by setting up a counterpart fund into which the proceeds from the sale of relief goods were to be paid and used to redeem bonds and debentures of the government's chief lending institution, the Reconstruction Finance Bank. Perhaps most important was Dodge's establishment of a firm exchange rate for the yen. He managed to balance the budget by June 1949, and a year later inflation was under control, but his deflationary policy had by then brought Japan to the brink of disaster. Production at that time was about a third of what it had been in 1931 and had grown stagnant.

Only the start of the Korean War truly saved the situation.

A New Divine Gift

"We had prepared the way without knowing what was coming," Kiichi Miyazawa told me years later. At the time, he was an assistant in the Finance Ministry and he subsequently held many important bureaucratic and political jobs, including running the Foreign Ministry and the Economic Planning Agency. "The war enabled us to deflate the deflation. For us, it was an undeniable boon."

It was more than a boon—it was a bonanza. Procurement orders, both for military material and for services for the Americans and the United Nations armed forces fighting in Korea, were valued at more than $338 million in the first year of the war, and amounted to about 40 percent of Japan's total exports for 1950. Hisato Ichimada, the Governor of the Bank of Japan, described the orders as "divine aid." Ten percent of the orders were for ordnance, which re-established the Japanese arms industry. By the end of 1950 the nation's trade balance, which had been deep in the red for four years, had become favorable. By the end of 1951 Japan's industrial production was up to the level of the 1934–1936 period, which was the goal set by Saburo Okita and the group of planners who had met clandestinely back in 1945. In 1951, iron and steel production had exceeded the prewar level and Japan had again become the world's leading textile exporter. Even though the big military orders tapered off after the war ended in 1953, they continued for the support of American troops left in Korea.

The Korean War, coming on top of the victory of the Communists in China, helped bring Japan another reward that stimulated its growth: a peace treaty formally ending World War II and the American occupation. The treaty was the crowning achievement of Yoshida, whose prewar training had been in diplomacy. (He had been Ambassador to England and Foreign Minister before his disapproval of the pact with the Axis powers and of militarist policy cast him into limbo, and eventually into jail.) A stubborn man of high principle who operated mostly by instinct, he had disapproved of many of the occupation's methods, such as the initial purges and the destruction of the *zaibatsu*, but he had strongly supported such programs as land reform. The new constitution, he felt, was far too much of an American rather than a Japanese instrument. Throughout his long months in office, he played a carefully contrived cat-and-mouse game with MacArthur. The two men, despite their strong egos, had a mutual respect and dealt bluntly and openly with each other.

As early as 1947 the Americans had begun informal discussions with the Japanese about a peace treaty, and they had made it increasingly clear that they were ready to move ahead without the Russians, if necessary, and to make a separate bilateral security arrangement with Japan as well. A few days before the Korean War began, John Foster Dulles, who had just been appointed a special adviser to the State Department by President Truman, arrived in Japan to open discussions for a settlement. Dulles, as a hard-line Cold Warrior, wanted the Japanese, as anti-Communist allies, to rearm. American military leaders, including General Omar Bradley, Chairman of the Joint Chiefs of Staff, and Defense Secretary Louis Johnson, on the other hand, wanted the Americans to retain a strong military presence on Japanese soil. Yoshida was against rearming, and MacArthur supported him. Yoshida had no qualms about aligning Japan with the United States and Great Britain against Russia and China, which had only recently signed their own alliance and still regarded Japan as a potential enemy. But he had to fight off his political opposition, whose members demanded a treaty everyone would sign, including the Russians and the Chinese, arguing that only in this way could Japan remain truly neutral and avoid being caught between the two emerging power blocs.

Since the first American divisions sent to Korea were occupation forces from Japan, it was soon clear that new provisions would have to be made to protect America's bases in Japan, as well as the 225,000 American civilians and dependents there. Dulles initially tried to sell Yoshida on a Japanese army of 300,000 men, but in the meantime it was agreed to establish a 75,000-man National Police Reserve. Though even the NPR appeared to violate Article 9 of the Japanese constitution, which stated that "land, sea and air forces, as well as other war potential, will never be maintained," the new police force soon received tanks, machine guns and mortars, and became the nucleus of today's Self-Defense Forces, which total about 240,000. In a secret message to Washington, Yoshida also suggested that "if the American side so proposed," Japan was "prepared to study ways of offering the United States military bases on Japanese soil."

This paved the way for the signing of the United States–Japan Security Treaty, which took place in San Francisco on September 8, 1951, the same day the peace treaty was signed; the security treaty was to go into effect on April 28, 1952, when the occupation formally ended and Japan regained its independence. Forty-nine nations signed the peace treaty, which amounted to "a peace for Asia without Asians," as one American commentator wrote, since China, Russia and India refused to participate. Though all three established relations with Japan on different levels, it was not until mid-1978 that China and Japan signed a treaty of peace and friendship, and no treaty between Russia and Japan has been signed as yet. The Americans, in their treaty, made a somewhat qualified statement that they would be available to defend Japan against attack; ultimately it was agreed that they would be allowed to keep a garrison force of up to 100,000 men in the country, but there was no assurance that the United States would be able to use Japanese bases in case of war. The Americans did gain the right to veto any proposal for the entry of the forces of a third power into Japan, and they maintained their hold on the strategic Ryukyu Islands, including Okinawa, which was not returned to the Japanese until 1972. The treaty was admittedly lopsided, but clauses promising continued economic aid, and the lack of insistence on rearmament, despite Dulles, were both positive contributions to Japanese growth.

Security and Rearmament

The Japanese opposition parties protested the peace treaty and the security pact, but were not strong enough to keep both from being approved by the Diet; the issues involved remained, and the security aspects divided the country politically. The revision of the security pact in 1960, even though in Japan's favor, caused severe riots. Under the continuing protection of the American "nuclear umbrella," and with its own defense costs less than 1 percent of its gross national product, Japan was frequently accused by American politicians and other critics of obtaining a "free ride" militarily, and there was an increasing body of opinion in the United States that the Japanese should share the burden of Pacific defenses more than they did, especially at sea. There was no doubt that by keeping its defense costs down, compared to those of other major nations, Japan was able to concentrate most of its energies and money on building up its economy. With the start of withdrawal of the remaining 40,000 American ground troops in Korea in 1978, and a further reduction of the American garrison in Japan and Okinawa to about 46,000—down from 85,000 in 1970 and 240,000 in 1952—renewed pressure was placed on the Japanese to beef up their military forces and to assist the American Seventh Fleet in defense of the western Pacific, beyond the Japanese islands and the surrounding seas.

Though the rearmament issue remained a touchy one for years in Japan, it became increasingly less so in the late seventies. Opinion polls in 1978 showed that more than 80 percent of the Japanese now favored both the security pact and the Self-Defense Forces, and it seemed likely that Japan would soon exceed the 1 percent of GNP allocated for defense purposes. The opposition parties were no longer adverse to a stronger defense posture. The quality and quantity of arms were already being markedly improved and increased with the purchase of more than a hundred supersonic F-15E fighter planes from the United States to replace older-model fighters, and forty-five PC-3 Orion antisubmarine patrol planes to keep track of the expanding Russian navy in the Pacific. The basic aim of the Fourth Defense Build-up Plan was to make Japan's armed forces more functional and efficient, but the line between a defensive and an offensive potential was becoming blurred, particularly concerning an offensive air capability. There was talk of building a number of small aircraft carriers and increasing the range of planes with air-to-air refueling tankers. To beef up the ground forces, some fifty modern tanks and a score of self-propelled howitzers were ordered, as well as additional helicopters. For the first time, despite the nuclear "allergy," suggestions were made that the Japanese might manufacture "defensive" nuclear weapons, and they already had the capacity to do so.

Short of a sudden and destructive nuclear attack, the country's defense elements were geared to hold off an invader for a week or so, until the Americans, in accordance with the provisions of the security treaty, came to Japan's aid. One thing seemed certain: a new war, involving Japan directly and initially, would be an altogether different proposition from the last Pacific war, when, after the attack on Pearl Harbor, the United States began the long road back through the central Pacific islands and from Australia up through New Guinea and the Philippines to Okinawa, and to Japan itself, where the surrender took place. If a new war broke out, it would probably be over much more quickly, given the proximity and strength of the most likely enemy, Soviet Russia.

For this reason some military experts, both in Japan and in the United States as well as in Europe, were suggesting closer collaboration, including joint American-Japanese military exercises, and consultations among the NATO powers and Japan on the linkage of European and Asian security matters. Even more significant, the Chinese let it be known that they were in favor of a stronger Japanese defense role, and the possibility of some sort of eventual triangular relationship between the United States, Japan and China was not to be foreclosed, particularly in the light of normalization between Washington and Peking following by four months the signing of the peace treaty between Tokyo and Peking. While this would not take the form of a military alliance, it could well be a nonaggression pact or an agreement banning the use of weapons against each other that might derive from the sale of technological materials and from information to China by Japan and the United States which could be employed for military purposes.

Despite the emergence of Japan as a burgeoning new military power for the first time since the end of the Pacific war, the rest of Asia seemed surprisingly unperturbed. If the United States and Japan continued to work together, particularly on a broader basis at sea, this was viewed by the Southeast Asian nations as a counterweight to growing Soviet sea power and as a force for stability. But if the Japanese went nuclear, that would pose a different and more ominous threat. It was still debatable, in 1979, whether the Japanese would alter their three non-nuclear principles prohibiting the production, possession or introduction into Japan of nuclear weapons, but they were determined to continue reprocessing uranium and plutonium derivatives in order to obtain new sources of energy and eliminate their total dependence on expensive imported oil. If, in any sense, they felt themselves isolated, the step to manufacturing nuclear weapons would be a small one, whether for defensive or offensive use. This would become a distinct possibility if South Korea went nuclear.

The Japanese did not hide their disappointment and concern over President Carter's plan to begin Korean withdrawals in 1978. Of the four factors that they kept most in mind with regard to their still-limited defense system, the stability of the Korean peninsula was by far the most important, outweighing the other less tangible three, i.e., the amorphous state of Soviet-American détente, the still strong possibilities of Sino-Soviet confrontation, and the not yet totally defined status of the new Sino-American relationship, especially regarding the future of Taiwan, with which Japan had retained close ties after establishing diplomatic relations with Peking—ties which were easier to retain because Tokyo, unlike Washington, had no defense treaty with the Taipeh government.

If even a limited war broke out on the Korean peninsula, Japan could not help but be directly affected as a result of its security arrangement with the United States, assuming that the Americans would live up to their pledge to assist the South Koreans and would seek to obtain Japanese approval for activation of the American bases on the Japanese islands and on Okinawa. What worried the Japanese about the potentially explosive Korean situation was not only the chance that if the major nations became openly involved again, Japan might not be able to avoid getting involved itself, but also the likelihood of a large influx of refugees from both parts of Korea. The Japanese already had some 600,000 Koreans on their soil, where in many ways they were regarded as social outcasts. Of those politically active, about 60 percent were pro–South Korean and the rest pro-North. This in itself created a tense atmosphere, with constant political overtones. If as many as a million more refugees poured into Japan, which is the general estimate, the situation could become unmanageable.

The full impact of the scheduled American troop withdrawal from Korea would not be felt until 1982, if indeed it was carried out by then and assuming that the tenuous peace on the Korean peninsula could be maintained in the interim. But despite the air and logistic support the Americans planned to leave behind, the withdrawals, however slowly they took place, seemed certain to lead to an intensification of the debate about how strong Japan's defense posture should be. It was conceivable, as a number of Japanese politicians of all parties still privately urged, that the reduction of American troops in Korea and a further reduction of American forces in Japan could result in a swing of the pendulum the other way—toward renunciation by the Japanese of maintaining a strong military posture. The far more likely alternative of Japan improving its defense capabilities further and cooperating more fully with the

Americans, particularly at sea, would inevitably depend on some of the other larger factors still undetermined, such as the evolution of Sino-American, Japanese-Russian and Sino-Soviet relations, and general progress toward disarmament, including the future of Strategic Arms Limitation Talks. The Japanese perception of their own evolving role in Asia was yet another factor that would bear upon the problem, particularly as concerned economic relations with Southeast Asia. And these questions, in turn, had a direct bearing on the changing attitudes toward rapid economic growth in Japan itself, which in the past had so often taken place at the expense of other nations. To appreciate this, one had to look back on what Japan had accomplished over the more than three decades since its abject surrender aboard the *Missouri*.

3-Growth, Change and Challenge

In the mid-1950s, having emerged from the first phase of the Cold War and the Korean War as perhaps the greatest beneficiary of each, Japan was on the verge of an amazing economic takeoff. Initially the Japanese had concentrated on rehabilitating their basic industries—coal, iron, steel, fertilizers and food production. But even by the end of the Korean War, despite exports having reached $250 million a year, the nation's goals were still modest. As Kiichi Miyazawa pointed out to me, "No one as yet was thinking in terms of rapid growth. We thought simply of maintaining a solid foreign-exchange position in order to earn enough for imports."

One of the first export industries to take off was textiles, and this was mostly the result of the soaring demands of American buyers of such articles as inexpensive blouses and shirts. Scores of buyers flocked to Japan from New York and other big cities in the early fifties and told the Japanese exactly what to design and mass produce. From 180,000. dozen cotton shirts imported to America in 1953, the figure soared to well over 1 million dozen in 1955. American manufacturers and cotton growers began protesting, with the result that the following year the first "voluntary" export quotas were reluctantly accepted by the Japanese. These became one of the most touchy perennial issues between the two governments—the subject of long and complicated negotiations that resulted in elaborate agreements and quotas for different kinds of garments.

Ever since the Meiji period (1867–1912) the Japanese had imported foreign technology and adapted it for local use. Now, as exports started booming, they turned abroad again for new machinery and techniques in order to modernize their plants. A large portion of the investment in equipment went into the iron-and-steel, electric-power and machine industries. Chemical fertilizers and shipbuilding also started to boom, and then electronics, petrochemicals, synthetic fibers, photographic and optical equipment, and automobiles (though the real auto boom did not begin until the sixties). Invariably, the Japanese made their own improvements on the technology they imported. As Saburo

Okita emphasized, "On many occasions, because of such improvements, factories originally built with foreign design in the course of time reached a much higher output than the designed capacity set by the foreign supplier of the 'know-how.' " Frequently the Japanese went to the United States and bought newly designed and as yet untested machinery, shipped it to Japan, assembled it in their own way, and started utilizing it even before the Americans. They also built their factories on or near the east coast, which made exporting easier.

Japanese investment in foreign equipment increased in 1956 by an astonishing 57.5 percent over the previous year, and shot up another 23.5 percent in 1957. Millions of dollars were paid out for patent rights. Much of this investment was financed by government banks, such as the Japan Development Bank, and by the Industrial Bank of Japan. The policies of these banks in turn stimulated private bank lending. Though the government initiated some efforts to control the expansion of credit, the eleven major so-called "city," or private, banks in Tokyo began the practice of overlending that periodically plagued the Japanese economy, bringing on tight-money policies leading to heavy losses and bankruptcy among many individual enterprises, especially small and medium-size firms. (Both large and small companies customarily borrowed between 60 and 80 percent of their capital.) Until the world-wide economic and financial crisis of 1973–1974, however, this unique credit-control mechanism, over which the central Bank of Japan sat like a calm and regal mother hen, served the Japanese well and was another important reason for the country's phenomenal growth.

In the mid-fifties the labor supply was overabundant, but with new factories springing up everywhere, the opportunities for jobs quickly multiplied. And as farm production increased, spurred by efficient miniature tractors and rapid improvement in the use of fertilizers, there was no longer the need to import quite so much food from abroad. Despite growing agricultural prosperity, many young people from the rural areas began moving to the cities to work in the new factories and lead more exciting lives. The population of Tokyo reached 7.5 million in 1955—more than double what it had been ten years before.

Three Electric Treasures

With the start of urbanization came a new hunger for consumer goods. Not only were people eating better but they wanted things that made life easier, particularly "the three electric treasures"—washing machines, refrigerators and television sets. The sales of washing machines quadrupled between 1953 and 1955, and doubled again in 1956. In March 1956 there were 156,000 television sets in Japan; by the end of 1957 the figure was 750,000, and by the end of 1958 it had more than doubled again. Much of the credit for the fast growth of the television industry belonged to a man named Matsutaro Shoriki, who had introduced professional baseball to Japan before the war and owned the *Yomiuri Shimbun,* one of the country's three major newspapers.

Shoriki was the first to think of developing a television industry, and at the end of 1951 he applied for a TV-station license. This prompted Nippon Hoso Kyokai, the publicly owned Japan Broadcasting Company, known as NHK, to speed up its own plans for starting a noncommercial network; it made its initial telecast in February 1963, beating Shoriki's Nippon Television (NTV) by half a year.

About this time a phenomenon that became an obsession in Japan began to be widely discussed—the generation gap. It was the theme of a 1956 novel, *Season of Violence,* by Shintaro Ishihara, who went on to become an icono-clastic right-wing member of the Diet, ran unsuccessfully for mayor of Tokyo, and later became Minister of Environment. The book dealt with the rejection by the young of the values and ethics of their elders and vividly described sexual acts as an expression of the new freedom. It became a best seller and made Ishihara an overnight cult hero.

Despite a general prosperity, however, poverty and low living standards had by no means vanished. The majority of people lived in apartments of one or two tiny rooms, or in little wooden houses, and the government program to build so-called *danchi*—four- to six-story concrete apartment houses—did little to alleviate the situation. Sewage facilities remained abysmal, there was a shortage of water in Tokyo and other large cities, and the poor quality of roads caused many accidents and horrendous traffic snarls. There were not enough schools and hardly any recreational facilities. Life in the big city, despite its glitter, was in many ways disorganized, drab and confining. The urban rehabilitation of West Germany far surpassed that of Japan—a compari-son often made by traveling Japanese.

The growth of large corporations increased in the sixties, stimulating urbaniza-tion further, but about three quarters of all Japanese enterprises remained small, having only one to four employees. The symbiotic relationship between big and small companies, known as the dual economic structure, was one of the signal features of Japan's unique enterprise system. And despite the diffi-culties the smaller firms had in times of trouble, when credit dried up and many of them went bankrupt, and despite the social and economic inequities the dual structure created, its enduring strength helped sustain the nation and characterize the society.

During one of my recent trips to Japan I visited both large corporations and small private enterprises to see how the dual system worked. First I went to the Kimitsu plant of the Nippon Steel Corporation, the biggest steel company in the world and Japan's largest manufacturing company. Kimitsu is situated on drab flatland reclaimed from the sea on a peninsula across the pollution-hazed bay south of Tokyo. It covers 1,800 acres and includes three of the world's biggest blast furnaces. About three quarters of the company's iron and steel had generally been used domestically, but when domestic demand for steel slumped, as it did during the recession of the mid-seventies, Nippon Steel tried to step up its exports to take up the slack.

Most employees at Kimitsu, like virtually all Japanese who worked for big concerns, stayed with Nippon Steel all their lives, though by the end of the seventies, life employment with one company was no longer quite as universally accepted. The average age of beginning workers at Nippon Steel was twenty-four, and they retired on a company pension at fifty-five. The typical employee was thirty-two years old and earned about $600 a month, plus semiannual bonuses, which are commonly given in Japan and as a rule equal a third of a year's pay. The 7,000 workers at Kimitsu enjoyed virtually rent-free housing in flats built by the company and costing only $15 a month—less than a tenth of what a similar apartment cost on the outskirts of Tokyo, let alone near the center of the city. Such cheap accommodations were typical of what Japanese firms began offering their employees as a lure when the boom cycle started in the mid-fifties.

There were twenty-four apartment buildings containing 4,500 company flats at Kimitsu, each consisting of three small rooms plus a kitchen-dining alcove, and on the ample space around the buildings were playgrounds, a swimming pool and a supermarket. But the whole area looked somehow deserted and unfinished, which is why some of the workers lived, or aspired to live, in three- or four-room private houses nearby that ranged from $27,000 to $33,000. I spoke with three families in one of the eleven-story apartment buildings. Though all workers were entitled to twenty days of paid vacation a year, the families I talked to said they did little traveling, and indicated they were more or less content to spend all their time at Kimitsu. They all owned the three "electric treasures." Most of their spare time, they said, was spent visiting other families and gossiping; the men kept active playing volley ball and other games, and the women took classes in cooking or dressmaking. They read newspapers and popular magazines, of which Japan has scores, and they spent a lot of time watching television. Only one of the wives I spoke with, who used to work, as did her husband, for the Self-Defense Forces in Tokyo before joining Nippon Steel, showed any discontent with what seemed to me the boring, confined life at Kimitsu. When I asked her if she was satisfied with her new life, she shrugged and replied, "Satisfaction is a different thing," but admitted that she sometimes reflected on the greater opportunities for entertainment in Tokyo.

Sometime after my trip to Kimitsu I went to the town of Kiryu, about fifty-five miles northwest of Tokyo, where weaving, first of silk, then of cotton (and more recently of synthetics), had been a tradition for hundreds of years. Though it was still the major industry, it was declining, largely because of import restrictions placed on Japanese textiles by the United States, and local manufacturers were making better profits from such things as electric appliances, auto parts and *pachinko,* or pinball machines, for which the Japanese have had a consuming passion for many years. But there were still more than eight hundred textile "factories" in Kiryu, most of them private homes where the owners, some of whom were part-time farmers, had installed a few textile machines. The majority of these small enterprises were making kimonos,

Japanese obis, or sashes, and neckties, and were weaving some cloth for export.

I spoke with a typical subcontractor, Soji Nakazato, who lived with his wife, their three teen-age daughters and his wife's mother in a spacious nine-room farmhouse on the edge of town. Nakazato, a burly, smiling, outdoors type, had six new electric textile machines in the main part of the house; he worked ten hours a day five or six days a week, with his wife as his only helper, weaving cloth and making kimonos for dolls under contract to a larger factory nearby. He said he averaged a net profit of about $4,000 a year. He hoped his daughters would help him when they graduated from high school so that he could devote more time to his original vocation, farming—he still grew his own rice and vegetables. This pattern of part-time work and part-time farming had become typical of the small entrepreneur in Japan. Though Tokyo was only two and a half hours away by train, Nakazato, who had worked there for a time as a young man, said he seldom went to the city anymore. "Life is a lot more pleasant here," he said. "It's more old-fashioned and it's quiet. I've got my electric washer, my refrigerator and my television set. I work in my garden when I can, and my weekends are taken up with weddings and funerals and other ceremonies—all the members of the cooperative here are really one big family."

This idea of the local cooperative as a family—just as all employees of a big company, such as Nippon Steel, considered themselves members of an industrial family—is one of the significant characteristics of Japanese work patterns. In fact, in addition to maintaining traditional personal loyalties—such as attachment to relatives, to drinking companions a man saw at his after-work bar, to members of one's university class, and so on—all Japanese regard themselves as belonging to a single huge family of 113 million people. This spirit of cohesiveness and homogeneity, of shared identity and destiny, dates back centuries.

One has only to stop on a busy Tokyo street on a weekday morning and watch thousands upon thousands of men and women rushing to work, their fixed expressions and determined gait as alike as their briefcases and clothes, to be aware of the compulsive galvanizing force that has moved Japan to a position of economic power. The Japanese have demonstrated a capacity for management and organization that is probably superior to that of any other nation in the world. Things worked because they made them work to suit their purposes, but when something went awry, as it did in the mid-seventies, they tended to panic because, as one leading economist admitted to me, "we lack the tactical and strategic ability to cope with drastic situations." Their defensive reaction was to go back to their drawing boards, or computers, to formulate more of their dozens of meticulous plans. But in a society as deeply focused on specific issues and goals as Japan is, it was difficult, as another Japanese friend pointed out, "for our establishment to rank our priorities and to relate our domestic interests and policies to our international problems and pursuits."

Business and Politics

Though the Japanese contemporary establishment was shaped in 1955, the system bears many resemblances to its nineteenth-century antecedents and can trace some of its traditions, bureaucratic as well as economic, even further back, into the feudal (Tokugawa) period. These traditions helped cast the political mold of postwar Japan. In November of 1955, following an earlier move by the right and left wings of the split Socialist Party to reunite, the Liberal and Democratic parties, at the instigation of the big-business leaders —the so-called *zaikai*, of the Keidanren, or Japan Federation of Economic Organizations—joined to form the Liberal Democratic Party. Through most subsequent years, until 1975, the Liberal Democrats maintained a clear majority of votes and a margin of approximately two to one in the Diet over the combined opposition parties, even though almost from the start their popularity slowly began to recede. The LDP owed most of its success to its rural base and to the large corporations, which also functioned independently but contributed heavily to the party's campaign funds and worked closely with the leading politicians and bureaucrats to further Japan's economic growth.

Beginning in 1974—1975, however, in the wake of the 1974 upper house elections, widespread criticism of flagrant big-business backing of the LDP led to a considerable reduction of donations on the part of some big companies and to a more restrained system of corporate contributions generally. A new electoral reform law limited such contributions to 150 million yen, or $500,-000, a year per corporation; they used to run to billions of yen. The new law, and the effects of the Lockheed scandal which broke in July 1976, combined to give the LDP a severe setback in the elections for the Lower House of the Diet that December, when it lost its outright majority for the first time in two decades, and sustained it on a working basis only with the support of eight independently elected representatives. Further, it lost its control of some important committees, including the Budget Committee. In July 1977 the party barely managed to cling to power in the upper house elections, losing three seats and requiring the votes of three independent councillors to hold off the opposition, whose views, in both Diet branches, it was now forced to take into consideration. With its popular vote continuing to decline, and facing more uncertainty about its future than at any time since its birth, partly because of the chastened attitude of big business, the LDP in mid-1977 faced an internal crisis of confidence. The close links between business corporations and conservative political leaders seemed bound to last, since they were mutually dependent and for the most part still agreed philosophically and practically about their objectives. But the foundations of the conservative establishment as a whole had been shaken, and it became apparent that new outlooks and orientations were required if it was to endure in its traditional shape and form.

In Japan's elaborate power structure, the most important element in many respects was the bureaucracy, a good many members of which eventually became politicians. Perhaps the best description I have read of the relationship that existed over the years between bureaucrats, businessmen and politicians was one given by Professor Chitoshi Yanaga, of Yale University, in his book *Big Business in Japanese Politics:* "Organized business is the playwright as well as the financier. The ruling party, as producer, director, and stage manager, adapts the play and makes sure that the production meets with the approval of the playwright-financier. It is also responsible for picking the leading actor, who must be *persona grata* to the financier. The administrative bureaucracy utilizes its expertise in looking after the technical details as well as the business end of the production."

In 1978 there were six major *zaikai* combines, led by the Mitsubishi, Mitsui and Sumitomo conglomerates, and they were the direct successors of the family-owned *zaibatsu* firms broken up after the occupation. Allied with them were such major concerns as Nippon Steel and the big private, or city, banks. In the pluralistic Japanese economic society, harmony and consensus remained the keynotes, and while the big companies naturally competed with one another, they did so on a principle of cooperation. Few decisions affecting the nation's economic course were reached without thorough consultation among business leaders both privately, often during dinners or in cabarets or geisha houses, and within the Keidanren and the three similar business organizations, the memberships of which conveniently overlapped. Important politicians maintained privately organized clubs to keep up their contacts with business-men. Nevertheless, it would be an oversimplification to say that the LDP had all along been solely the party of big business, for it also represented many other interest groups, such as the farmers banded together in Nokyo. In other respects as well, the party was no longer a monolithic organization.

For many years the LDP was divided into a half-dozen major factions, and some smaller ones. These factions were a reflection in some ways of traditional and feudal leadership groups, and they always fought bitterly for the party presidency, which automatically led to the prime-ministership. Although most of the factions were formally disbanded in 1977, they maintained so-called study groups, which met regularly to discuss specific topics and tactics, and in effect, the factions endured. While the party covered an increasingly wide spectrum of opinion from highly conservative to relatively liberal, and while it made an earnest effort to turn itself into more of a grass-roots organization, alliances and deals made at the top and siphoned down through loyal ranks continued to dominate political life. However, because of the wider divergence of views and opinions, and because the old guard of factional leaders was slowly giving way to a younger and more mixed fluid and "modernized" group of potential leaders, the former system of alliances and channels was no longer the sole conduit of political power.

By the same token, wider differences of opinion, both political and eco-nomic, were being expressed within the business community. Many corpora-tion executives, still-hidebound conservatives, continued to think solely of mounting profits and greater growth. But others, particularly some of those in their fifties who were beginning to come into the limelight at a faster pace than before, were far more aware of the changes taking place in Japan and of the need for business to adjust to them, not only from its own point of view but with regard to changing social and human components and factors. One of the more far-seeing men I met on several trips to Tokyo was Toshio Doko, the octogenarian head of the Keidanren. A lifelong Buddhist who always rose each morning at four o'clock to read religious scriptures, Doko expressed his liberal-conservative philosophy by placing the support of his organization behind the policy of restructuring Japanese industry and building nonpolluting, resource-conserving enterprises to help create more of a welfare state under conditions of a slower annual growth rate. When I saw him in the spring of 1977 he spoke frankly of the "moral transgressions" that the old political faction system had led to as it became "overpersonalized," and of the salutary effects the Lockheed case had had on the overweening money-politics alliance.

"We want the LDP to remain the stable base of government," he said, "but no longer with the enormous sums from business. The opposition parties have not matured enough and are not suitable to govern present-day Japan. But the LDP must develop progressive economic policies of its own, and cleanse itself, if it wants a bright future."

Japan's bureaucracy is often caught in the middle between the multiple demands of businessmen and politicians, and sometimes it is immobilized by tensions between them—as it was to a considerable extent during the period of the Lockheed-scandal revelations, when everything seemed to come to a standstill for a time. Nevertheless, it has played a unique historical role through its enduring capacity for what Professor Yanaga has described as "executive supremacy." Possessed of attributes both of rigidity and flexibility that have helped it endure for two thousand years, it can sometimes be creative and innovative, and also, at times of stress or drift, unimaginative and constrained. Like most bureaucracies, it works within a huge web of red tape, but day in and day out it serves as the balance wheel of Japan's successful consensus system. Unlike most other bureaucracies, including the American civil service, it has very little turnover except when its members retire or go into politics, and being a thoroughly professional body with its own set standards and ways, it does not welcome advice from outsiders, seldom—far too seldom, its critics maintain—seeking the views of academics and other specialists. In all fairness, however, it has to be said that with the exception of a few academic specialists, most professors choose to remain in their ivory towers and do not try to participate in making decisions, confining themselves, for the most part, to aloof criticism and analysis.

During the seven years of the occupation, the government bureaucrats, having survived the purges better than the politicians and businessmen, acted as middlemen between them and the occupation authorities. Subsequently, as the *zaikai* gained new power, the government ministries, especially the Finance Ministry and the Ministry of International Trade and Industry, came to create policies and administrative machinery that served the purposes of the business world. Usually, when legislation was required, it was the bureaucrats of the thirteen principal ministries who prepared it and guided it through the Diet, of whose members between a third and a half were ex-bureaucrats. The pervasive influence of the bureaucracy has been attested to by the fact that most of Japan's fourteen postwar prime ministers were formerly bureaucrats. As the Japanese economic machine became more complex, the experts of the bureaucracy controlled much of it, both administratively and legislatively— the former by means of periodic "administrative guidance," a euphemistic phrase for a directive that is tantamount to an order. In addition to drafting most bills for the Diet, the bureaucrats prepared the draft of the national budget, as well as government contracts and other documents. They did all the detailed planning for which the Japanese had such a predilection, and then they wrote constant summaries of how and why the plans succeeded or failed. This process was a neatly self-perpetuating one.

Shocks in the System

For more than two decades the Japanese power structure functioned smoothly, with its three principal components each playing what appeared to be an almost ordained role. But as a result of the series of shocks that started with the oil crisis, and on the basis of long talks with scores of bureaucrats and politicians, I became convinced that while the system would undoubtedly go on functioning, it would either have to change or be altered if it was to cope with the new challenges Japan was facing at home and abroad. For one thing, if the country were ruled by a multiparty system, or even if the opposition parties merely maintained a greater leverage under a continuing LDP umbrella, the bureaucracy would have to spread its wings and keep abreast of what the other parties were doing and thinking, of where new areas of compromise lay. These included not only building a more welfare-oriented society at home, which everyone agreed was necessary, but making those adjustments to the multipolar world Japan was being forced by circumstances and events to acknowledge as unavoidable.

The inability to meet these challenges sooner was due to the rigidity that was the backbone of the so-called vertical Japanese society: the intricate mechanism of organization based on passive and complete obedience and respect for one's superiors, as well as on promotion by slow stages on the basis of age and rank rather than merit (though by the late seventies merit was being taken more into consideration). Still, the system had precluded the sort of cross-fertilization that could enable bold new ideas to be implemented. Such ideas were expressed from time to time, but too often they remained unexplored. The tendency within the bureaucracy was for each new problem to be considered in turn, passed up and down the administrative ladder, discussed and rediscussed in endless committee meetings, and at last brought to a point of decision by consensus, after invariably being narrowed down in scope instead of broadened. Various options were thus discarded in favor of a single central emphasis, which was not necessarily the most relevant or useful solution, and risks or unorthodox opinions were seldom accepted.

During the Meiji period the bureaucrats were the principal agents of change. Over the years they gradually relinquished that role, or it was taken away from them. If they can take advantage of the new elements of change brought on by political and social flux, and by shifts in economic emphases and goals, including new foreign-policy approaches, they may again play a more creative part in the evolution of a more mobile and outgoing Japanese democracy. "Up until now, consensus was really collusion," one scholar pointed out, "but now we have a more open society. There will consequently be more bargaining, politically and otherwise, and as we develop a more pluralistic society and a more multivalued way of life, no longer oriented solely toward domestic growth, the bureaucrats can, in fact, gain a greater leverage than they ever had before if they are freshly motivated and grasp the chance." But if they don't, then what? He agreed that the whole delicate mechanism could fall apart.

With such a tremendous concentration of money and power in Tokyo, where virtually all important decisions in business, politics and administration are made, it was no accident that three other major institutions of the country were also centered there. These were the media—the three biggest newspapers and the main television stations, as well as hundreds of monthly and weekly magazines; the big labor unions; and the principal universities, headed by the prestigious Tokyo University. The press, always part of the establishment in modern Japan, gained full freedom of expression after World War II, but it did not really come into its own until after the Korean War, when newsprint became plentiful. Competition between the three major dailies—*Asahi*, *Yomiuri* and *Mainichi*—became fierce, and the first two amassed morning circulations alone of more than six million daily, and afternoon circulations of not much less. But despite this competition for readers, the Japanese press operated with almost as much rigidity as the rest of the system. Although the big papers covered events at home and abroad with a thoroughness unequaled by all but a few of the best American dailies, there was a dreary sameness to them, and their lack of distinctiveness served to emphasize the homogeneity that characterized so much of Japanese life. This was largely due to the "club" system, whereby reporters from all papers covering a ministry, agency or the Prime Minister's office, for example, collectively agreed to select and share each day's news and avoid scoops. Investigative reporting was virtually unknown until recently, when a monthly magazine's disclosure of the wealth and manipulations of former Prime Minister Kakuei Tanaka led to his resignation and helped set the stage for the Lockheed scandal.

The press criticized the government frequently, but it did so blandly and with restraint, tending to be carping and negative rather than constructive and positive. As for television, it involved itself in even fewer controversial issues than the newspapers did. Although there were some good educational channels, including linguistic instruction hours, the commercial channels were primarily devoted to often erotic entertainment, including scatalogical jokes and risqué skits, to interminable talk and audience-participation programs, and to sumo wrestling, baseball and other sports. The government-owned NHK presented plenty of news and some analysis but did not permit its staff to express any firm editorial opinions.

The Japanese labor movement, one of the largest and most paternalistic in the world, had 12 million members by 1978, almost half of whom belonged to Sohyo, the most militant of the four national federations. Though not as radical as they were in the immediate postwar years, many of the unions that belonged to Sohyo or worked with it, such as the teachers union, were still Marxist-oriented, and Sohyo as a whole gravitated ideologically toward the left-wing socialists, who in the political spectrum were closer to the Communists than to the right-wing socialists. While Sohyo believed in utilizing political struggles to achieve economic gains, the more moderate Japanese Workers Confederation, or Domei—which, with 2.25 million members, was the second most influential of the four major federations—was in favor of democratic unionism and was more willing than Sohyo to work out compromises with management. Since the Japanese unions were organized by company units rather than horizontally on an industry-wide basis, as in the United States and Europe, the annual spring "offensive," called *shunto,* was primarily a political-pressure exercise but not a class struggle, and despite short, symbolic work stoppages, final negotiations were usually resolved amicably between individual companies or groups of companies and unions, although sometimes the settlements covered a broader industry-wide scope.

During the 1974 spring *shunto,* 6 million workers combined to conduct the most effective short strikes in years. The resulting 33 percent average wage increases did much to worsen inflation. In the ensuing four years, in deference to the slowdown in the economy, the unions reverted to a more moderate course and the wage increases averaged between 9 and 12 percent. Increasingly over the past few years, labor has stressed the need for more welfare programs and for broader pension systems. As its orientation became more middle-class, and as workers demanded more leisure time in a lower-growth society, their ideas about participation in politics were likely to alter some of the rigidities that had marked their voting habits to date. And as the opposition party spectrum shifted, if these parties gained a greater voice in decision making, and proved their maturity, the responses of workers, as of others, were bound to change as well.

Crisis in Education

The third Tokyo institution with vast national influence is Tokyo University, or Todai for short, whose alumni, it has often been said, runs Japan. Eight of the country's fourteen postwar prime ministers, up to and including Masayashi Ohira, were graduated from Todai—a nationally financed institution—along with a third to a half of the ranking members of the bureaucracy and a high proportion of the top business executives. Considering the fact that there are more than a hundred state and public universities in the country, and nearly three hundred private institutions, this is an inordinately high percentage, and the influence of Todai far exceeds that of Oxford and Cambridge in England, or of the Ivy League universities in America. One of the few other institutions with anywhere near this influence is Kyoto University, though many of the better private universities, such as Keio and Waseda, also in Tokyo, train leading businessmen as well as senior executives of various ministries. Founded in 1877 as Tokyo University and renamed Tokyo Imperial University in 1897, Todai was designed to create an administrative elite for government service, and although in the postwar period a growing number of students from poor families were able to pass its difficult entrance examinations—the toughest in the country—by far the majority of students were still sons and daughters of the rich and powerful. Particularly influential were graduates of the Todai law school, who became the dominant force in the Japanese power hierarchy.

One of the major changes taking place in Japan in the late seventies was a move toward relaxing and democratizing the rigid educational system all the way up from the elementary to the university level. This began in 1974 when, during the maverick and reformist prime-ministership of Takeo Miki, the Education Ministry was headed by a prominent newspaper commentator and educator named Michio Nagai, and it continued when Prime Minister Takeo Fukuda took over and Toshiki Kaifu, one of the younger liberal LDP leaders, headed the ministry. The reforms instituted by Nagai and carried on by Kaifu were nothing short of revolutionary and, if implemented fully, would undoubtedly prove to be as significant as any other instrumentalities of change in Japanese society.

Education in Japan, after it was released from the rigid formulas of the past under the occupation, soon became as highly competitive and remorseless an enterprise as industrial growth. Beginning at the kindergarten level, youngsters were subjected to constant strains and pressures all of which were geared to climbing the ladder of success—ultimate acceptance in business or government as part of the establishment. Stringent examinations to get into the best schools and colleges, and then to do well enough to progress from rung to rung toward the goal of a good job, created psychological and emotional strains which drove both parents and students to the brink of nervous collapse, and not infrequently to suicide. Failing an examination at any one of the rungs became a family disaster. Cram schools to prepare for examinations or to win an applicant a second chance became a national institution. Educational success was not only a goal but a mania. Mothers, driving their sons and daughters up the education ladder while their husbands were engaged in similar struggles in the business world, were known as "Education Mammas." As a result of the passion for education, 40 percent of high school graduates, or about one of every four young men and women between eighteen and twenty-two, attended a college or university.

The goals outlined by Nagai and then by Kaifu included the establishment, by 1979, of uniform entrance tests for candidates to 120 so-called national, municipal and prefectural universities. The 300 private senior colleges and universities were more reluctant to join the program but the government hoped to obtain their compliance gradually, and meanwhile it was instituting plans, under a new law, to give more financial assistance to these schools because many of them were in trouble. One of the overall objectives, according to Nagai, was to diversify the university structure. "We want more peaks than just Todai," he says. "Mount Fuji may be beautiful, but a mountain of eight peaks instead of just one is far more beautiful." In addition, the curriculum for primary and secondary schools was transformed, starting in 1978, to include the rewriting of textbooks by 1980. The objective, Nagai said, was to reduce the school workload by 10 percent. "In the sixties and early seventies, there was rapid growth and we had a technological and informational revolution. Too much was forced down students' throats—they had too big a menu. Now we want to make things simpler and less demanding, and we will be more selective and concentrate on basic knowledge."

In cooperation with the more liberal elements in the big-business federations, the reformist educators, who still faced a strong opposition in the traditionally conservative Ministry of Education, hoped to persuade the big corporations to change their ways, and to accept and promote young university graduates on the basis of their ability and aptitude rather than their academic background alone. "All of this will take a generation to achieve," Kaifu said, "but we have at least made a start. We want to retain our national sense of diligence and hard work among students, but increase their sense of social responsibility."

The educational reforms, while on the whole commendable, might serve to increase university attendance further, but might also lower the prestige of students, which had been on the decline anyway. Already, with 1.7 million students in colleges and universities, there was a serious surplus, according to some critics. Herbert Passin, of Columbia University, one of America's foremost experts on Japan, has noted: "One result is that the universities have become even more stratified than they used to be in terms of social ranking, facilities, quality of faculty, quality of students, and the kinds of access they open up into Japanese society." There were not enough "suitable" jobs for university graduates, he added, and consequently they "are obliged to lower their aspirations several steps and go into work careers that often leave them feeling demeaned and cheated." More and more of them were forced to take blue-collar jobs instead of managerial posts, competing with middle-school graduates, and at the white-collar level, with high school graduates. "If the rate of university attendance continues to rise, the problem will be very serious indeed," Passin said.

The demand by students entering the work force for "more purpose and meaning in their lives, and in their work as well, for more visible rewards, and more adventure out of their work," was leading to a questioning of traditional values and authority. As the younger generation became less compliant and demanded more participation in the making of decisions, the consensus system itself was likely to be challenged, becoming horizontal instead of purely vertical. While the Japanese seem passive, their sense of rebellion is always latent, and there is no doubt that dissatisfaction with the quality and nature of government is growing; witness statistics that showed 40 percent of all voters no longer having any party preferences. Young voters in particular were expressing their political apathy. Whether this might lead to an actual breakdown of the parliamentary system, as some authorities suggested, seems a still-doubtful proposition. But the general discontent and restlessness that was pervasive among Japanese youth was something that was not to be discounted, and it could, if the current economic and social strains continued, have serious political consequences, provoking a new and perhaps even a dangerous instability and a further questioning of fundamental precepts.

From Kishi to Ikeda

Periods of social rebellion and instability had occurred before in postwar Japan, but they invariably were of short duration. At the end of the seventies, however, the issues were broader, more universal and more complicated. Many Japanese political leaders, both past and present, had become increasingly aware that in the era of economic change education, for example, was only one of the many facets of a society in a state of transition. In a long illuminating conversation I had with Nobosuke Kishi (who became Prime Minister early in 1957 and held the office for three critical years), he said that, in retrospect, he felt the economy had grown too fast and had overstimulated Japanese society as a whole. In his eighties, but still sharp and spry, Kishi, who was one of the principal engineers of the merger that created the Liberal Democratic Party, said, "I was actually an advocate of a stable growth rate of about eight percent a year, but the boy was fed too much and got too fat. One of the results has been the assumption in Japan that money can buy anything and everything. We have to recover the old Japanese virtues of thrift and saving, as well as develop our own resources. The people's sense of morality has been badly neglected. We attained economic prosperity without enough spiritual development."

As Prime Minister, Kishi had tried to force through a new system whereby teachers in all elementary and secondary schools would be rated by their superiors according to aptitude and attitude and ability to introduce moral education in the schools, something the occupation had more or less eliminated. His approach, however, was too traditional and was fought by the leftist Japanese Teachers Union, which conducted a number of strikes throughout the country, some of which were violent. Eventually a national rating system was dropped in favor of a compromise whereby local districts could decide how to handle the problem. Kishi then ran into trouble when he tried to ram a bill through the Diet to increase the powers of the police by giving them the right to search individuals for concealed weapons and to take "preventive" steps to forestall crimes and disorders. The opposition felt that such a measure would pave the way for the re-establishment of a police state, and when Kishi forced an extension of the Diet to try to pass the bill, a general strike of 4 million workers took place, and the refusal of the Socialists to participate in further discussion of the measure led to rejection of the bill.

Less than two years later, in the spring of 1960, Kishi faced his greatest struggle over the revision of the 1951 security treaty with the United States. The treaty issue prompted not only the sharpest confrontation between left- and right-wing elements since the end of the war, but also involved was the basic and still continuing conflict between the desire of many Japanese to re-establish their full independence, their identity in Japanese terms, and the urge to maintain a close relationship with their American tutors and protectors. Kishi drove ahead mercilessly and forced a vote of approval through the lower house amid partisanship so intense that there were physical struggles among members. The reaction led to a general strike of 5.5 million workers and to demonstrations by 6 million students and union members. It was the biggest confrontation in postwar Japan. As a result of the opposition action, the scheduled visit of President Dwight Eisenhower was canceled, and though Kishi won his fight for approval of the treaty, his harsh approach and tough tactics led to his resignation. In a significant and frank comment to me fifteen years later, he said, "I should have dismissed the Diet sooner, waited until tempers died down, and allowed the people to express their ideas in a new election."

The experience had been a traumatic one for all the Japanese, let alone Kishi, and after it was over, they wanted a period of calm and fresh concentration on what they were best at—rapid economic growth. The man who took Kishi's place as Prime Minister, Hayato Ikeda, was ideally suited for that purpose. Where Kishi was the last of the prewar old guard, Ikeda was a representative of the postwar world. A favorite of the *zaikai,* he was at the same time a more outgoing, gregarious person, a Kyoto graduate with a precise mathematical mind. As one Japanese friend of mine put it, "After the Harvard-Yale types from Todai, he was the man from Detroit." Adopting a low profile, Ikeda listened to and followed the advice of an exceptionally able bureaucratic brain trust he gathered around him, which conceived the "income doubling" policy, whereby the Japanese people were to double their incomes in a decade. The principal authors of the policy were Saburo Okita and another brilliant economist named Osamu Shimomura. The two men projected a 7 or 8 percent annual growth rate, but as it developed, the average rate of growth for the first four years after 1960 was 11 1/2 percent, despite a recession in 1962, and the income-doubling policy was revised upward. After another recession in 1965, when the "overheated" economy had to be slowed down by government credit restrictions, the country's average yearly growth was 12 1/2 percent from 1966 through 1969. The basic economic philosophy behind the long-term plan that was devised, Okita explained, lay in its emphasis on importing more technology and applying it to domestic production, with the result that productivity would increase faster than consumption or wages and thus make Japanese prices more competitive at lower prices abroad.

As domestic demand increased with higher wages, so did foreign demand for better Japanese products at reasonable prices. The range of exports expanded quickly to include more high-quality consumer goods, such as cameras and electronic devices, and then heavy-industrial products, including steel and ships. The international climate for most of these products was consistently favorable, and as trade increased around the world, Japan became the chief beneficiary, despite a strict policy of limiting imports. The "economy first" principle adopted by both government and business meant that official policy was always oriented to more production, fed by more and more imported raw materials, while the low value of the yen gave the busy Japanese an added competitive advantage. Productivity became a higher goal than profits as Japan competed in more and more fields, and individual ambition was subjugated to the greater good of raising the annual gross national product, which by the early seventies was third only to that of the United States and the Soviet Union, reaching $400 billion. Invading foreign markets with more and more goods became, in effect, a holy crusade; the fact that this made the Japanese increasingly unpopular did little to slow down the process.

Impacts of Change

The description "Japan, Inc." came to be commonly used to describe the national purpose and achievement, and one American management consultant, James Abegllen, wrote that the term denoted "a special kind of corporation: a conglomerate in United States terms. . . . a *zaibatsu* of *zaibatsu.*" However, not all economists accepted the Japan, Inc. thesis unquestioningly. The Brookings Institution, for example, in a lengthy series of essays published in 1976 under the title "Asia's New Giant—How the Japanese Economy Works," pointed out that while a consensus between business and government on economic goals and the means of obtaining them certainly had existed all along, as well as a common ideology and set of values, it could not simplistically be said that government controlled business in Japan—the Japan, Inc. thesis —or that business controlled government, which was the "monopoly capitalism, or 'America, Inc.' thesis." The government was not monolithic or united, the authors argued, since there were "substantial differences between the LDP and the central government administrative bureaucracy," while there was not total consensus among the government ministries either because "each ministry in fact has its own special constituency and its own perception of the 'national interest.' " Business, too, was competitive, and experienced its own conflicts of interest. The authors logically concluded that "a pluralist interpretation of the distribution of power in economic decision-making was more useful in understanding Japan's contemporary political economy."

While these arguments became more tenable in the past few years of recession and change, my own view has been that a basic and functional consensus on all important matters affecting the role of business and government is still extremely strong, and that at least in these areas Japan remains, in effect, a guided elitist autocracy. If the political landscape changed drastically—as a result of the rising discontent among young voters and women voters, among other reasons—the Japan, Inc. thesis undoubtedly would be further weakened, and it might also lose its validity if Japan was persuaded by increasing international pressure to be less of a driven "economic animal" and became more of an international partner with Europe and the United States, both in matters of trilateral trade and in approaches to the developing nations. If, on the other hand, the Japanese reacted differently and felt themselves impinged upon and treated unfairly, and if they consequently were made to feel more isolated and apart than they have always felt historically, the Japan, Inc. philosophy and psychology could be defensively resuscitated, with undoubted dire results that not only could provoke economic warfare but could prompt a move by Japan to rearm and possibly go nuclear. The interplay of these various countervailing forces, ranging from a sense of rebelliousness among young people to a stubborn, defensive reaction within the establishment over maintaining Japan's economic prerogatives, has created a potentially dangerous and explosive situation. The arguments in 1978 and 1979 about protectionism and a reduction of Japanese exports were manifestations of this growing conflict.

The affluence of the sixties and early seventies—the period that led to the predicaments of the later era of questionable affluence and protectionism—brought about many changes in Japan. As more money became available to spend, and was more evenly distributed, the Japanese began to enjoy themselves with a sense of abandon they had never displayed before, buying vast amounts of consumer goods, packing movies and night clubs, and taking trips around the country and abroad—invariably, as is their way, in groups. The 1964 Olympics in Tokyo symbolized the new national success, and the Japanese prepared for them with their customary vigor and zeal, building a fine new stadium and superhighways, though they hardly finished the construction in time. The Olympics spurred the purchase of hundreds of thousands of color television sets; the other new treasures of this period, cars and air conditioners, also enjoyed an upswing in sales. The Games were a way for Japan to display its prosperity and achievements to the rest of the world, and the Japanese took full advantage of the opportunity. But there were problems, too. Rapid growth had brought about a sharp increase in the size of the major cities—particularly Tokyo, Osaka and Nagoya, which together received more than 14 million migrants from the countryside in little over a decade. As more and more young people left the rural areas, farming began to be carried on by women and grandparents, and only improved mechanization and technology enabled productivity to be maintained. The government rice monopoly kept raising the price paid to farmers to avoid a further decline in the rural population, and as early as 1967, rice cost consumers twice as much as it had a decade earlier, and twice what it cost abroad. Aside from overcrowding in industrial cities, air, water and noise pollution increased rapidly, reaching a danger point and forcing the government to pass strict new measures to control them.

The Olympics marked a sort of watershed for Japan, epitomizing its success as a world economic power. The day after the Games ended, Ikeda resigned as Prime Minister because he was ill with cancer; he was succeeded by Eisaku Sato, who was Nobosuke Kishi's younger brother (the difference in names originated when Nobosuke was adopted by his wife's family, this being a common practice in Japan). Sato, another Todai man and then a bureaucrat before he entered politics as a protégé of former Prime Minister Yoshida in 1948, was not an innovator like Ikeda, but he was an extremely cautious, conservative man who, if he lacked brilliant ideas of his own, knew how to adapt and carefully apply those of others, always with an acute finger to the political wind. Though he served nearly eight years—longer than any other postwar Prime Minister—he failed to come to grips with the new problems of urbanization, which were beginning to affect the popularity of the rurally oriented LDP. Sato died in June 1975, but shortly before that, I was fortunate in having two long talks with him at his spacious house in Tokyo, where he had lived for thirty years. Like his brother Kishi and others, he admitted that "we may have placed too much emphasis on economic growth, and forgotten other vital things," though he took apparent personal pride in having shepherded Japan through the second half of the sixties' growth period and into the early seventies. He seemed to be somewhat ambivalently caught between this pride and a delayed recognition of his having failed to comprehend sooner some of the problems which Japan was facing. His chief accomplishment was his successful negotiation of the return of Okinawa to Japan by the Americans, which took place in 1972, and which he hailed as "the real end of the postwar period."

It would be more logical, from an economic point of view, to designate the oil crisis of 1973–1974 and the recession that followed as the significant turning point, or at least as the end of Japan's almost uninterrupted period of postwar growth. These facts, and the political events that marked the decline of the LDP and its struggle to revivify itself in the face of shifting tides and fortunes and such shocks as the Lockheed scandal, will be examined in a final section on Japan. Along with the continuing attempt by the Japanese to define a new world role for themselves, these critical domestic factors have constituted the most serious challenges the country has faced since the end of World War II. They took place at a time when subtle and surprising changes were occurring in Japanese society.

4-A Society Unto Itself

Perhaps more than any other people in the world, the Japanese have an insatiable curiosity about themselves, and a passion for self-analysis. Sometimes this only goes skin-deep and is part of their addiction to fads, involving both self-mockery and self-reassurance, but for the most part it is a genuine search for their own identity—a word, incidentally, that those who speak English often use but that has no counterpart in Japanese, save for one that conveys the meaning of "identical," or the notion of sameness. There is irony here, for the Japanese are constantly aware that they are different from other people, including other Asians. In many ways they would like to be not so different, and yet in most respects they are inordinately proud of their differences, and of their traditions that have engendered and protected the qualities and characteristics that have set them apart. There is a further paradox in the fact that despite their compulsion for modernization—what some observers have described as their "hunger mentality" to catch up with the West economically—they retain nostalgic images and romantic notions of their past, of what they sometimes call the "true Japan."

Part of this is attributable to their earlier and still residual belief that, as Kano Tsutomo, the editor of the *Japan Interpreter,* a quarterly published in English, has written, "The nation is not simply a collectivity of individuals" but "an entity that transcends the people both in time and space." No matter what the postwar constitution says, Tsutomo adds, "The emperor is the symbol of that transcendence," and "this concept of the nation as a suprahistorical entity" is more than just a remnant right-wing manifestation and is "something broadly Japanese." Even though the idea of a "true Japan" has become somewhat obscure, "it still exists somewhere in the depths of the Japanese mind," he says, "and every time the pendulum swings inward, this image is called back into active service."

When World War II ended, the Japanese were in a self-deprecatory mood, condemning not only themselves but many of their traditions, including that of *bushido,* which had helped provoke their costly militarist aberration. By the sixties, their rapid economic growth had provoked a new sense of nationalism and a "big power" mentality. The brief period of anti-Americanism espoused by the left wing gave way both to competition with and a new overdependence on the United States. The Japanese thereupon slowly regained their confidence and their belief in their old virtues and values. A somewhat similar process took place after the Meiji Restoration of 1868, when Japan was brought out of the isolation fostered by the Tokugawa Shogunate and began to accept and imitate Western patterns of industrialization, as well as many other Western forms and habits. Then they began to criticize the West; a rising nationalism led to the denunciation of the inequitable treaties that had been forced upon the country, and successful wars were waged against China and Russia. Ultimately, however, this led to ultramilitarism, dictatorship, and to the disastrous war against the United States and the West.

Modern Japan, as Tsutomo among others has noted, "has been neither fully Western nor fully Asian and yet it has aspired to more than full membership" in both worlds, and he cites this as "one of the most important sources of our identity crisis." Some commentators who have deplored Japan's having become an "economic beast" have been less than charitable in their analyses. Shintaro Ishihara, the author and sometime politician, has decried the "spiritual void at the core of the Japanese nation, a moral degradation that characterizes everything that happens in this society," adding that "Japanese have lost the heart of their ideological and spiritual frame of reference, and nothing has been found to substitute, not even after thirty years." This may be a bit harsh, though Ishihara is not alone in his opinions. Nevertheless, the sudden national curiosity about the Japanese personality and about the changes taking place in Japanese life—what intellectuals have called an "introspection boom" (the Japanese phrase is *nihonjin-ron*)—reflected a healthy if sometimes overheated concern about things that were previously considered rather private.

The Japanese sense of privacy derives from a number of things. Because Japanese society is multidimensional and multilayered but at the same time extremely compartmentalized, each member of it feels insecure in the expression of his own ego until he can clearly define his exact relationship with those with whom he regularly lives and deals, whether in the immediate surroundings of his family or in the larger context of the groups with which he has a professional connection. By thus charting the structure of his mutual dependence early in life—there is a special word for it, *amae*—the Japanese finds both strength and confidence, and once he has established his bearings he is more than likely to remain on course for the rest of his life, even as he grows older and the order of dependency alters. While this process is primarily a domestic phenomenon, it has also affected the conceptions that Japanese have of themselves in relation to the outside world, about which they have become increasingly less certain but with which they have begun to try harder to come to terms.

While the Japanese retain a strong sense of their superiority and rectitude, as well as pride in their ancient appreciation of beauty (despite the ugliness of most of their modern industrial cities), they seldom engage in the kind of specious self-praise and assertiveness that marked their prewar society, though these are qualities that sometimes still seem to come through in their dealings with foreigners. When this happens, and an "ugly Japanese" image emerges, it in fact masks a far greater degree of skepticism about the future and about themselves than they had a few years ago when they were riding high and when the same sort of image was more carelessly projected. After the oil crisis and recession sent their economy skittering, they were chastened but didn't really know what to do next, which is why they panicked initially and sent emissaries scurrying all over the Middle East in pursuit of Arab friendship. In the more rational introspective phase they are going through nowadays, they have become aware that their compulsive economic success of the past twenty years has failed to bring many amenities they should have had sooner, such as better housing and more social benefits. They have also suffered growing self-doubts about the vapidity, and even vulgarity, of much of their current cultural life, and about the negative effect their vaunted prosperity has had on both their professional and personal lives. One manifestation of this, despite an outward craving for participation in group activity whether travel, golf and tennis, attending baseball games or just sitting around coffee shops or drinking in cafés and bars, is a growing inclination to turn inward again and seek the refuge of one's own small dwelling—what some have called "my home–ism." Thus sometimes the pendulum seems to swing both ways simultaneously.

Tokyo's Melting Pot

The casual observer is not readily apt to discern these many contradictions in Japanese society. For example, a visitor to Tokyo, which, with the probable exception of Shanghai, is the biggest city in the world, has the feeling of moving up and down a giant escalator in a huge emporium where there are myriad enticing goods to see, touch and smell. With its flowing crowds and cars, its modern, highly efficient subways and trains, its never-ending construction and reconstruction, Tokyo is probably the busiest-sounding, though not necessarily the noisiest, of capitals—the most perceptible auditory sensation being a steady hum of activity not unlike the whirring of a tremendous generator that never stops. To escape this generator, which epitomizes their propulsive economic force, the urban Japanese have a particular private passion for quietude which they seldom reveal to foreigners but which has sustained them as a people apart from others, a people whose language is more silent than oral. The meaning of what they say to each other is often imparted, as they put it, "through the belly" (the Japanese word is *haragei*) and understood intuitively. While this privacy of communication has helped to keep them isolated, as they have been through the centuries more by choice than necessity, they have, especially in the last few years of flux and crisis, become increasingly aware not only of their apartness but also of the inherent fragility of their modern society. Hence the new introspection boom, which has resulted in dozens of books and hundreds of articles. Each new shock, such as the Lockheed scandal, projects a whole new spate of such publications, and a fresh orgy of self-criticism, even of flagellation. But these short-term phenomena of deprecatory self-appraisal are not to be confused with their more lasting search to find out who and what they are and where they are going in a disoriented and disjointed world.

In their constant effort to find out more about themselves and what they think, want and respect, the Japanese have developed a positive mania for conducting surveys on every conceivable subject. To judge by such data, they are not satisfied with their way of life, and the more comprehensive of these surveys, including the most recent of a series taken every five years by the Education Ministry, reveal a growing dissatisfaction, attributed mainly to overurbanization. (A Tokyo government study disclosed that the three greatest concerns were rising prices, pollution, and a lack of sufficient housing, followed in sequence by complaints about insufficient health care, inadequate garbage disposal, poor facilities for the aged, insufficient anti-disaster preparations—particularly for serious earthquakes—a paucity of parks and playgrounds, poor traffic controls, and the poor quality of schoolteachers.) Though the latest Education Ministry survey disclosed a continuing belief in *giri ninjo* —the traditional Japanese sense of duty and devotion, especially of obligation to one's family—it also showed a mounting distrust of government and a consequent political and social apathy. Whereas in 1963, at the start of Japan's rapid economic surge, a similar poll showed that 30 percent felt that scientific and technological growth could lead to a loss of "humanity," 50 percent felt this to be the case in 1973; 54 percent felt that while Japan had surpassed most Western countries as an economic power, it rated either "fairly bad" or "very bad" in richness of mind and spirit, and 64 percent felt that "peace of mind" would decrease further. Demonstrating the growing trend toward "my home– ism," 81 percent said they were generally satisfied with their home life, but only 26 percent were satisfied with the society in general.

Japanese youth, who were rebellious during the sixties, have diminished their activism over such larger issues as the security pact and the Vietnam war in recent years. But student demonstrations against such problems as higher fees, especially in the private colleges, where fees are five or six times higher than in the national universities, still take place on campuses, and small radical groups that used to form part of broader political fronts still engage in occasional violent and sometimes deadly internecine warfare. Although Japan has no serious drug problem by most European or American standards, recent statistics show that drug pushing is growing. In the last decade the amount of heroin impounded by the police increased by about ten times, and of hashish and grass thirteen times. The use of amphetamines is also on the rise, especially among adults. The police keep a careful watch on all drug traffic, but as Passin has pointed out, Japanese youth travel a lot more than they used to and "Japanese young people are very responsive to trends in the youth culture all over the world, and drugs, like marijuana, may be hard to keep out."

A government survey in 1971, before the current societal strains began to show, pointed out that while a large majority of youths questioned had close family ties, they felt themselves to be considerably closer to their mothers than to their fathers, no doubt because so many Japanese men after working all day spend their evenings together in restaurants or bars, or with their mistresses. Once enrolled in a decent college, however, many students tend to drift away from their families more than they used to, but since they don't establish particularly close substitute relationships with their teachers, they seem to sublimate their desire for companionship by joining athletic or social clubs or by meeting in coffee shops. Anthropologist Chie Nakane remarked, "Young people still search for security and they find it by belonging to groups, to more leisure as well as work groups. That's healthy because they can enjoy life more." Nakane added the interesting comment that because of Japan's continuing homogeneity and sense of isolation, "no real social comparison with others is possible, so we seek assurance of what we are."

The search for self-confidence and assurance, though it remains a dominant factor among contemporary Japanese youth, is accompanied by an increasing restlessness as well as a diminishing work ethic. A recent survey by the Prime Minister's office indicated that while 61 percent of college graduates were "fairly contented," they had no particularly strong psychological or emotional attachment to the companies they worked for—a significant shift from traditional Japanese attitudes. Complaints included insufficient wages, not enough vacations, and lack of close relationships with superiors. Younger employees seemed to feel that their special abilities were not taken advantage of and that the long climb up the promotional ladder toward retirement was no longer as worthwhile as it had once seemed. A general apathy was reflected in a widely expressed preference for easier, less tense and more pleasurable lives instead of just making money. Another survey, early in 1979, revealed that major corporations, for the first time in their postwar experience, were having difficulty recruiting young workers, while they were also having trouble persuading older employees to retire at fifty-five instead of at fifty-eight or sixty.

In two long conversations I had with groups of students in Tokyo and Kyoto, many of them expressed a need to define their own moral standards and values. As one youth put it, "There are a lot of ideas and ways of life we want to understand and explore that are different from those of our parents, who came from the generation of defeat and then of economic boom. The country is still in a state of digestion, and if we want to change things we have to digest more ideas from abroad, because there are so few we can find here." Most of those I talked with said they were not interested in politics but that they had, as one student pointed out, "tested the waters of radicalism in college, because a lot that our parents told us wasn't right." Then, realizing that they somehow had to make a living and prepare to support a family, they had been forced to "follow regulations" and plan to go to work. Others, however, wanted to get part-time jobs—some already had, even as waiters and waitresses, so they could make enough to get by and save for a trip abroad. "I'm proud of being a Japanese, but I don't want to be trapped and hemmed in," one said. "There is a danger, of course, of drifting too long, but I think a year or two of wandering would be right."

Attitudes of Youth

In speaking of the generation gap, many of the students cited contrasts in vocabulary as evidence. They use words and phrases not known by their mothers and fathers, they said, including titles and phrases from popular songs and cartoons, as well as such words as *resubian*—which is borrowed from English, like many words in modern Japanese, and means "lesbian." Incidentally, lesbianism, and homosexuality in general, is on the increase, especially in large cities like Tokyo; so is sexual freedom as a whole. A high percentage of the young men and women I saw, the men in particular, had no compunctions about premarital sexual relations, unlike their elders, despite the fact that their fathers have a long tradition of extramarital sex. While the well-off male can afford to keep a mistress, those who earn less money take full advantage of the love hotels and massage parlors that abound all over Japan. The traditional double standard is fully accepted, with wives relegated to home and duty while men are free to indulge in whatever pleasures they seek to pursue, including the demimonde, or *mizu-shobai*, of prostitutes and bar girls. But there are growing signs that the sexual revolution is catching up with women too. As traditional institutions break down, including family ties to a considerable extent, Japanese women are becoming far more independent and are demanding more equality. A women's-lib movement has burgeoned in the past few years, and women are playing an increasingly active role in leading consumer groups and other such organizations, and to some extent are becoming more active in politics. In the upper house election of July 1977, a Japan Woman's Party appeared for the first time and ran ten candidates, but it disbanded after failing to win any seats.

Despite these various manifestations of a greater personal freedom, Japanese society is still cast in a basically conservative mold. Old habits and forms of conduct seem bound to remain even as new ones impinge on them. The whole organized ritual, for example, of bowing according to rank, of exchanging business cards, of exchanging greetings and gifts in an exaggerated and formal manner still prevails, and in many ways it is part of the shell beneath which the individual hides his private self from all but his intimates. Drinking with friends in a favorite bar, the ordinary Japanese businessman sticks his head out of this shell for a few hours, often to engage in indiscriminate, disconnected and trite conversation. A deeper frustration with the hardships of life can lead to suicide or to running away, and there are thousands of cases a year of people, usually unhappy husbands and wives, simply disappearing; the police track down most of them.

The younger generation gives vent to its frustrations in various ways, sometimes moving to the edge of violence. There has been an upsurge of wild hot-rod motorcyclists and souped-up–sports-car gangs, called *sahkitto-zoku,* or "circuit-racing tribes." There are about five hundred such groups in the country, and more than two hundred in Tokyo alone, with names like Massacre, Black Emperor, Spectre, Medusa and Outlaw. The favorite weekend pastime of such tribes, whose members ordinarily wear leather jackets, blue jeans and rock-age hairdos, is to tear through the city's traffic mazes at the highest possible speed or to engage in highly competitive drag racing. Some of the hot-rodders have established relationships with local gangsters and engage in fights to "defend their turf," and in 1976 the police reported fifty cases in which young girls, lured by the fascination of the new breed of speed demons, were gang-raped.

The overall Japanese crime rate, especially in the big cities, is astonishingly low compared to the incidence of crime in foreign cities, though after decreasing for several years, it took a swing upward in 1976, when police reported a sharp increase in murders and crimes committed by women as well as in juvenile crimes. Statistics on petty theft and "intellectual crimes," mostly bribery, also showed some increase. And the level of corruption rose, partly in connection with the competition for scarce land and with the profiteering that was contributing to rampant inflation. But the still generally low rate of crime is attributed to various factors, including rigid gun control, the dominant national sense of self-discipline and duty, and the sense of shame if one is arrested. The 42,500 members of Tokyo's highly efficient police force function mainly through a network of more than 1,200 police boxes, called *koban,* which cover every neighborhood, and the police have the voluntary help of civilian block captains, each of whom is responsible for about thirty households. This is a mild reflection of the old neighborhood surveillance system of the prewar and wartime days, but today's police are invariably mild-mannered and helpful, treating drunks and other disorderly persons far more leniently than New York police do.

Fumihiko Kunashima, one of Tokyo's top police superintendents, told me, when I asked him why there was relatively little violent crime in Japan, "We are all Japanese here. We have strong family and mutual relationships, and are accustomed to helping each other, to working hard and supporting ourselves." Nevertheless, not to be discounted is the existence of more than 2,500 organized gangs called *boryokudan,* and this gang world, known as the *yakuza,* is akin to the Mafia in the West, controlling prostitution, gambling and some sports, as well as engaging in widespread black marketeering and blackmail. The police do very little about the *yakuza,* and, in fact, are often tied into it, since the top leaders, such as Yoshio Kodama, one of the principal defendants in the Lockheed scandal, have been deeply involved in politics and are still regarded as powerful and influential Godfather figures.

Changing Population Trends

Japanese society over the past twenty years has been affected in many ways by population changes. Following a postwar baby boom, in which the population soared from 72 million to 80 million in three years, the birth rate declined by half during the fifties, due chiefly to the Eugenic Protection Law of 1948, which permitted abortions for specified physical and economic reasons. By 1965 contraception was more important in limiting births, but because of a shortage of younger workers in the past few years it has become more difficult to obtain abortions for economic reasons, and while contraceptive pills are available in drugstores, they are theoretically supposed to be sold only to regulate menstruation but not to prevent conception. In the past twenty years the birth rate has remained fairly stable, at about 18 per 1,000, but the death rate has declined from nearly 11 per 1,000 in 1950 to 7 per 1,000, and the natural increase in the country's population, now 113 million, is about 12 per 1,000 a year, or roughly 1 percent.

In the coming five to ten years, the government has warned, "the change that will occur in the age distribution of the population will be extremely irregular and will probably give rise to profound economic and social consequences." The segment of the population aged between fifteen and twenty-nine will drop by 4 million, while the thirty-to-forty bracket will increase by the same amount; the group between forty-five and fifty-nine will rise by 5.7 million; and the number of those over sixty will increase by about 1 million. The government says that no other country has ever experienced such an irregular change of the population over a decade, and that these demographic shifts will make it "extremely difficult to supplement the younger labor force." While more women are seeking jobs—they now represent more than a third of all employees—they are also attending universities in greater numbers than ever before, which has delayed their entry into the work force.

During the early sixties, when the movement from rural to metropolitan areas was at its height, the six largest cities in Japan increased in population by 50 percent. People moved to the urban centers primarily to find better jobs, with the search for better living conditions a secondary factor. Sociologists have pointed out that urbanization and industrialization in Japan caused less social disruption than it did in the cities of Western Europe and the United States, and that this has been due to basic community concepts such as work groups and other social or religious organizations that helped supplement family networks. However, there are recent signs that the urban community structure is beginning to break down. In the seventies, during what the government calls the "second internal migration," people evinced a greater desire to seek a good residential environment. As this attitude grew stronger, the attraction of living in big polluted cities diminished, and life in the rural areas no longer seemed so unrewarding. Migration to the larger cities has continued, but the pace has slackened, and many villagers decided to stay put and seek part-time jobs in nearby towns instead. In the years ahead, the internal migration pattern is expected to show a return of individuals and families to their regions of origin, though not necessarily to their hometowns. This is what Japanese demographers call a "J turn"—in contrast to a "U turn," which denotes those who do go back to their old villages. Already many small communities are trying to lure former residents back by finding new jobs for them, at home or in nearby places.

Part of this movement away from crowded cities represents a manifestation of the search for old values, what some experts describe as a coming revival of localism, and this is likely to have interesting political as well as social implications. Kimitada Miwa, a professor at Sophia University, in Tokyo, believes that historically, Japanese nationalism may have been the result of the suppression of local or regional desires and aspirations. Eventually, he thinks, the ultranationalists subverted the process, and as they became stronger, used local issues and traditions for their own purposes. "You could say that Japanese pan-Asianism before and during the Second World War was the result of suppressed localism," Miwa says. "Now there is an effort to recapture local characteristics and identities."

Hajime Nakamura, a well-known professor of Oriental philosophy, commented that "a lot of people want to restore the lost spirit of the nation, but it has to be done properly, and not demagogically." He noted that while Shintoism is no longer a state religion, it remains popular, and many young people go to Shinto shrines. "The bedrock remains," he said. "People get married in a Shinto ceremony, and when they die they have Buddhist funerals. Meanwhile our conservative leaders often cite Zen aphorisms when they want to be elusive and evasive." More people are also taking an interest in famous shrines as part of the revival of traditionalism. Each year the crowds get larger at the Sengakuji temple, in Tokyo, where they burn incense and throw flowers over the graves of the forty-seven brave *ronin*—the loyal warriors who, early in the eighteenth century, avenged the hara-kiri of their lord by killing the evil official who had forced him to it, and then committed mass suicide. Similarly, the Japanese revere the Ise Grand Shrine, which for the past thirteen centuries has been rebuilt every twenty years. Shoichi Suzuki, one of the priests, says, "Ise is a place for the Japanese to pause, to put aside their technical skills for a moment, their moneymaking, their Western masks, and to become Japanese again."

This attachment to the past, much of which has a pantheistic motivation, also includes a nostalgic retention of ceremonial forms, partly as a kind of convenient defense mechanism. One of them is the *miai*, the system of professional matchmaking: a young man and a young woman will be formally introduced by a matchmaker even if they have met before and become interested in each other, or the matchmaker will make a ritualistic appearance at the engagement ceremony. Form is thus preserved, though the matchmaker becomes little more than a master of ceremonies.

Otis Cary, an American-born professor of literature at Doshisha University, in Kyoto, who has lived in Japan more than a quarter of a century, is among the small group of long-time foreign residents who is acutely aware of the changes taking place in Japanese society at the same time that older values are retained. "In particular, personal relationships are being altered," he says. "But there are many fundamental strains that remain—what I call 'subterranean passages' of the society. These include some basic supports that a Japanese can count on, and that anchor him back into the culture whenever he feels the need for it. Among them are such things as Nō and kabuki plays, judo, *kempo*, karate, flower and tea ceremonies, sand painting, the cultivation of bonsai, calligraphy, and so on. These are the things that help shore the Japanese up, that keep them from falling into a void."

Another perceptive American observer, Donald Richie, a literary, film and theater critic, is impressed by the fact that while they have doubts about their world role, the Japanese "never seem to doubt their Japaneseness." He adds, "Behind any single Japanese looms his country and his culture, the larger order, or tribe, of which he is a member. His individual decisions are always tempered, if not dictated by this. Socially and politically the Japanese is not his own man because he is such a loyal member of the home team, a rooter and a booster. Japan remains a primitive tribe which has achieved extraordinary technology. By primitive one means basic, that is, adjusted, in this case to a natural world that no longer exists. It is the technology itself which has destroyed it, but, oddly, not the primitive social structure upon which it is presumably based. The country, moreover, has a remarkable adhesive quality: same color hair, nearly same color eyes, the last homogeneous culture—this country of cousins. It makes for the most extraordinary cooperative displays. After a disaster the Japanese band together like ants after a flood. And yet, at the same time, the Japanese seem to have more 'selves' than the Westerner could ever have. The Japanese has a social self—he willingly and happily can become what we'd call a cog, a mere unit in a corporation, and he can do this with no fear or apparent loss. He can melt into a demonstration, or a crowd. On the other hand, the same person has his own 'self'—the solitary person that he is and no one else. The Japanese thus has, by Western standards, a plethora of selves, but his larger sense of loyalty constantly applies itself not only to country but to such country-surrogates as school, factory, and so on. So selflessness, in this sense, beyond being a virtue, is one of the essential qualities of being Japanese. And an experienced foreigner comes to realize that by dealing with *a* Japanese one is eventually dealing with *the* Japanese—all of them."

The Importance of Amae

One of the most important aspects of the Japanese personality, and a key to an understanding of the whole society, is *amae*, the sense of mutual dependence. *Amae* has been thoroughly explained by Dr. Takeo Doi, a brilliant clinical psychiatrist, with whom I had two fascinating talks in his office at Tokyo University; his book *The Anatomy of Dependence* is regarded throughout the world as one of the best analyses of the Japanese character. The *amae* relationship, according to Dr. Doi, starts in infancy, when a child begins to *amaeru* (this is the verb) toward his mother, depending on her breast for food. In this, the infant is no different from infants elsewhere, but subsequently, in the special hierarchical Japanese society—involving the highly intricate relationships a man establishes with his peers and with those above and below him in rank and status, both on an individual basis and within the group-oriented world that dominates so much of his life—*amae* becomes the determining force of an adult's actions and responses. Most Japanese behavior is thus influenced by such dependency relationships and also, conversely, by the frustration of an unfulfilled relationship. The vocabulary, logic and pathology of *amae*, Dr. Doi says, are peculiarly Japanese, and there are no Western words or concepts that can specifically explain their substance and meaning.

Closely related to awareness of self (the Japanese word is *jibun*), *amae* is also associated with that other fundamental Japanese characteristic, *giri ninjo*, which Dr. Doi defines as "social obligation and human feeling." The relationships that the Japanese establish throughout their lives are, in essence, defined by these words, and a man lives by affirming or denying his capacity to *amaeru*. "We are all *amae*-ridden," Dr. Doi told me. John Bester, the English translator of Dr. Doi's book, aptly sums this up at the end of his foreword: "Only a mentality rooted in *amae* could produce a people at once so unrealistic yet so clear-sighted as to the basic human condition; so compassionate and so self-centered; so spiritual and so materialistic; so forebearing and so wilful; so docile and so violent—a people, in short, that from its own point of view is preeminently normal and human in every respect."

In present-day Japan, Dr. Doi feels, "social relationships no longer allow the individual to *amaeru* as easily as in the past; or, he adds, "it may be that society has become so complex that it is no longer easy to discover the rules whereby one may *amaeru* with ease." At the same time, he does not regard the generation gap as serious except insofar as it represents "the older generation's loss of self-confidence." But, as a psychiatrist, he has numbers of patients who demonstrate depression—rather than anxiety—deriving from a loss of firm goals in their lives and from the inability, as they have expressed it, "to melt into others"; that is, to *amaeru* successfully. He has also observed an increasing incidence of a phobia expressed in a morbid fear of crowds and public places, and he thinks this may partly account for the growing "my home–ism," or turning inward. The apathy of many students and their desire to drift, he says, also reflect this.

The Japanese consensus society is "a token satisfaction of *amae*," in Dr. Doi's terms. Similarly, *amae* accounts for the fact that legal differences between individuals are invariably settled out of court, and corporate cases by arbitration. The whole process is closely tied to special ways of communicating and to the language itself. Elsewhere, Dr. Doi has written: "That the Japanese language is so constructed as to be particularly conducive to the effect of ambiguity is well known. For instance, Japanese verbs come at the end of the sentence. Therefore, unless and until you hear the whole sentence, you wouldn't know where the speaker stands. This apparently gives him a psychological advantage, as he can change his position in anticipation of your possible reaction to it. However, it may happen that you are often left wondering whether he really means what he says."

The lack of pronouns in everyday conversation also results in ambiguity, while conjunctions, which in English provide logical connections, in Japanese "more often . . . serve only to cement and induce the speaker's free associations." Masao Kunihiro, a cultural anthropologist, says that "in Japanese, there is a sense of leisurely throwing a ball back and forth and observing each other's response," whereas, in contrast, "in the language of the West, logic and reason are continuously tossed between speaker and listener as if one's identity were constantly being questioned, and throughout there is a sense of reinforcing each other's independence." Kunihiro, who speaks fluent English, says that even so, when he does, "I feel like Dr. Jekyll and Mr. Hyde, as if somehow I have put on a disguise . . . something akin to the enjoyment of wearing a mask." The Japanese refer to "round" and "square" language. When they talk seriously, especially with foreigners but also among themselves, they use "square" language; when they relax, in bars or elsewhere, they talk "round," giving vent to their personal feelings. In serious conversations among themselves, their frequent long silences represent a fishing for clues to determine where each participant stands. They may also hesitate or hold back because of their fear that what they say will be disagreeable to others, especially when they have to express dissent, and this is also related to *amae*, for dissent destroys the proper sense of dependence, or overpresumes. As Dr. Doi says, "Americans hate silence, whereas Japanese can sit together comfortably without saying a word to one another," gathering by intuition what they mean and feel. Dr. Doi says that when he first went to the United States, "I was greatly surprised, almost perturbed, by the fact that Americans love to talk incessantly whenever they get together, even during the meal. As a matter of fact, they sounded to me almost hypomanic."

Professor Chie Nakane believes that the sense of *amae* is decreasing somewhat because "of lack of time, among other reasons, and because we want more things constantly. Excitement is necessary here whether it's bad or good —though a lot of the desire for change is superficial—and we can't stay with one thing too long." The increasing freedom to act in different ways challenges the group structure and, to a degree, diminishes efficiency, but she feels that what she calls the "vertical principle," which she elaborated in her book *Japanese Society,* will not be seriously altered. The principle is shaped by what she calls the "attribute" and the "frame"—the frame is the locality, the institution or the company, while the attribute refers to the situation and condition of those within it. Thus, a lathe operator and his foreman represent attributes, and the company they work for is the frame. The company becomes the *ie,* or the household, as Professor Nakane sees it, and dominates a man's existence, both socially and professionally. His *amae* relationship has been transferred from family to firm, and the spirit and purpose of the company pervade the life of all employees, who engage, for example, in the fervid singing of company songs.

In the vertical society, rank applies outside the company as well as within it, so that a man of lower status and his wife, if they meet a fellow employee of higher position in a restaurant or on the street, will defer to him, bowing lower. An employee seeking a decision or an opinion will never leap-frog over his immediate superior to obtain it, for that would be considered insulting and detrimental to his own fortunes. This paternalistic *oyabun-kobun* (literally, parent-child) relationship predominates in all areas of Japanese life, as does the system of group loyalties. This helps sustain the discipline needed for tremendous material progress, but it also has disadvantages. Because various competing groups have limited links with one another, "they lack a sociological framework on which to build up a complete and integrated society," Professor Nakane says. Central authority is so overweening that it "implants in the Japanese a ready submissiveness, alongside fear and hostility." Obedience becomes total submission. Opposition to authority is usually seen as a form of heroism; intellectuals hail it as "democratic action," but it seldom works, and is often opposition for opposition's sake alone. More often a company employee, faced with the vast rigidity of daily life, turns to his colleagues for consolation, and they protect and side with him, whether he is right or wrong, in his personal and sometimes his professional affairs. This is perhaps the main reason the after-work bar is so important in Japan. Men openly admit, "I can't live without a bar," and the bar has a function of its own, which neither wife nor mistress can duplicate.

A Yearning to Belong

Both Professor Nakane and Dr. Doi spoke of the growth of old and new Buddhist sects in Japan over the past several years, agreeing that this was a sign of people seeking fresh outlets for their frustrations and new sources of identity. The largest of these groups is Soka Gakkai, which has 20 million members in the country and is based on the tenets of the thirteenth-century priest Nichiren Daishonin. Dr. Doi does not consider Soka Gakkai politically dangerous, as some others do, "because it is too religious a movement to go either left or right," but he admits that a certain danger could arise if "those who run it and belong to it become too self-righteous." Professor Nakane made the point that though Soka Gakkai cuts across the hierarchical structure—its members come from all walks of life—it, too, is thoroughly organized along vertical lines, with a member's loyalty belonging to the person who converted him and to the particular small group, or cell, to which he is attached. Most of its members belong to the urban lower-middle or poorer classes, and it has considerably more women than men. Each member is urged to contribute to society as best he can by, among other things, converting others in his neighborhood, school or factory to Soka Gakkai's cause. Despite its essential religious character, Soka Gakkai plays an important, behind-the-scenes political role by means of Komeito, the Clean Government Party, which became its political arm in 1964 but has since severed formal relations while welcoming its continued support. Komeito members in the Diet and in local prefectures are active in promoting welfare plans and other reforms, and the party, while it is unlikely to become a dominant force, is an increasingly important part of the opposition, though it has recently moved closer to the LDP and could eventually be a major part of a new conservative or middle-of-the-road coalition, especially if the LDP continues to slip in popularity.

The leader of Soka Gakkai until he suddenly resigned in April 1979 was Daisaku Ikeda—he had been president since 1960. I had a long interview with him in 1975 just after he had returned from a visit to China and was preparing to go to the Soviet Union with a view to promoting peace. Ikeda is an impressive, heavy man in his late forties, with a broad face, deep brown eyes and a resonant voice. He was dressed impeccably, in a blue suit with a white shirt and blue tie, which made him look like any other Japanese executive, and he greeted me with an elaborate bow and handshake at the entrance of one of the many offices and temples that Soka Gakkai has throughout Tokyo and elsewhere (including a large university campus on the city's outskirts). Ikeda is a prolific writer, and having written several books on Buddhist doctrine, had just finished the eighth volume of a historical novel about the movement. At the outset of our talk he discussed the contrast between the great progress Japan has made in the past twenty years and "the lack of purpose in our lives." He said that he looked upon Soka Gakkai as "middle-of-the-road Buddhism, based on the principle of humanism," and added that "our main aim is to avoid any extremism of left or right in the country—we can serve as an important buffer." He had visited thirty-five countries over the past few years, and the two men he had met who had impressed him most were Arnold Toynbee and André Malraux.

I came away from our conversation impressed with Ikeda's sincerity and graciousness but with a lingering reservation about the Soka Gakkai movement as a whole. With its amorphous, largely ignorant and inchoate membership, ranging from bar girls to discontented employees of big companies, it could at a time of stress become someone else's political instrument. Though Ikeda, in mid-1975, conducted a long public dialogue with Kenji Miyamoto, chairman of the Presidium of the Japan Communist Party, during which the two men agreed to respect each other's viewpoints and seek further mutual understanding, Soka Gakkai remains probably more of a potential right-wing than a left-wing threat. Now under new leadership, its future is more difficult to predict.

A number of people I spoke with in Japan referred to "togetherness" as "the cancer of the country," and it is certainly true that despite their penchant for withdrawing into themselves, the Japanese, whether through such organizations as Soka Gakkai or within the all-consuming confines of their big companies, demonstrate a basic fear of doing things alone. The new leisure boom, encouraged by the increasing prevalence of the five-day week (until around 1970, the six-day week was the rule), has produced a restlessness and a sense of fretful unfulfillment. "The Japanese don't know what to do with their growing independence and leisure," critic Donald Richie says. "They read comics, watch television, go to *pachinko* parlors, and tend to fritter away their time. Part of this derives from their double-decker life, their peculiar mixture of Western and Japanese habits and ways. It is true that many of them, older people particularly, still go home at the end of the day, have their Japanese baths, and get into their kimonos and relax, but the number is decreasing. The distinction between Western suits and kimonos, rugs and tatami, sake and Scotch whiskey is becoming blurred. In a sense, by becoming steeped in Western culture while trying to remain themselves, they've spread themselves too thin. They function now with a certain frenzy, but without healthy self-mockery. Until ten or fifteen years ago, for example, their films and plays had a wild, rambunctious quality—or represented what they call *mono no aware,* a sympathetic sadness. There was an appreciation of mutability, of transience. Now there's a denial of all those things. On television, soap operas reign supreme—the dead hand of Andy Hardy. The humor is scatalogical, raucous and slapstick. It always comes out in a scream."

Writers in Japan

According to Richie, Japan has never had an objective literature such as the West has had, one in which actual facts are made to appear uncolored by the writer's thoughts or feelings. "Literature has, from the first, been subjective," he says. "It is precisely the writer's thoughts and feelings which have been prized—and much of it has consequently remained a refuge for the Japanese, art for art's sake. Both traditional and much modern literature is written in the first person singular, and is confined to what the narrator knows or has observed. With the exception of a few Marxist authors, the writer has, at least until very recently, never played a social role. There are no Dreisers, no Dos Passoses—perhaps only Yukio Mishima presumed a social role, and he was the first person to use Western psychological methods in writing a novel."

Mishima, the modern Asian writer most widely translated into English, committed suicide by hara-kiri, with the assistance of members of his small private army, the Shield Society, on November 25, 1970, a few moments after he had harangued the Self-Defense Forces from a balcony at their headquarters in a theatrical effort to stir their patriotism and their vanishing samurai spirit, in the face of what he deemed Japan's flagrant economic waste and spiritual emptiness. He had often spoken and written of suicide before. His friend Donald Keene, one of the best Western critics of Japanese writing, afterward said that in taking his own life, Mishima was "governed by aesthetic, not political reasons." Other critics regarded his act as a manifestation of his highly confused erotic impulses—he was a homosexual—and as a bathetic sacrifice. Although he wrote plays, essays and even kabuki dramas, his finest talents were displayed in his novels, and in these highly lyrical, moralistic books, through which the theme of death and rebirth ran steadily, he ranked on a par with his Nobel Prize-winning contemporary, Yasunari Kawabata, who also committed suicide, but in a much less dramatic way.

After Mishima, the Japanese writer best known in the West today is Kobo Abé, who is concerned, in his novels and plays, both with what he deems the nightmarish quality of modern Japan and with universal aspects of modern life, in the manner of Kafka, Pinter and Beckett. Abé, born in Tokyo in 1924 and raised in Manchuria, where his father was a doctor, is best known for *The Woman in the Dunes* and *The Ruined Map*, both novels that deal, in an often bizzare but wry and humorous fashion, with themes of victimization, alienation, homelessness, loneliness, the hunter and the hunted. Without any of Mishima's posturing or self-glorification, Abé has a tragicomic view of life that often, especially in his plays, is expressed in absurd terms and situations; people are trapped, or trap themselves, in ridiculous positions and conditions, and neither love nor death provide solutions—they are in effect confronted, suspensefully, and either happily or unhappily, with their own fates.

After reading two of Abé's novels and seeing two of his macabre and humorous short plays, I spent a couple of delightful evenings with him. On the first occasion we simply drank at his private club and talked at random —he seldom likes to talk about himself—about such things as the return to Japan of Lieutenant Hiroo Onoda, the World War II intelligence officer who had spent twenty-nine years hiding out in the Philippines. Abé found him a ridiculous—indeed, almost despicable—figure. "He belongs to the international fraternity of spies," he said. "He should now get a job as a spy for a big company." (Onoda, in fact, found the new Japan too much for him and went off to manage a cattle ranch in Brazil.)

On the second occasion Abé sat, owlish-looking—he wears heavy horn-rimmed glasses—on a sofa in his actors' studio in the Shibuya section of Tokyo, where I had just seen one of his plays, and we talked of his work. "Japan is changing so quickly," he said. "Each individual is helplessly inundated by change. He can't digest or react to it, so therefore he is uptight. It's part of the country's personality, but if we were robbed of it, there would probably be even more suicides. All that remains, somewhere, is the inner man, but in an everyday sense, Japanese just float in their uptightness. Their relationship to society as a whole remains tenuous, and in a way they don't even know what they are alienated from."

In Kyoto I spent an afternoon and evening with another well-known Japanese writer, Sakyo Komatsu, a forty-three-year-old author of science fiction, whose 1973 book *Submersible Japan* sold more than four million copies and was later published in America. The book is a prophecy of the national death and destruction that many Japanese fear will actually take place, and thus it typifies the doomsday books that are highly popular today, vying for attention with nostalgic and escapist and historical works and books about the dangers of another world war instigated by a Russian attack on Japan. *Submersible Japan* chronicles the destruction of the nation following a series of titanic volcanic explosions—the whole country simply sinks into the Pacific, carrying with it forty million people (the rest have been evacuated in time). When I saw Komatsu, he had just completed a second long stint of research on a new book about another Ice Age sweeping over the whole globe. Over drinks and a steak dinner in a small Kyoto restaurant, he, too, spoke in depressed terms of modern Japan. "Our prosperity is a cancer on the sun," he said. "The Japanese learn quickly, but they also forget quickly. We are too timid about the world. We need a whole new approach, a new world, but I'm not sure a new world needs Japan. We have come to the end of our season of heroes."

One can obtain almost as many opinions about Japan as one wishes, but there is little doubt that the nation today is subject to more strains and stresses than at any point since the end of World War II, and that its social as well as its economic stability is threatened more than it has been before. A man who impressed me as knowing as much about Japan as any foreigner I talked to was Father Joseph Roggendorf, a Jesuit priest who has lived in the country for some forty years. He felt strongly that the Japanese will have to integrate better with the rest of the world or be condemned "to being forever a kind of fringe country." He added that "the Japanese have always shut the world out or been hostile, and have been accustomed to thinking of the world in terms of strong and weak people, but they can't do it anymore. Instead of considering themselves as Japanese looking out on foreigners, they will have to change their world view, or else they won't even be able to trade. They are not used to colloquy, and they're still trying to keep the barbarians away, but they will have to change or perish. It's debatable how much the younger generation understands this need for larger change. There are some hopeful signs. One of them is that 'loss of face,' which always meant shame, doesn't matter so much anymore. They no longer go to bed in tears to hide their frustrations. There seems to be a new variety of Japanese that understands that they can no longer live apart in a hothouse atmosphere."

Whether the Japanese will be able to achieve a greater degree of integration in the world without stepping on others' toes, as well as avoid having their own stepped on, remains one of the key questions as we approach the twenty-first century—which futurologist Herman Kahn believes will be the Japanese Century. Along with a number of others, I disagree with Kahn. The Japanese will not be ready to assume such a role, in my opinion, for reasons more important than economic ones alone. It seems to me that their continuing struggle to seek their own identity and then relate, in psychological as well as practical and political terms, to the rest of the world is a serious and difficult one that will take considerable time; it will involve internal and external challenges and conflicts that may prove insurmountable.

The Japanese may continue to prosper, but their prosperity will be tempered, if not guided, by mixed factors of fragility and strength which have not yet been resolved, and which could cause them, and the rest of us, problems. One of those factors or issues which the Japanese have not yet come to terms with concerns conflicts between traditional and modern forces and influences in their own society. These conflicts, latent or active, are pervasive, and while they are part of the attractiveness and mystery of Japan, they also provoke domestic discontent and divisiveness. The Japanese will not feel comfortable with the rest of the world, with other Asians or with Westerners, and they may feel increasingly less comfortable with themselves as well, until and unless these problems and paradoxes are clarified and solved.

5-The Lockheed Case, and the Road Ahead

More than Watergate, which had a violent purging effect on the American political and social scene, the Lockheed scandal in Japan challenged some of the basic tenets of Japanese democracy at a time when the country was already undergoing a period of self-questioning and doubt. Coming on top of the oil and energy crisis that began late in 1973 and the recession that followed, and involving as the chief defendants former Prime Minister Kakuei Tanaka and Yoshio Kodama, the most notorious of the postwar *kuromaku,* or fixers, Lockheed acted as a catalyst and a conscience-stirring phenomenon, accelerating the process of reappraisal in which the Japanese were already engaged. There is a saying in Japan that no scandal or sensation of any kind lasts more than seventy-five days. Lockheed proved otherwise, and while public interest in the case gradually slackened after a year or so—it broke in February 1976 as a result of testimony and evidence brought forth during hearings of the United States Senate Subcommittee on Multinational Corporations—it provoked a healthy catharsis that manifested itself in various ways, culturally and psychologically as well as politically. Though Japan was likely to remain fundamentally conservative and democratic, the symbiotic relationship between big business and party politics, notably those of the LDP whose unilateral hold on government was no longer so certain, was being thoroughly scrutinized and questioned; and what Japanese scholars and commentators referred to as "structural corruption" was widely debated in magazines and newspapers.

The Japanese have a strong resiliency in their character, which fits their traditional sense of harmony and adaptability, and they do not like to shake the boat. Nor do they enjoy taking an adversary position about themselves, which again is why so many civil suits are settled out of court. For this reason most previous postwar scandals, including those involving major political figures, petered out, one way or another, either by being dropped or through the prolonged process of legal appeal. The Lockheed trials, however, the ultimate results of which, involving a total of sixteen defendants, would not be determined for several years, proved different from any other criminal cases since World War II. This was due to a number of factors that happened to coincide in time, among them political and social malcontent and economic uncertainty, and some accidental elements as well.

Once the case had received its initial impetus from America—to the surprise and chagrin of the Japanese, since despite their involvement in corrupt payoffs in Southeast Asia and South Korea, no recent domestic scandals of such magnitude had been uncovered—their sense of shame emerged. This was so especially because the chief accused, Tanaka, had been a Prime Minister, albeit a maverick one who had climbed the ladder of success as a wheeler-dealer businessman rather than as a traditional politician or bureaucrat. As for Kodama, opinion was even sharper. He had been a wartime profiteer in smuggled metals from China and had been jailed for the first three years of the occupation; then he became a behind-the-scenes political powerbroker as well as the leader of the murky Japanese underworld. Those who remembered the war resented his sustained affluence and power, and others who were younger and simply looked askance at the continuing underground influence of ultraright-wing leaders in the convoluted world of Japanese politics and business, jointly regarded his involvement in the Lockheed case as a national disgrace and as indicative of moral flaws in the modern democratic system.

Charges against Tanaka

Unlike Richard Nixon, who in the wake of Watergate resigned as President of the United States in August 1974, Tanaka, who resigned three months after Nixon as a result of the same sort of journalistic exposure that initiated Nixon's downfall, continued to be a powerful force in Japanese politics. Had it not been for the revelations at the Senate hearings about Lockheed's bribes abroad, totaling about $38 million and including $12.6 million paid out in Japan, most of it to Kodama, Tanaka might even have become Prime Minister again. As it was, while still on trial, he remained a kingmaker whose political maneuvering was largely responsible for the election of Masayashi Ohira as Party President and Prime Minister of Japan in December 1978.

Tanaka's name had not come up at the Senate hearings, but as a result of information turned over by the United States Department of Justice and other federal agencies at the request of the Japanese government to its prosecutors, he was arrested some six months later, early on the morning of July 27, 1976, immediately jailed, and then, three weeks afterward, indicted and released on high bail for violating Japan's Foreign Exchange Law and for accepting a bribe of 500 million yen, or $1.6 million, from Lockheed to help sell its Tri-Star transport planes to All Nippon Airways, the country's largest domestic carrier. According to the charges, the bribe had been offered to Tanaka four years earlier, shortly after he had become Prime Minister, by two top officers of the Marubeni Corporation, Japan's fourth largest trading company and Lockheed's official agents in Japan; the money, provided by Lockheed, was said to have been paid in four installments, in the second half of 1973 and the early part of 1974, to Toshio Enomoto, Tanaka's private secretary, who was also indicted.

Lockheed was only one of three hundred American corporations that admitted paying bribes to obtain contracts in foreign countries, a practice which has since been curtailed as a result of federal legislation and voluntary codes of conduct. The company felt itself singled out unfairly, both during the Senate investigations and because it was subjected to a thorough self-investigation at the direction of the Securities and Exchange Commission and then forced to make a full report of its activities abroad and of the payments it had made in more than a dozen countries. If it was, in fact, subjected to more unfavorable publicity than other firms, Lockheed was probably the most flagrant in the use of illegal payments to sell its airplanes, a notoriously competitive business in which the line between outright bribes and exorbitant commissions to middlemen has tended to be a narrow one.

In 1958 the company began paying large commissions to Kodama to obtain his help in selling its F-104 fighter planes called Starfighters to the Japanese government, and Kodama swung the deal despite the fact that the Grumman Aircraft Corporation had originally had the inside track for the sale of its F-11F Supertiger fighters. Kodama remained Lockheed's secret agent thereafter, ultimately receiving a total of nearly $7 million dollars for his efforts, none of which he was ever asked by Lockheed to account for—he simply signed receipts for most, though not all, of the money. At the time the case broke, having been instrumental in arranging the sale of the first of twenty-one Tri-Stars to All Nippon Airways, he was still engaged in an even bigger deal to sell Lockheed's Orion PC-3 antisubmarine patrol planes to Japan's Defense Agency, and he was to receive higher commissions if he succeeded. (As it turned out, Lockheed broke its contract with Kodama and sold the Orions to Japan without his further help while Kodama was still on trial for tax evasion and violation of the exchange laws.)

In fact, though A. Carl Kotchian, Lockheed's former president, told the Senate hearing that he was convinced Kodama's help was necessary in order to do business in Japan (Kotchian later said that he would do the same again under the circumstances in which he was then operating), it seemed obvious that Lockheed went to undue extremes and, to say the least, was profligate in dispensing money among the Japanese. In addition to paying Tanaka a large bribe, which was passed off as a political contribution, the company paid another $1.6 million to a wealthy businessman named Kenji Osano, a friend of Tanaka's who also was placed on trial separately, on a charge of having perjured himself in testimony he gave to the Japanese Diet about his role in the case. The other defendants in the four trials were three of Tanaka's political associates accused of helping push the Tri-Star sales, Kodama's secretary, three former officials of Marubeni, and six officials of All Nippon Airways.

Effects of Lockheed Scandal

The Lockheed case illuminated the whole money-party alliance that had for so long been the foundation of postwar Japanese politics, especially of the close relationship between the LDP and large corporations. When Takeo Miki, who was Prime Minister during the height of the case, pushed hard for full disclosure, as well as for election reforms and a stronger antimonopoly law, he did so to the displeasure of most of his fellow LDP members, including his major factional opponents. There was irony in the fact that though Miki succeeded in obtaining the cooperation of the Americans in moving the Lockheed case into the Japanese courts, personally ordering the arrest of Tanaka, he was forced to resign after the lower house elections of December 1976, in which the LDP lost its outright majority partly because of public reaction against the party in the wake of the Lockheed revelations.

Takeo Fukuda, who took over from Miki, and Ohira subsequently, promised to continue efforts to disclose all the facts of the case. But unlike Miki, a reformist all his life, Fukuda, a traditional conservative who came into politics through the bureaucratic ranks, was not eager to encourage any investigations involving additional payoffs or bribery—particularly since some LDP Diet members had been accused of accepting money not only from Lockheed but from South Korean and Indonesian businessmen as kickbacks. When I saw Fukuda early in 1977 he said, contrary to what a number of opposition party members of the Diet had told me, that he didn't think there was any truth to the South Korean and Indonesian "rumors" but that he regarded the Lockheed case as "a blessing in disguise," since it had provoked the LDP into a long-delayed housecleaning and spurred it to adopt a new and "more dynamic grass-roots approach" to the public. There was irony here, too, since the "grass roots" methods the party introduced led directly to Fukuda's defeat by Ohira at the end of 1978.

To what degree the Lockheed scandal helped dissipate what the Japanese call the "black mist" of corruption remained uncertain, but it was probably true, as anthropologist Kunihiro pointed out, that "the public is no longer so gullible regarding the legitimacy and propriety of the government." There was a fresh awareness of the need, Kunihiro added, for "countervailing forces in institutional terms," and this was reflected in the formation of several new political or quasi-political parties and groups such as the Society for the Building of a New Japan and the Socialist Citizens League, composed of politicians and academics who were serious about searching for new formulas to modify some of the old institutions, notably the money-power alliance, and to counteract attitudes of apathy and drift. However, Kunihiro and others with whom I spoke, including several dozen members of the Diet as well as academic leaders, bureaucrats, writers and lawyers, also believed that unless the reformist campaign maintained enough momentum, the "black mist" impact of Lockheed would dissipate without sufficient corrective measures having been taken. Some of these fears were dispelled by the surfacing, early in 1979, of a similar scandal involving efforts by the Grumman Aircraft Corporation to sell its planes in Japan. Once again, American investigators were responsible for bringing the case to light when they revealed that Grumman may have paid unusually high commissions to promote the sale of its EC2 early-warning defense planes to the Japanese. The charges, which the Japanese investigators were quick to follow up, concerned the Nissho-Iwai Company (like Marubeni a major foreign sales organization), which allegedly agreed to pay 40 percent of $1 million, to be obtained from Grumman, to an American promoter named Harry Kern, a former editor of *Newsweek* and a friend of many Japanese politicians, if he could arrange the sale of the Grumman planes to the Defense Agency. A report of the Securities and Exchange Commission in Washington indicated that "an American retained by Grumman International in Japan" (presumably Kern) may have agreed to pay part of his fee to Japanese officials if the plane deal went through. This new scandal came to a head when one of Nissho-Iwai's top executives committed suicide by jumping from his office window in Tokyo. The suicide and subsequent revelations about Grumman's operations in Japan through Nissho-Iwai served to renew interest in the Lockheed case, particularly as the time approached for Tanaka to take the stand in his own defense, and furnished the Japanese newspapers with fresh material to attack the money-power alliance.

While there was wide acclaim for the manner in which the Japanese prosecutors had moved boldly and persistently in the Lockheed case, there was considerable talk but no action about setting up new rules for Diet committees to conduct effective investigations with the help of hired legal staffs, as is done by U.S. Senate and House of Representative committees and subcommittees. Historically, the Diet has never functioned smoothly in Japan, being subject to a peculiar and typically Japanese mixture of sub rosa consensus and subtle discipline, which was effective as long as the LDP factions held the reins and commanded a solid majority. But when that majority evaporated and the factions were disbanded, if only formally, and the party had to begin including the opposition in the consensus-making process, along with the bureaucrats who themselves had become less certain of their role, discipline began to break down.

Some of those most concerned with these matters, such as Wataru Hiraizumi, one of the more effective LDP members of the lower house, who was in favor of flexibility as well as reform, warned of the danger of "overpruning the tree." At the height of the Lockheed case, Hiraizumi made the comment to me that "politics aren't perfect, but neither is the public, and we have to make sure that Lockheed is deprived of its sensational elements because if they get out of hand, they could lead to the destruction of the whole democratic structure itself." In mid-1979, though the trials were still in progress, there seemed little danger of this. Even so, Hiraizumi, like Kunihiro and others, was worried that if the process of reform and readjustment was not carefully guided, and if emotional and extremist reactions took place, Japan, still a volatile nation, could again swing to the right. Kunihiro described this danger as one of "going Fascistic in a democratic way." The possibility would be enhanced, he said, if Japan felt itself hemmed in economically by the protectionist policies of other nations—for which it was itself largely responsible as a result of its propulsive export drive—and by the effect of such measures as the 200-hundred-mile fishing limits announced by a growing number of nations, including the Soviet Union and North Korea, which sizably cuts the annual catch of Japanese fishermen in this fish-consuming nation. These are only symptoms of the larger changes impinging on Japan, but they are serious ones, stimulating fears of rejection and deeper isolation which the Japanese are so prone to, and which cause them to worry about the future. Traditionally the Japanese have rejected change—they have always wanted to keep things as they are. As their national character became increasingly bourgeois and middle-class, and shifts in habits and attitudes took place, the idea of having to confront the challenge of change in an adversary manner and to adopt postures that were new to them, both in their domestic stance and in their international behavior, was more discomfiting than rewarding. Yet they are responding to this dual challenge in their own unique way, and any look into the future has to take into consideration both parts of the equation.

Fissures in the LDP

To consider the domestic scene first—always paramount with the Japanese— one could detect a number of things that pointed to a reevaluation of Japanese democracy as it was initially superimposed on the country's Confucian-Buddhist society by the Americans more than thirty years ago. The critics and doomsayers who adopted a negative approach pointed to a moral decline, or at best a selfish amorality, that progressively increased during the boom years and earned the Japanese their reputation as "economic animals"—the late Charles de Gaulle, in an only slightly milder condemnation, described them as a nation of "transistor salesmen." To some, such as author Shintaro Ishihara, Tanaka was the "symbol of ruin and confusion in Japanese affairs," the epitome of the *nouveaux riches* elements which rose to prominence between the mid-sixties and early seventies and who, in effect, bought their way to power. Tanaka's boldly proclaimed but never implemented plan for "Remodeling the Japanese Archipelago" by spreading industry and development around the islands did nothing so much as encourage vast speculations in land, from which he himself benefited, as he at the same time built his personal fortune in various other ways as a means of financing his political ambitions. The fall of Tanaka, which preceded the Lockheed case and which was the result of a brilliant exposé of his business manipulations and his profligate personal life in the monthly magazine *Bungei Shunju*—a unique and outstanding example of investigative reporting of a sort the Japanese press had never before practiced—in many ways marked the end of an era.

When Miki took over in 1974, unexpectedly as a result of a stalemate between Fukuda and Ohira in the contest for Party President, very few people believed that in his own altogether different maverick fashion, he would last as long as he did, about two years. It was Lockheed that kept him in office, and whether he will ultimately prove to have been only an aberrational figure in Japanese politics or a transitional one of greater importance, he provided time for the LDP to look at itself in the mirror and regard its sagging flesh. After so many years, as Miki himself, with a benign smile that hovered between cynicism, pride and regret, told me after Fukuda had replaced him, "deficiencies were bound to come to the fore." The public, he said, was "tired of one-party rule," and its changing sense of values were such that "one party alone can no longer cope with the situation." Only if divergent views could be allowed to surface, and if the reformist elements within the LDP maintained their momentum, could it avoid "the unity of the graveyard." He spoke, as Fukuda did subsequently, of bringing individual party members and supporters into the process of selecting the party president, replacing factional contests, compromises and decision making by a handful of party elders. With its original rural base eroded, and its popularity in the big metropolitan areas at best uneven—the mayors of Japan's major cities, including Tokyo, had been Socialists or Communists or independents for several years—the LDP was obviously in need of a drastic face-lifting.

The trouble with a face-lifting for the LDP was that it had too many faces. If Japan itself was still a homogeneous nation, the same could no longer be said for the party that had controlled its destinies for most of the postwar period. Even before the Lockheed case, which served to emphasize the fissures in the party, it was already divided not only by its growing factional conflicts but by ideology, strategy and tactics. By and large its old-line leaders—the Fukudas, Ohiras and others of their generation who were in their mid-sixties or seventies—were still the dominant figures. But when Miki, who was of the same generation, became Prime Minister, he drew support not only from his own faction but from many younger members of the party who favored reform, and from some who were beginning to veer toward a position of independence. Among the latter, for example, was Tokuma Utsonomiya, a party elder who resigned and became an independent partly because he favored full disclosure of the widely reported Korean bribery of Diet members and Japanese businessmen, and believed in international cooperation to reduce tensions on the Korean peninsula, including full and open elections in South Korea and new approaches to North Korea.

A growing number of younger party members, those in their forties and fifties, such as Tetsuo Kondo, remained loyal to the party but were determined to change its image by adopting bold new positions not only on such issues as Lockheed and other brewing scandals but on a variety of domestic and foreign questions. When I spoke with Kondo he said he was particularly worried about the party's diminishing image among Japanese youth, which with women, who are now a majority of voters, comprise a total of 40 percent of the so-called floating vote—those who no longer admit to supporting any party but cast their ballots on the basis of personalities and issues of the moment. A Miki supporter, like the older Utsonomiya, Kondo felt that the younger party elements should push much harder for novel reforms, even if this resulted in tarnishing the LDP's outworn image and possibly led to evolution of a new conservative force and even a new conservative party. This possibility, of two conservative parties emerging within a few years, was one that many observers considered likely, in keeping with what one discerning American diplomat described as Japan's desire not for "an alternative to conservatism but for a conservative alternative."

Such an alternative was offered in mid-1976 when one of the brightest young luminaries in the LDP, Yohei Kono, whose father twenty years earlier almost became Prime Minister, left the party to form a new one, the New Liberal Club, which surprised everyone by winning 17 seats (out of twenty-five candidates who ran) in the lower-house elections of December 1976. The NLC didn't fare as well in the upper house elections of July 1977, when it ran thirteen candidates and only won 3 seats, but the party, though it lacked organization and funds, had established itself as a true alternative to the LDP, or as an ally in a coalition with it or with a middle-of-the-road group of parties, notably Komeito, that within the next few years could emerge as a genuine threat to the LDP's long solitary supremacy. Kono, who at forty was young in Japanese political terms but already regarded as a potential Prime Minister, was accused of vagueness in his party's platform, but in two long discussions with him I did not find this to be the case.

"After thirty years of the LDP and the bureaucracy working together in harmony and consensus, the Lockheed case hit us like a bombshell," he said. "People suddenly became suspicious of privilege, and it became clear that we, as politicians, had underestimated the sources of dissatisfaction. Part of this is due to the relationship between the political and administrative systems, which are separate in the United States but are blurred in Japan. It has become clear that political parties themselves, and within the Diet collectively, should play a different role. They should consider basic policies and priorities more than they have in the past, and the bureaucracy should stop getting bogged down in the details of long-range planning. The system needs altering because our rhythm has been stopped. We must think in terms of a better mechanism for the future. For one thing, the upper house should revert to its original purpose, which was to act as a watchdog rather than simply as the weaker partner in a bicameral legislature.

"If you look at the political situation today, it's ten years behind the level of people's consciousness, and we must bring it up to that level. We decided to leave the LDP because we felt it would never really change. We try to operate on the principle of wanting to know what the people think, of seeking a new national consensus, and when the climate is changing, as it is now, this requires a thorough review of the whole social structure. For the past thirty years the assumption has been that only the LDP can preserve our liberal society. We no longer agree with that assumption. A liberal society must offer and reflect equal opportunity for the people to select voluntarily the programs they prefer. The LDP has been lacking in this regard. There should be less control from the top, more decentralization. We must trust our private sector more, for one thing, and there must be more communication between politicians and the people, and less bureaucracy for bureaucracy's sake."

Though Kono, as an individual, enjoyed a wide range of supporters, many doubted that his party would continue to prosper because it lacked both substance and an organizational structure. Whether it would remain a force to be reckoned with would largely depend on how well the LDP recovered from its old-age doldrums. By losing only three seats in the July 1977 upper house elections instead of an expected seven or eight, the party made what some considered a comeback after the lower house vote six months earlier. But others deemed its performance more defensive than offensive and attributed its clinging to power, with the help of a few independents, to the continuing inability of the opposition parties, notably the Socialists and the Communists, to gain strength. In fact, the voting trend in recent years, which has shown the LDP also losing votes overall but marshaling its candidates better in the mixed national and local constituency system—some candidates run singly on a national basis, while others from the same party run locally against each other as well as against candidates from other parties—has been toward the center. Komeito, the Buddhist-oriented party, and the Democratic Socialists both have gained strength, and together with the New Liberal Club and some right-wing Socialists, formed a potential centrist element that could in time become the basis of a new middle-of-the-road coalition party. The Socialists, considered for years to be an alternative ruling party, showed signs of having virtually destroyed themselves by divisiveness, and their left wing in 1978 was actually more Marxist than the Communists, whose fortunes were also declining despite solid strength in some rural areas.

Ohira's Surprise Victory

The contest for the Presidency of the LDP—and the prime-ministership —at the end of 1978 was more a postponement of a crisis than a resolution of the party's basic problems. Ohira's unexpected victory over Fukuda in what, for the first time, was an opening round akin to a primary, in which 1.5 million party members and supporters throughout the country expressed their choice, was, if in part a successful "democratization" of the party at the grass-roots level, to a greater degree a reaffirmation of the old money-politics alliance in what could prove to be a final show of strength by old-guard faction leaders. With the help of his friend Tanaka's still powerful machine, Ohira won 550,891 votes to Fukuda's 472,523: under the new system, the "points" won by the other two candidates, Yasuhiro Nakasone and Toshio Komoto, were split by the two leaders, which resulted in Ohira's winning 748 points to Fukuda's 638. Fukuda promptly conceded, thus averting a final showdown in what would have been a second round whereby the LDP members of the Diet, voting along what would obviously have been factional lines, picked the Prime Minister.

The son of a farmer from Shikoku Island, Ohira had worked his way through a relatively obscure college and then climbed the bureaucratic ladder in typical political style. While organizing his own faction, he served as Finance Minister, Foreign Minister and Minister of Trade and Industry. A slow-moving, laconic man of sixty-eight, he often gave the impression, in his rambling speeches, of being sleepy and vague, but this was somewhat misleading. An avid reader, a Christian and a teetotaler in a country of heavy drinkers, he was, in fact, highly studious and deliberate; if he lacked charisma, he had an avuncular quality that among the Japanese, with their many subterranean perceptions of character, lent him a special quality of leadership.

It was unlikely, however long he lasted as an essentially transitional figure, that Ohira would change the course Japan was following, domestically or abroad. The country, he said, was passing through "an age of uncertainty" that called for caution. "I am an ordinary man, I want to do ordinary things, I do not want to do anything spectacular or unusual," he said of himself. Like Fukuda before him, he pledged to "forge harmony and unity in the party" and "not depend on power." He chose his cabinet carefully, alloting the factions of Fukuda, Tanaka and Nakasone their share of ministries, but ran into trouble on some posts, notably the important secretary-generalship of the party, when opposition right-wing elements forced him to back down on his first choice, the chief lieutenant of his own faction. It seemed probable that both factionalism and internal party strife on a personal as well as ideological level would make his tenure as Prime Minister a difficult one. He managed to weather his first hundred days in his professed "slow but steady" fashion. Japan, he maintained, had passed through its "age of politics" under Prime Minister Yoshida and its "economic age" under Prime Minister Ikeda, Ohira's *sensei*, or teacher, and was now about to enter what he called the "cultural age." To pave the way, he summoned about 200 scholars and bureaucrats, most of them young men in Japanese terms, averaging forty-four years in age, to study nine basic fields or subjects, among them the "pluralized society," the future of "garden cities," overseas economic policy and "pan-Pacific cooperation." This large brain trust, adopting both theoretical and realistic methods, is to prepare a series of reports about Japan's future by June 1980.

The "uncertainty" Ohira spoke of was manifest in many ways, economically at home and abroad, and with respect to Japan's political and military posture. While the economic situation was slowly improving domestically, Ohira quickly admitted that the 7 percent growth rate both he and Fukuda had earlier promised would be achieved in 1978–1979 was no longer attainable; most predictions were for a rate of about 5 percent. As for Japan's world role, Ohira went through the customary affirmations of close ties with the United States, but having been one of the original supporters of close ties with China, too, he strongly backed the new treaty of peace and friendship Tokyo had signed with Peking in mid-August of 1978—Fukuda's proudest accomplishment. He promised to prosecute Japan's predominant new economic and financial relationship with the Chinese, which, as a result of profitable contracts for trade and for technological assistance to Peking in return for oil and coal, might go far toward alleviating economic distress at home. He spoke, somewhat vaguely, of responding to the rising demands for the country to strengthen itself militarily, as a reaction to the acknowledged Soviet threat. But at the same time he said he would "energetically strive to promote understanding between Japan and the Soviet Union" in what was an obvious attempt to ameliorate Moscow's anger over the Peking-Tokyo agreement which included the phraseology the Chinese had long sought—for cooperation to guard against the efforts of any nation (meaning Russia) to establish "hegemony" in the region.

Following closely in Fukuda's footsteps, though perhaps adopting a somewhat more moderate and liberal course, Ohira was, all in all, engaged from the outset in a carefully contrived effort to assure the LDP's survival as the most dominant political force in Japanese politics. But his success was by no means assured, the more so because it was no longer certain that the party would be able, as it had for more than two decades, to pass leadership on from one generation to the next smoothly. On the basis of my own observations, I predict that the LDP will have increasing difficulty surviving by itself and will have to either make a contract with the Democratic Socialists, with Komeito, and perhaps with Kono's New Liberal Club, or accept the fact that Japan will have two competing conservative parties—the LDP as one, and a coalition of the centrist parties as another. Such a development would enable the consensus sytem to continue functioning but with less ease and simplicity than before, and the existence of a sizable opposition on the left—and a smaller one on the far right—could create a dangerous polarization and lead to serious economic and social conflicts, including labor and generational ones, that would threaten Japan's inherent stability. If the LDP ultimately recovers and regains cohesive power, as some predict it will under younger leadership, Japan could revert to its present political course, but even so, this course would probably be altered by changing moods and circumstances. An indication of the future trend was the election for local and gubernatorial offices in April 1979, when with the help of the centrist parties—splitting and sharing some candidates with them—the LDP did surprisingly well, sweeping all fifteen gubernatorial races and backing victorious mayoralty candidates in the key cities of Tokyo and Osaka. But without Komeito, in particular, the LDP would not have done as well as it did, and the party would probably have to solidify this new tenuous alliance to win the important lower house elections, which might be held as early as the fall of 1979. These elections would furnish a true test of the LDP's survival and of its ability to continue ruling alone or only in alliance with the centrists.

If Japan's economic well-being is threatened by further oil shocks or recession and conditions in northeastern Asia grow more tense and unsettled, this will inevitably have an effect on domestic politics. The Japanese economy, in a transitional state as it moves toward a lower growth plateau and confronts the challenge of restructuring itself to new types of investment, is perhaps the least predictable of any in the major industrial nations today. This is so not because of any lack of ability on the part of the Japanese, but because of the difficulties they face in trying to balance a demand by other nations that they reduce exports, on which they have so heavily depended for so long, and compensate by policies of reflation and revived consumption. With their balance-of-trade and balance-of-payments figures so highly in their favor vis-à-vis both the United States and Europe, they continue to face protectionist constraints from their major trading partners in a variety of products, including color television sets, other electronic goods and autos. As an economic power of increasing military strength, and locked into a tenuous geopolitical position in northern Asia, with its Pacific ally, the United States, on one flank and the two Communist powers, China and Russia, on the other, not to mention the two contesting parts of Korea, Japan is not unlike a tethered Gulliver bound by conflicting interests of other nations, large and small, on whom its fortunes so largely depend. This is why the Japanese are trying to make fresh forays in Southeast Asia, Latin America and in the Middle East. But how successful they will be remains moot. While they got the jump on the Americans in China, normalization between Washington and Peking in December 1978 presents the threat of long-term economic competition for a dominant share of the expanding Chinese market.

Even before the oil crisis, which quadrupled Japan's oil bill from $5 billion to $20 billion a year, there was a growing awareness, partly for environmental reasons, that the nation's economy would have to be restructured to meet the requirements of a lower growth rate and simultaneous demands for an improvement in the quality of people's lives, including more and better housing and a wider variety of social consumption goods. Although the Japanese are seeking to diversify their energy resources, both from nuclear and solar sources and from the importation of more coal, what the country needs, the experts agree, is less heavy, energy-consuming industry and more knowledge-intensive, or highly technological, production, such as computers, aviation products, and so on. According to the Economic Planning Agency, in its plan for the second half of the seventies geared "toward a stable society," a relatively high level of exports can be maintained by concentrating on more sophisticated products, including transferable plants and machinery, and by improving processing of such goods as textiles and sundries. The hope of the EPA was that through a gradual mixture of new private plant investment, private consumer expenditure, public works, and other government-fixed capital formation, an annual growth rate in the range of 7 percent can eventually be sustained and that both inflation and unemployment—for the first time since the postoccupation days a problem that arose during the cutbacks of the recession—can be controlled.

Most of the economists I spoke with in 1977 and 1978, such as Saburo Okita, felt that there was enough "flexible dynamism" in the nation's economy to meet the new challenges and sustain a "realistic" rate of growth as well as make the adjustment to a better balance of exports and imports to meet the complaints of the United States and the European nations. Part of this improved balance, they felt, would come from establishing better and more diversified trade relations, with Southeast Asia in particular. The difficulty is that the Japanese still do not feel at ease with most other Asians, let alone most other people, which is one reason they so often seem to act precipitately and without sufficient thought as to what effect their actions are likely to have on others. As Masataka Kosaka pointed out, "When the Japanese learn to consider the position of their trading partners and understand that occasional short-term concessions can bring them long-term gains, then they will truly have achieved self-confidence." Kosaka, however, also rightfully added that Japan has not always been to blame, and that in its relations with America, for example, the Americans have gradually changed their attitude of benevolence as the Japanese became strong competitors.

A New World Role

Japan would like to regard itself as a Pacific Basin power, maintaining its close alliance with the United States, solidifying the new China relationship, and looking ahead to a growing triangular alliance with Washington and Peking while seeking to allay Moscow's fears of Asian encirclement. There appears to be little doubt that the Chinese are trusted while the Russians are not, although the Japanese were upset by the Chinese invasion of Vietnam. Beyond the cultural affinity between the Chinese and the Japanese, and notwithstanding their different political systems, the two peoples for the most part share some fundamental perceptions of Asia and other Asians and understand and get along with each other on a workmanlike and practical basis. If the Chinese continue to follow a moderate course in the post-Mao period, the chances are that the Sino-Japanese relationship will develop apace, with each nation increasingly able to help the other in ways that are easier to implement practically, due to proximity alone, than between China and the United States. On the other hand, in world-power terms, because of the Sino-Soviet conflict, Peking needs Washington more than it needs Tokyo.

The Russians have not gone out of their way to initiate an era of good feeling between themselves and the Japanese, and the mood has remained one of intransigence, criticism and some tension ever since World War II. As of the start of 1979, there were no prospects of a treaty between Moscow and Tokyo formally ending the war. The Russians remained adamant in refusing any concessions about the four small islands off northern Hokkaido they continued to claim, refusing to recognize Japan's right to regain them, and they took the lead in establishing a 200-hundred-mile fishing zone, which was a blow to Japanese fishermen. The Japanese would like to help develop Russia's rich Siberian mineral and other resources, and some joint projects were started, but no major ones, such as the Tyumen gas and oil fields, with their vast potential production. Moreover, American participation was sought by the Japanese for such large-scale development, and Washington has not yet expressed any firm interest, undoubtedly because of its own balancing of détente between Moscow and Peking and because of the tenuous and uncertain Korean problem. Above all, disturbing to both the Americans and the Japanese has been the growing power of the Russian naval fleet in the western Pacific, particularly its missile-carrying submarines.

The Americans and the Japanese are fond of telling one another that their bilateral relations are on as sound a footing as possible and that, bolstered by the twenty-five-year-old security treaty, according to which both parties retain the right to terminate on one year's notice, their Pacific alliance is one of the world's firmest. This mutual exercise in polite reassurance masks the fact that there are a number of areas of trade and communication wherein serious differences and shortcomings exist, as well as some signs that on matters of military strategy and tactics, the alliance is not as tight as it once was. Late in April 1979 Ohira visited Washington to discuss economic, political and military matters with President Carter and to patch up the somewhat tarnished alliance prior to Carter's state visit to Japan in June, which was followed by an economic summit with the Europeans and the United States. Chances are that despite concessions by both Tokyo and Washington—and the same holds true for Japan and its European trading partners—protectionist trends are likely to increase as patterns and modalities of commercial and industrial exchange, and the international monetary picture, grow more complicated in an ever-more competitive climate. The Japanese are likely to try to maintain their exports at as high a level as possible, and their balance of trade and payments surpluses, which will probably continue to plague the Americans and Europeans, as they also disturb the non-Communist Southeast Asian nations.

As for military questions, much will depend on how efficaciously the American troop withdrawals from Korea are executed, how successfully the South Koreans will strengthen and stabilize themselves, politically as well as militarily, and on whether the whole fragile condition on the Korean peninsula can be ameliorated. Japan's capacity for feeling vulnerable should not be underestimated, and the effect in Japan of America's mishandling of the Vietnam question, and its ultimate defeat, does not enhance admiration for American methods and judgments. If the American posture in the western Pacific should become uncertain—a peculiar mixture of withdrawal and suspended retention of some troops and of air, naval and nuclear power whose level of sufficiency was likely to be a growing source of debate—then the American-Japanese alliance might slowly erode further and even disintegrate. Whether the Japanese would thereupon seek out the Chinese more assiduously, or even the Russians, would become moot questions.

For the next five years, until the mid-eighties, Japan will probably try to maintain the status quo in the best of all possible worlds, balancing off its major economic concerns, including higher investments at home and abroad and continued ready access to raw materials, with political expediency and compromise. As Yonosuke Nagai, a foreign-policy expert, aptly wrote: "Japanese diplomacy has no unified, long-range aspect which could be called 'national interest' or 'policy.' Japan merely has a sheaf of 'interests' in the form of commercial relations, foreign investment, foreign assets, exchange of technical information and persons, and foreign aid, which are loosely organized around a vague commitment to the 'Free World.'" What Professor Nagai offered as the worst scenario was "the specter of American neo-isolationism and trade protectionism on the one hand, coinciding with a resurgence of Japanese nationalism and militarism on the other."

If such a dire prognosis still seems unlikely, some of the telltale signs bear watching. For the time being, even as they venture more carefully and cautiously into the world and try to project, if they do not always succeed in executing, a broader policy of integration and cooperation, the Japanese remain not doers but reactors. When they feel frustrated, they invariably turn back inward and do what comes naturally to them, which is to promote their national business interests and let broader foreign-policy issues and questions take their course, which is often one of drift. The protective American umbrella enabled them to do this for many years, but if the umbrella is removed, or springs some leaks, it will no longer be as easy for the Japanese to follow this convenient and practical path. If and when that happens, Japan's changing domestic political situation would project new foreign-policy evaluations and decisions, the nature of which would in all probability be less practical and more erratic and would, as a consequence, have an unpredictable and possibly damaging impact and influence on the rest of Asia. It remains a paramount question, as the uncertain eighties approach, whether the United States, which has not always established a reputation of its own for being innovative or imaginative, can, at a potential moment of Japanese crisis, play a new Pacific role which it has not yet clearly projected or defined for itself.

Conclusion–
Asia in the
Eighties

When I left Asia to move back to the United States, at the end of 1978, it was with mixed feelings of regret and relief. At least for the time being I had witnessed enough turbulence, upheaval, misery and destruction. The end of the Vietnam war had been an emotional as well as a political watershed for all of us, and after my traumatic departure from Saigon by helicopter I experienced a depressing sense of anticlimax. For Americans, Vietnam had been an abject defeat and failure, not only in itself but as a reflection of United States policy failures over several decades in Asia. My own momentary mood of withdrawal was reflected in the low profile adopted back home, including those engaged in the salvage of statecraft, as well as tired and cynical editors who began shunting news about Asia to the back pages.

As I traveled back and forth between 1975 and 1978 from North to Southeast Asia, revisiting all the countries I had seen so many times before, in an effort to reappraise and reinterpret them in the confused and uncertain post-Vietnam atmosphere, anticlimax was accompanied by a feeling of déjà vu. On the surface, so many issues and problems—poverty, corruption, development —seemed the same, and if the cities had exploded into noisy concrete jungles, the jungles themselves and the remote rural areas where the peasants still toiled away their lives in quiet oblivion were for the most part unaltered. But I soon discovered that significant changes were taking place. From Japan to Indonesia, the political and social ground was shifting, and new economic imperatives and challenges brought on by the aftermath of the 1973–1974 oil shock and world-wide recession were everywhere apparent. Despite the plethora of problems, a fresh spirit of self-reliance and resilience slowly burgeoned. If there was trouble ahead, as in Cambodia, and if confrontational crises posed continuing dangers, as in Korea and on the Sino-Vietnamese border, and if ethnic tensions smoldered, as in the Philippines and Malaysia, Asia as a whole was like a great turning wheel. The hub and spokes revolved in a special rhythm that was continentally unique, at once moving slowly forward toward yet elusive goals and producing fresh, uneven furrows in the backroads of history and time.

After having spent half of my journalistic career covering Asia and the Pacific, including three major wars and half a dozen smaller ones, and watching the long revolutions unfold and blend together, I still felt, as I had at the outset, that Asia is the most fascinating and most important continent. If another war started in Europe, it would probably end in Asia again. Conversely, if a system of enduring peace could somehow be created and tested, I hoped, with some remnant romanticism that belied my skepticism, that it would be fostered in Asia, and that it could serve as a beacon for the rest of the world.

Realistically, it is all too apparent today that new wars and revolutions can just as easily begin in Asia and spread elsewhere, perhaps even causing a Sino-Soviet war. But whatever happens, Asia—and particularly China—will be on center stage, and its population, more than half the world's, is bound to be the single largest moving force in determining the future.

Impact of China

I have not dealt in this book with China as a separate entity, for that would require a book in itself, but I have included the impact of Chinese foreign policy on the individual countries of Asia. Although in most respects the Chinese revolution has been an inward-turning upheaval that has convulsed the mainland for most of the twentieth century, its effects are being felt one way or another in every Asian nation, and it has been a guiding force in a number of them—most notably in Korea, Vietnam and Indonesia. For the remainder of the century, certainly in the decade of the eighties ahead, events in China are bound to have an even greater effect not only in Asia but in other parts of the world as well, including Africa. Under certain circumstances China may prove to be a force for stability, less interested in exporting revolution than in establishing a framework for economic peace and security, perhaps even prosperity, as it modernizes its own economy and triangulates its policies with those of the United States and Japan. But other circumstances could just as readily prevail: modernization might fail in China, or simply prove too slow a process, and revolutionary dynamics and dialectics might again take over internally and spill across its borders. Moreover, the looming shadow of the Soviet "polar bear" is unlikely to disappear. If a Sino-Soviet war cannot be discounted, neither can some degree of accommodation or rapprochement between the two Communist powers be precluded. All of these possibilities concern the rest of Asia, and Japan and the United States as Pacific allies in particular.

The formal establishment of diplomatic relations between Washington and Peking on January 1, 1979, was a delayed landmark move that would have been accomplished sooner had it not been for the vagaries of American politics (if one can call Watergate a vagary). But as it turned out, the vagaries of

Chinese politics were an equal factor. The phoenixlike return to power, for the third time, of the indomitable Teng Hsiao-ping as Vice Premier, Vice Chairman of the Communist Party and Army Chief of Staff provided the positive impetus for normalization. To a certain extent, a negative stimulus was President Jimmy Carter's need for a foreign-policy coup in the face of disappointing delays in accomplishing a Middle East peace and the signing of a SALT II agreement with the Russians, and as a somewhat belated counterthrust to the signing of the Soviet-Vietnamese treaty.

Despite the howls raised by the pro-Taiwan members of Congress and by other Americans, and the fact that the Taipeh government was only given eight hours' notice, it had long been apparent in Taiwan that normalization was coming, and the less rigid Kuomintang leaders had already resigned themselves to it. Although the Americans accepted all of Peking's conditions as set forth in the Shanghai Communiqué of February 1972 (that Washington abrogate its defense treaty with Taiwan, recognize Peking's sovereignty over all of China, including Taiwan, and remove the remaining American advisers, already down to seven hundred), Washington did manage to obtain Peking's agreement for a year's delay before the treaty lapsed, in accordance with its original language on termination, and for continuing to resupply Taiwan with defensive weapons. While Peking refused formally to renounce the use of force in joining Taiwan to the mainland, there seemed little or no chance that it would have such a capability for five years or more. In one of his many interviews, Teng himself said that only Russian intervention or Taipeh's protracted refusal to negotiate would prompt a Chinese attack or invasion. It has long been my opinion that the advantages of normalization far outweigh the embarrassment, moral or otherwise, of altering the relationship with Taiwan; that American prestige will suffer little in the tough, pragmatic, even amoral climate of today's world; and that a new workable series of arrangements can be reached with the Taipeh regime that will enable it to continue flourishing economically, and help it retain for the medium future the relative autonomy that Peking has now also promised.

What is of far more importance, beyond the twinges of guilt over Taiwan, is the impact of normalization and its contribution to China's bold four-ply modernization program: in agriculture, industry, science and technology, and defense. Here, along with others, I have a number of doubts and reservations. From the standpoint of internal Chinese politics, it is apparent that the doughty, feisty Teng Hsiao-ping, in his third reincarnation, is engaged in the climactic political battle of his life. At the age of seventy-four, he does not have much time left to consolidate his power and simultaneously set in motion and implement the modernization plan to the point where its priorities will be rationally channeled to China's capabilities and resources, including its human as well as material resources. During his American tour in mid-January 1979, over and above his showmanship in the style of an American politician on the campaign trail, his constant references to the dangers of the "polar bear," and to the need for America and China to stand firmly together against the Soviets (which caused Carter some embarrassment because of the pending SALT II agreement), Teng gave every indication that he was both a man in a hurry and not yet completely sure of his personal power. It was partly a case of his protesting too much, as he revealed in his response to a question during a television interview when he insisted that he had succeeded in acquiring a thorough consensus both in the upper and middle echelons of the Communist Party hierarchy.

No matter how many crystal balls one uses, it is patently impossible to foresee the future evolution of the Chinese Communist Party. The historic proclamation of the Central Committee was made public late in December 1978; a careful reading of it in the light of the political jockeying that was still going on within the committee and the Politburo, and a study of the highly unusual public reaction to the promises of more democracy and human rights, greater free enterprise and better educational opportunities, produces as much of a feeling of uncertainty and unreality as confidence in a bright new future. Considering what China has been through since the Cultural Revolution of 1966–1969 and its bitter aftermath (culminating in the arrest of the "Gang of Four" following the deaths of Mao Tse-tung and Chou En-lai), plus the military, party and regional cleavages that still existed in the country, in addition to the obvious confusion of purpose and design, let alone ideology, the chances of maintaining a smooth course in an altogether new direction toward modernism and moderation seem slim. Yet Western yardsticks of progress are not applicable. Depending mostly on how the leadership at the top holds together, and of how traditional habits and generational conflicts in Chinese life, both Communist and pre-Communist, will be affected and resolved by the startling changes prescribed and proposed, the Chinese may, after all, be able to begin what they grandiloquently are calling a New Long March. But the likelihood is that, as was the case with the famous Long March of the mid-thirties, which Mao led from southeastern to northcentral China, not everyone will survive, and those who do may end by fighting one another and then choosing a different revolutionary path.

There is much in the Central Committee statement that bears the mark of Teng Hsiao-ping, such as the pledge "to strengthen democracy in party life and in the political life of state," to clarify "the dialectical relationship between democracy and centralism," to eliminate "the overconcentration of authority" and "overcome egalitarianism" in building "a new socialist economy." But the fact that there had been important compromises is implicit in the decision "to close the large-scale nationwide mass movement to criticize Lian Piao and the Gang of Four" and to shelve the debate about Mao's "errors" and "the shortcomings and mistakes" that had already been noted "in the actual course of the revolution"—that is, the Cultural Revolution. If Teng and Chairman Hua Kuo-feng, Mao's chosen successor, have reached fundamental agreement on the broad program to modernize China by the year 2000, their latent personal rivalry, or competition for sources of political power, is still an important factor that seems likely to be further tested in the immediate period ahead. For example, Teng succeeded in diminishing the power but not altogether eliminating the influence of such Politburo members as Wu Teh, the former mayor of Peking, who had led the boisterous and often vitriolic fight against him, and who was a friend of Hua's; of Wang Tung-hsing, the former commander of Mao's bodyguard; and of Chen Hsi-lien, commander of the Peking military region. Teng did achieve a major victory in obtaining the appointment to the vacant job of party secretary-general of a close associate of many years, Hu Yao-pang, who along with Teng had been purged at the start of the Cultural Revolution. The sixty-two-year-old Hu, a trained administrator and technocrat, also became head of the Propaganda Department and was elevated to the Politburo, and he seems in a good position to succeed Teng and to compete for power with Hua Kuo-feng if a new showdown takes place in the post-Teng era.

Will Modernization Succeed?

The debate over whether a power struggle does or does not still exist below the surface is probably secondary to the fundamental question of whether China can finance and absorb the vast amount of technology and capital assistance—some $600 billion worth between 1979 and 1985, an estimated third of which will be applied for the acquisition of plants, equipment and services from abroad, primarily from Japan, the United States and Western Europe. A whole series of imponderables relates to this problem. In a report at the end of 1978, the Central Intelligence Agency cited "economic realities" as posing "formidable obstacles" to the modernization scheme, whose 120 large-scale planned projects—among them ten iron and steel complexes, six new trunk railways and five new harbors—could only be completed success-fully by 1985 "under the most auspicious conditions." Among the obstacles mentioned was an antiquated labor force, 70 percent of which was still en-gaged in backward agriculture, whose productivity potential was difficult to gauge and whose demand for more consumer goods was rising. Another factor was the paucity of skilled technicians and managers for operating the billions of dollars of modern equipment scheduled to be purchased. China's credit rating at the moment was good, chiefly because it had no foreign debts and because it stood to earn additional foreign exchange from its oil production, projected to increase fourfold by 1988 to more than 400 million tons a year. But no one can tell how much of this oil supply, let alone gas and coal, will have to be used to fuel the country's planned industrial expansion and to run its enlarged transportation system, and how much would be left over for export. Foreign-exchange reserves in 1979 were only about $2 billion. Foreign banks, particularly the Japanese, are willing and eager to lend China cash and offer credit, but how much permanent strain can be placed on the new system of so-called "deferred-payment financing"? And how will the foreign-exchange pie—even if it grows larger as a result of the profits derived from joint ventures with the Japanese and Western nations—be divided among the competing sectors of industry, the military and agriculture, particularly as the country's foreign debt increases to $20 or $30 billion, as seems highly likely within a decade?

Of China's population of nearly 1 billion people, three quarters are peasants. In January 1979, thousands of them from all of the country's twenty-nine provinces descended on Peking and marched through the streets of the capital carrying banners saying "We don't want hunger, we don't want to suffer anymore, we want human rights and democracy." During the moves toward relaxation, which were soon curtailed as the popular surge for democracy was deemed to have gone too far, edicts were issued to end discrimination against "landlords, rich peasants, counterrevolutionaries and bad elements" and to afford them equal access to schools and universities, to jobs and party membership. At the same time, a new and broader system of payments and incentives to ordinary peasants was introduced, based on their productive output. But as reported early in 1979 in the *New York Times* by Edward Friedman, a political scientist from the University of Wisconsin who had just returned from a tour of northern rural China, the traditional peasants seemed to prefer the older planned economy and "their own incentive system over the new one that enhanced individual incentives." Friedman suggested that "remnant ultras among power elites could someday join with the traditional peasants and provide a legitimate rationale for a takeover by military, party and government officials whose arbitrary powers for cruel and corrupt action are being undercut by the Teng Hsiao-ping campaign against abuses of power. An anti-Teng platform could seem to stress the rural, the poor and the semi-educated against the urban, the rich and the professionals." Despite higher wages and improvements both in the quality of consumer goods and services, and in agricultural technology, including an increase in farm mechanization, there is no guarantee that the rising urban-rural tensions can be controlled or that Teng and his modernization cohorts can retain the support of the ranking military and party representatives who either claim to speak for, or hold ascendancy over, the inchoate rural masses.

China's Great Leap Forward of the late fifties, which proved a disaster only equaled by the Cultural Revolution that soon followed, is now being matched by what has been described as the Great Leap Outward. But even here, aside from the possible financial problems that will probably come to bear in the mid- or late eighties, imponderables and uncertainties exist, and many of them concern the United States. There is little hesitation on the part of other nations to sell China almost any sort of modern technology; and in Europe some of the NATO nations, with America's blessing, have contracted to sell the Chinese both light and heavy military equipment, which neither Japan nor the United States will do—Tokyo for constitutional reasons prohibiting it, and Washington for political reasons, chiefly the desire not to arouse the Russians. Some American experts, however, have recommended that defensive weapons be made available to the Chinese if U.S.-Soviet relations were to deteriorate, and that China should have immediate access to military-related technology which would enable it to catch up with Russia in military strength in the interest of promoting a better balance of power. The danger in doing this, others maintain, lies in pushing Moscow toward taking pre-emptive measures against Peking, or in encouraging the Chinese to adopt an aggressive posture not only toward Taiwan but toward South Korea and some of the Southeast Asian nations, including Vietnam.

Certainly one thing was clear at the outset of normalization: the Sino-American relationship is bound to be more abnormal than normal, not only as it pertains to trade and technology, but also as it concerns human exchange. The Chinese anticipate sending as many as 20,000 or 30,000 students and experts to America, most of them potential or practicing scientists and technicians, and this in itself presents something of a political problem. For example, some might defect. On the other hand, China still speaks openly of preparing for an inevitable war against the Russians. Would the Chinese, as the Japanese did forty years ago, take advantage of American hospitality and gullibility to act as agents in obtaining military secrets or simply gather as much published material as they can lay their hands on for adaptation back home, perhaps with the help of Japanese technology? The temptations to do so will be enormous. At the same time, while welcoming American tourists as a source of foreign exchange, will the Chinese establish bans or limitations on the type of American experts who wish to visit China, notably social scientists seeking to study the rural society and economy in depth? There are already signs that such experts are not especially welcome, also for political reasons.

The options open to the United States for fostering or containing the new China relationship are thus manifold. It seems to me that the best course is to proceed with caution and not, in typical historical American fashion, fall victim to euphoria. The myth of a vast China trade has survived the years of enmity and isolation, and it is entirely possible that it will remain a myth, despite the initial excitement over multimillion-dollar deals for building hotels, and steel mills and other projects. In fact, some of these tentative arrangements, based on Chinese "letters of intent" rather than firm contracts, were already, in the spring of 1979, being delayed. Tensions are bound to arise over deals consummated and unconsummated, over rivalries between Japan and the United States for the China market. (The Japanese already have an initial jump as a result of their $20 billion trade pact with the Chinese, which promises in a relatively short time to reach a volume of $60 billion.)

Even under the best of circumstances, it will not be easy for Washington to prosecute its relations with China and Russia without offending one or the other—or very likely both. At the outset of the eighties, American diplomacy is neither bipartisan nor unified within the Administration itself—witness the different approaches of Secretary of State Cyrus Vance and National Security Adviser Zbigniew Brzezinski, as well as differences across the whole spectrum of Congress. If a policy of care and caution were adopted toward developing the China connection, there would be no reason why economic relations between Peking and Washington should not slowly prosper, with each partner feeling his way, and why the United States should not offer its technology and assistance, within prescribed limits, to help China modernize itself. For the time being, the disadvantages of military sales appear to outweigh the advantages. With its poor human rights record and its political unpredictability in the post-Maoist era, China is scarcely a trustworthy military ally, short of the United States being forced to make a dangerous choice in the event of a serious conflict with Russia.

But this does not mean that the United States cannot and should not encourage China to play a larger Asian and even global role. As self-styled leaders of the Third World, and professed friends of ASEAN, the Chinese are in a position to use their leverage, not only among the 15 million overseas Chinese in Southeast Asia but also in such far-off places as Africa and the Middle East, to promote peaceful settlements of disputes. Regardless of their unrenounced support of party-to-party relations and of insurgency movements, they can work in behalf of stability. There are obvious danger spots, such as Vietnam, and the Chinese attack in mid-February 1979, setting in motion the long-threatened punitive invasion in retaliation against alleged Vietnamese border attacks into China, clearly showed, on top of the Vietnamese invasion of Cambodia, how tenuous peace was in Indochina. While the Chinese objectives were limited and an all-out war seemed unlikely, there were inherent wider dangers in this second confrontation in less than two months of Communists against Communists in Southeast Asia. Sino-Soviet tensions, already aggravated by Cambodian situation, were increased further, and the possibilities of the proxy war on the Indochina peninsula exploding into a larger conflict could not be ignored. For this reason the United States was in a unique position to do more than simply urge caution, and to play a more substantial balancing role by following up recognition of Peking by finally recognizing Hanoi. But it seemed in no hurry to do so.

In northeastern Asia, though reluctant to push the North Koreans into the hands of Moscow, Peking might yet be prevailed upon by the United States and Japan to take part in a broader conference that can help bring peace to the still-explosive Korean peninsula. It is unlikely that, in the foreseeable future, the Chinese can be persuaded to join in conferences to reduce either conventional or nuclear arms—at least not until they have improved their own weak military posture by modernizing their army, navy and air force. But there are other areas of international concern, such as the distribution of food and the control of energy and raw materials, in which their cooperation might be obtained sooner.

In sum, the adventure of exploring the new relationship with the Chinese in the eighties calls both for prudence and imagination, qualities of diplomacy for which the United States in its recent past has not distinguished itself. But if Japan and the United States can stand together and avoid becoming rivals for China's affection, the triangular relationship may prove to be a real force for peace and stability in Asia. At the same time, modernization of China will perhaps achieve limited and gradual success if internal Chinese political and societal frictions are contained.

The Japan Relationship

These two "ifs" remain considerable. While China has become the keystone of both American and Japanese foreign policy in Asia, the Washington-Tokyo relationship is likely to get worse before its gets better. Despite pledges to decrease exports and increase imports, and to stimulate domestic consumption, Japan had a trade surplus of about $12 billion with the United States in 1978—a near 50 percent jump over 1977—and its world-wide trade surplus was twice that amount, while the United States had a world-wide deficit of more than $34 billion. Protectionist sentiment in Congress was on the rise as faith in the Japanese to make a more consistent effort to balance trade diminished, and as the predicted pace of economic growth at a rate of 6.3 percent for fiscal 1979 did not, in the opinion of Westerners, lay sufficient stress on domestic restructuring of the highly organized Japanese economy. The result is that economic tensions between the two Pacific allies have continued to acquire inevitable political overtones. The Japanese Diet also faces protectionist pressures, particularly from the agricultural sector on which the ruling Liberal Democrats most depend for continuing support. Despite the Ohira-Carter talks and the Tokyo economic summit, trade relations between Japanese and American officals are likely to remain touchy and to further inhibit the once harmonious Japanese-American dialogue.

For more than two decades the American-Japanese relationship has been predicated on United States military support, with the security umbrella, both nuclear and non-nuclear, enabling the Japanese to push their economic growth virtually to ceilings of their own choosing. If this is no longer the case in the wake of the oil crisis and the recession, there is no indication that Japanese business and government circles are willing to risk domestic crises, including problems of unemployment, by cutting back their production quotas to levels more consonant with creating better overall balances and fostering a healthier international atmosphere. The astronomical appreciation of the yen, especially versus the declining dollar, has been another source of contention.

While it would be an exaggeration to say that the Japanese are showing signs of becoming anti-American, there are growing indications of a diminishing American influence. Instead of accepting and responding to everything American in a positive and exuberant way, as they have been doing for so long, the Japanese are testing other waters. They are broadening their markets and their interests, looking to the West European nations, for example, not only for new avenues of trade but also for cultural stimulation, and for such things as innovations in fashions. Also, as many or more Japanese are traveling to Europe as to America for pleasure as for business. This trend seems likely to continue in the eighties, and to become a two-way procedure as more non-Americans visit Japan. Moreover, as the Japanese become more confident of their own high-skilled technological products, such as computers, and measure themselves against the Germans rather than against the Americans, they will no longer demonstrate an exclusive dependence on the United States for technology.

The speed-up in Japanese rearmament, though still largely dependent on the purchase of American planes and other equipment, is accompanied by new demands that the Japanese be allowed to build planes themselves under licensing agreements, and that domestic manufacturers, such as Mitsubishi Heavy Industries, be awarded military contracts. In the seventies, Japanese defense spending rose sevenfold, to about $10 billion in 1979, and if one included such non-hardware items as housing and pensions, was close to the NATO estimate of West German expenditures. As opposition parties dropped their pacifist orientation, the long-accepted limit of spending no more than 1 percent of the gross national product for military purposes was no longer regarded as an unbreachable barrier. As the Japanese become a military power capable of taking some offensive as well as defensive action, particularly in the air, they are bound to assume a more independent and perhaps even hostile posture. If the Russian build-up at sea, and to some extent on land in the north, was the principal reason cited for rearming, there were other, more subtle reasons as well, including a growing degree of nationalist sentiment and a romantic harking back to the past. At the same time, the American withdrawal from South Korea and Taiwan, despite Washington's repeated efforts to underline the importance which the United States still attaches to its security arrangements with Japan, prompted Japanese doubts about how firm that commitment really is, and how it would stand up under pressure. In many ways, given the American preoccupation with domestic concerns and with other parts of the world, they could not be blamed for having some misgivings.

Though the Japanese have been expanding their interests in the rest of Asia, and showing more concern for the feelings of ASEAN, they cannot yet be said to have established themselves as a welcome Asian superpower. They are still too much of an inward-turning island nation to achieve that status. As the eighties will test their ability to surmount their homogeneous island prejudices, and to play a larger diplomatic and political role in international affairs generally, they will continue to be called upon to play a role for which they are psychologically and historically ill prepared. In the realm of diplomacy, except when their own interests are directly at stake, they are still followers rather than doers. The opening with China is likely to stimulate a more positive thrust, but it remains to be seen whether this will prove to be purely competitive on a limited basis or lead to the broader degree of cooperation envisaged by some American specialists. Japan, in the eighties, will thus be studying its own image in a multisided mirror. By the end of the decade, the Japanese will probably reach a new comprehension of themselves, one that might enhance their leadership role in Asia or, alternatively, result in their turning further inward and adopting a more defensive and aggressive attitude of self-preservation.

Asia and the United States

As one looks at the rest of Asia on the eve of the eighties, it seems apparent that the authoritarian regimes of the right and center will have to contend increasingly with the spreading influence of Communism. If armed revolutionary conflicts occur, they will most likely be provoked by economic and social discontent brought to a boil by mounting insurgencies. These may have a right- as well as a left-wing orientation, as in the southern Philippines and perhaps in parts of Malaysia, but it does not seem likely that they will be of overriding importance. They will more probably be spotty and noncohesive eruptions, lacking central direction and coordination. But they may ultimately prove to be debilitating and destructive, and given the absence or weakening of authority as a result of internal political conflicts, they may also explode into chaos as time goes by.

Thus, in Thailand, the prospects of stability under Prime Minister Kriangsak were weakened by the Vietnamese capture of Cambodia, which, if the newly installed Samrin regime were consolidated and the Vietnamese remained as its overseers, would place the Thais on a direct line of attack against the central plains that lead to Bangkok. The return of the Thai military to absolute power, which remains a strong possibility, would only enhance the threat of an internal or external Communist response.

If Thailand becomes shaky, both Malaysia and Singapore will be affected. In spite of the broad endorsement received by Prime Minister Hussein Onn in the 1978 elections in Malaysia, he was still confronted by severe racial strains and problems. His program of "bumiputranization" (boosting the economic condition of the Malay sons of the soil) would almost certainly run into more trouble by the mid-eighties as the Chinese complaints of discrimination and neglect on economic and educational issues came to a head. A marriage of convenience is not inconceivable between disaffected members of Hussein's predominantly Moslem (Barisan) front and the new Chinese middle-of-the-road and leftist parties or groups, and perhaps of some of the minority Indian elements as well. The growing differences between the Malay poor and the Malay elite may prove another destabilizing factor. While the Communist insurgency is contained for the moment, trouble in Thailand could easily revive it, and upset the equilibrium further. Should that happen, mostly Chinese Singapore under Lee Kuan Yew across the southern causeway would grow more authoritarian in desperation, and its economic status and survival, on which it justifiably prides itself, would be jeopardized.

The two island republics of Indonesia and the Philippines are likely to remain immersed in their own problems of political succession and economic and social adjustment. Each faces potentially serious internal Islamic threats to stability; in addition, the Philippines still has to contend with a small but stubborn Communist insurgency movement. Neither nation has as yet really begun to resolve the deep endemic crisis of poverty and social justice that riddles its social fabric, poses continuing threats to long-range prosperity, and diminishes the luster of 6 to 8 percent annual growth rates mostly based on the development of the modern sector. The next few years will test both the capacity of these and other nations to make good on long-standing promises of reform and also their ability to implement economic plans designed to benefit the many rather than the few, and to at least make some inroads against still-rampant and almost systemic corruption. Both countries have reached what might be described as plateaus of authoritarianism, at once static and stagnant in many of their manifestations, and both suffer from a lack of vibrant political activity—something which, if it were allowed to surface, might provide a better hope for the future.

Regional cooperation in Southeast Asia, through ASEAN, began to show some signs of progress after the fall of Vietnam to the Communists. For the first decade of its existence, ASEAN was little more than a fractious debating society, engaging in far more talk than action. The disparate and competitive nature of the economies of the five members overrode sporadic attempts to reach even limited trade agreements, and political antipathies and rivalries (as between the Philippines and Malaysia over historic claims to Sabah) almost destroyed the organization. But starting with the Bali Conference of the ASEAN heads of state in 1976—the first ever held—it acquired more of a *raison d'être*. Economic cooperation among the five countries gradually led to some agreements to reduce tariffs on a preferential basis, though progress on key items remained slow. More important, the group reached a consensus about dealing with the major industrial nations of Europe and with Japan on such matters as establishing a Common Fund to stabilize the prices of key export commodities such as rubber and tin, and building industrial plants in the ASEAN countries that would be complementary rather than competitive. The United States, whose trade with ASEAN was not voluminous, nevertheless supported the group's regional objectives and expressed a continuing interest in Southeast Asia, something that the five members had come to doubt after Vietnam.

Despite ASEAN's apparent coming of age, the organization still fell short of qualifying as a regional success story, and differences among its members on economic and trade matters outnumbered agreements. After Vietnam it held together more out of political necessity than anything else, and the relative cohesion it developed in dealing with the separate blandishments of Hanoi and Peking lent it a unity it had not previously achieved. The Vietnamese assault on Cambodia and the Chinese attack on Vietnam brought the ASEAN nations closer, as much out of nervousness and fear as anything else; at the same time disagreements surfaced about the advisability of adopting joint military policies. On a bilateral basis, Malaysia and Thailand, and Malaysia and Indonesia, had successfully conducted joint operations; the former pair, in particular, achieved success after several false starts in confronting the Communist insurgency on the Thai-Malaysian border. But the fact remained that Vietnam alone was stronger militarily than the five ASEAN nations' combined forces.

Both the Cambodian invasion and the Chinese punitive move against Vietnam did little to assure ASEAN of the inviolability of its borders or of stability in the region, nor did the American withdrawal from Taiwan. Whether, during the eighties, ASEAN will slowly evolve into more of a political-security alliance depends on the future course of Sino-Vietnamese and Sino-Soviet hostilities. Certainly peace rather than conflict between the Communist blocs is a more desirable formula, while economic growth by itself for the ASEAN nations is no guarantee of stability.

The retention of American bases in the Philippines, and limited amounts of military aid rendered by Washington to the Philippines, Indonesia and Thailand, as well as increased use by the Americans of Singapore base facilities for naval repair, refueling and air reconnaissance, offer some reassurance to ASEAN, but not enough to dispel the mood of uncertainty among its members. Such uncertainty seems bound to grow as Communist tensions mount, and to detract from the organization's fundamental aims of achieving social justice and eliminating economic inequities. The fact that American foreign-policy interests are for the most part concentrated on Europe, the Middle East and Africa does little to assuage Asian sensibilities.

Asia remains of prime importance to the United States and to the future of world peace. Unfortunately, although it was a major and positive move, normalization with China served to aggravate rather than diminish tensions in Southeast Asia because it accelerated the Sino-Soviet conflict. The United States was unprepared for the consequences. As was evident during both the invasions of Cambodia and Vietnam, Washington adopted a halting if not negative policy based on what one senior State Department official later defined as a "quarantine strategy." Its purpose is to stay as aloof as possible from conflicts between Communist nations and thereby to limit their impact on American security interests. This approach, which has the further apparent design of helping pro-Western nations in the area avoid being pressured into aligning themselves with either Peking or Moscow and of reducing the dangers of polarization accordingly, is in effect a lesser version of Washington's diminishing security umbrella policy in Northeast Asia. It pretends to be a corollary of that policy as revised by the Carter Administration to include the encouragement of Japanese rearmament while American withdrawal from Korea is being temporarily delayed and U.S. naval strength in the Pacific, contrary to earlier reports, is to be kept at its present levels. But demands for the Seventh Fleet's presence in the Indian Ocean and the Middle East at the same time make this a dubious strategy.

What the quarantine approach, supported by relatively small military- and economic-aid programs in Southeast Asia, amounts to is an expedient holding operation while Washington sorts out its difficult options elsewhere in the world. It is neither a positive nor a negative policy but something in between that sounds better than it is. In that sense it typifies the Administration's attitude of restraint—or of what has been widely criticized as weakness and incoherence in the general conduct of foreign policy, despite occasional bold forays such as promoting formulas for Israeli-Egyptian peace. The criticism, while in many ways justified, is perhaps somewhat unfair. What has been lacking in Washington is consistency and good management rather than incoherence, though the last derives from the failure to practice the first two successfully. As Professor Stanley Hoffman, of Harvard University, has pointed out, there is a peculiar failure of nerve in the prosecution of American foreign policy today, an indecisiveness based partly on hesitation or incapacity to exploit tensions within the Communist world in an effective way, and partly on an American moral conflict over where and how to draw the line between "a desire to play standard-bearer and a policy of non-intervention, a clash between a desire to promote institutions that reflect our principles and a detachment bred from a fear that our intervention will lead to abuse."

American policy makers on Asia retain a tendency, in the wake of Vietnam, to avoid facing the realities of limitation. The fact remains that, despite Washington's expressed obligations, the American people would probably refuse to go to war over Korea today, or, for that matter, over Japan. It is true that if there is a fresh outbreak of fighting in Korea, it would no doubt all be over in less than the sixty-day time span allowed the President to dispatch troops and air and naval support simply after "consulting" Congress. But I'm not at all sure that any American President would intervene in Asia to the degree necessary to withstand a major attack by the Russians, the most likely aggressors, or by the North Koreans or Vietnamese with Moscow's approbation. Americans would far more readily come to the support of Western Europe, particularly England, and perhaps Israel. But the United States, in desperation or out of impatience, might again use nuclear weapons in Asia to stem the tide of aggression, or in the mistaken belief that it would put an end to a brush war that threatened to get out of hand. That would be a hazardous move, one that could easily trigger a wider nuclear war in Europe and elsewhere.

Beyond quarantining aggressors in Asia—to use the old Rooseveltian phrase—the United States needs to define more clearly its role and relationship in the emerging four-power balance structure in the area, and particularly to assess carefully its new relationship with both China and Japan. This may take some time, but the sooner the effort is made, the sooner both the the non-Communist and Communist nations of Asia will know the limits and strengths of the more powerful nations, of which the United States is only one, to whom they would normally turn for support or consolation. Certainly the chances of America subverting Communist regimes in Asia are all but nonexistent. By the same token, the chances of reforming authoritarian regimes may be just as slight. But these limitations call for something more than a policy of drift and vacillation. The pursuit, politically and militarily, of a balance of power in Asia as in Europe and the Middle East may be the logical solution, but it is at best only part of the game. Unless it is accompanied by a clear affirmation of what the United States is really prepared to do about such vital matters as alleviation of Asian poverty and hunger, about the environment and about the spread of corruption, a balance-of-power concept in today's unstable and explosive climate is bootless and ineffectual.

Whatever the United States or the other major powers do, the revolutionary wheel in Asia will surely continue to turn in its own way, but in what direction is difficult to tell. There are, indeed, wheels within wheels, and they all turn in their separate ways toward different destinations. The destinies of Asian countries are more than ever intermeshed, and what happens in one part of the continent is bound to affect what takes place in another. But the grease of nationalism remains a more common lubricant than the dream of a common market or the lure of nonalignment. In much of Southeast Asia, Islam is providing a grease of its own, and other elements of race and religion are by no means dormant factors there or elsewhere. The containment of conflict is perhaps the best that can be hoped for in what promises to be another turbulent decade. But if serious confrontations can be avoided, and if there are no other frightful aberrations like Cambodia, Asia, with all its problems and all its imponderables, stands a good chance of finding its way toward some sort of order and tranquillity. A watershed of peace, after half a century of war, is as much as one can ask, and no part of the world deserves or needs it more.

Index

About the Author

ROBERT SHAPLEN was born in Philadelphia in 1917, received degrees from the University of Wisconsin and Columbia University, and was a Nieman Fellow at Harvard in 1947–48. After starting his professional career on the New York *Herald Tribune*, he became a war correspondent in the Pacific and opened a Shanghai bureau for *Newsweek* in September 1945. He began writing for *The New Yorker* in 1943 and since then has published more than one hundred and thirty articles for the magazine. From 1962 to 1978 he served as *The New Yorker*'s Far Eastern correspondent, based in Hong Kong.

Mr. Shaplen has won five Overseas Press Club awards, as well as special citations from Wisconsin and Columbia. He now lives in Princeton, New Jersey, with his wife and children.